Anxand
Jeccer

DEBATING VARIETIES OF CAPITALISM

Debating Varieties of Capitalism

A Reader

Edited by
BOB HANCKÉ

OXFORD
UNIVERSITY PRESS

OXFORD

UNIVERSITY PRESS

Great Clarendon Street, Oxford OX2 6DP

Oxford University Press is a department of the University of Oxford.
It furthers the University's objective of excellence in research, scholarship,
and education by publishing worldwide in

Oxford New York

Auckland Cape Town Dar es Salaam Hong Kong Karachi
Kuala Lumpur Madrid Melbourne Mexico City Nairobi
New Delhi Shanghai Taipei Toronto

With offices in

Argentina Austria Brazil Chile Czech Republic France Greece
Guatemala Hungary Italy Japan Poland Portugal Singapore
South Korea Switzerland Thailand Turkey Ukraine Vietnam

Oxford is a registered trade mark of Oxford University Press
in the UK and in certain other countries

Published in the United States
by Oxford University Press Inc., New York

British Library Cataloguing in Publication Data

Data available

Library of Congress Cataloging in Publication Data

Data available

Typeset by SPI Publisher Services, Pondicherry, India
Printed in Great Britain
on acid-free paper by
Clays Ltd, St Ives plc

ISBN 978–0–19–956967–0 (Hbk.)
978–0–19–956966–3 (Pbk.)

1 3 5 7 9 10 8 6 4 2

Acknowledgements

My thanks go to many colleagues and students with whom I have discussed most of the issues raised in the Introduction over the last decade, but especially to Martin Rhodes and Mark Thatcher for their help in a collaborative project where many of the points made here were voiced for the first time, to Jonathan Zeitlin for constructive criticism of this project at the inception stage, and to Michel Goyer and Steven Coulter for comments on the Introduction. The usual exculpations apply.

Bob Hancké
London, 2009

The following chapters originally appeared in books published by Oxford University Press: Chapter 1 is adapted from *Varieties of Capitalism: The Institutional Foundations of Comparative Advantage*, edited by Peter A. Hall and David Soskice (2001), © Oxford University Press. Chapter 2 is adapted from *Capitalist Diversity and Change: Recombinant Governance and Institutional Entrepreneurs* by Colin Crouch (2005), © Colin Crouch. Chapter 3 is adapted from *Beyond Continuity: Institutional Change in Advanced Political Economies*, edited by Wolfgang Streeck and Kathleen Thelen (2005), © Oxford University Press. Chapter 9 is adapted from *Beyond Varieties of Capitalism: Conflict, Contradictions, and Complementarities in the European Economy*, edited by Bob Hancké, Martin Rhodes, and Mark Thatcher (2007), © Oxford University Press.

The following chapters were originally published in *Socio-Economic Review*, and are © Oxford University Press and the Society for the Advancement of Socio-Economics: Chapter 5 appeared under the same title in volume 4, issue 1 (2006). Chapter 8 appeared under the same title in volume 7, issue 1 (2009).

Chapter 4 was originally published under the same title as a Max Planck Institute for the Study of Societies Discussion Paper 04/5, Cologne.

Chapter 6 was originally published under the same title in *Industry and Innovation*, 6/1 (1999), © Taylor & Francis Ltd. It is reprinted here with kind permission of the publisher.

Chapter 7 was originally published under the same title in *International Organization*, 58 (2004), © The IO Foundation. It is reprinted here with kind permission of the publisher.

Contents

Introducing the Debate

Bob Hancké

Globalization, European integration, shifting macro-economic policy paradigms, clamours for supply-side restructuring, and active institutional borrowing by social-democratic as well as conservative governments seem to
define our era. The often inescapable conclusions of analyses based on these
deep socio-economic trends have been that advanced capitalist economies
will become more alike in their institutional make-up in order to compete
successfully in a global economy, and that the deregulating neo-liberal
political–economic model would ultimately trump the more coordinated
and frequently more socially oriented continental European and South-East
Asian economic development models. Almost a decade ago, Peter Hall and
David Soskice (2001) developed an approach to comparative political economy that led to a very different argument. Advanced capitalist economies not
only were not converging on a single (neo-liberal) type, globalization in
fact pushed them further apart as a result of the comparative institutional
advantages associated with different socio-economic models. Their approach,
labelled 'varieties of capitalism' (henceforth VoC), quickly became one of
the most central theories in comparative political economy, spawning a wide
critical literature which ranged from supportive applications of the perspective in new areas to profound criticism of the basic arguments of VoC. In
a few years, VoC changed the terms of the debate in comparative political
economy: prestigious journals organized symposia on the approach, the book
was reviewed in every major political science journal and even some news-
papers, and within a few years a rich critical literature emerged.

This Reader's basic purpose is to bring together nine key texts on VoC,
starting from Hall and Soskice's (2001) seminal introduction to *Varieties of
Capitalism: The Institutional Foundations of Comparative Advantage* and
working all the way up to the state of the debate in 2009. Many of the texts
collected here have found a place on reading lists for graduate and advanced

undergraduate seminars on comparative capitalism, and so bringing them together in one place seemed like a good idea. While limited in number, the texts cover the main critiques and debates surrounding VoC and, combined, they give a good picture of this literature. In addition, the bibliography to this volume can be seen as close to an exhaustive list of the most relevant readings surrounding VoC and thus also a guide to further reading. This introduction frames the texts that are included in this Reader. It starts with a short analytical summary of the VoC argument, emphasising the key conceptual building blocks. The debate that VoC responded to and which followed from the Hall and Soskice (2001) volume make up the bulk of this intro-duction in Section 2. VoC is of course not the only attempt to map capitalist diversity and Section 3 discusses some related but analytically different conceptual frameworks. Section 4 concludes by presenting the texts in this volume.

1. KEY ELEMENTS OF 'VARIETIES OF CAPITALISM'

The VoC approach starts – axiomatically – with the firm at the centre of the analysis. In contrast to standard economic analyses, however, it treats the firm as a relational network: the firm, operating in its markets and other aspects of the relevant environment, is institutionally embedded. These institutional frameworks, in turn, are mutually attuned in systemic ways, leading to insti-tutional complementarities, and conferring comparative and competitive advantages to countries. These are reinforced through specialization in rapidly integrating international markets. What emerges, in ideal-typical form, are two (or more, but at least two) institutional equilibria: one where coordination takes the form of contractual relations (liberal market economies – LMEs) and another which relies on strategic forms of coordination (coordinated market economies or CMEs).

By placing the firm at the core of the analysis, VoC explores capitalism from the vantage point of what it considers to be its central actor – business. Where other perspectives have focused on descriptive macro-level attributes, and to a large extent have read the shape of markets and the nature of market parti-cipants as a function of these macro-structures, VoC instead starts with the analytics underlying the coordination problems that firms face in their stra-tegic environment. That world, according to VoC, is riddled with information and hold-up problems: how do owners know that managers maximize their profits, managers that workers perform to the level of their abilities, and who or what guarantees workers that owners will not fire them after they have put in their effort? The solution to these potentially debilitating information asymmetries is offered by the historically given institutional frameworks within which firm management finds itself. Firms find themselves permanently exposed to markets – product markets which structure relations between firms and their customers; labour markets where workers and management meet; and capital markets which provide firms with capital – and these markets take very different shapes in different capitalist economies. Labour markets in Germany, Sweden, and other countries in north-western Europe, for example, are highly structured arrangements, where strong employers associations meet strong trade unions and collectively negotiate wages. Capital provision has, up until very recently, been organized through banks in those countries, and even if international investors have made a dramatic and massive appearance on these capital markets over the last decade, the relations between firms and banks have remained highly coordinated. Compare this with the dispersed shareholder systems associated with the City of London and Wall Street, or with the loose hire-and-fire labour market regulations in most Anglo-Saxon (but very few continental European) economies, and the differences are clear. Firms in these two types of systems do not operate in the same labour and capital markets.

This is not a coincidence: it makes little sense to provide firms with long-term capital along the lines of what banks usually offer and have short-term, highly deregulated labour markets or vice versa. Long-term investors are usually very willing to invest in the provision of specific skills for workers and accept that regulated labour markets are a useful way of doing so. Nervous institutional investors such as hedge funds, on the other hand, are loath to sink capital into a long-term training project with uncertain (and often even longer-term) pay-offs and that tie their capital to the effort and skills of workers. The crucial issue is that, once labour and product markets are linked in such systemic ways, the options for a company in terms of product markets are considerably narrower as well. Building machine tools in a competitive way, for example, requires that both employer and employee invest in skills that further a deep knowledge of the technology deployed and of the type of customers that would want to buy such complex capital goods. Specific skills and long-term capital are combined, in other words, in ways that produce important competitive advantages in narrow market niches, where long-term, relationship-specific links between producers and consumers emerge.

VoC systematizes this insight into a key argument: the presence of several 'correctly calibrated' institutions that govern different markets determines the efficiency of the overall institutional framework. This argument of 'institutional complementarities' implies that for a framework to have the desired strong effect, the constituent institutions in the different markets – between labour relations and corporate governance, labour relations and the national training system, and corporate governance and inter-firm relations – reinforce each other. The tightness of the links between these institutional complementarities between institutional subsystems determines the degree to which a political economy is 'coordinated'. Coordinated market economies (CMEs) are characterized by the prevalence of non-market relations, collaboration, and credible commitments among firms. The essence of its 'liberal market economy' (LME) antithesis is one of arms-length, competitive relations, formal contracting, and supply-and-demand price signalling (Hall and Soskice 2001b; Hall and Gingerich 2004). VoC argues that these institutional complementarities lead to different kinds of firm behaviour and investment patterns. In LMEs, fluid labour markets fit well with easy access to stock market capital, producing 'radical-innovator' firms in sectors ranging from bio-technology, semi-conductors, software and advertising to corporate finance. In CMEs, long-term employment strategies, rule-bound behaviour and the durable ties between firms and banks that underpin patient capital provision predispose firms to 'incremental innovation' in capital goods industries, machine tools and equipment of all kinds. While the logic of LME dynamics is centred on mobile 'switchable assets', whose value can be realized when diverted to multiple purposes, CME logic derives from 'specific or co-specific assets' whose value depends on the active co-operation of others (Hall and Soskice 2001b; Hall and Gingerich 2004).

The persistence of capitalist diversity is largely attributed to the 'positive feedbacks' referred to above: the different logics of LMEs and CMEs create different incentives for economic actors which, in turn, generate different politics of economic adjustment. 'In the face of an exogenous shock threatening returns to existing activities, holders of mobile assets will be tempted to "exit" those activities to seek higher returns elsewhere, while holders of specific assets have higher incentives to exercise "voice" in defence of existing activities' (Hall and Gingerich 2004: 32). In LMEs, holders of mobile assets (workers with general skills, investors in fluid capital markets) will seek to make markets still more fluid and accept further deregulatory policies. In CMEs, holders of specific assets (workers with industry-specific skills and investors in co-specific assets) will more often oppose greater market competition and form status-quo supporting cross-class coalitions (Hall and Gingerich 2004: 28–9). Globalization thus reinforces this logic of divergent adjustment instead of undermining it (Hall and Soskice 2001b; Gourevitch and Hawes 2002). Since FDI will flow to locations rich in either specific or co-specific assets, depending on the sector or firm-specific requirements that investors are searching for, globalization will often reinforce comparative institutional advantage. CMEs and LMEs are therefore likely to be located at different points in international production chains: high value-added, high skill-dependent, high-productivity activities will tend to remain in the core CMEs, while lower-value-added, lower-skill, price-oriented production will relocate to lower-cost jurisdictions.

The final step in the argument, therefore, links the development of these coherent institutional frameworks to the processes of economic integration associated with globalization and, at a more modest but also more tangible level, European integration. It builds on two key insights in classical political economy. Ricardo's theory of comparative advantage suggests that if two trading nations specialize in what they do relatively better, the overall outcome will be beneficial. VoC suggests that in today's world the intricate institutional frameworks in different capitalist economies confer such comparative advantages. Adam Smith's idea that the division of labour is determined by the extent of the market – the larger the market, the more market participants specialize – is the second. Globalization increases the size of the market, and therefore nations will specialize according to their comparative advantages.

2. MAPPING THE DEBATE

VoC has been heralded as one of the most important recent theoretical innovations in the comparative social sciences both by its critics and more sympathetic commentators. The combination of systematically constructed micro-foundations, innovations in game theory, and historical institutionalism offered political economy a toolbox that allowed it to hold its ground alongside mainstream economics, while at the same time being more sensitive to empirics, and gave us a way of thinking about capitalism beyond simple neo-liberal convergence arguments. The substantive arguments that linked comparative institutional advantage and institutional complementarities, and which used globalization as a driver of divergent adjustment, opened an entirely new perspective on the evolution and future of advanced capitalism. Some of those elements, however, were also a provocation to many others who were less sanguine about the micro-foundations of a macro-theory, rejected the theoretical basis in rational choice, and questioned the almost exclusive attention to capital at the expense of labour and the state. The critiques of VoC can perhaps best be divided along three broad themes. The first is one where the very idea of capitalist variety itself is questioned. From different angles, liberal convergence theorists, social constructivists, and historical institutionalists have attacked the key idea of institutionally driven divergence. The second broad strand of criticism does not so much question the idea of different capitalist models, but critically reviews the constituent elements of VoC: the largely absent state, the nature of complementarities, trade specialization, and comparative institutional advantage. The third and final way to organize the literature argues for different, often conceptually richer, approaches to capitalist diversity.

The first group of critics, which can be labelled 'liberal convergence theorists', questions the very idea of institutional divergence among capitalist economies. Their basic position has been around at least since Adam Smith, and was expressed perhaps most cogently by Marx and Engels in the first two chapters of the *Communist Manifesto*: the more capitalist economies at different stages of development become integrated in one world market, the more competition, the driver of capitalism as an economic system, will impose institutional convergence. This simple notion cyclically resurged by the 1990s, when it was picked up again by commentators such as Thomas Friedman (2000), and has become the cornerstone of arguments by politicians in the UK and the USA, increasingly across continental Europe, in the European Commission, in the ECB, and other international economic and financial institutions such as the OECD and the IMF. A more sophisticated version of this idea was recently expressed almost simultaneously by Nobel Prize winner Edmund Phelps (2007) and Berkeley economist Barry Eichengreen (2007): a significant level of non-market coordination in capitalist economies, they argue, may have allowed economic and political elites to mobilize the resources associated with the need for fast growth in the post-war era. Non-market coordination could have taken many forms, from authoritarian central planning via directive state planning as in France to associational governance mechanisms as in Germany. If growth was primarily *extensive* growth – a larger number of inputs leading to higher output – then such non-market coordination had enormous advantages because it allowed for fine-tuning across different social actors that represented the factors of production. However, when growth turns from primarily extensive to primarily *intensive* growth – relying on the intensity and productivity of factors of production – in a more volatile economic environment, such a coordinated system slows down the pace of adjustment. In the end, therefore, the innovative capacity of liberal, market-based solutions will trump the coordinated market economies in which associations and the state play a much stronger part.

Not surprisingly, neo-Marxian authors make a parallel point: since the mid-1970s, the world political economy has taken a turn in favour of business, and everywhere this finds an expression in the way policies and institutions that made workers less dependent on income from markets are being rolled back: the attacks on organized labour, the decentralization of wage bargaining, and the redesign of the welfare state are but the most obvious expressions of this new class war. Talking about 'variety' of capitalism, understood as different simultaneously coexisting models, is misleading, and better understood as reflecting differences in class relations, and therefore of different positions on a single trajectory toward neo-liberalism. One of the subtlest versions of this argument, at least as much inspired by Polanyi (1944) as by Marx can be found in a recent book by Wolfgang Streeck (2009) which provisionally concludes his ever more pessimistic assessments of the leading CME, Germany. Streeck's claim is that Germany no longer is the coordinated market economy that VoC makes it out to be. What has happened in the last two decades, instead, is a slow process of reintroducing basic capitalist mechanisms into a political economy and society that appeared to have conquered, until the early 1990s, the efficiency–equality trade-off which has haunted most modern capitalist economies.

Constructivist critiques of VoC are different: for these authors, 'convergence' and 'divergence' are concepts that simply do not offer a very useful framework for understanding economic activity in advanced capitalist economies. Instead, they argue, actors engage in pragmatic experimentation, trying out different solutions within the broad institutional and normative paradigm that they find themselves in, while both trying to maximize their returns and relying on those strategies to change the institutional framework they found themselves in (Sabel and Zeitlin 1997). Since these experiments are localized, categories such as 'national framework' and even 'capitalism' blend out too much of the internal diversity: some of the economic orders may be contractual and market-based, for example, while others reflect cooperation and mutual trust, but an approach based on single models (rather than hybrids) fails to understand those internal incongruencies – which may even be necessary conditions for the national system as a whole to survive. Put differently, for these authors, the national-level aggregation of these distinct local orders is a limiting exercise with little added value. Crouch (2005; Chapter 2 below) has adapted and elaborated this argument. Governance, he claims, rather than institutions, is the central category for an analysis of contemporary capitalist economies. Like other constructivists, he insists on the fundamental ambiguity and openness that characterizes modern economic activity rather than the institutionally based path dependency that VoC-inspired neo-institutionalists emphasize. Instead of one or two types, these authors argue, there is a potentially infinite number of local, regional, and national governance mechanisms. Focusing on national types simply implies aggregating these different modes (in a somewhat arbitrary way), but with the result that the empirical wealth existing at these lower levels is blended out.

Many others, though, agree with the broad idea that different forms of capitalism persist despite pressures for convergence, and that national institutional frameworks play a large role in that variation. However, they look for the sources of diversity elsewhere – in politics, history, or culture rather than in the micro-structure of market economies. The disagreements within this broad family of divergence theorists can perhaps best be mapped using three central issues. The first deals with the written and unwritten assumptions underlying the VoC approach, the second questions the notion of institutional complementarities, and the third addresses the issues of comparative institutional advantage and international specialization.

The key actor in VoC – and therefore also the key level of analysis on which others are built – is the firm. While very few critics fundamentally disagree with the idea of paying attention to the strategic choices of firms and business more generally, most of them would argue that the conditions under which firms operate, and especially the nature of the state, the role of labour law and collective bargaining, and the institutionalized power of labour unions, are as crucial in understanding the modern capitalist world as the choices that capitalists make. The innovation that VoC introduced – the relational view of the firm at the basis of the approach – has been overemphasized, they claim, and often at the expense of the more conventional macro political–economic frameworks that were at the basis of comparative political economy up until then. Bringing states (and labour) back into the analysis has therefore become a central part of the work of all VoC critics.

Raising the relative absence of the state and thus politics from the framework heralds a wider problem. Understanding the world as a set of coordination problems among firms and between firms and owners, employees and customers may be helpful to model the interactions between these different actors, but misses the simple point that one of the defining characteristics of capitalism is not so much the *absence of coordination* as the *presence of distributive conflict* (Howell 2003). Portraying, for example, skill acquisition and wage bargaining as mutually reinforcing coordination games in a high-skill, high-wage economy, or the welfare state as a means of securing investment in specific assets, simply ignores that all of these are results of struggles by a more or less organized working class. The power-resources school (Korpi 2006; Esping-Andersen 1990), in fact, sees different models of capitalism as occupying different positions on a continuum, and that position is to a large extent determined by the ability of organized labour to protect wage-earners from the vagaries of the market.

This critique of the theoretical foundations of VoC, and especially of the specific role of politics in the theory, has led both to spirited defences and revisions of the framework. In their reply to critics in a *Comparative European Politics* symposium, Hall and Soskice (2003) pointed out many misunderstandings and offer clarifications and revisions. Iversen (2005) and Iversen and Soskice (2006) responded by explicitly paying attention to politics, in this case how economic arrangements influence choices of policies, electoral systems, and their distributive effects. Hall (2007) used the framework to shed light on long-term national adjustment paths in four political economies in Europe, paying particular attention to how politics and the economy mutually conditioned and constrained each other in that process. And the review in Hancké et al. (2007; Chapter 9 below) offers a wide menu of VoC-compatible revisions and amendments that explicitly pay attention to class, politics, and systemic friction points as well as complementarities.

A second critical strand in the literature may share the scepticism of their colleagues, but instead of having broad theoretical concerns about the level of analysis and the approach as a whole, concentrates on what it sees as specific weaknesses in the framework. Especially the key building blocks of VoC – institutional complementarities and comparative institutional advantage – have been the subject of important debates. One of the key notions in VoC that has come under fire in this regard is that of institutional complementarities: 'two institutions can be said to be complementary if the presence (or efficiency) of one increases the returns from (or efficiency of) the other' (Hall and Soskice 2001: 17). Several questions have been raised with regard to this idea and they found an early expression in the pages of the *Socio-Economic Review* (Höppner 2005). The first issue addressed what exactly this concept refers to (cf. Crouch 2005): elements in a political–economic system that mutually compensate for individual deficiencies; a situation in which change in one element has immediate implications for other elements that are linked to it; or simply similarity? Streeck (2005) emphasizes the need to combine a systemic notion of complementarities with (actor-centred) contingencies, and thus warns against overly functionalist readings of the linkages between different elements in an economy. Others (Boyer 2005; Deeg 2005; Amable 2005; Börsch 2007) raise the issue of distinguishing between compatibility, coherence, and complementarity. All three ideas point in the same direction, but have different implications for understanding the inter-relatedness of different capitalist subsystems.

Somewhat surprisingly, the question becomes more rather than less complicated in empirical terms. Hall and Gingerich (Chapter 4 below) test the hypothesis that complementarities – mutually calibrated institutions in different spheres of the economy that reinforce each others' positive effects, measured through the strength of interaction terms in multivariate analysis – explain long-term economic performance. Their finding that growth rates are higher on the extremes of a continuum, roughly coinciding with what VoC calls LMEs and CMEs, suggests that some systemic complementarity is at work in different capitalist systems. But Kenworthy (2006; Chapter 5 below) disagrees. He reclassifies the cases, many of which he considers less internally coherent than Hall & Gingerich do, replicates the analysis, and finds that complementarities play at best a very small role in explaining economic performance. His results in fact suggest that the long-term economic performance of hybrids is at least as good, and possibly better, than that of the very few pure capitalist types.

One of the responses by VoC authors to this critique of the links between complementarities and change has been to demonstrate how constellations of institutions influenced adjustment paths of different political economies (see especially Hall 2007; Iversen 2005; Hall and Thelen 2009; Chapter 8 below; the argument goes back to Katzenstein 1978). Institutional frameworks not only defined and translated the pressures that different countries have experienced since the Second World War, but also offered distinct adjustment scenarios as a result. Thus, despite the destruction that Germany faced in 1945, labour markets could relatively easily be reconstructed by combining training systems, workplace-level co-decision schemes and industry-level collective bargaining (Hall 2007: 46–7). And in France the responses to the crises of the 1970s and 1980s entailed a wholesale abandonment of previous attempts at decentralized decision-making and a return to the labour-exclusionary model that had characterized the post-war era, all against the background of large firms leading while supported by the central state (Hancké 2002; Hall 2007: 54–6). Change, in other words, reflected differences in the institutional frameworks, and the elements in these frameworks seemed to be linked in systemic ways – both in terms of what they offer as possibilities and what they exclude. Expanding this key neo-institutionalist point, Hall and Thelen (2009; Chapter 8 below) argue that institutional change need not undermine the capacity of companies to coordinate.

A second heated debate addresses the idea that product market strategies differ in systematic ways across advanced capitalist countries. 'Comparative institutional advantage' and the related notions of specialization in radical and incremental innovation are central dynamic concepts in VoC. The first refers to the idea that national institutional frameworks impose a relatively narrow set of choices on the competitive strategies that firms in them adopt, and that different countries therefore specialize in particular export activities. For example, whilst the US car industry suffered from Japanese competition in the 1980s, the German car industry managed to weather that threat by shifting upwards in terms of quality and price (Streeck 1989, 1996), relying on the constructive system of labour relations in the industry (Turner 1991). Or, when deciding on where to locate particular activities in the value chain, multinational corporations will arbitrage between different institutional environments: design and engine manufacturing (requiring higher specific skills) will move to countries like Germany, while low-value-added activities such as assembling may move to low-cost jurisdictions in central Europe (Hall and Soskice 2001; Borrus and Zysman 1998). In a comparison of supplier relations in Germany and the USA, however, Herrigel and Wittke (2005) found that the notion of comparative institutional advantage may be significantly overstated. Manufacturing firms in automotive and other engineering industries, supposedly a paradigmatic sector where differences are very pronounced, not only face very similar problems but are also trying out similar organizational changes in response to new forms of manufacturing. Since Germany and the USA are each other's polar opposites in the VoC classification, such a convergence in terms of strategies raises questions about the basic categories that organize VoC.

A second central insight of VoC is that institutional frameworks condition types of innovation: LMEs excel in radical innovation while CMEs specialize in incremental innovation. This argument takes shape both in cross-national comparisons of sectoral innovation activity and dynamically in the way new technologies are moulded to take advantage of different skills in different advanced capitalist nations (Casper et al. 1999; Chapter 6 below). German bio-technology firms, for example, specialize in the more stable market segments that rely on customizing complex technology for other bio-tech firms: with some (slight) exaggeration, one could say that they produce the machine-tools for other firms in the pharmaceutical industry (Casper 1999). However, Taylor (2005; Chapter 7 below) criticizes the distinction between radical and incremental innovation: attributing technological types to sectors, he claims, misses the point that sectors can and often do encompass elements of both radical and incremental innovation; moreover, including the USA, which is an outlier in the data, produces a much starker contrast between LMEs and CMEs than the remainder of the cases warrant.

Considering this barrage of criticism and data, it is tempting to condemn the complex of ideas related to comparative institutional advantage and specialization (especially if conferred through complementary institutions) wholesale. Yet this evidence needs to be put alongside other research that suggests more systematic divergence in product market strategies and a direct link to the way constellations of institutions shape the context of competitive and comparative advantages. In a careful econometric analysis, for example, Carlin et al. (2001) suggest that the large residual left when explaining export performance in the OECD through standard economic variables such as cost and technology, reflects systematic differences in national institutional frameworks. In a similar vein, Hancké and Herrmann (2007) argue that the shifts in institutional frameworks that originated as a result of the Maastricht Treaty have led to a significant adjustment of aggregate competitive strategies in the EMU member states, more directly in line with the constraints imposed by the institutional frameworks. And in a study of regulatory reform in the Single European Market, Thatcher (2007) suggests that these reforms adopted paths reflecting the previously existing tight technological and organizational linkages between utility companies and their suppliers. These and other analyses address the mechanism through which institutional complementarities lead to comparative advantage more systematically and, most importantly perhaps, more dynamically than many of the VoC critics. The debate about institutional complementarities and their effects in terms of specialisation and comparative advantage is, therefore, far from settled.

3. ALTERNATIVE PERSPECTIVES ON CAPITALIST VARIETY

All this intellectual activity with regard to the understanding of capitalist economies has both been based on and led to different broad approaches. Where VoC is closely linked to the intersection of political science and standard economics, these other approaches usually have roots within different social sciences and emphasize the role of broad societal structures, historical legacies, and normative frameworks. What distinguishes these is that many of them are primarily concerned with empirically proving that convergence toward a single institutional system is not taking place, and that institutions are 'sticky', in the sense that they survive shocks and their effects thus remain powerful even under the assault of increased global competition (e.g. Lane 1995; Schmidt 2005). But they are, therefore, mostly theories of non-convergence, not theories of divergence.

Among these alternative typologies, two stand out because of their systematic character and the way they prefigure parts of the VoC argument. The 'National Business Systems' (NBS) perspective (Whitley 1999; Morgan, Whitley and Moen 2005) organizes diversity within capitalist systems along two dimensions: the provision of capital (via direct ownership, banks or stock markets, etc.) and the relations between management and workers (cooperation, dependence, conflict, etc.). Relying on a wide variety of different constellations of capital provision and employment relations, he identifies six types of business systems (Whitley 1999: 42). One, a fragmented business system, characterized by small owner-managed firms that have few long-term links with other firms and therefore cooperate little, and who do not develop long-term links with their workforce and customer base. Two, a coordinated industrial district business system, which also consists of small firms, but where both labour and capital inputs are better organized, and where a firm's flexibility depends to a large extent on the abilities of employees. Compartmentalized business systems are the third type Whitley identifies: these are large-firm led, often with a semi-autarchic (in-house) provision of labour and capital, and protected product markets. Large firms also play an important role in the fourth type, the state-organized business system. Large firms and the state jointly drive the economy, with the state acting both as a channel for cheap credit and a forum for coordination among different firms. Collaborative business systems display important capacities for collective organization and cooperation at the level of industrial sectors, while the labour market is governed through dense training systems and collectively bargained wages. The final type is the 'highly coordinated' business system, which includes dense horizontal and vertical coordination of capital and labour and where product market strategies are integrated with capital and labour markets. Different capitalist countries are close to different types of business system: South Korea, for example, is a state-organized business system, Germany (at least until recently) a collaborative model, and the Third Italy a coordinated district business system. In contrast to the LME/CME typology in VoC, which has a primarily analytical and heuristic function, the national business system approach is more empirically grounded, based on stylized facts that claim to capture the essence of economic relations and institutions in a given political economy. For anyone familiar with the VoC formulation of capitalist variety, both the key differences and similarities are easy to spot. VoC uses similar initial categories to distinguish between different types (capital, labour, and training figure prominently in the Hall and Soskice model), and even many of the empirical types can be considered as subtypes of LMEs and CMEs. The basis of the typology is also part of the differences, however. NBS may identify more, and more finely defined types, but to some extent at the extent of the elegant conceptual and analytical simplicity of VoC. Labour appears in many different guises in the NBS approach, as does capital, and some of the types appear perhaps more historically specific than others.

This concern with staying close to empirical data also informs the French *Régulation*-inspired 'Social Systems of Innovation and Production' (SSIP) approach (Amable, Boyer and Barré 1997; Amable 2003; Boyer 2005). Instead of relying on a small number of analytical distinctions, as VoC does, or on stylized representations as the NBS approach does, SSIP are built on analytics that bear some resemblance to VoC, but over more relevant dimensions, and with data which are more systematically gathered than those that the NBS approach is built on. Amable's analysis (2003) examines five spheres in an economy: product market competition, wage-setting systems and labour markets, finance and corporate governance, social protection and the welfare state, and the educational system (Amable 2003: 14). His approach establishes close mutual links through correlation analysis and then uses statistical methods (principal component analysis) to bring out underlying commonalities that tie the different dimensions into coherent models. He thus identifies five capitalist models where the different spheres are articulated in a complementary way: the market-based, the social-democratic, the continental European, the Mediterranean, and the Asian models. Amable (2003: 15–16) thus works through these complementarities in the different models:

Product-market competition is an important element of the market-based model. It makes firms more sensitive to adverse shocks which cannot be fully absorbed by price adjustments. Quantity adjustments will matter, which implies that competitiveness is based on labour-market flexibility. This allows firms to react quickly to changing market conditions. Financial markets are also instrumental in this capacity of firms to adapt to new competitive environments. They also supply individuals with a large range of risk-diversification instruments which are particularly welcome in the absence of a well-developed Welfare State. The social-democratic model is organized according to very different complementarities. A strong external competitive pressure requires some flexibility in the labour force. But flexibility is not simply achieved through lay-offs and market-based adjustments. Protection of specific investments of employees is realized through a mixture of moderate employment protection, a high level of social protection, and easy access to retraining thanks to active labour-market policies. A coordinated wage-bargaining system allows a solidaristic wage-setting which favours innovation and productivity. The Continental European model possesses some common features with the social-democratic model. It is based on a higher degree of employment protection and a less developed Welfare State. A centralized financial system facilitates long-term corporate strategies. Wage bargaining is coordinated and a solidaristic wage policy is developed, but not as much as in the social-democratic model. Workforce retraining is not as easy as in the social-democratic model, which limits the possibilities for an 'offensive' flexibility in the labour market. The Mediterranean model of capitalism is based on more employment protection and less social protection than the Continental European model. Employment protection is made possible by a relatively low level of product-market competition and the absence of short-term profit constraints as a result of the centralization of the financial system. However, a workforce with a limited skills and education level does not allow for the implementation of a high wages and high skills industrial strategy. The Asian model of capitalism is highly dependent on the business strategies of the large corporations in collaboration with the State and a centralized financial system, which allows the development of long-term strategies. Workers' specific investments are protected by a de facto protection of employment and possibilities of retraining and career-making within the corporation. Lack of social protection and sophisticated financial markets make risk diversification difficult and render the stability provided by the large corporation crucial to the existence of the model.

What the many attempts since the early 2000s to identify different types of capitalism share is that most of them see at least three modes of economic governance: market-based, state-centred, and associational, thus covering, by and large, three of the main European economies: the UK, France, and Germany (e.g. Schmidt 2005; Amable 2003). Finer-grained distinctions would then include the USA – a deregulated, primarily market-based economy like the UK – conglomerate-led Japan (or Korea), distinguished by the presence of large, integrated holding groups serving as a key economic governance mechanism, and family-based Mediterranean models such as Italy or Spain (Whitley 1999). One of the problems with such expanding typologies is that ultimately one could claim that every capitalist country has produced its own 'variety', in which at least one institution or combination of institutions is historically specific, and therefore different from other related types. But such attempts raise the question of whether the gains in empirical coverage and possibly even depth outweigh the losses in terms of analytical sharpness. In a recent contribution, Molina and Rhodes (2007) attempt to remain close to the analytically parsimonious spirit of VoC while extending the empirical range to include what they call Mediterranean market economies (MMEs). The state, they claim, is crucial in those economies in large measure because of the weakness of parts of the other economic coordination and governance mechanisms, and compensates, often financially and through regulation, but occasionally also through the support or provision of institutions, for the gaps in coordination mechanisms that might hold up economic development.

Alongside competing typologies which are more or less convincing, two critical contributions stand out because of the way they address similar questions as VoC, but use a very different angle. Since both are included in this Reader, their presentation can be relatively short. Crouch (2005; Chapter 2 below) emphasizes that 'national models' of capitalism virtually always consist of many very different modes of economic governance, which may even be mutually contradictory – one part relying almost exclusively on the market, for example, and another, equally crucial subsystem relaying on state-induced cooperation. Since there may be many relevant subsystems which can be combined, and since a 'national model' consists of the aggregation of these different subsystems, there are in principle an almost unlimited number of possible models – which makes that category slightly redundant. Streeck and Thelen (2005; Chapter 3 below) focus on institutional change. The concern they voice is that theories of capitalism such as VoC may excel in comparative statics, but fail to understand dynamically how change in institutional frameworks takes place. Too often, they complain, significant changes in function may be disguised as continuity in form and thus pass unnoticed, while impoverished notions of change prevent us from understanding subtle shifts. Their core claim is that institutional frameworks never entirely disappear, are reorganized wholesale, or are invented anew; instead, new elements are introduced into existing frameworks without each one of them necessarily undermining them. But, as more of these novel elements accumulate, the logic of the initial set-up and its effects change dramatically in nature. The upshot for the debate on comparative capitalism is that national models are probably not stable enough over the long haul to characterize them adequately. The German model, as Streeck (2009) argues, no longer is the highly coordinated social market economy that figures so prominently in VoC, but has been transformed because of many small changes in the operation of the underlying institutional framework.

4. OUTLINE OF THE READER

Many of these debates are presented in this Reader, organized along three overarching themes. Part I explores different ways of understanding capitalist diversity, and includes the foundational Hall and Soskice (2001) text, as well as Crouch's (2005), and Streeck and Thelen's (2005) contributions to the debate on comparative political economy and VoC. Together, they highlight both commonalities and differences in the comparative study of capitalism, and suggest ways of enriching the field. Part II shifts focus slightly by presenting narrower, mostly empirically informed debates on specific arguments developed by VoC authors. The paper by Hall and Gingerich (2004) in Chapter 4 constitutes a first test with systematic data of the hypothesis that institutional complementarities lead to better economic performance. Kenworthy's (2006) critique of the coding by Hall and Gingerich, and the substantive implications of such a recoding, follows in Chapter 5. Chapter 6 is a somewhat older but still relevant paper by Casper, Lehrer, and Soskice (1999), exploring different dimensions of the implications of VoC for the comparative study of innovation and, more generally, the institutional embeddedness of innovation systems. Despite its somewhat advanced age, this paper remains the most coherent statement of VoC with regard to innovation. Taylor's (2005) critique in Chapter 7 addresses directly and indirectly some of the key points in Chapter 6, but also suggests areas where different institutional approaches might complement each other and even converge. Part III, then, presents texts that offer amendments to VoC which respond to many of the debates presented in this introduction and in the preceding chapters. It starts with a very recent contribution by Hall and Thelen (2009) that tries to span different dimensions of critiques of VoC. Its basic point is that institutions in advanced capitalism usually have both stabilizing systemic effects and are the result of reform and reconfiguration that reflect the distributive gains and losses of coalitions that underpin them. Chapter 9 by Hancké, Rhodes, and Thatcher (2007) introduced a recent volume of essays that took VoC as a starting point to understand challenges in the European political economy, and offers paths to address many of the critiques of VoC.

Part I

Capitalist Diversity

1

An Introduction to Varieties
of Capitalism

Peter A. Hall and David Soskice

1. INTRODUCTION

Political economists have always been interested in the differences in economic and political institutions that occur across countries. Some regard these differences as deviations from 'best practice' that will dissolve as nations catch up to a technological or organizational leader. Others see them as the distillation of more durable historical choices for a specific kind of society, since economic institutions condition levels of social protection, the distribution of income, and the availability of collective goods – features of the social solidarity of a nation. In each case, comparative political economy revolves around the conceptual frameworks used to understand institutional variation across nations.

On such frameworks depend the answers to a range of important questions. Some are policy-related. What kind of economic policies will improve the performance of the economy? What will governments do in the face of economic challenges? What defines a state's capacities to meet such challenges? Other questions are firm-related. Do companies located in different nations display systematic differences in their structure and strategies? If so, what inspires such differences? How can national differences in the pace or character of innovation be explained? Some are issues about economic performance. Do some sets of institutions provide lower rates of inflation and unemployment or higher rates of growth than others? What are the trade-offs in terms of economic performance to developing one type of political economy rather than another? Finally, second-order questions about institutional change and stability are of special significance today. Can we expect technological progress and the competitive pressures of globalization to inspire institutional convergence? What factors condition the adjustment paths a political economy takes in the face of such challenges?

The object of *Varieties of Capitalism* is to elaborate a new framework for understanding the institutional similarities and differences among the developed economies, one that offers a new and intriguing set of answers to such questions.[1] We outline the basic approach in this Introduction. Subsequent chapters extend and apply it to a wide range of issues. In many respects, this approach is still a work-in-progress. We see it as a set of contentions that open up new research agendas rather than settled wisdom to be accepted uncritically, but, as the contributions to *Varieties of Capitalism* indicate, it provides new perspectives on an unusually broad set of topics, ranging from issues in innovation, vocational training, and corporate strategy to those associated with legal systems, the development of social policy, and the stance nations take in international negotiations.

As any work on this topic must be, ours is deeply indebted to prior scholarship in the field. The 'varieties of capitalism' approach developed here can be seen as an effort to go beyond three perspectives on institutional variation that have dominated the study of comparative capitalism in the preceding thirty years.[2] In important respects, like ours, each of these perspectives was a response to the economic problems of its time.

The first of these perspectives offers a *modernization approach* to comparative capitalism nicely elucidated in Shonfield's magisterial treatise of 1965. Devised in the post-war decades, this approach saw the principal challenge confronting the developed economies as one of modernizing industries still dominated by pre-war practices in order to secure high rates of national growth. Analysts tried to identify a set of actors with the strategic capacity to devise plans for industry and to impress them on specific sectors. Occasionally, this capacity was said to reside in the banks but more often in public officials. Accordingly, those taking this approach focused on the institutional structures that gave states leverage over the private sector, such as planning systems and public influence over the flows of funds in the financial system (Cohen 1977; Estrin and Holmes 1983; Zysman 1983; Cox 1986). Countries were often categorized, according to the structure of their state, into those with 'strong' and 'weak' states (Katzenstein 1978b; Sacks 1980; Nordlinger 1981; Skocpol and Amenta 1985). France and Japan emerged from this perspective as models of economic success, while Britain was generally seen as a laggard (Shonfield 1965; Johnson 1982).

During the 1970s, when inflation became the preeminent problem facing the developed economies, a number of analysts developed a second approach to comparative capitalism based on the concept of *neo-corporatism* (Schmitter and Lehmbruch 1979; Berger 1981; Goldthorpe 1984; Alvarez et al. 1991). Although defined in various ways, neo-corporatism was generally associated with the capacity of a state to negotiate durable bargains with employers and the trade union movement regarding wages, working conditions, and social or economic policy.[3] Accordingly, a nation's capacity for neo-corporatism was generally said to depend on the centralization or concentration of the trade union movement, following an Olsonian logic of collective action which specifies that more encompassing unions can better internalize the economic effects of their wage settlements (Olson 1965; Cameron 1984; Calmfors and Driffill 1988; Golden 1993). Those who saw neo-corporatist bargains as a 'political exchange' emphasized the ability of states to offer inducements as well as the capacity of unions to discipline their members (Pizzorno 1978; Regini 1984; Scharpf 1987, 1991; cf. Przeworski and Wallerstein 1982). Those working from this perspective categorized countries largely by reference to the organization of their trade union movement; and the success stories of this literature were the small, open economies of northern Europe.

During the 1980s and 1990s, a new approach to comparative capitalism that we will term a *social systems of production* approach gained currency. Under this rubric, we group analyses of sectoral governance, national innovation systems, and flexible production regimes that are diverse in some respects but united by several key analytic features. Responding to the reorganization of production in response to technological change, these works devote more attention to the behavior of firms. Influenced by the French regulation school, they emphasize the movement of firms away from mass production toward new production regimes that depend on collective institutions at the regional, sectoral, or national level (Piore and Sabel 1984; Dore 1986; Streeck and Schmitter 1986; Dosi et al. 1988; Boyer 1990; Lazonick 1991; Campbell et al. 1991; Nelson 1993; Hollingsworth et al. 1994; Herrigel 1996; Hollingsworth and Boyer 1997; Edquist 1997; Whitley 1999). These works bring a wider range of institutions into the analysis and adopt a more sociological approach to their operation, stressing the ways in which institutions generate trust or enhance learning within economic communities. As a result, some of these works resist national categories in favor of an emphasis on regional success of the sort found in Baden-Württemberg and the Third Italy.

Each of these bodies of work explains important aspects of the economic world. However, we seek to go beyond them in several respects. Although those who wrote within it characterized national differences in the early post-war era well, for instance, some versions of the modernization approach tend to overstate what governments can accomplish, especially in contexts of economic openness where adjustment is firm-led. We will argue that features of states once seen as attributes of strength actually make the implementation of many economic policies more difficult; and we seek a basis for comparison more deeply rooted in the organization of the private sector.

Neo-corporatist analysis directs our attention to the organization of society, but its emphasis on the trade union movement underplays the role that firms and employer organizations play in the coordination of the economy (cf. Soskice 1990a; Swenson 1991). We want to bring firms back into the center of the analysis of comparative capitalism and, without neglecting trade unions, highlight the role that business associations and other types of relationships among firms play in the political economy.

The literature on social systems of production accords firms a central role and links the organization of production to the support provided by external institutions at many levels of the political economy. However, without denying that regional or sectoral institutions matter to firm behavior, we focus on variation among national political economies. Our premiss is that many of the most important institutional structures – notably systems of labor market regulation, of education and training, and of corporate governance – depend on the presence of regulatory regimes that are the preserve of the nation-state. Accordingly, we look for national-level differences and terms in which to characterize them that are more general or parsimonious than this literature has generated.[4]

Where we break most fundamentally from these approaches, however, is in our conception of how behavior is affected by the institutions of the political economy. Three frameworks for understanding this relationship dominate the analysis of comparative capitalism. One sees institutions as *socializing agencies* that instill a particular set of norms or attitudes in those who operate within them. French civil servants, for instance, are said to acquire a particular concern for the public interest by virtue of their training or the ethos of their agencies. A second suggests that the effects of an institution follow from the *power* it confers on particular actors through the formal sanctions that hierarchy supplies or the resources an institution provides for mobilization. Industrial policy-makers and trade union leaders are often said to have such forms of power. A third framework construes the institutions of the political economy as a *matrix of sanctions and incentives* to which the relevant actors respond such that behavior can be predicted more or less automatically from the presence of specific institutions, as, for instance, when individuals refuse to provide public goods in the absence of selective incentives. This kind of logic is often cited to explain the willingness of encompassing trade unions to moderate wages in order to reduce inflation.

Each of these formulations captures important ways in which the institutions of the political economy affect economic behavior and we make use of them. However, we think these approaches tend to miss or model too incompletely the *strategic interactions* central to the behavior of economic actors. The importance of strategic interaction is increasingly appreciated by economists but still neglected in studies of comparative capitalism.[5] If interaction of this sort is central to economic and political outcomes, the most important institutions distinguishing one political economy from another will be those conditioning such interaction, and it is these that we seek to capture in this analysis. For this purpose, we construe the key relationships in the political economy in game-theoretic terms and focus on the kinds of institutions that alter the outcomes of strategic interaction. This approach generates an analysis that focuses on some of the same institutions others have identified as important but construes the impact of those institutions differently as well as one that highlights other institutions not yet given enough attention in studies of comparative capitalism.

By locating the firm at the center of the analysis, we hope to build bridges between business studies and comparative political economy, two disciplines that are all too often disconnected. By integrating game-theoretical perspectives on the firm of the sort that are now central to microeconomics into an analysis of the macroeconomy, we attempt to connect the new microeconomics to important issues in macroeconomics. Ours is a framework that should be of interest to economists, scholars of business, and political scientists alike. We turn now to an elucidation of its basic elements.

2. THE BASIC ELEMENTS OF THE APPROACH

This *varieties of capitalism* approach to the political economy is actor-centered, which is to say we see the political economy as a terrain populated by multiple actors, each of whom seeks to advance his interests in a rational way in strategic interaction with others (Scharpf 1997a). The relevant actors may be individuals, firms, producer groups, or governments. However, this is a firm-centered political economy that regards companies as the crucial actors in a capitalist economy. They are the key agents of adjustment in the face of technological change or international competition whose activities aggregate into overall levels of economic performance.

2.1. A Relational View of the Firm

Our conception of the firm is relational. Following recent work in economics, we see firms as actors seeking to develop and exploit *core competencies* or *dynamic capabilities* understood as capacities for developing, producing, and distributing goods and services profitably (Teece and Pisano 1998). We take the view that critical to these is the quality of the relationships the firm is able to establish, both internally, with its own employees, and externally, with a range of other actors that include suppliers, clients, collaborators, stakeholders, trade unions, business associations, and governments. As the work on transactions costs and principal–agent relationships in the economics of organization has underlined, these are problematic relationships (Milgrom and Roberts 1992). Even where hierarchies can be used to secure the cooperation of actors, firms encounter problems of moral hazard, adverse selection, and shirking. In many cases, effective operation even within a hierarchical environment may entail the formation of implicit contracts among the actors; and many of a firm's relationships with outside actors involve incomplete contracting (cf. Williamson 1985). In short, because its capabilities are ultimately relational, a firm encounters many coordination problems. Its success depends substantially on its ability to coordinate effectively with a wide range of actors.

For the purposes of this inquiry, we focus on five spheres in which firms must develop relationships to resolve coordination problems central to their core competencies. The first is the sphere of *industrial relations* where the problem facing companies is how to coordinate bargaining over wages and working conditions with their labor force, the organizations that represent labor, and other employers. At stake here are wage and productivity levels that condition the success of the firm and rates of unemployment or inflation in the economy as a whole. In the sphere of *vocational training and education*, firms face the problem of securing a workforce with suitable skills, while workers face the problem of deciding how much to invest in specific skills. On the outcomes of this coordination problem turn not only the fortunes of individual companies and workers but the skill levels and competitiveness of the overall economy.

Issues of coordination also arise in the sphere of *corporate governance*, to which firms turn for access to finance and in which investors seek assurances of returns on their investments. The solutions devised to these problems affect both the availability of finance for particular types of projects and the terms on which firms can secure funds. The fourth sphere in which coordination problems crucial to the core competencies of an enterprise appear is the broad one of *inter-firm relations*, a term we use to cover the relationships a company forms with other enterprises, and notably its suppliers or clients, with a view to securing a stable demand for its products, appropriate supplies of inputs, and access to technology. These are endeavors that may entail standard-setting, technology transfer, and collaborative research and development. Here, coordination problems stem from the sharing of proprietary information and the risk of exploitation in joint ventures. On the development of appropriate relationships in this sphere, however, depend the capacities of firms to remain competitive and technological progress in the economy as a whole.

Finally, firms face a set of coordination problems vis-à-vis their own *employees.* Their central problem is to ensure that employees have the requisite competencies and cooperate well with others to advance the objectives of the firm. In this context, familiar problems of adverse selection and moral hazard arise and issues of information-sharing become important (see Milgrom and Roberts 1992). Workers develop reservoirs of specialized information about the firm's operations that can be of value to management, but they also have the capacity to withhold information or effort. The relationships firms develop to resolve these problems condition their own competencies and the character of an economy's production regimes.

2.2. Liberal Market Economies and Coordinated Market Economies

From this perspective, it follows that national political economies can be compared by reference to the way in which firms resolve the coordination problems they face in these five spheres. The core distinction we draw is between two types of political economies, liberal market economies and coordinated market economies, which constitute ideal types at the poles of a spectrum along which many nations can be arrayed.[6]

In *liberal market economies,* firms coordinate their activities primarily via hierarchies and competitive market arrangements. These forms of coordination are well described by a classic literature (Williamson 1985). Market relationships are characterized by the arm's-length exchange of goods or services in a context of competition and formal contracting. In response to the price signals generated by such markets, the actors adjust their willingness to supply and demand goods or services, often on the basis of the marginal calculations stressed by neoclassical economics.[7] In many respects, market institutions provide a highly effective means for coordinating the endeavors of economic actors.

In *coordinated market economies,* firms depend more heavily on non-market relationships to coordinate their endeavors with other actors and to construct their core competencies. These non-market modes of coordination generally entail more extensive relational or incomplete contracting, network monitoring based on the exchange of private information inside networks, and more reliance on collaborative, as opposed to competitive, relationships to build the competencies of the firm. In contrast to liberal market economies (LMEs), where the equilibrium outcomes of firm behavior are usually given by demand and supply conditions in competitive markets, the equilibria on which firms coordinate in coordinated market economies (CMEs) are more often the result of strategic interaction among firms and other actors.

Market relations and hierarchies are important to firms in all capitalist economies, of course, and, even in liberal market economies, firms enter into some relationships that are not fully mediated by market forces.[8] But this typology is based on the contention that the incidence of different types of firm relationships varies systematically across nations. In some nations, for instance, firms rely primarily on formal contracts and highly competitive markets to organize relationships with their employees and suppliers of finance, while, in others, firms coordinate these endeavors differently. In any national economy, firms will gravitate toward the mode of coordination for which there is institutional support.

2.3. The Role of Institutions and Organizations

Institutions, organizations, and culture enter this analysis because of the support they provide for the relationships firms develop to resolve coordination problems. Following North (1990: 3), we define institutions as a set of rules, formal or informal, that actors generally follow, whether for normative, cognitive, or material reasons, and organizations as durable entities with formally recognized members, whose rules also contribute to the institutions of the political economy.[9]

From this perspective, markets are institutions that support relationships of particular types, marked by arm's-length relations and high levels of competition. Their concomitant is a legal system that supports formal contracting and encourages relatively complete contracts, as the chapters in *Varieties of Capitalism* indicate. All capitalist economies also contain the hierarchies that firms construct to resolve the problems that cannot be addressed by markets (Williamson 1985). In liberal market economies, these are the principal institutions on which firms rely to coordinate their endeavors.

Although markets and hierarchies are also important elements of coordinated market economies, firms in this type of economy draw on a further set of organizations and institutions for support in coordinating their endeavors. What types of organizations and institutions support the distinctive strategies of economic actors in such economies? Because the latter rely more heavily on forms of coordination secured through strategic interaction to resolve the problems they face, the relevant institutions will be those that allow them to coordinate on equilibrium strategies that offer higher returns to all concerned. In general, these will be institutions that reduce the uncertainty actors have about the behavior of others and allow them to make credible commitments to each other. A standard literature suggests that these are institutions providing capacities for (i) the *exchange of information* among the actors, (ii) the *monitoring* of behavior, and (iii) the *sanctioning* of defection from cooperative endeavor (see Ostrom 1990). Typically, these institutions include powerful business or employer associations, strong trade unions, extensive networks of cross-shareholding, and legal or regulatory systems designed to facilitate information-sharing and collaboration. Where these are present, firms can coordinate on strategies to which they would not have been led by market relations alone.

The problem of operating collaborative vocational training schemes provides a classic example. Here, the willingness of firms to participate depends on the security of their beliefs that workers will learn useful skills and that firms not investing in training will not poach extensively from those who do, while the participation of workers depends on assurances that training will lead to remunerative employment. As Culpepper's chapter in *Varieties of Capitalism* indicates, it is easier for actors to secure these assurances where there are institutions providing reliable flows of information about appropriate skill levels, the incidence of training, and the employment prospects of apprentices (Finegold and Soskice 1988; Culpepper and Finegold 1999).

Similarly, the terms on which finance is provided to firms will depend on the monitoring capacities present in the economy. Where potential investors have little access to inside information about the progress of the firms they fund, access to capital is likely to depend on highly public criteria about the assets of a firm of the sort commonly found on balance sheets. Where investors are linked to the firms they fund through networks that allow for the development of reputations based on extensive access to information about the internal operations of the firm, however, investors will be more willing to supply capital to firms on terms that do not depend entirely on their balance sheets. The presence of institutions providing network reputational monitoring can have substantial effects on the terms on which firms can secure finance.

In short, this approach to comparative capitalism emphasizes the presence of institutions providing capacities for the exchange of information, monitoring, and the sanctioning of defections relevant to cooperative behavior among firms and other actors; and it is for the presence of such institutions that we look when comparing nations.

In addition, examination of coordinated market economies leads us to emphasize the importance of another kind of institution that is not normally on the list of those crucial to the formation of credible commitments, namely institutions that provide actors potentially able to cooperate with one another with a capacity for *deliberation*. By this, we simply mean institutions that encourage the relevant actors to engage in collective discussion and to reach agreements with each other.[10] Deliberative institutions are important for several reasons.

Deliberative proceedings in which the participants engage in extensive sharing of information about their interests and beliefs can improve the confidence of each in the strategies likely to be taken by the others. Many game-theoretic analyses assume a level of common knowledge that is relatively thin, barely stretching past a shared language and familiarity with the relevant payoffs. When multiple equilibria are available, however, coordination on one (especially one that exchanges higher payoffs for higher risks) can be greatly facilitated by the presence of a thicker common knowledge, one that extends beyond the basic situation to a knowledge of the other players sufficiently intimate to provide confidence that each will coordinate on a specific equilibrium (Eichengreen 1997). Deliberation can substantially thicken the common knowledge of the group.

As Scharpf (1987: ch. 4) has pointed out, although many think only of a 'prisoner's dilemma' game when they consider problems of cooperation, in the political economy many such problems take quite different forms, including 'battle of the sexes' games in which joint gains are available from more than one strategy but are distributed differently depending on the equilibrium chosen. Distributive dilemmas of this sort are endemic to political economies, and agreement on the distribution of the relevant gains is often the prerequisite to effective cooperation (Knight 1992). In some cases, such as those of collaborative research and development, the problem is not simply to distribute the gains but also the risks attendant on the enterprise. Deliberation provides the actors with an opportunity to establish the risks and gains attendant on cooperation and to resolve the distributive issues associated with them. In some cases, the actors may simply be negotiating from positions of relative power, but extensive deliberation over time may build up specific conceptions of distributive justice that can be used to facilitate agreement in subsequent exchanges.

Finally, deliberative institutions can enhance the capacity of actors in the political economy for strategic action when faced with new or unfamiliar challenges. This is far from irrelevant since economies are frequently subject to exogenous shocks that force the actors within them to respond to situations to which they are unaccustomed. The history of wage negotiations in Europe is replete with examples. In such instances, developments may outrun common knowledge, and deliberation can be instrumental to devising an effective and coordinated response, allowing the actors to develop a common diagnosis of the situation and an agreed response.

In short, deliberative institutions can provide the actors in a political economy with strategic capacities they would not otherwise enjoy; and we think cross-national comparison should be attentive to the presence of facilities for deliberation as well as institutions that provide for the exchange of information in other forms, monitoring, and the enforcement of agreements.

2.4. The Role of Culture, Informal Rules, and History

Our approach departs from previous works on comparative capitalism in another respect.[11] Many analyses take the view that the relevant outcomes in economic performance or policy follow more or less directly from differences in the formal organization of the political economy. Particular types of wage settlements or rates of inflation and unemployment are often said to follow, for instance, from the organizational structure of the union movement. Because we believe such outcomes are the products of efforts to coordinate in contexts of strategic interaction, however, we reject the contention that they follow from the presence of a particular set of institutions alone, at least if the latter are defined entirely in terms of formal rules or organizations.

As we have noted, the presence of a set of formal institutions is often a necessary precondition for attaining the relevant equilibrium in contexts of coordination. But formal institutions are rarely sufficient to guarantee that equilibrium. In multi-player games with multiple iterations of the sort that characterize most of the cases in which we are interested, it is well known that there exist multiple equilibria, any one of which could be chosen by the actors even in the presence of institutions conducive to the formation of credible commitments (Fudenberg and Maskin 1986). Something else is needed to lead the actors to coordinate on a specific equilibrium and, notably, on equilibria offering high returns in a non-cooperative context.[12] In many instances, what leads the actors to a specific equilibrium is a set of shared understandings about what other actors are likely to do, often rooted in a sense of what it is appropriate to do in such circumstances (March and Olsen 1989).

Accordingly, taking a step beyond many accounts, we emphasize the importance of informal rules and understandings to securing the equilibria in the many strategic interactions of the political economy. These shared understandings are important elements of the 'common knowledge' that lead participants to coordinate on one outcome, rather than another, when both are feasible in the presence of a specific set of formal institutions. By considering them a component of the institutions making up the political economy, we expand the concept of institutions beyond the purely formal connotations given to it in some analyses.

This is an entry point in the analysis for history and culture. Many actors learn to follow a set of informal rules by virtue of experience with a familiar set of actors and the shared understandings that accumulate from this experience constitute something like a common culture. This concept of culture as a set of shared understandings or available 'strategies for action' developed from experience of operating in a particular environment is analogous to those developed in the 'cognitive turn' taken by sociology (Swidler 1986; DiMaggio and Powell 1991). Our view of the role that culture can play in the strategic interactions of the political economy is similar to the one Kreps (1990) accords it in organizations faced with problems of incomplete contracting.

The implication is that the institutions of a nation's political economy are inextricably bound up with its history in two respects. On the one hand, they are created by actions, statutory or otherwise, that establish formal institutions and their operating procedures. On the other, repeated historical experience builds up a set of common expectations that allows the actors to coordinate effectively with each other. Among other things, this implies that the institutions central to the operation of the political economy should not be seen as entities that are created at one point in time and can then be assumed to operate effectively afterwards. To remain viable, the shared understandings associated with them must be reaffirmed periodically by appropriate historical experience. As Thelen emphasizes in *Varieties of Capitalism*, the operative force of many institutions cannot be taken for granted but must be reinforced by the active endeavors of the participants.

2.5. Institutional Infrastructure and Corporate Strategy

This varieties of capitalism approach draws its basic conceptions of how institutions operate from the new economics of organization. We apply a set of concepts commonly used to explain behavior at the micro-level of the economy to problems of understanding the macroeconomy (Milgrom and Roberts 1992). One of the advantages is an analysis with robust and consistent postulates about what kind of institutions matter and how they affect behavior. Another is the capacity of the approach to integrate analysis of firm behavior with analysis of the political economy as a whole.

However, there are at least two respects in which our account deviates from mainstream views in the new economics of organization. First, although we make use of the influential dichotomy between 'markets' and 'hierarchies' that Williamson (1975) has impressed on the field, we do not think this exhausts the relevant variation. Markets and hierarchies are features of LMEs and CMEs but we stress the systematic variation found in the character of corporate structure (or hierarchies) across different types of economies and the presence of coordination problems even within hierarchical settings (Milgrom and

Roberts 1992). Even more important, we do not see these two institutional forms as the only ones firms can employ to resolve the challenges they confront. In coordinated market economies in particular, many firms develop relationships with other firms, outside actors, and their employees that are not well described as either market-based or hierarchical relations but better seen as efforts to secure cooperative outcomes among the actors using a range of institutional devices that underpin credible commitments. Variation in the incidence and character of this 'third' type of relationship is central to the distinctions we draw between various types of political economies.[13]

Second, it is conventional in much of the new economics of organization to assume that the core institutional structures of the economy, whether markets, hierarchies, or networks, are erected by firms seeking the most efficient institutions for performing certain tasks. The postulate is that (institutional) structure follows (firm) strategy (cf. Chandler 1974; Williamson 1975, 1985; Chandler and Daems 1980). In a restricted sense, this is certainly true: firms can choose whether to contract out an endeavor or perform it in-house, for instance, and they enjoy some control over their own corporate form.

However, we think it unrealistic to regard the overarching institutional structures of the political economy, and especially those coordinating the endeavors of many actors (such as markets, institutional networks, and the organizations supporting collaborative endeavor), as constructs created or controlled by a particular firm. Because they are collective institutions, a single firm cannot create them; and, because they have multifarious effects, it may be difficult for a group of firms to agree on them.[14] Instead, as Calvert (1995) observes, the construction of coordinating institutions should be seen as a second-order coordination problem of considerable magnitude. Even when firms can agree, the project may entail regulatory action by the government and the formation of coalitions among political parties and labor organizations motivated by considerations going well beyond efficiency (Swenson 1991, 1997).

As a result, the firms located within any political economy face a set of coordinating institutions whose character is not fully under their control. These institutions offer firms a particular set of opportunities; and companies can be expected to gravitate toward strategies that take advantage of these opportunities. In short, there are important respects in which strategy follows structure. For this reason, our approach predicts systematic differences in corporate strategy across nations, and differences that parallel the overarching institutional structures of the political economy. This is one of the most important implications of the analysis.

Let us stress that we refer here to broad differences. Of course, there will be additional variation in corporate strategies inside all economies in keeping with differences in the resource endowments and market settings of individual firms. The capabilities of management also matter, since firms are actors with considerable autonomy. Our point is that (institutional) structure conditions (corporate) strategy, not that it fully determines it. We also agree that differences in corporate strategy can be conditioned by the institutional support available to firms at the regional or sectoral levels (Campbell et al. 1991; Hollingsworth et al. 1994; Herrigel 1996). Many of the works making this point are congruent with our own in that they stress the importance of the institutional environment to firm strategy, even though there has been fruitful disagreement about which features of that environment matter most (cf. Streeck 1992b).[15]

However, we emphasize variations in corporate strategy evident at the national level. We think this justified by the fact that so many of the institutional factors conditioning the behavior of firms remain nation-specific. There are good reasons why that should be the case. Some of the relevant institutions were deeply conditioned by nationally specific processes of development, as are most trade unions and employers' associations. In others, the relevant institutions depend heavily on statutes or regulations promulgated by national states, as do many institutions in the financial arena and labor market, not to mention the sphere of contract law.

In sum, we contend that differences in the institutional framework of the political economy generate systematic differences in corporate strategy across LMEs and CMEs. There is already some evidence for this. For instance, the data that Knetter (1989) has gathered are especially interesting. He finds that the firms of Britain, a typical LME, and those of Germany, a CME, respond very differently to a similar shock, in this case an appreciation of the exchange rate that renders the nation's goods more expensive in foreign markets. British firms tend to pass the price increase along to customers in order to maintain their profitability, while German firms maintain their prices and accept lower returns in order to preserve market share.

Our approach predicts differences of precisely this sort. We would argue that British firms must sustain their profitability because the structure of financial markets in a liberal market economy links the firm's access to capital and ability to resist takeover to its current profitability; and they can sustain the loss of market share because fluid labor markets allow them to lay off workers readily. By contrast, German firms can sustain a decline in returns because the financial system of a coordinated market economy provides firms with access to capital independent of current profitability; and they attempt to retain market share because the labor institutions in such an economy militate in favor of long-term employment strategies and render layoffs difficult.

These are only some of the ways in which the institutional arrangements of a nation's political economy tend to push its firms toward particular kinds of corporate strategies. We explore more of these below with special emphasis on innovation.

To put the point in the most general terms, however, firms and other actors in coordinated market economies should be more willing to invest in *specific* and *co-specific assets* (i.e. assets that cannot readily be turned to another purpose and assets whose returns depend heavily on the active cooperation of others), while those in liberal market economies should invest more extensively in *switchable assets* (i.e. assets whose value can be realized if diverted to other purposes). This follows from the fact that CMEs provide more institutional support for the strategic interactions required to realize the value of co-specific assets, whether in the form of industry-specific training, collaborative research and development, or the like, while the more fluid markets of LMEs provide economic actors with greater opportunities to move their resources around in search of higher returns, encouraging them to acquire switchable assets, such as general skills or multi-purpose technologies.[16]

2.6. Institutional Complementarities

The presence of *institutional complementarities* reinforces the differences between liberal and coordinated market economies. The concept of 'complementary goods' is a familiar one: two goods, such as bread and butter, are described as complementary if an increase in the price of one depresses demand for the other. However, complementarities may also exist among the operations of a firm: marketing arrangements that offer customized products, for instance, may offer higher returns when coupled to the use of flexible machine tools on the shop floor (Jaikumar 1986; Milgrom and Roberts 1990, 1995).

Following Aoki (1994), we extend this line of reasoning to the institutions of the political economy. Here, two institutions can be said to be complementary if the presence (or efficiency) of one increases the returns from (or efficiency of) the other.[17] The returns from a stock market trading in corporate securities, for instance, may be increased by regulations mandating a fuller exchange of information about companies.

Of particular interest are complementarities between institutions located in different spheres of the political economy. Aoki (1994) has argued that long-term employment is more feasible where the financial system provides capital on terms that are not sensitive to current profitability. Conversely, fluid labor markets may be more effective at sustaining employment in the presence of financial markets that transfer resources readily among endeavors thereby maintaining a demand for labor (cf. Caballero and Hamour 1998; Fehn 1998). Casper explores complementarities between national systems of contract law and modes of inter-firm collaboration, and we identify others in the sections that follow.

This point about institutional complementarities has special relevance for the study of comparative capitalism. It suggests that nations with a particular type of coordination in one sphere of the economy should tend to develop complementary practices in other spheres as well.[18] Several logics may be operative here. In some cases, the institutions sustaining coordination in one sphere can be used to support analogous forms of coordination in others. Where dense networks of business associations support collaborative systems of vocational training, for instance, those same networks may be used to operate collective standard-setting. Similarly, firms may pressure governments to foster the development of institutions complementary to those already present in the economy in order to secure the efficiency gains they provide.

If this is correct, institutional practices of various types should not be distributed randomly across nations. Instead, we should see some clustering along the dimensions that divide liberal from coordinated market economies, as nations converge on complementary practices across different spheres. Figure 1.1 presents some support for these propositions. It locates OECD

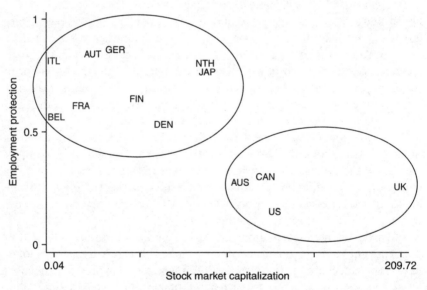

Figure 1.1. Institutions across sub-spheres of the political economy

Note: Employment protection refers to the index of employment protection developed by Estevez-Abe, Iversen, and Soskice in *Varieties of Capitalism*. Stock market capitalization is the market value of listed domestic companies as a percentage of GDP.

Source: International Federation of Stock Exchanges, *Annual Report*.

nations on two axes that provide indicators for the character of institutions in the spheres of corporate finance and labor markets respectively. A highly developed stock market indicates greater reliance on market modes of coordination in the financial sphere, and high levels of employment protection tend to reflect higher levels of non-market coordination in the sphere of industrial relations.[19] Although there is some variation within each group, a pronounced clustering is evident. Nations with liberal market economies tend to rely on markets to coordinate endeavors in both the financial and industrial relations systems, while those with coordinated market economies have institutions in both spheres that reflect higher levels of non-market coordination.

Among the large OECD nations, six can be classified as liberal market economies (the USA, Britain, Australia, Canada, New Zealand, Ireland) and another ten as coordinated market economies (Germany, Japan, Switzerland, the Netherlands, Belgium, Sweden, Norway, Denmark, Finland, and Austria) leaving six in more ambiguous positions (France, Italy, Spain, Portugal, Greece, and Turkey).[20] However, the latter show some signs of institutional clustering as well, indicating that they may constitute another type of capitalism, sometimes described as 'Mediterranean', marked by a large agrarian sector and recent histories of extensive state intervention that have left them with specific kinds of capacities for non-market coordination in the sphere of corporate finance but more liberal arrangements in the sphere of labor relations (see Rhodes 1997).

Although each type of capitalism has its partisans, we are not arguing here that one is superior to another. Despite some variation over specific periods, both liberal and coordinated market economies seem capable of providing satisfactory levels of long-run economic performance, as the major indicators of national well-being indicate. Where there is systematic variation between these types of political economies, it is on other dimensions of performance. We argue below that the two types of economies have quite different capacities for innovation. In addition, they tend to distribute income and employment differently. As Figure 1.2 indicates, in liberal market economies, the adult population tends to be engaged more extensively in paid employment and levels of income inequality are high.[21] In coordinated market economies, working hours tend to be shorter for more of the population and incomes more equal. With regard to the distribution of well-being, of course, these differences are important.

To make this analytical framework more concrete, we now look more closely at coordination in the principal spheres of firm endeavor in coordinated and liberal market economies, drawing on the cases of Germany and the United States for examples and emphasizing the institutional complementarities present in each political economy.

3. COORDINATED MARKET ECONOMIES:
THE GERMAN CASE

As we have noted, we regard capitalist economies as systems in which companies and individuals invest, not only in machines and material technologies, but in competencies based on relations with others that entail coordination problems. In coordinated market economies, firms resolve many of these problems through strategic interaction. The resulting equilibria depend, in part, on the presence of supportive institutions. Here, we use the case of Germany to illustrate how non-market coordination is achieved in each of the principal spheres of firm endeavor. Of course, the institutions used to secure coordination in other CMEs may differ to some extent from those of Germany.

(i) The *financial system* or *market for corporate governance* in coordinated market economies typically provides companies with access to finance that is

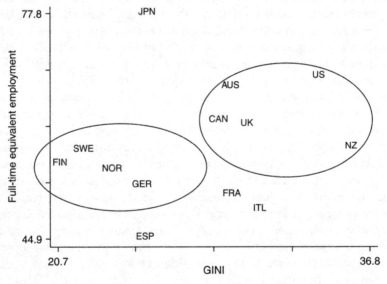

Figure 1.2. Distributional outcomes across political economies

Note: Full-time equivalent employment is defined as the total number of hours worked per year divided by full-time equivalent hours per year per person times working age population. GINI refers to the Gini coeffficient measuring post-tax, post-transfer income inequality.

Sources: For full-time equivalent unemployment: OECD (1996a). For GINI index: Spain, Japan, New Zealand are from Deiniger and Squire (1996); the remaining countries are from OECD (1996a).

not entirely dependent on publicly available financial data or current returns. Access to this kind of 'patient capital' makes it possible for firms to retain a skilled workforce through economic downturns and to invest in projects generating returns only in the long run. The core problem here is that, if finance is not to be dependent on balance-sheet criteria, investors must have other ways of monitoring the performance of companies in order to ensure the value of their investments. In general, that means they must have access to what would normally be considered 'private' or 'inside' information about the operation of the company.

This problem is generally resolved in CMEs by the presence of dense networks linking the managers and technical personnel inside a company to their counterparts in other firms on terms that provide for the sharing of reliable information about the progress of the firm. Reliability is secured in a number of ways. Firms may share information with third parties in a position to monitor the firm and sanction it for misleading them, such as business associations whose officials have an intimate knowledge of the industry. Reputation is also a key factor: where membership in a network is of continuing value, the participants will be deterred from providing false information lest their reputation in the network and access to it suffer. CMEs usually have extensive systems for what might be termed 'network reputational monitoring' (Vitols et al. 1997).

In Germany, information about the reputation and operation of a company is available to investors by virtue of (*a*) the close relationships that companies cultivate with major suppliers and clients, (*b*) the knowledge secured from extensive networks of cross-shareholding, and (*c*) joint membership in active industry associations that gather information about companies in the course of coordinating standard-setting, technology transfer, and vocational training. Other companies are not only represented on the supervisory boards of firms but typically engaged closely with them in joint research, product development, and the like. In short, firms sit inside dense business networks from which potential funders can gain a considerable amount of inside information about the track record and projects of a firm.[22]

The overall structure of the market for corporate governance is equally important. Since firms often fund their activities from retained earnings, they are not always sensitive to the terms on which external finance is supplied. But they can be forced to focus on profitability and shareholder value if faced with the prospect of hostile takeover by others claiming to be able to extract more value from the company. Thus, the corporate strategies found in many CMEs also depend on tax provisions, securities regulations, and networks of cross-shareholding that discourage hostile mergers and acquisitions, which were very rare until recently, for instance, in Germany.

(ii) The *internal structure* of the firm reinforces these systems of network monitoring in many CMEs. Unlike their counterparts in LMEs, for instance, top managers in Germany rarely have a capacity for unilateral action. Instead, they must secure agreement for major decisions from supervisory boards, which include employee representatives as well as major shareholders, and from other managers with entrenched positions as well as major suppliers and customers. This structural bias toward consensus decision-making encourages the sharing of information and the development of reputations for providing reliable information, thereby facilitating network monitoring.

In the perspective we present, the incentives facing individuals, whether managers or workers, are as important as those facing firms. In CMEs, managerial incentives tend to reinforce the operation of business networks. Long-term employment contracts and the premium that firm-structure places on a manager's ability to secure consensus for his projects lead managers to focus heavily on the maintenance of their reputations, while the smaller weight given to stock-option schemes in managerial compensation in CMEs relative to LMEs inclines them to focus less on profitability than their counterparts in LMEs. The incentives for managers are broadly aligned with those of firms.

(iii) Many firms in coordinated market economies employ production strategies that rely on a highly skilled labor force given substantial work autonomy and encouraged to share the information it acquires in order to generate continuous improvements in product lines and production processes (Sorge and Warner 1986; Dore 1986). However, companies that adopt such strategies are vulnerable to 'hold up' by their employees and the 'poaching' of skilled workers by other firms, while employees who share the information they gain at work with management are open to exploitation.[23] Thus, CMEs need *industrial relations* institutions capable of resolving such problems.

The German industrial relations system addresses these problems by setting wages through industry-level bargains between trade unions and employer associations that generally follow a leading settlement, normally reached in engineering where the union is powerful enough to assure the labor movement that it has received a good deal. Although union density is only moderately high, encompassing employers' associations bind their members to these agreements. By equalizing wages at equivalent skill levels across an industry, this system makes it difficult for firms to poach workers and assures the latter that they are receiving the highest feasible rates of pay in return for the deep commitments they are making to firms. By coordinating bargaining across the economy, these arrangements also limit the inflationary effects of wage settlements (Streeck 1994; Hall and Franzese 1998).

The complement to these institutions at the company level is a system of works councils composed of elected employee representatives endowed with considerable authority over layoffs and working conditions. By providing employees with security against arbitrary layoffs or changes to their working conditions, these works councils encourage employees to invest in company-specific skills and extra effort.

(iv) Because coordinated market economies typically make extensive use of labor with high industry-specific or firm-specific skills, they depend on *education and training systems* capable of providing workers with such skills.[24] The coordination problems here are acute, as workers must be assured that an apprenticeship will result in lucrative employment, while firms investing in training need to know that their workers will acquire usable skills and will not be poached by companies that do not make equivalent investments in training. CMEs resolve these problems in a variety of ways.

Germany relies on industry-wide employer associations and trade unions to supervise a publicly subsidized training system. By pressuring major firms to take on apprentices and monitoring their participation in such schemes, these associations limit free-riding on the training efforts of others; and, by negotiating industry-wide skill categories and training protocols with the firms in each sector, they ensure both that the training fits the firms' needs and that there will be an external demand for any graduates not employed by the firms at which they apprenticed. Because German employer associations are encompassing organizations that provide many benefits to their members and to which most firms in a sector belong, they are well placed to supply the monitoring and suasion that the operation of such a system demands as well as the deliberative forums in which skill categories, training quotas, and protocols can be negotiated. Workers emerge from their training with both company-specific skills and the skills to secure employment elsewhere.

(v) Since many firms in coordinated market economies make extensive use of long-term labor contracts, they cannot rely as heavily on the movement of scientific or engineering personnel across companies, to effect technology transfer, as liberal market economies do. Instead, they tend to cultivate *inter-company relations* of the sort that facilitate the diffusion of technology across the economy. In Germany, these relationships are supported by a number of institutions. Business associations promote the diffusion of new technologies by working with public officials to determine where firm competencies can be improved and orchestrating publicly subsidized programs to do so. The access to private information about the sector that these associations enjoy helps them ensure that the design of the programs is effective for these purposes. A considerable amount of research is also financed jointly by companies, often in collaboration with quasi-public research institutes. The common technical standards fostered by industry associations help to diffuse new technologies, and they contribute to a common knowledge-base that facilitates collaboration among personnel from multiple firms, as do the industry-specific skills fostered by German training schemes (Lütz 1993; Soskice 1997b; Ziegler 1997).

Germany has also developed a system of contract law complementary to the presence of strong industry associations that encourages relational contracting among companies and promotes this sort of technology transfer. Because of the many contingencies that can arise in close inter-firm relationships involving joint research or product development, tightly written, formal contracts are often inadequate to sustain such relationships. However, the German courts permit unusually open-ended clauses in inter-firm contracts on the explicit condition that these be grounded in the prevailing standards of the relevant industry association. Thus, the presence of strong industry associations capable of promulgating standards and resolving disputes among firms is the precondition for a system of contract law that encourages relational contracting (cf. Casper 1997).

In these respects, German institutions support forms of relational contracting and technology transfer that are more difficult to achieve in liberal market economies. One of the effects is to encourage corporate strategies that focus on product differentiation and niche production, rather than direct product competition with other firms in the industry, since close inter-firm collaboration is harder to sustain in the presence of the intense product competition that tends to characterize LMEs.

The complementarities present in the German political economy should be apparent from this account. Many firms pursue production strategies that depend on workers with specific skills and high levels of corporate commitment that are secured by offering them long employment tenures, industry-based wages, and protective works councils. But these practices are feasible only because a corporate governance system replete with mechanisms for network monitoring provides firms with access to capital on terms that are relatively independent of fluctuations in profitability. Effective vocational training schemes, supported by an industrial-relations system that discourages poaching, provide high levels of industry-specific skills. In turn, this encourages collective standard-setting and inter-firm collaboration of the sort that promotes technology transfer. The arrows in Figure 1.3 summarize some of these complementarities. Since many of these institutional practices enhance the effectiveness with which others operate, the economic returns to the system as a whole are greater than its component parts alone would generate.

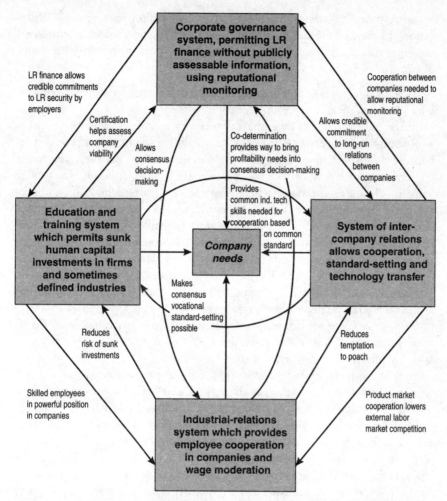

Figure 1.3. Complementarities across subsystems in the German coordinated market economy

4. LIBERAL MARKET ECONOMIES: THE AMERICAN CASE

Liberal market economies can secure levels of overall economic performance as high as those of coordinated market economies, but they do so quite differently. In LMEs, firms rely more heavily on market relations to resolve the coordination problems that firms in CMEs address more often via forms of non-market coordination that entail collaboration and strategic inter-action. In each of the major spheres of firm endeavor, competitive markets are more robust and there is less institutional support for non-market forms of coordination.

(i) Several features of the *financial systems* or *markets for corporate govern-ance* of liberal market economies encourage firms to be attentive to current earnings and the price of their shares on equity markets. Regulatory regimes are tolerant of mergers and acquisitions, including the hostile takeovers that become a prospect when the market valuation of a firm declines. The terms on which large firms can secure finance are heavily dependent on their valuation in equity markets, where dispersed investors depend on publicly available information to value the company. Liberal market economies usually lack the close-knit corporate networks capable of providing investors with inside information about the progress of companies that allows them to supply finance less dependent on quarterly balance sheets and publicly available information. The relevant contrast is with CMEs, where firms need not be as attentive to share price or current profitability in order to ensure access to finance or deter hostile takeovers.

Of course, there are some qualifications to these generalizations. Com-panies with readily assessable assets associated with forward income streams, such as pharmaceutical firms with a 'pipeline' of drugs, consumer-goods companies with strong reputations for successful product development, and firms well positioned in high-growth markets, need not be as concerned about current profitability. New firms in high-technology fields can often secure funds from venture-capital companies that develop the resources and tech-nical expertise to monitor their performance directly and trade ownership stakes in these firms for the high risks they take.[25] On the whole, however, the markets for corporate governance in LMEs encourage firms to focus on the publicly assessable dimensions of their performance that affect share price, such as current profitability.

(ii) In the *industrial relations arena*, firms in liberal market economies generally rely heavily on the market relationship between individual worker and employer to organize relations with their labor force. Top management normally has unilateral control over the firm, including substantial freedom to hire and fire.[26] Firms are under no obligation to establish representative bodies for employees such as works councils; and trade unions are generally less powerful than in CMEs, although they may have significant strength in some sectors. Because trade unions and employer associations in LMEs are less cohesive and encompassing, economy-wide wage coordination is generally difficult to secure. Therefore, these economies depend more heavily on macroeconomic policy and market competition to control wages and inflation (Hall and Franzese 1998).

The presence of highly fluid labor markets influences the strategies pursued by both firms and individuals in liberal market economies. These markets make it relatively easy for firms to release or hire labor in order to take advantage of new opportunities but less attractive for them to pursue production strategies based on promises of long-term employment. They encourage individuals to invest in general skills, transferable across firms, rather than company-specific skills and in career trajectories that include a substantial amount of movement among firms.

(iii) The *education and training systems* of liberal market economies are generally complementary to these highly fluid labor markets. Vocational training is normally provided by institutions offering formal education that focuses on general skills because companies are loath to invest in apprenticeship schemes imparting industry-specific skills where they have no guarantees that other firms will not simply poach their apprentices without investing in training themselves. From the perspective of workers facing short job tenures and fluid labor markets, career success also depends on acquiring the general skills that can be used in many different firms; and most educational programs from secondary through university levels, even in business and engineering, stress 'certification' in general skills rather than the acquisition of more specialized competencies.

High levels of general education, however, lower the cost of additional training. Therefore, the companies in these economies do a substantial amount of in-house training, although rarely in the form of the intensive apprenticeships used to develop company-specific or industry-specific skills in CMEs. More often, they provide further training in the marketable skills that employees have incentives to learn. The result is a labor force well equipped with general skills, especially suited to job growth in the service sector where such skills assume importance, but one that leaves some firms short of employees with highly specialized or company-specific skills.

(iv) *Inter-company relations* in liberal market economies are based, for the most part, on standard market relationships and enforceable formal contracts. In the United States, these relations are also mediated by rigorous antitrust regulations designed to prevent companies from colluding to control prices or markets and doctrines of contract laws that rely heavily on the strict interpretation of written contracts.

Extensive reputation-building is generally more difficult in economies lacking the dense business networks or associations that circulate reputations for reliability or sharp practice quickly and widely. Because the market for corporate governance renders firms sensitive to fluctuations in current profitability, it is also more difficult for them to make credible commitments to relational contracts that extend over substantial periods of time.

How then does technology transfer take place in liberal market economies? In large measure, it is secured through the movement of scientists and engineers from one company to another (or from research institutions to the private sector) that fluid labor markets facilitate. These scientific personnel bring their technical knowledge with them. LMEs also rely heavily on the licensing or sale of innovations to effect technology transfer, techniques that are most feasible in sectors of the economy where effective patenting is possible, such as biotechnology, microelectronics, and semiconductors. The prominence of this practice helps to explain the presence of venture-capital firms in liberal market economies: one success at standard-setting can pay for many failed investments (Borrus and Zysman 1997).

In LMEs, research consortia and inter-firm collaboration, therefore, play less important roles in the process of technology transfer than in CMEs where the institutional environment is more conducive to them. Until the National Cooperative Research Act of 1984, American firms engaging in close collaboration with other firms actually ran the risk of being sued for triple damages under antitrust law; and it is still estimated that barely 1 to 7 per cent of the funds spent on research and development in the American private sector are devoted to collaborative research.

It should be apparent that there are many institutional complementarities across the sub-spheres of a liberal market economy (see Figure 1.4). Labor market arrangements that allow companies to cut costs in a downturn by shedding labor are complementary to financial markets that render a firm's access to funds dependent on current profitability. Educational arrangements that privilege general, rather than firm-specific, skills are complementary to highly fluid labor markets; and the latter render forms of technology transfer that rely on labor mobility more feasible. In the context of a legal system that militates against relational contracting, licensing agreements are also more effective than inter-firm collaboration on research and development for effecting technology transfer.

Special note should be taken of the complementarities between the internal structure of firms and their external institutional environment in liberal and coordinated market economies. In LMEs, corporate structures that concentrate authority in top management make it easier for firms to release labor when facing pressure from financial markets and to impose a new strategy on the firm to take advantage of the shifting market opportunities that often present themselves in economies characterized by highly mobile assets. By contrast, in CMEs, where access to finance and technology often depends on a firm's attractiveness as a collaborator and hence on its reputation, corporate structures that impose more consensual forms of decision-making allow firms to develop reputations that are not entirely dependent on those of its top management. By reducing the capacity of top management to act arbitrarily, these structures also enhance the firm's capacity to enter credibly into relational contracts with employees and others in economies where a firm's access to many kinds of assets, ranging from technology to skills, may depend on its capacity for relational contracting.

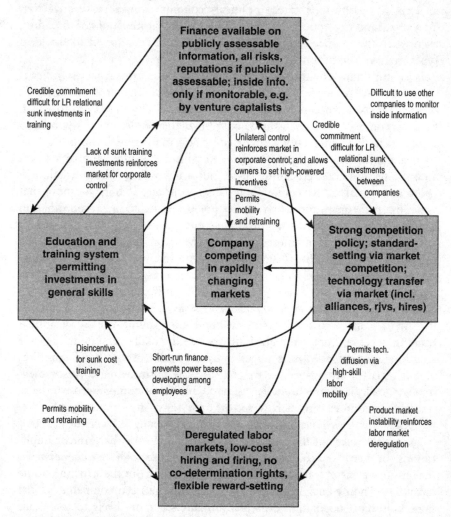

Figure 1.4. Complementarities across subsystems in the American liberal market economy

5. COMPARING COORDINATION

Although many of the developed nations can be classified as liberal or coordinated market economies, the point of this analysis is not simply to identify these two types but to outline an approach that can be used to compare many kinds of economies. In particular, we are suggesting that it can be fruitful to consider how firms coordinate their endeavors and to analyze the institutions of the political economy from a perspective that asks what kind of support they provide for different kinds of coordination, even when the political economies at hand do not correspond to the ideal types we have just outlined.

It is important to note that, even within these two types, significant variations can be found. Broadly speaking, liberal market economies are distinguishable from coordinated market economies by the extent to which firms rely on market mechanisms to coordinate their endeavors as opposed to forms of strategic interaction supported by non-market institutions. Because market institutions are better known, we will not explore the differences among liberal market economies here. But a few words about variation in coordinated market economies may be appropriate, if only to show that variation in the institutional structures underpinning strategic coordination can have significant effects on corporate strategy and economic outcomes.

One important axis of difference among CMEs runs between those that rely primarily on *industry-based coordination,* as do many of the northern European nations, and those with institutional structures that foster *group-based coordination* of the sort found in Japan and South Korea. As we have seen, in Germany, coordination depends on business associations and trade unions that are organized primarily along sectoral lines, giving rise to vocational training schemes that cultivate industry-specific skills, a system of wage coordination that negotiates wages by sector, and corporate collaboration that is often industry-specific. By contrast, the business networks of most importance in Japan arc built on *keiretsu,* families of companies with dense interconnections cutting across sectors, the most important of which is nowadays the *vertical keiretsu* with one major company at its center.

These differences in the character of business networks have major implications. In Germany, companies within the same sector often cooperate in the sensitive areas of training and technology transfer. But the structure of the Japanese economy encourages sharp competition between companies in the same industry. Cooperation on sensitive matters is more likely to take place within the *keiretsu,* that is, among firms operating in different sectors but within one 'family' of companies. The sectoral cooperation that takes place usually concerns less sensitive matters, including recession cartels, licensing require-ments, and entry barriers as well as the annual wage round (Soskice 1990a).

This pattern of *keiretsu*-led coordination also has significant implications for patterns of skill acquisition and technology transfer. Serious training, technology transfer and a good deal of standard-setting take place primarily within the vertical *keiretsu*. Workers are encouraged to acquire firm- or group-specific skills, and notably strong relational skills appropriate for use within the family of companies within which they have been trained. In order to persuade workers to invest in skills of this specificity, the large firms have customarily offered many of them lifetime employment. And, in order to sustain such commitments, many Japanese firms have cultivated the capacity to move rapidly into new products and product areas in response to changes in world markets and technologies. This kind of corporate strategy takes advantage of the high levels of workforce cooperation that lifetime employ-ment encourages. To reinforce it, Japanese firms have also developed company unions providing the workforce with a voice in the affairs of the firm.

Japanese firms tend to lack the capacities for radical innovation that Ameri-can firms enjoy by virtue of fluid market settings or for sector-centered technology transfer of the sort found in Germany. Instead, the group-based organization of the Japanese political economy has encouraged firms there to develop distinctive corporate strategies that take advantage of the capacities for cross-sector technology transfer and rapid organizational redeployment pro-vided by the *keiretsu* system. These translate into comparative institutional advantages in the large-scale production of consumer goods, machinery, and electronics that exploit existing technologies and capacities for organizational change. Although Japan is clearly a coordinated market economy, the institu-tional structures that support group-based coordination there have been con-ducive to corporate strategies and comparative advantages somewhat different from those in economies with industry-based systems of coordination.

The varieties of capitalism approach can also be useful for understanding political economies that do not correspond to the ideal type of a liberal or coordinated market economy. From our perspective, each economy displays specific capacities for coordination that will condition what its firms and government do.

France is a case in point. Collaboration across French companies is based on career patterns that led many of the managers of leading firms through a few elite schools and the public service before taking up their positions in the private sector. The top managers of many French firms, therefore, have close ties to the state and weak ties to the rest of the enterprise. As a result they are less likely to pursue the corporate strategies found in Britain or Germany and more likely to look to the state for assistance than their counterparts in other nations. However, in the case of vocational training, there are clear limits to what states can do in the absence of strong business associations capable of monitoring their members. Large French firms adapt to these limits by taking industrial reorganization upon themselves, sometimes devising new networks to coordinate their activities.

In sum, although the contrast between coordinated and liberal market economies is important, we are not suggesting that all economies conform to these two types. Our object is to advance comparative analysis of the political economy more generally by drawing attention to the ways in which firms coordinate their endeavors, elucidating the connections between firm strategies and the institutional support available for them, and linking these factors to patterns of policy and performance. These are matters relevant to any kind of political economy.

6. COMPARATIVE INSTITUTIONAL ADVANTAGE

We turn now to some of the issues to which this perspective can be applied, beginning with a question central to international economics, namely, how to construe comparative economic advantage. The theory of comparative economic advantage is important because it implies that freer trade will not impoverish nations by driving their production abroad but enrich them by allowing each to specialize in the goods it produces most efficiently and exchange them for even more goods from other nations. It can be used to explain both the expansion of world trade and the patterns of product specialization found across nations. The most influential version of the theory focuses on the relative endowment of basic factors (such as land, labor, and capital) found in a nation and suggests that trade will lead a nation to specialize in the production of goods that use its most abundant factors most intensively (Stolper and Samuelson 1941).

However, recent developments have dealt a serious blow to this account of comparative economic advantage. The most important of these include the expansion of intra-industry trade and increases in the international mobility of capital. If the theory is correct, nations should not import and export high volumes of goods from the same sector; and there is a real possibility that international movements of capital will even out national factor endowments. As a result, some economists have become skeptical about whether comparative advantages really exist, and many have begun to seek other explanations for the expansion of trade and the geographic distribution of production.

Some explain the growth of trade, and intra-industry trade in particular, as the result of efforts to concentrate production in order to secure returns to scale (Helpmann 1984). Others explain the concentration of particular kinds of production in some nations as the result of firms' efforts to secure the positive externalities generated by a group of firms engaged in related endeavors at the same site, whether in the form of appropriate labor pools, the availability of relevant intermediate products, or technological spillovers. This approach predicts that companies making similar products will cluster together, whether in Silicon Valley or Baden-Württemberg (Krugman 1991).

However, while both of these theories explain why the production of some kinds of goods might be concentrated in a nation, they say little about why production of *that* type should be concentrated in *that* particular nation, while other nations specialize in other kinds of production. We still need a theory that explains why particular nations tend to specialize in specific types of production or products.

We think that such a theory can be found in the concept of *comparative institutional advantage*. The basic idea is that the institutional structure of a particular political economy provides firms with advantages for engaging in specific types of activities there. Firms can perform some types of activities, which allow them to produce some kinds of goods, more efficiently than others because of the institutional support they receive for those activities in the political economy, and the institutions relevant to these activities are not distributed evenly across nations.

The contention that institutions matter to the efficiency with which goods can be produced receives considerable support from the growing body of work on endogenous growth. Many economists have observed that national rates of growth cannot be explained fully by incremental additions to the stock of capital and labor and fixed rates of technical change. Endogenous growth theorists have suggested that the institutional setting for production also seems to matter to national rates of growth; and various efforts have been made to specify what features of that setting might be important. There is now widespread recognition that the institutional context can condition rates of growth and technological progress.

To date, however, most efforts to specify these institutions have concentrated on market relationships and the legal framework for them, neglecting the non-market relations that may be equally important to such outcomes. The latter receive more emphasis in the literature on national innovation systems and some analyses of competitive advantage (Dosi et al. 1988; Porter 1990; Barro and Sala-i-Martin 1995; Edquist 1997). Most of this literature, however, looks for the ingredients of *absolute* advantage, that is, it identifies factors more of which will improve the performance of any economy. We seek institutional features that might confer *comparative* advantage and, thus, be better suited to explaining cross-national patterns of product or process specialization (Zysman 1994).

The basic logic of our approach should be apparent. We have argued that, in some political economies, firms make more extensive use of non-market modes of coordination to organize their endeavors, while in others, firms rely mainly on markets to coordinate those endeavors. Broadly speaking, these differences correspond to the level of institutional support available for market, as opposed to non-market, coordination in each political economy. Using a distinction between liberal and coordinated market economies, we have identified many of the institutional features of the political economy relevant to these differences and suggest that these correspond to cross-national differences in corporate strategy.

The important point to be added here is that the availability of these different modes of coordination conditions the efficiency with which firms can perform certain activities, thereby affecting the efficiency with which they can produce certain kinds of goods and services. In short, the national institutional frameworks examined in this volume provide nations with comparative advantages in particular activities and products. In the presence of trade, these advantages should give rise to cross-national patterns of specialization.

Although there may be types of comparative advantage that these institutional frameworks confer that we have not yet explored, we focus here on their impact on *innovation* since a firm's capacity to innovate is crucial to its long-run success. The key distinction we draw is between *radical* innovation, which entails substantial shifts in product lines, the development of entirely new goods, or major changes to the production process, and *incremental* innovation, marked by continuous but small-scale improvements to existing product lines and production processes. Over the medium to long term, efficiency in the production of some kinds of goods requires a capacity for radical innovation, while, in other kinds of goods, it requires a capacity for incremental innovation.

Radical innovation is especially important in fast-moving technology sectors, which call for innovative design and rapid product development based on research, as in biotechnology, semiconductors, and software development. It is also important to success in the provision of complex system-based products, such as telecommunications or defense systems, and their service-sector analogs: airlines, advertising, corporate finance, and entertainment. In the latter, competitiveness demands a capacity for taking risks on new product strategies and for the rapid implementation of such strategies within large, tightly coupled organizations that employ a diverse personnel.

Incremental innovation tends to be more important for maintaining competitiveness in the production of capital goods, such as machine tools and factory equipment, consumer durables, engines, and specialized transport equipment. Here, the problem is to maintain the high quality of an established product line, to devise incremental improvements to it that attract consumer loyalty, and to secure continuous improvements in the production process in order to improve quality control and hold down costs.

Coordinated market economies should be better at supporting incremental innovation. This follows from the emphasis we have put on the relational requirements of company endeavors. It will be easier to secure incremental innovation where the workforce (extending all the way down to the shop floor) is skilled enough to come up with such innovations, secure enough to risk suggesting changes to products or process that might alter their job situation, and endowed with enough work autonomy to see these kinds of improvements as a dimension of their job. Thus, incremental innovation should be most feasible where corporate organization provides workers with secure employment, autonomy from close monitoring, and opportunities to influence the decisions of the firm, where the skill system provides workers with more than task-specific skills and, ideally, high levels of industry-specific technical skills, and where close inter-firm collaboration encourages clients and suppliers to suggest incremental improvements to products or production processes.

The institutions of coordinated market economies normally provide high levels of support for these relational requirements. Highly coordinated *industrial-relations systems* and *corporate structures* characterized by works councils and consensus decision-making provide employees with the guarantees that elicit their cooperation. The *training systems* of CMEs typically provide high skill levels and the requisite mix of company-specific and more general technical skills. Appropriate *contract laws* and *dense networks of inter-corporate linkages* allow firms to form relational contracts with other firms; and *systems of corporate governance* that insulate firms against hostile takeovers and reduce their sensitivity to current profits encourage long employment tenures and the development of the inter-firm and employee relations that foster incremental innovation. By encouraging corporate strategies based on product differentiation rather than intense product competition, these inter-corporate networks also tend to promote incremental, rather than radical, innovation. A reputation for risk-taking or cut-throat competition is rarely an asset in such networks.

By contrast, although some can occur there, the institutional features of liberal market economies tend to limit firms' capacities for incremental innovation. Financial market arrangements that emphasize current profitability and corporate structures that concentrate unilateral control at the top deprive the workforce of the security conducive to their full cooperation in innovation. Fluid labor markets and short job tenures make it rational for employees to concentrate more heavily on their personal career than the firm's success and on the development of general skills rather than the industry- or company-specific skills conducive to incremental innovation. The complexion of contract law and antitrust laws discourages inter-firm collaboration in incremental product development.

However, the institutional framework of liberal market economies is highly supportive of radical innovation. *Labor markets* with few restrictions on layoffs and high rates of labor mobility mean that companies interested in developing an entirely new product line can hire in personnel with the requisite expertise, knowing they can release them if the project proves unprofitable. Extensive *equity markets* with dispersed shareholders and few restrictions on mergers or acquisitions allow firms seeking access to new or radically different technologies to do so by acquiring other companies with relative ease, and the presence of venture capital allows scientists and engineers to bring their own ideas to market. *Inter-firm relations* based primarily on markets enhance the capacities of firms to buy other companies, to poach their personnel, and to license new products—all means of acquiring new technologies quickly.

By contrast, in CMEs, although dense inter-corporate networks facilitate the gradual diffusion of technology, they make it more difficult for firms to access radically new technologies by taking over other companies. Corporate structures characterized by strong worker representation and consensus decision-making make radical reorganization of a firm more difficult, as each of the affected actors contemplates the consequences for his relationship to the company. The long employment tenures that such institutions encourage make it less feasible for firms to secure access to new technologies by hiring in large numbers of new personnel.

In short, the institutional frameworks of liberal market economies provide companies with better capacities for radical innovation, while those of co-ordinated market economies provide superior capacities for incremental innovation. Therefore, to the extent allowed by transport costs and the efficiency of international markets, there should be national patterns of specialization in activities and products; and these should reflect rational responses to the institutional frameworks identified here rather than random geographic agglomeration.

We have focused on innovation here because it is one of the most crucial dimensions of economic success. However, the institutional structures of LMEs and CMEs may confer other kinds of comparative advantages yet to be explored. Firms in coordinated market economies, for instance, are well placed to secure high levels of quality control, by virtue of their close relationships with workers and suppliers; and such a capacity may give them advantages in products for which demand turns more heavily on quality relative to price. Conversely, the ease with which firms in liberal market economies can cut costs by releasing workers, given fluid labor markets and high levels of managerial prerogative, may provide them with advantages in products for which demand is highly price-sensitive.

Economists have also long believed that skill levels can be important to comparative advantage, and our analysis suggests that the availability of labor with particular types of skills will be dependent on precisely the kinds of institutions that distinguish liberal from coordinated market economies. The extensive facilities for inter-firm collaboration that foster high levels of industry-specific skills in some CMEs and company-specific skills in others may provide those nations with advantages for producing goods that require such labor, while the fluid labor markets and support for the development of general skills in LMEs may make the production of goods and services that require less skilled but lower-cost labor more viable there.

We have stressed the paradigmatic cases of liberal and coordinated market economies, but the perspective can be extended to institutional variation of other types. As we have noted, for instance, the group-based coordination characteristic of some CMEs provides firms with better capacities for diffusing technology across sectoral boundaries than do industry-based systems of coordination; and these capacities may give nations with group-based coordination special advantages in particular industries (Soskice 1994a). We have provided an explicit basis for understanding how comparative institutional advantage might operate, but there are many dimensions to it that remain to be investigated.

7. NEW PERSPECTIVES ON COMPARATIVE PUBLIC POLICY-MAKING

Comparative political economists have been as interested in patterns of economic policy-making as in problems of economic performance. Accordingly, it is appropriate to note that the analytical framework developed in *Varieties of Capitalism* also opens up substantial new perspectives on both economic and social policy-making with relevance for the domestic arena and international relations.

7.1. Economic Policy-Making

The approach we take to the political economy suggests some important revisions in the way we normally think about the problematic facing economic policy-makers, especially on the supply side of the economy. A substantial literature in comparative political economy, going back to Shonfield (1965), construes the problem facing policy-makers as one of settling on the actions that firms or other private-sector actors should take in order to improve economic performance and then devising a set of incentives, whether regulatory or financial, to induce them to take those actions. This was what the 'strong' states of France and Japan were once said to be so effective at doing (Johnson 1982; Zysman 1983). Broadly speaking, the problem was seen as one of inducing economic actors to cooperate with the government.

From our perspective, however, the principal problem facing policy-makers is quite different: it is one of inducing economic actors to cooperate more effectively with each other.[27] This follows from our view of the economy as an arena in which multiple actors develop competencies by devising better ways of coordinating their endeavors with one another. When firms coordinate more effectively, their performance will be better, and the result will be better overall economic performance. In some cases, more effective coordination among other actors, such as trade unions and employers, will also enhance performance.[28] Accordingly, one of the principal ways in which policy-makers can improve national economic performance is to secure better forms of coordination among private-sector actors.

In some cases, markets can be used to secure this coordination, and so the task facing policy-makers is to improve the functioning of markets. This is not always easy, but there are some well-known techniques for accomplishing this task. However, there are other cases in which firms can perform certain endeavors well (whether wage-bargaining, collaborating with other firms in research and development, or the like) only by coordinating with others in contexts of strategic interaction. Here, the problem is one of improving the equilibrium outcomes that arise from strategic interactions, and less is known about how to accomplish that. Culpepper describes this problem as one of securing 'decentralized cooperation'. It entails persuading private-sector actors to share information, improving their ability to make credible commitments, and altering their expectations about what others will do. As we have noted, the development of supportive institutions and the cultivation of a base of common knowledge may be crucial here (Ostrom 1990; Ramirez-Rangel 2000; Culpepper 2003).

This formulation highlights the difficulties facing economic policy-makers, especially when they are seeking to enhance non-market coordination. In such contexts, states cannot simply tell economic actors what to do, not only because the outcomes are too complex to be dictated by regulation but because states generally lack the information needed to specify appropriate strategies. In many cases, effective strategic coordination depends on the presence of appropriately organized social organizations, such as trade unions and employer associations, that governments can encourage but not create. As Culpepper's analysis of vocational training shows, effective cooperation also requires common knowledge that may develop only out of experience over time. Where norms and institutions supporting effective cooperation already exist, policy-makers may be able to improve its operation with complementary regulations, but it is difficult to induce such cooperation *ex nihilo* (Culpepper 1998).

It follows that economic policies will be effective only if they are *incentive compatible*, namely complementary to the coordinating capacities embedded in the existing political economy (Wood 1997). In liberal market economies, where coordination is secured primarily through market mechanisms, better economic performance may demand policies that sharpen market competition, while coordinated market economies may benefit more from policies that reinforce the capacities of actors for non-market coordination. Because the institutional context of the British economy encourages the acquisition of general skills and militates against sectoral coordination, its government is likely to enhance skill levels more by expanding formal education than by trying to foster sectoral training schemes modeled on the German. Conversely, competition policies that serve Britain well might erode the capacities of German firms for non-market coordination.

Wood (1997) goes beyond this to argue that the viability of policy depends not only on the organization of the political economy but on the organization of the political realm (see also Katzenstein 1978b, 1987).[29] Let us distinguish between 'market incentive' policies and 'coordination-oriented' policies. The former rely on market-based incentives to induce actors to perform more effectively. The latter attempt to improve the competencies of firms, such as their skill levels or technological capabilities, by addressing firm needs with relative precision. Thus, coordination-oriented policies must be based on high levels of information about the activities of the firm. But, as Wood points out, firms are reluctant to share such information with governments whose position as powerful actors under a range of unpredictable influences raises the risks that they will defect from any agreement and use the information they have acquired against the firm. In short, this kind of policy-making is marked by information asymmetries, high transaction costs, and time-inconsistency problems.

The governments of coordinated market economies have taken advantage of the strong business associations, trade unions, and other para-public organizations in their political economies to resolve these problems. Because such associations are independent of the government and responsible to their member-firms, the latter are more inclined to trust them with enough private information to administer a coordination-oriented or 'framework' policy effectively. And because these associations are in a good position to monitor and even gently sanction their members, they can often secure the coordination that a policy demands with lower transaction costs. Thus, producer-group organizations enter into 'implicit contracts' with the government to administer the policy, drawing some benefits of their own in the form of enhanced resources and authority.

This is where the organization of the political realm matters. Business associations and their members will be willing to form such contracts, which usually entail some information-sharing, only if the government's commitment to abide by them is credible. As Wood (1997) observes, however, that commitment will be more credible where the relevant producer groups have enough structural influence to punish the government for any deviations from its agreements. This structural influence may rest on a number of bases: the authority of producer organizations inside political parties, the entrenchment of neo-corporatist practices in enough spheres of policy-making that defection in one can be punished in another, or policy-making procedures decentralized enough to allow producer groups many points of access and some veto points. Of course, the influence of producer groups will also depend on the character of those groups themselves: they must be encompassing and powerful enough to mobilize a serious constituency if they need to sanction the government. In short, coordination-oriented policies should be more feasible in nations with both a coordinated market economy and a political system in which producer groups enjoy substantial structural influence.

Coordination-oriented policies will be more difficult to implement in liberal market economies because their business and labor associations usually lack the encompassing character required to administer such policies well. In addition, producer groups may be less willing to enter into such implicit contracts in nations where they do not possess enough structural influence to sanction the government for deviations from them. This should be an especially important problem in nations where the powers of the state are highly concentrated in the political executive or where the influence of producer groups inside political parties is very limited.

In contradistinction to some others, then, this analysis suggests that the attributes normally associated with the 'strength' of a state may prevent governments from implementing many kinds of policies effectively. Wood (1997) shows that the failures of successive British schemes for industrial rationalization were rooted, not in the 'weakness' of the British state, as many who underline the limited levers in the hands of the authorities have suggested, but in its very strength: the Westminster system concentrates so much power in the political executive that producer groups were reluctant to trust it (cf. Sacks 1980; Leruez 1975; Shonfield 1965).

In general, liberal market economies should find it more feasible to implement market-incentive policies that do not put extensive demands on firms to form relational contracts with others but rely on markets to coordinate their activities. Because of the bluntness of the instruments available to states and the importance of markets to these economies, deregulation is often the most effective way to improve coordination in LMEs.

This analysis of institutional complementarities between political regimes and political economies raises some intriguing issues about the patterns observable in the developed world. Many liberal market economies have Westminster systems of government that concentrate power in the political executive, while coordinated market economies tend to be governed by consociational, coalitional, or quasi-corporatist regimes. If regimes that provide structural influence to encompassing producer groups find it more feasible to implement coordination-oriented policies, while states in which power is highly concentrated have more success with market-incentive policies, the character of the political regime may contribute to the development of a particular type of economy. Levy (1999a) argues forcefully for a variant of this view in the case of France.

To put a similar point in more general terms, the character of the political regime may condition the levels of asset specificity found across nations (see Alt et al. 1996). We have already argued that the institutional structure of the economy encourages certain kinds of investments. The fluid market settings of liberal market economies encourage investment in switchable assets, while the dense institutional networks of coordinated market economies enhance the attractiveness of investment in specific or co-specific assets. Political regimes characterized by coalition governments, multiple veto points, and parties that entrench the power of producer groups may also be more conducive to investment in specific assets than ones that concentrate power in highly autonomous party leaders, because (i) regimes of this sort are well positioned to provide the framework policies that sustain the institutions supporting specific investments and (ii) because they provide producers with more direct influence over government and the capacity to punish it for deviating from its agreements, such regimes offer investors more assurance that policy will not shift in such a way as to damage the value of assets that cannot readily be switched to other uses.[30] Thus, we should expect to find more investment in specific assets in nations with such regimes. These are issues that merit further investigation.

7.2. Social Policy

The varieties of capitalism approach to political economy also opens up new perspectives on social policy. In particular, it highlights the importance of social policy to firms and the role that business groups play in the development of welfare states. Convention associates the development of social policy with organized labor and progressive political parties, on the assumption that business generally opposes such initiatives. However, Mares (1998a) shows that business groups have played key roles in the development of social policy for over a century and develops a parsimonious model to explain the policies in which various types of firms will have interests. Her work advances an important literature exploring the contribution that business groups have made to the construction of welfare states (Pierson 1995a; Martin 1999; Swenson 1997, 2001; Mares 1997b, 1998; Estevez-Abe 1999a).

The relational approach we take to company competencies naturally draws attention to the support that social policies can provide for the relationships firms develop to advance their objectives. Social policy is often thought to interfere with labor markets by raising labor costs or the reservation wage. But the contributors to *Varieties of Capitalism* explore the ways in which social policies can improve the operation of labor markets, notably from the perspective of the firm. Unemployment benefits with high replacement rates, for instance, can improve the ability of firms to attract and retain pools of labor with high or specific skills. Disability benefits and early retirement benefits can allow firms that operate production regimes requiring employee loyalty to release labor without violating implicit contracts about long-term employment. There are many respects in which social policies can be crucial to the relational strategies of firms.

For this reason, there should be a correspondence between types of political economies and types of welfare states. And that appears to be the case. Virtually all liberal market economies are accompanied by 'liberal' welfare states, whose emphasis on means-testing and low levels of benefits reinforce the fluid labor markets that firms use to manage their relations with labor (Esping-Andersen 1990). Liberal social-policy regimes also encourage individuals to develop the general, rather than specific, skills that corporate strategies in LMEs tend to require.

Although the social-policy regimes that accompany coordinated market economies are more varied, there are many respects in which their distinctive features lend support to the corporate strategies found in such economies. Large companies in Japan find it easier to secure employee loyalty and company-specific skills because they provide many of the social benefits that might otherwise be the responsibility of the state (Estevez-Abe 1999a). Many of the firms in CMEs operate product market strategies and associated production regimes that require a workforce equipped with high levels of industry-specific skills. Workers must be persuaded to invest in such skills, however, especially given the risk that, if they are laid off and must take employment in another sector, they may never realize their investment. In such contexts the pension and unemployment-benefit schemes offering generous replacement rates closely tied to wages often found in coordinated market economies help to assure workers that they can weather an economic downturn without having to shift to a job in which their investment in specific skills does not pay off.

Governments introduce social legislation for many reasons, some of them conditioned by partisan competition and the demands of labor. But business also has important interests in social policy and a role in its development. Mares (1998) traces the way in which social policy emerges from alliances between business groups, trade unions, and public officials in Germany and France, while Estevez-Abe (1999a) and Iversen and Soskice (2000) explore the politics that leads specific types of political economies toward distinctive welfare states. In the sphere of social policy, the varieties of capitalism approach is helping to open up several new research agendas.

7.3. National Interests in the International Arena

The international arena is also an important sphere for policy-making. What states cannot secure domestically, because of political resistance or transnational externalities, they often seek in negotiations about international regimes (Krasner 1983b; Keohane 1984; Putnam 1988). These regimes now have a substantial impact on national societies, especially in Europe where the regulations of the European Union have become almost as important as national policies. For this reason, it is important to understand how the rules or regulations of such regimes are determined, and a number of approaches can be taken to that problem. One of the most influential, however, argues that the character and regulations of regimes and of the EU are determined by their member states, operating from conceptions of national interest (Moravcsik 1991).

Analysts have taken several approaches to identifying the conceptions of national economic interest that motivate governments in international negotiations. Some formulations associate them with prevailing economic conditions, such as the levels of inflation or unemployment in the nation (Moravscik 1998). Others employ neoclassical economic doctrine to specify the welfare gains likely to accrue to the nation from a particular outcome, such as freer trade (Frieden and Rogowski 1996). Most who take this approach use an economic theory to identify the impact a decision will have on particular sectors and an institutional theory to predict which sectors will have more influence over the government (Milner 1988, 1997; Frieden 1991; Garrett and Lange 1996).

There is some value in all these approaches, especially for specific cases, but the conceptions of national interest they generate can be nebulous or of limited generality. Varieties of capitalism suggests that their stance toward new regulatory initiatives will be influenced by judgements about whether those initiatives are likely to sustain or undermine the comparative institutional advantages of their nation's economy. Governments should be inclined to support such initiatives only when they do not threaten the institutions most crucial to the competitive advantages their firms enjoy.[31]

Fioretos (1998) applies this perspective to the positions taken by states in negotiations over the Maastricht Treaty. For instance, he argues that Britain's opt out from the social charter sprang from its efforts to secure a competitive edge for its firms and preserve the institutions of its liberal market economy. Germany's reluctance to accept deep financial regulation may have derived from a concern to preserve the capacities for network monitoring that sustain the terms on which domestic capital is available to its firms (cf. Storey and Walter 1997).

In terms of the wider development of the EU, since the success of national economies hinges on whether the institutions of their states supply the right economic policies to sustain them, its members may share a concern with whether EU-wide economic policies are compatible with these. Thus, states and actors from coordinated market economies can be expected to seek institutions conducive to the formation of implicit contracts between public authorities and business associations, while those from liberal market economies should want to avoid agencies interventionist enough to interfere with the operation of market mechanisms.

This perspective may help explain why it has been so difficult for the EU to secure full regulatory harmonization and why it has resorted, instead, to the 'mutual recognition' of national regulations (Nicolaides 1993). Transaction costs alone do not seem to provide enough of an explanation. If the structure of the European economies were broadly similar, it should be possible to agree on 'best practice', allowing a transition period for laggards to catch up. But there are profound institutional differences among the political economies of Europe, on which the firms of each nation have come to rely for competitive advantage. This suggests that, despite some significant effects, international negotiations are unlikely to be vehicles for the cross-national institutional convergence that some expect from them.[32]

8. THE DYNAMICS OF ECONOMIC ADJUSTMENT

Although we have emphasized differences among political economies that have been relatively durable, ours is not a static conception of the political economy. On the contrary, we expect the corporate strategies, policies, and institutions of each nation to evolve in response to the challenges they face, and our approach contains a number of conceptual tools for understanding both the nature of contemporary challenges and the shape this evolution is likely to take. In this section, we discuss some of the dynamic elements of the analysis that are covered in more detail in subsequent chapters.

8.1. The Challenge of Globalization

For political economy, the principal issue raised by globalization (defined as the internationalization of trade and finance with the threat of exit) concerns the stability of regulatory regimes and national institutions in the face of heightened competitive pressure (Boyer and Drache 1996; Rodrik 1997). Will institutional differences among nations of the sort we have identified remain significant or will the processes of competitive deregulation unleashed by international integration drive all economies toward a common market model?

To these questions, the conventional view of globalization prominent in the press and much of the literature gives an ominous answer. It is built on three pillars. First, it sees firms as essentially similar across nations at least in terms of basic structure and strategy. Second, it associates the competitiveness of firms with their unit labor costs, from which it follows that many will move production abroad if they can find cheaper labor there. And, third, these propositions generate a particular model of the political dynamic inspired by globalization, of the following type.

In the face of threats from firms to exit the economy, governments are said to come under increasing pressure from business to alter their regulatory frameworks so as to lower domestic labor costs, reduce rates of taxation, and expand internal markets via deregulation. The precise effects that each nation suffers in the face of globalization will be determined by the amount of political resistance that labor and the left can mount to proposals for change. But, because international interdependence provides capital with more exit opportunities than it does for labor, the balance of power is said to have shifted dramatically toward capital. In short, this is a model that predicts substantial deregulation and a convergence in economic institutions across nations. Conventional views of globalization contain a 'convergence hypothesis' analogous in force, but considerably less sanguine in implications, to an earlier one based on theories of industrialism (Kerr et al. 1960; Graubard 1964).

8.2. Reconsidering Globalization

The varieties of capitalism approach calls into question each of the assumptions underpinning the conventional view of globalization. First, it suggests that firms are not essentially similar across nations. On the contrary, firms in LMEs and CMEs develop distinctive strategies and structures to capitalize on the institutions available for market or non-market coordination in the economy. There is substantial evidence that firms in different types of economies react differently to similar challenges (Knetter 1989). Thus, we should not expect identical responses from them to globalization.

Second, our perspective suggests that firms will not automatically move their activities off-shore when offered low-cost labor abroad. Cheaper labor that comes with commensurate skill and productivity levels is always attractive, but firms also derive competitive advantages from the institutions in their home country that support specific types of inter- and intra-firm relationships. Comparative institutional advantages tend to render companies less mobile than theories that do not acknowledge them imply.

Of course, with international liberalization, there will be some movement of corporate activities across national borders, as firms seek access to new markets and new sources of supply, but our approach suggests dimensions to this movement that conventional views do not anticipate. It implies, for instance, that firms based in LMEs may be more inclined to move their activities abroad to secure cheaper labor than companies based in CMEs, as the latter often pursue corporate strategies that rely on high skills and institutional infrastructure difficult to secure elsewhere.

Our concept of comparative institutional advantage also suggests that firms may exploit new opportunities for movement to engage in a form of *institutional arbitrage.* By this, we mean that companies may shift particular activities to other nations in order to secure the advantages that the institutional frameworks of their political economies offer for pursuing those activities. Thus, companies may move some of their activities to liberal market economies, not simply to lower labor costs, but to secure access to institutional support for radical innovation. Conversely, companies may locate other activities in coordinated market economies in order to secure access to the quality control, skill levels, and capacities for incremental innovation that their institutional frameworks offer. Over time, corporate movements of this sort should reinforce differences in national institutional frameworks, as firms that have shifted their operations to benefit from particular institutions seek to retain them.

Finally, our perspective predicts one dynamic in liberal market economies and a different one in coordinated market economies. In the face of more intense international competition, business interests in LMEs are likely to pressure governments for deregulation, since firms that coordinate their endeavors primarily through the market can improve their competencies by sharpening its edges. The government is likely to be sympathetic because the comparative advantage of the economy as a whole rests on the effectiveness of market mechanisms. Therefore, the balance of power is likely to tilt toward business. The result should be some weakening of organized labor and a substantial amount of deregulation, much as conventional views predict.

In coordinated market economies, however, the political dynamic inspired by globalization should be quite different. Here, governments should be less sympathetic to deregulation because it threatens the nation's comparative institutional advantages.[33] Although there will be some calls for deregulation even in such settings, the business community is likely to provide less support for it, because many firms draw competitive advantages from systems of relational contracting that depend on the presence of supportive regulatory regimes. In these economies, firms and workers have common interests to defend because they have invested in many co-specific assets, such as industry-specific skills. Thus, the political dynamic in CMEs is likely to center around the formation of cross-class coalitions, as firms and workers with intense interests in particular regulatory regimes align against those with interests in others (cf. Swenson 1991, 1997).[34]

This analysis explains several outcomes in the spheres of policy and politics that are otherwise puzzling. Globalization was expected to weaken trade unions across the industrialized world. But comparative data show that trade union membership and the locus of collective bargaining has dropped far more substantially in some nations than in others (Lange et al. 1995; Ebbinghaus and Visser 2000). Our analysis predicts most of the patterns observed. Trade unions have been weakened by business initiatives and deregulation in LMEs but remain strong in CMEs where cross-class coalitions help to preserve them and some degree of wage coordination.

Instead of the monolithic movement toward deregulation that many expect from globalization, our analysis predicts a bifurcated response marked by widespread deregulation in liberal market economies and limited movement in coordinated market economies.[35] This is precisely the pattern of policy across the OECD in recent decades. Deregulation has been far-reaching in the liberal market economies of Britain, the United States, New Zealand, Canada, and Australia but much less extensive in the coordinated market economies of northern Europe and east Asia (Vogel 1996; Ellis 1998; Story and Walter 1997; Wood 1997; King and Wood 1999).[36] Moreover, Wood and Thelen report finding just the sort of politics this approach would lead one to expect in both liberal and coordinated market economies in recent years (Wood 1997; Thelen 2000).

Ultimately, it is not surprising that increasing flows of trade have not erased the institutional differences across nations. After all, world trade has been increasing for fifty years without enforcing convergence. Because of comparative institutional advantage, nations often prosper, not by becoming more similar, but by building on their institutional differences.[37]

8.3. Developments in the Market for Corporate Governance

There is another side to globalization, however, with effects that some argue are more ambiguous. It lies in the pressures stemming from the internationalization of finance, where developments have recently been dramatic, if not unprecedented.[38] International flows of capital have grown exponentially in the past two decades, raising levels of both direct and portfolio investment (cf. Simmons 1999). This puts pressure on the institutions of coordinated market economies in several ways. International financial markets have become increasingly important sources of capital for large firms. But, lacking the facilities to monitor the progress of a company closely, distant investors usually prefer to supply capital on arm's-length terms that emphasize transparent, balance-sheet criteria. Therefore, firms seeking access to these funds face pressure to revise their accounting standards, appoint independent directors, and deliver the high rates of return associated with 'shareholder value'.

Even more important is the wave of international merger and acquisition activity that has taken place over the past decade. Firms based in coordinated market economies, such as Germany, that have usually not been as concerned about their rate of return on capital or share price as American firms have acquired a new interest in such matters because many hope to use their own shares to make foreign acquisitions to consolidate their competitive position in global markets that are opening and reconfiguring rapidly.[39] Shares that are highly valued can be a significant asset in merger and acquisition contests.

Similarly, some of the large banks and insurance companies in CMEs that once cultivated close relations with manufacturing firms have been disengaging from them in order to free up resources for global expansion. The German government has recently facilitated such moves by lowering capital-gains taxes on the sale of corporate shareholdings. Where steps such as these reduce cross-shareholding enough to undercut the protection it provides firms against hostile takeovers or government regulations on such acquisitions are relaxed, the heightened dangers of takeover could also prompt firms to become more attentive to the value of their shares and earnings in order to deter takeovers.

These developments threaten traditional practices in CMEs in several ways. On the one hand, they could disrupt the intricate systems of cross-shareholding and inter-corporate linkage that provide capacities for network monitoring, thereby reducing the access of firms to capital that is not tied to current profitability. On the other, they could force firms whose strategies and structure have reflected responsiveness to a wide range of stakeholders, including employees, to become more attentive to shareholders and rates of return; and this might reduce their capacity to make credible commitments to long-term collaborative relationships. That could engender shifts in strategy extending all the way down to production regimes.

However, while important, the impact of international financial developments can easily be misinterpreted. There is no doubt that large companies in CMEs will have to make the long-run, risk-adjusted real rates of return demanded by world financial markets. But that is not inconsistent with internal management practices that maximize comparative institutional advantage. These pressures have led many companies to develop closer relationships with works councils rather than the reverse, simply because employee cooperation becomes more, not less, important in such contexts. Moreover, it is not a rational strategy for shareholders to insist on Anglo-Saxon management practices if that has the effect of lowering rates of return.

The market for corporate governance is changing but at a pace that may allow firms to retain many aspects of their long-standing strategies.

8.4. Analyzing Change in National Systems

Much of the work on comparative capitalism lacks developed conceptions of how national systems change. As a result, the literature on globalization tends to cluster around two poles. On one side are works that focus on the static nature of institutions and the ways in which they reproduce stable patterns of behavior. On the other are works that attribute great force to the pressures of globalization, and see national practices as inertial factors to be transformed by these.

Our approach offers a more dynamic conception of national political economies in the sense that it anticipates change in them and contains specific propositions about the processes through which it will occur. However, it may be useful to summarize some of the key implications about dynamics in this approach.

We see national political economies as systems that often experience external shocks emanating from a world economy in which technologies, products, and tastes change continuously. These shocks will often unsettle the equilibria on which economic actors have been coordinating and challenge the existing practices of firms. We expect firms to respond with efforts to modify their practices so as to sustain their competitive advantages, including comparative institutional advantages. Thus, much of the adjustment process will be oriented to the institutional recreation of comparative advantage. In its course, firms and individuals will modify their relational investments, seeking new competencies that entail new relations with other firms or employees.

To do so, they will call on the existing institutional structures supporting coordination in the economy, including those that allow for deliberation and the making of credible commitments. In many cases, firms will need the cooperation of government, but we expect governments to be responsive to efforts to restore coordination, because they will come under pressure from producer groups and voters with substantial interests in existing institutions to do so (Iversen and Soskice 2000). If coordination entails strategic interaction, however, more than institutional support is required to establish it. As we have noted, this sort of coordination also depends on the presence of a common knowledge-set of beliefs that reflect relatively complete understandings of the roles and interests of the participants in the arrangement, as well as some confidence in the trustworthiness of the relevant institutions. Economic shocks and interim attempts to cope with them can unsettle such understandings. Therefore, their restoration will be a crucial, and difficult, component of the adjustment process.

Several points follow from this perspective. First, although we expect firms to attempt to sustain or restore the forms of coordination on which their competitive advantages have been built, after an economic shock, these efforts may entail changes to existing institutions or practices in the economy. Second, the importance of common knowledge to successful strategic interaction implies some asymmetry in the development potential of these systems. LMEs, which lack this, will find it difficult to develop non-market coordination of the sort common in CMEs, even when the relevant institutions can be put into place. However, there is no such constraint on CMEs deregulating to become more like LMEs. However, we have noted that some firms in CMEs want to retain competitive advantages that depend on high levels of regulation.

Institutional complementarities should play an important, if ambiguous, role in these processes of adjustment. On the one hand, they raise the prospect that institutional reform in one sphere of the economy could snowball into changes in other spheres as well. If the financial markets of a CME are deregulated, for instance, it may become more difficult for firms to offer long-term employment. That could make it harder for them to recruit skilled labor or sustain worker loyalty, ultimately inspiring major changes in production regimes (cf. Aoki 1994). Financial deregulation could be the string that unravels coordinated market economies. On the other hand, institutional complementarities generate disincentives to radical change. Firms and other actors may attempt to preserve arrangements in one sphere of the economy in order to protect complementary institutions or synergies with institutions elsewhere that are of value to them.

The types of adjustment problems encountered in a coordinated market economy are well illustrated by some of the recent difficulties afflicting the German system of wage coordination.[40] For many years, the capacity of this system to generate wage increases moderate enough to sustain the competitiveness of German industry has depended on the ability of employers' associations to mount resistance to exorbitant wage demands, if necessary orchestrating lockouts of the workforce. In many cases, the major firms in a sector would resist high industry settlements, even if they could afford them, in order to maintain solidarity with smaller firms that could not afford them, increasing their own workers' wages only after an industry agreement had been reached.

In some sectors, the large firms responded to higher levels of international integration, moving some operations off-shore and reconfiguring supply chains. As a result, they have become increasingly sensitive to interruptions in production and inclined to veto lockouts. But this shift in stance has disrupted the existing equilibrium. Without the cooperation of large firms, employers' associations can no longer mount effective resistance to wage demands. As a consequence, some smaller or less efficient firms are dropping out of them; and moderate and solidaristic trade union leaders are now finding themselves unable to compromise because of pressure from their militants.[41] The result has been a deterioration in the effectiveness of wage coordination and of employers' associations in some German sectors (Thelen and Kume 1999a; Thelen and Wijnbergen 2000; see also Manow and Seils 2000).

This is the type of adjustment problem that often arises in coordinated settings. However, there are good reasons for thinking that effective coordination can be restored in most such cases. Such problems are not unprecedented in coordinated market economies. The equilibrium outcomes on which actors coordinate have been unsettled by economic shocks many times in the past. In each case, new equilibria have been found through processes of negotiation and compromise. The presence of institutions that entrench the power of employers and trade unions increase cooperation and deliberative institutions facilitates coordination.

In 'negotiated economies' such as these, adjustment is often slower than it is in economies coordinated primarily by markets; but markets do not necessarily generate superior outcomes. Where encompassing producer groups have extensive 'strategic capacity' and strong incentives to reach agreement, the results can be equally satisfactory.[42] Coordinated market economies have a track record of meeting these kind of challenges (Hall 1997; Global Economic Forum 2000). In Sweden, for instance, peak-level bargaining broke down during the 1980s because it was no longer meeting the needs of firms facing new technologies and greater international competition; but the trade unions and employers developed new forms of wage-bargaining recoordinated at the sectoral level rather than revert to purely liberal arrangements (Pontusson and Swenson 1996).

In sum, this is an approach to political economy designed not only to identify important patterns of similarity and difference across nations but also to elucidate the processes whereby national political economies change. It anticipates institutional change in all the developed democracies, as they adjust to contemporary challenges, but provides a framework within which the import of those changes can be assessed.

NOTES

1. We concentrate here on economies at relatively high levels of development because we know them best and think the framework applies well to many problems there. However, the basic approach should also have relevance for understanding developing economies as well (cf. Bates 1997).
2. Of necessity, this summary is brief and slightly stylized. As a result, it does not do full justice to the variety of analyses found within these literatures and neglects

some discussions that fall outside them. Note that some of our own prior work can be said to fall within them. For more extensive reviews, see Hall (1999, 2001).

3. An alternative approach to neo-corporatism, closer to our own, which puts less emphasis on the trade union movement and more on the organization of business was also developed by Katzenstein (1985a, 1985b) among others (Offe 1981).

4. One of the pioneering works that some will want to compare is Albert 1993, which develops a contrast between the models of the Rhine and America that parallels ours in some respects. Other valuable efforts to identify varieties of capitalism that have influenced us include Hollingsworth and Boyer 1997; Crouch and Streeck 1997b; Whitley 1999.

5. There are a few notable exceptions that influence our analysis, including the work of Scharpf (1987, 1997a) and Przeworski and Wallerstein (1982).

6. In other works by the contributors to *Varieties of Capitalism*, 'organized market economy' is sometimes used as a term synonymous with 'coordinated market economy'. Although all of the economies we discuss are 'coordinated' in the general sense of the term, by markets if not by other institutions, the term reflects the prominence of strategic interaction and hence of coordination in the game-theoretic sense in CMEs.

7. Although we do not emphasize it here, this is not meant to deny the observation of Granovetter (1985) and others that market relations are usually underpinned by personal relationships of familiarity and trust.

8. This point applies with particular force to market relationships in which one or more of the participants has substantially more market power than the others, as in cases of oligopoly, oligopsony, and the relations found in some supplier chains. We are not arguing that all markets in LMEs are perfectly competitive.

9. Note that, from time to time, we refer loosely to the 'institutions' or 'organization' of the political economy to refer to both the organizations and institutions found within it.

10. One political economist who has consistently drawn attention to the importance of deliberation is Sabel (1992, 1994) and the issue is now the subject of a growing game-theoretic literature (see Elster 1998).

11. Here we depart from some of our own previous formulations as well (cf. Hall 1986; Soskice 1990b).

12. Culpepper (1998, 2001) documents this problem and explores some solutions to it.

13. Williamson (1985) himself acknowledges the presence of institutionalized relationships extending beyond markets or hierarchies, albeit without characterizing them precisely as we do here.

14. At the sectoral or regional level, of course, large firms may be able to exercise substantial influence over the development of these institutions, as Hancké (2001) shows (see also Hancké 2002).

15. It is possible to apply the general analytical framework of *Varieties of Capitalism* to variations at the regional or sectoral level, as Hancké (2001) does in some respects. From the perspective of *Varieties of Capitalism*, institutional variation at the regional

or sectoral level provides an additional layer of support for particular types of coordination and one that enhances a nation's capacity to support a range of corporate strategies and production regimes.

16. For examples in one sphere, see Estevez-Abe, Iversen, and Soskice (2001).

17. Conversely, two institutions can be said to be 'substitutable' if the absence or inefficiency of one increases the returns to using the other. Note that we refer to total returns, leaving aside the question of to whom they accrue, which is a matter of property rights, and we define efficiency as the net returns to the use of an institution given its costs.

18. Of course, there are limits to the institutional isomorphism that can be expected across spheres of the economy. Although efficiency considerations may press in this direction, the presence of functional equivalents for particular arrangements will limit the institutional homology even across similar types of political economies, and the importance to institutional development of historical processes driven by considerations other than efficiency will limit the number of complementarities found in any economy.

19. The employment protection index developed by Estevez-Abe, Iversen, and Soskice (2001) is a composite measure of the relative stringency of legislation or collective agreements dealing with hiring and firing, the level of restraint embedded in collective dismissal rules, and the extent of firm-level employment protection. Stock market capitalization is the market value of listed domestic companies as a percentage of GDP.

20. Luxembourg and Iceland have been omitted from this list because of their small size and Mexico because it is still a developing nation.

21. The Gini Index used in Figure 1.2 is a standard measure for income inequality, measured here as post-tax, post-transfer income, reported in the Luxembourg Income Study for the mid- to late 1980s. Full-time equivalent employment is reported as a percentage of potential employment and measured as the total number of hours worked per year divided by full-time equivalent hours per person (37.5 hours at 50 weeks) times the working-age population. It is reported for the latest available of 1993 or 1994.

22. In previous decades, the German banks were also important contributors to such networks by virtue of their control over large numbers of shares in industrial firms (Hall 1986: ch. 9). In recent years, the role of the large commercial banks has declined, as they divest themselves of many holdings (Griffin 2000).

23. 'Hold up' is Williamson's (1985) term for the withdrawal of active cooperation to back up demands.

24. Compared to general skills that can be used in many settings, industry-specific skills normally have value only when used within a single industry and firm-specific skills only in employment within that firm.

25. Note that we avoid a distinction often drawn between countries in which firms can raise 'long-term' capital versus those in which only 'short-term' capital is available because this distinction is rarely meaningful. Many companies in LMEs

with established market reputations can raise capital for projects promising revenues only in the medium to long term, and firms often finance the bulk of their activities from retained earnings. Of more relevance are the rules governing hostile takeovers, whose prospect can induce firms to pay more attention to corporate earnings and the price of their shares.

26. Partly for this reason, the market valuation of firms in LMEs often depends more heavily on the reputation of its CEO than it does in CMEs.

27. The formulations in these paragraphs are influenced by the work of Pepper Culpepper (1998, 2003) and owe a good deal to conversations with him.

28. Here, as elsewhere in this chapter, when we refer to 'more effective' coordination, we mean coordination by the actors on actions providing equilibria that are Pareto-superior to those that preceded them in the sense that they make at least some of the actors better off without making others worse off.

29. The analysis in the following paragraphs owes a great deal to Wood (1997) as well as his chapter in this volume.

30. Katzenstein (1987) shows how the structural features of the German political system hem in most governments, while Gamble and Walkland (1987) show how frequently British governments have changed regulatory regimes important to business.

31. Note, of course, that governments can misperceive the impact of a proposed regulation and that other factors will often also enter into calculations of national interest. These formulations are deeply influenced by the work of Fioretos (1998).

32. As Streeck (1996b) and Scharpf (1995: ch.2) have pointed out, precisely because they cannot legislate regulatory convergence, international regimes and the EU may resort to measures that enhance market competition, thereby intensifying the presures for convergence that come from another direction, namely via process of competitive deregulation. There is much to be said for this view. For further discussion, see the section on 'globalization' below.

33. Note that we are not claiming all types of non-market institutions contribute to the efficiency of the economy. We have identified some specific types of inter- and intra-firm relations and supporting institutions that we associate with effective firm performance. There are other 'non-market' institutions in many economies that simply generate economic rents or detract from economic efficiency. The point is to distinguish among them and not to label all 'non-market' institutions efficient or inefficient.

34. Note that this observation corresponds to the predictions of Frieden and Rogowski (1996) that class conflict is more likely in economies where switchable assets predominate and sectoral conflict characterized by cross-class coalitions more likely in economies where asset specificity is high. However, because firms and workers share some interests in all economies, we do not exclude the possibility that some cross-class coalitions will also be formed in liberal market economies, as Swenson (1997) suggests.

35. We use 'deregulation' as a convenient shorthand to refer to policies that remove regulations limiting competition, expand the role of markets in the allocation of

resources, or sharpen market incentives in the economy. Of course, we recognize that all deregulation is implicitly a form of reregulation (Vogel 1996).

36. We predict some, if more limited, deregulation in CMEs because, alongside non-market institutions, they also use market mechanisms whose operation can be improved by a measured amount of deregulation.

37. The effects of trade integration seem to have fallen, less substantially on the differences between CMEs and LMEs, and more heavily on practices of state intervention of the sort once prominent in France and the developing world, as governments found that *dirigiste* policies cannot ensure competitiveness on international markets (cf. Hall 1990; Ziegler 1997; McArthur and Scott 1969).

38. As Zevin (1992) points out, international capital markets were probably more integrated in the decades before World War I than they have ever been since.

39. We are grateful to Michel Goyer for drawing our attention to this point (see Goyer 2001).

40. We owe this example to Kathleen Thelen (see Thelen and Kume 1999a; Thelen and Wijnbergen 2000).

41. Of course, with the advent of economic and monetary union, the Bundesbank no longer has the capacity to discipline union members by threatening tighter monetary policies, and the capacity of the European central bank to do so is much lower now because it stands at one remove from the German economy (see Hall and Franzese 1998).

42. By 'strategic capacity', we mean the capacity to formulate a collective strategy for the group and to mobilize support for it among the group. Typically, this entails highly articulated organization.

2

Typologies of Capitalism

Colin Crouch

That capitalist economies might take diverse forms has been long recognized by some scholars. Sometimes this diversity has been seen as a matter of evolutionary development. This was true of Max Weber's ideal type approach, that of the advocates of post-war modernization theory, and of those who followed Antonio Gramsci's identification of a Fordist phase of capitalism that was deemed to succeed the classic free-market form. This last idea flourished particularly in the French *régulationiste* school (Boyer and Saillard 1995). These approaches, different from each other though they are, all see some forms of capitalism superseding, and as therefore in some sense superior to, earlier modes. Hence these are not theories of a true diversity in the sense of a continuing multiplicity of forms, the historical superiority of any of which might never come to an issue.

Analysts willing to adopt this latter, less grand approach have been rarer. The modern *locus classicus* was Shonfield's work (1964), which examined the role of various institutions surrounding the economy – various branches of the state, banks, stock exchanges – in a number of western European countries, the USA, and Japan. Although he thought some were more efficient than others – in particular he was impressed by those that inserted some elements of planning into otherwise free markets – he did not talk in terms of historical transcendence.

When more theoretically inclined political scientists and sociologists returned to considering economic questions in the 1980s, they resumed Shonfield's concern with national politico-economic systems and hence national varieties of capitalism. Occasionally subtypes would be recognized within a national economy (mainly with regard to Italy and Spain), but these themselves have nearly always been geographically subdivided, so the concept of territorially based economies has been retained. This does not mean that each nation state has been seen as embodying its own unique form of capitalism; rather, national cases are grouped together under a small number of contrasted types.

This literature has many achievements. It has provided an intellectual counterweight to easy arguments about globalization, which predict an inevitable trend towards similarity among the world's economies. Whether globalization theorists predict a convergence based on US hegemony or an endogenous and voluntary aspiration towards a prosperous and rational new world, or whether they do not distinguish between these two, they have little time for arguments which insist on the viability of continuing differences. Neo-institutionalist accounts of diversity have provided both theoretical arguments and some empirical demonstrations to suggest that these may be great oversimplifications. However, I have argued previously (Crouch 2005: ch. 1) that, if we are to model the diversity of economic institutions more scientifically, and particularly if we are to study institutional change and innovation, we need to deconstruct the taken-for-granted wholes of contemporary neo-institutionalism and discover their constituent elements – elements which are able to survive in combinations other than those identified in the taken-for-granted wholes.

The fundamental point is: *empirical cases must be studied, not to determine to which (singular) of a number of theoretical types they should each be allocated, but to determine which (plural) of these types are to be found within them, in roughly what proportions, and with what change over time.* This alternative is less ambitious than the current fashion, in that it does not enable us to map the economic world with a few parsimonious categories. But it is also more ambitious, partly because it corresponds more closely to the requirements of scientific analysis, but also because it is able to accommodate and account for change taking place within empirical cases. This is something which most of the neo-institutionalist literature on capitalist diversity finds difficult to do, leading to the functionalism and determinism of much of its analysis.

More specifically, we can identify certain methodological flaws of the neo-institutionalist approach. Whatever else they do, schemes for analysing the diversity of capitalism usually answer two fundamental questions: How many types of capitalism do they perceive? And how extensive is the range of institutions their model covers? In answering the first, many theories derive their types in a dubious way. In tackling the second, they often make a flawed use of the concepts of elective affinity and complementarity. From these defects follow an oversimple relationship between types and cases and a reluctance fully to accept empirical heterogeneity. These further combine with an uncritical application of theories of path dependence to culminate in an inability to anticipate endogenous change and hence the emergence of a less static range of capitalist forms. In this chapter we shall concentrate on the first of the two initial flaws—deduction of the number of types. We shall consider problems of elective affinity and complementarity and their further consequences.

1. PITFALLS IN THE FORMULATION OF TYPES

The smallest number of theoretical types consistent with the idea of diversity is two. For almost all authors, one is always the free-market model of neoclassical economics. This constitutes the principal intellectual antagonist for neo-institutionalists, even when they argue that it accounts for only a highly specific form of capitalism (Boyer 1997). There must be at least one other form to make a theory of diversity: hence dichotomies. At the other extreme there is no theoretical limit to the number of forms that might be identified, but theories rarely propose more than five or six. Given the relatively small number of empirical cases of advanced capitalism for those tied to a national case approach (currently around twenty-five), it is difficult to sustain more than a handful of types without lapsing into empiricism.

The work of Albert (1991), who made the original contribution to dualistic analysis, is typical. He modelled two types of capitalism, which were seen in an antagonistic relationship. They are labelled in geo-cultural terms as Anglo-Saxon and *rhénan* (Rhenish). The former defines free-market capitalism, considered to be embodied in the anglophone countries.[1] The second takes its name from certain characteristics considered to be common to the riparian countries of the Rhine: Germany, the Netherlands, Switzerland, and more problematically France. However, not only is the author uncertain whether France's institutions fully belong to this type (an anxiety which was one of his main motives in writing the book), but Japan and Scandinavia are considered to be part of it. More disconcerting (at least from our perspective) than an image of the Rhine rising under Mount Fuji and entering the sea at Saltsjöbaden is the broad institutional range being gathered together to form this second type. The essential idea is a capacity to make long-term decisions that maximize certain collective rather than individual goods. But this means ignoring differences among the very diverse forms of collectivism found.

It is important to note that this dualism in the identification of types of economy parallels the debate between political philosophies – neoliberalism and social democracy – which lies behind the analysis and behind most contemporary political debate (Campbell and Pedersen 2001c). This has created some confusion over whether neo-institutionalism's confrontation is with neoclassical economics, and therefore at the analytical level only; or with neoliberal politics, implying an ideological confrontation; or with all political practices associated with the anti-Keynesian and pro-capitalist forces which came to prominence during the period.

Neoclassical analysis considers how economic actors would behave if a world of perfect markets existed. It usually but not necessarily incorporates the normative assumption that both economy and society would be improved were institutions to take this form, but neoclassical economists are at liberty to consider that this may not always constitute a practical proposition. They are not bound by their analytical approach to any particular policy conclusions, or to consider that the world in reality takes a certain form. It is neoliberalism which, as a political creed rather than a form of analysis, not only definitely adopts a positive normative evaluation of markets, but also believes that they could always be introduced in practice.

But in practice not even neoliberals do this. A by-product of the ideological dominance of neoliberalism since the 1980s, and in particular its association with the most powerful nation-state on earth – the USA – is a tendency among even serious analysts to assume that certain practices and institutions constitute part of the neoliberal paradigm just because they are found in the USA. The characteristics of the neoliberal model are derived from empirical observation of what is thought to be its main empirical example. But it is logically impossible to derive the characteristics of a theoretical category from the characteristics of an example of it, as the theoretical characteristics have to be known before a case can be considered to be such an example.

For example, an extremely powerful, scientifically oriented military sector, tying a number of contracting firms into close and necessarily secretive relations with central government departments, is a fundamental attribute of the US economy, and central to much of its innovative capacity in such sectors as aerospace and computing. The operation of such a military sector has nothing to do with the principles of either neoclassical economics or neoliberal politics. Analysts respond to this in two ways. Some just ignore the existence of this sector and its special characteristics in their account of the US economy. For example, the OECD (1994) felt able to describe the USA as a country lacking any close support from government for industry. Alternatively they argue that the defence sector is somehow part of the US 'liberal' model, without noting the difficulties of such an assumption (e.g. Amable 2000). At the level of US political ideology, it is significant that neoconservatism is replacing neoliberalism as the dominant force. The former has no difficulties with a dominant state-supported military sector.

As Campbell and Pedersen (2001c) argue, at the practical level neoliberalism has not been the monolith that both its advocates and opponents set it up to be. Within it have been contained a diversity of practices, some not particularly coherent with others. Kjær and Pedersen (2001) point to clear differences from the normally presented model in the form taken by so-called neoliberalism in Denmark. King and Wood (1999) have even demonstrated clear differences between the neoliberalisms of 1980s UK and USA, two cases normally seen as joint paradigms.

The collection of studies edited by Hall and Soskice (2001b) under the name *Varieties of Capitalism* represents the most ambitious and significant contribution to date of the dualist approach. It draws much from Albert, though it barely acknowledges his contribution. Their book has become the emblematic citation for all studies of diversity in capitalist economies. It is also an example of the preoccupation of many neo-institutionalists with coming to terms with and, in this case, eventually becoming absorbed by, an idealized version of neoliberalism. It seeks, not only to allocate every developed capitalist economy to one or other of two categories, but derives from this account a theory of comparative advantage and a list of the kind of products in which the country will specialize (Hall and Soskice 2001a: 36–44). This is achieved with the aid of certain assumptions concerning what constitutes radical and what incremental innovation—a characteristic which is considered to differentiate whole classes of goods and services. It is this factor, combined with its use of this sectoral analysis to account for certain important developments in different national economies during the 1990s, which has made the account so appealing.

Despite some ambiguity about a possible third model, these authors work with an essentially dualist approach along the rationale outlined above. They specify (Hall and Soskice 2001a), first, a liberal market economy (LME) identified with neoliberal policies, radical innovation, new sectors of the economy, and the anglophone countries (Australia, Canada, Ireland, New Zealand, the UK, but primarily the USA). Germany is at the centre of a second type, called a coordinated market economy (CME), where social and political institutions engage directly in shaping economic action. This form is linked to social democracy, incremental innovation, declining economic sectors, and non-anglophone countries.

It is odd that the core linguistic uniting characteristic of the LMEs, the only generalization that really works, is never actually discussed as such. More aware of Irish sensitivities than most authors, Hall and Soskice always talk of 'Anglo-Saxon and Irish' economies. But, perhaps because like others they resist the far simpler and more accurate 'Anglophone', they miss some serious potential implications of this. For example, one of the most impressive pieces of evidence cited by them to support their contention that radical innovation is concentrated in LME countries and only incremental innovation in CMEs is work carried out for them on patent citations (Estevez-Abe, Iversen, and Soskice 2001: 174–5). This reveals a strong statistical tendency for patents taken out in anglophone countries to cite scientific sources, while those taken out in continental Europe and Japan tend to cite previous patents or non-scientific sources. The six leading countries out of eighteen studied are all anglophone (headed by Ireland). Prima facie, the distinction between radical and incremental innovation does seem to be well proxied by that between academic and product citations, and one can see this being related to the character of research in firms, research centres, and universities. But it is also possible that firms in anglophone countries are more likely to cite chapters in the overwhelmingly anglophone literature of global science than those in other countries. Further, liberal market economies are largely defined by their having characteristics determined by common-law traditions; these also encourage the use of patenting of innovations to a greater extent than civil-law systems. Therefore, higher levels of patenting – as a legal device, not necessary a reflection of actual innovation – will be most widespread in common-law, and hence liberal market, systems. This distortion may help explain why, according to Estevez-Abe, Iversen, and Soskice (2001: 175), New Zealand has more radical technological innovative capacity than Germany, Sweden, or Switzerland.

The LME type of economy depends on labour markets that set wages through pure competition and permit very little regulation to protect employees from insecurity, and on a primary role for stock markets and the maximization of shareholder value in achieving economic goals. Such an economy is considered by the authors to be poor at making minor adaptive innovations, because employers make inadequate investment in employee skills which might produce such innovations; but it excels at radical innovations, because the combination of free labour markets and external shareholders makes it relatively easy to switch resources rapidly to new and profitable firms and areas of activity. A CME, featuring corporatist wage-setting, strongly regulated labour markets and corporate financing through long-term commitments by banks, follows exactly the reverse logic.

The authors stress strongly that they are depicting two *enduring* forms of capitalism, because each has different comparative advantages. However, those of the CME form are located solely in minor adaptations within traditional and declining industries, while LMEs have assigned to them all future-oriented industries and services sectors. In the end therefore this is a neo-institutionalism that fully accepts the logic of neoclassicism set out above: in the long run all institutions other than the pure market fail to cope with the future. Since these different forms of capitalism are considered to have been the products of historical *longues durées*, it also means that the

German economy *never was* radically innovative in the past, which requires explaining away many past events in the economic history of such German industries as chemicals, machinery, steel, motor vehicles, when these sectors were at the forefront of technological advance.

This brings us to a further fundamental point: typologies of this kind are fixed over time; they make no provision for changes in characteristics. As Zeitlin (2003) puts it, approaches like that of Hall and Soskice render learning almost impossible. Or, as Bertoldi (2003) says, they ignore any impact of change in the world economy and make no allowance for evolutionary development (see also Regini 2003; Lütz 2003). As Hay (2002) has it, this literature tends to take either a spatializing approach (the elaboration of models, as in the cases we are discussing here) or a temporalizing one (identifying historical phases, and therefore probably giving more scope to actors' capacity to change, but ignoring synchronic diversity). It is not necessary for neo-institutionalist analysis to be as rigid as this.

Hall and Soskice also assume automatically that all innovation within new industries represents radical innovation, while all within old ones can represent only incremental innovation. This is because they use different sectors as proxies for different types of innovation. According to such an approach, when Microsoft launches another mildly changed version of Windows it still represents radical innovation, because information technology is seen as a radical innovation industry; but when some firms eventually launch the hydrogen-fuelled motor engine, this will only be an incremental innovation, because the motor industry is an old industry. Further, the authors do not confront the leading position of two clearly CMEs (Finland and Sweden) in new telecommunications technologies and the Nordic countries generally in medical technologies (Amable 2003: ch. 5; Berggren and Laestadius 2000). Boyer (2004a, 2004b) has shown that the institutional pattern found in the Nordic countries can favour high-technology growth in information and communication technologies as much as the Anglo-American one. This is completely lost in accounts that insist on dualism and an a priori allocation of institutional patterns. Instead of the a priori paradigm case methodology, Boyer (ibid.) and Amable (2003), who reaches similar conclusions, used Ragin's Boolean techniques (Ragin 2000) to derive institutional patterns empirically.

A further serious flaw in the varieties of capitalism approach is that it misunderstands the work of individual innovative companies. While engaging in radical innovation, firms usually also need to bring out products with minor improvements in order to sustain their position in markets while they wait for a radical innovation to bear fruit; but according to the Hall–Soskice model it is not possible for firms within an LME to succeed at incremental innovation. It is a major advance of the approach that they focus on the firm as an actor, rather than take a macroeconomic approach to the study of economic success. However, many of the advantages of this are vitiated by the fact that their model allows the firm virtually no autonomy outside its national macroeconomic context. This problem is further considered by Crouch (2005, ch. 3).

These authors further follow conventional wisdom in arguing that the superiority of American (or anglophone) firms over German ones results from the fact that in the anglophone countries all managerial power is concentrated in the hands of a chief executive (CEO) who is required to maximize shareholder value, with employees engaged on a hire-and-fire basis with no representative channels available to them. Here they are failing to distinguish between the firm as an organization and as a marketplace. By seeing the CEO's power as being solely to maximize share values by the use of a hire-and-fire approach to management, they are able to present the firm in an LME as solely the latter and not as an organization. They can therefore dispense with the knowledge accumulated in the theory of the firm, which distinguishes between market and organization, and presents at least the large firm as an organization with personnel policies, and with management having a wider range of discretion and possibilities than just maximizing share values.

This is significant. In reality firms differ considerably in the extent to which they construct organizational systems, internal labour markets, and distinctive ways of working, even developing specific corporate cultures, rather than simply establishing themselves as spaces where a number of markets intersect. For example, a firm that develops a distinctive approach to work among its workforce as part of its competitive strategy cannot depend on a hire and fire personnel policy. Employees need to be inducted into the firm's approach, and are likely to demand some understandings about security if they are to commit themselves in the way that management wants. Rapid hire and fire meets neither of these needs. This fundamental difference in corporate strategy has nothing at all to do with differences between LMEs and CMEs; both can exist within either, particularly the former. Neglect of the firm as an organization is a weakness of much neo-institutionalist analysis. It is caused by the obsession already noted with a dichotomy between two mutually incompatible politico-economic ideologies, a dichotomy in which the distinction between firm and market is not at issue. At times Hall and Soskice (2001a: 9) seem to regard the organizational structure of the firm (or corporate hierarchy) as a characteristic of both LMEs and CMEs, and therefore an irrelevant variable – though the relevant passage is worded ambiguously:

All capitalist economies also contain the hierarchies that firms construct to resolve problems that markets do not address adequately (Williamson 1985). In liberal market economies, these are the institutions on which firms rely to develop the relations on which their core competences depend.

They seem here to be building into their model a functionalist balancing item, implying that hierarchy will exist to the extent that it can 'resolve problems'. In that case, why does their theory not build into the features of both LMEs and CMEs those that they would respectively need in order to have them cope with the kinds of innovation that their theory says is impossible for them? At the level of type-building one should not pick and choose which institutional features automatically receive compensation and which do not. As Weber originally formulated the concept, ideal types are 'one-sided accentuations', pressing home the logical implications of a particular kind of structure. The aim is not to provide an accurate empirical description, but a theoretical category, to be used in the construction of hypotheses. Again, the authors are not building their theory deductively, but are reading back empirical detail from what they want to be their paradigm case of an LME – the USA – into their formulation of the type. It is simply not possible within their methodological approach to ask the question: 'Is everything important that occurs in the US economy the embodiment of free markets?'

One contributor to the Hall and Soskice volume, Tate (2001), provides an analysis of standard setting in a number of countries which, because of its acute empirical observation, completely breaks the bounds of the master framework. Differences between France, Germany, the UK, and the USA simply cannot be contained within the LME/CME dichotomy. He points out the tendency to monopoly power embedded in the lack of authoritative public standards in the USA and subsequent need for regulation, and the strong role of the military arm of the state in establishing US standards. When he then tries to fit his subtle analysis to the dichotomy, he is forced to strange conclusions. For example, he labels as 'liberal' the tendency of the British Standards Institution to develop member-only services (ibid.: 448), while the tendency of the German standards institution (DIN) to develop universal standards is seen as a non-market characteristic (ibid.: 453–5). One could attribute the labels in the opposite way with at least equal plausibility.

Similarly, Tate (ibid.: 467–8) cites the current US approach to standardization, whereby the standards of individual corporations become national or even global, as an example of a liberal market process. But it is a defining characteristic of a liberal market that no one firm is able to impose conditions on others. If a single firm is able to impose such a thing as a standard on an entire market, there is not perfect competition, and that firm has been able to impose entry barriers. This is not regulation by the free market, but, again, by corporate hierarchy. An important aspect of the economic history of the

standard

initial triumph of the market model in the USA concerned the way in which many basic standards were imposed, usually by law, in a *neutral* manner that ensured a level playing field across a vast country and made market entry relatively easy. This did secure the true conditions of a competitive market. The establishment of national or super-national standards for electrical voltage and fittings, gas pressures, sizes of paper, and a myriad other things by public authorities or business associations enabled new firms to enter a market and consumers to choose their products without adapting a mass of other non-compatible equipment. This was true market-making by public infrastructures. The contemporary trend in, for example, computing and telecommunications for individual giant firms to use their market dominance to impose private standards and thereby erect large entry barriers against rivals is a mark of the rise of corporate hierarchy over both the market and public authority.

The path dependence literature has demonstrated how successful early standardization establishes the increasing returns that prevent the emergence of neoclassical equilibria (Arthur 1990, 1994). Much of the success of US firms in the new information economy of the 1990s consisted of such combinations of first-mover advantage with the large scale and international political weight of the country. This does demonstrate an important characteristic of the US variety of capitalism and helps explain its success in many new economy sectors, but it is misdescribed if it is defined as 'liberal market'. It *could* certainly be described as a strong instance of 'coordination' by corporate hierarchy and state leadership – qualities lacking *per definitionem* in an LME.

In practice the number of countries discussed at any length in the empirical chapters of Hall and Soskice's collection is very small—though a wider range appears in statistical tests. The UK (in eight chapters) and USA (four chapters) are the only LMEs subjected to any detailed analysis. As cases of CMEs there are Germany (eleven chapters), Italy (one chapter), and Sweden (one chapter). France appears in four chapters, always with serious question marks about its relation to the theory, and Japan similarly in two. In reality, therefore, this is a comparison between the UK/USA and Germany. But Germany is at times a problematic paradigm CME. It is the only large country among what the authors see as unambiguous European CMEs, and one with a very high degree of federalism. As Schmidt (2002: ch. 4) notes, because of its federalism, German network relations and the German state's enabling relations with economic actors are considerably less closely integrated and less influential than in most of the smaller countries. So the paradigm case is an outlier on a crucial aspect of the coordination variable. Another characteristic of the German economy is its tough anticartel law—one of many examples of how the post-war German economic constitution explicitly balanced the system's use of associative devices with mechanisms to ensure that these did not interfere with free competition. This is ignored by the authors of *Varieties of Capitalism*. Instead, antitrust law designed to prevent companies from colluding to control prices or markets is seen as typical of an LME model, and contrasted with the corporatist inter-firm relations of CMEs (Hall and Soskice 2001a: 31).

These authors do briefly consider diversity within the CME form. Apart from Germany, they also see Japan, Switzerland, the Netherlands, Belgium, Sweden, Norway, Denmark, Finland, and Austria as unproblematic—though differences between what they call 'industry-based' coordination of the German type and 'group-based' coordination found in Japan and Korea (ibid.: 34) are recognized. In an earlier work Soskice (1999) fully recognized these two distinct forms of CME: a northern European model, and the 'group-coordinated' East Asian economies. ('Northern Europe' is here defined by Soskice to include Italy but not France.) But not much is made of the distinction in the full development of theory or cases.

A 'Mediterranean' group (France, Italy, Spain, Portugal, Greece, and Turkey) is also given some recognition by Hall and Soskice. Like Albert (1991) before them, they accept that France is somehow different (Hall and Soskice 2001a: 35), and consider that a so-called southern European group (including France) probably constitutes a third, state-led, post-agrarian model. This at least makes matters more differentiated, though it produces a type curiously unable to distinguish between the French state and the Italian or Greek ones. Sometimes this 'Mediterranean' group is seen as being empirically poised somewhere between the LME and CME model, which enables the authors to insist that LME and CME remain the only points which require theoretical definition. But elsewhere the Mediterranean countries are treated as examples of CMEs; Thelen (2001), for example, treats Italy as almost unambiguously a 'German-type' 'coordinated' economy. One of the starting points of the Hall–Soskice model was an earlier paper by Soskice (1990) criticizing the Calmfors and Driffill (1988) model of wage-bargaining. This model had contrasted economies with centralized and decentralized collective bargaining arrangements, classing the French, Italian, and Japanese among the latter. Soskice pointed out that although these three countries were not as coordinated as Germany or Sweden, one could identify within them various mechanisms that ensured some coordination of wage-bargaining. He found (within the sample of countries being considered) that only the UK and the USA lacked such mechanisms; therefore all other cases were classified as CMEs. Both here and in Hall and Soskice, the basic drive of the dichotomy is to confront the neoclassical model with a single rival type.

2. BEYOND DICHOTOMIES

Some contributors to the study of capitalist diversity have gone beyond dichotomies. Schmidt (2002) has three models of European capitalism: 'market' (very similar to the LME model); 'managed' (with an 'enabling' state that encourages economic actors to co-operate, more or less the CME model); and 'state' (an interventionist state of the French kind). The last is designed to remedy the neglect of this form by Hall and Soskice. Acknowledging that the role of the state has declined considerably in France in recent years, she points out that its background role and historical legacy remain of considerable importance in enhancing national economic capacity. But indeed much the same could be said of the US state, whose role in the vast defence-related sector could well be defined as 'state enhancement' of economic capacity.

Schmidt (ibid.: ch. 2) also manages to be sensitive both to change and to its *timing*—an unusual attribute among institutionalists. She studies how countries embodying each of these types respond to the challenges of globalization and Europeanization. A central hypothesis is that these challenges do not lead to simple convergence. Governments of the various countries have responded in complex ways, producing new forms of diversity. If there is any overall convergence it is mainly towards a loss of extreme characteristics and thus some sharing of attributes from the various models. And these diversities are full of interesting paradoxes. The UK, having had in many respects the weakest economy of the three, was thus the earliest to be forced to come to terms with the pressures of globalization. As a result, it now appears better prepared to face that challenge than Germany which, being initially the strongest economically, could delay adjustment.

A second hypothesis fundamental to her study is that political discourse has been particularly important in shaping national responses to the challenge. By this Schmidt means not just that different substantive discourses were adopted, but that these took different forms. She distinguishes between 'communicative' and 'coordinating' discourse forms. The former, more suited to centralized systems like the British and French, inform the public of what needs to be done; the latter, more typical of Germany, is used to develop consensus among powerful actors who cannot be controlled from the centre.

This work therefore marks a refreshing shift towards an actor-centred and non-determinist account. Schmidt by no means discounts the existence of very strong structures, within which her actors need to operate. But these are malleable by innovative actors, in particular by politics. She criticizes particularly effectively the oversimplified accounts that characterize much rational choice work in international political economy. This, she argues, is a curiously depoliticized form of study of politics, assuming as it does that the interests of nation states can be modelled in a straightforward way, with fixed, consciously held preferences. She demonstrates effectively how governments in the three countries of concern to her study developed very varied positions in relation to Europeanization: For example, the UK was quickest to respond to many of the single market initiatives, but slowest to the single currency. This can all be explained, and she provides good explanations, but these require tactical and historically contingent political actors.

But Schmidt still follows the practice of identifying empirical cases as standing for ideal types. This is unfortunate, because her own actual practice is well able to cope with the implications of seeing cases as amalgams of types: her actors are creative political schemers, looking for chances to change and innovate, not automata acting out the parts the theorist has set for them. And, as noted, she succeeds in showing how over time individual countries have moved around the triangular space which her particular model of types of capitalism allows them.

Several other authors present three or more forms of capitalism, or of elements of capitalism, nearly always retaining a geo-cultural approach. Esping-Andersen's analysis (1990) of different types of welfare state embodies variables relating to the outcomes of political struggle, or dominant political traditions, which avoids some of the functionalist implications of the varieties of capitalism model (Chapter 3 of Crouch 2005). Again, one starting point is free-market or liberal capitalism associated with the anglophone group of countries, and another is Germany, producing a conservative, 'continental European' model. There is however a third, social-democratic pole, geographically associated with Scandinavia.

Critics of Esping-Andersen's model have concentrated: on identifying mixed cases (Castles and Mitchell 1991); on stressing how the treatment of women in different systems does not seem to correspond to the simple typology (Daly 2000); or on breaking up the overextended 'conservative continental' category. A fourth type has now been clearly established, separating southern European welfare states from this one on the basis of their particularly large role for the family (Naldini 1999) and other informal institutions (Ferrera 1997). Ebbinghaus (2001), concentrating on policies for combating early exit from the labour market, which he sees as deeply related to the form of the overall welfare regime, adds a fifth type based on Japan. All these works continue to depend on the characteristics of paradigm cases, which can be highly misleading. Viebrock (2004), in a study of different forms of unemployment benefit systems, has shown how Sweden – usually the absolute paradigm case of social democracy – has for reasons of political history retained a role for voluntary associations alongside the state in the organization of its unemployment insurance system.

A strong move away from dualism, which neither starts from nor privileges the free-market model, is the scheme of Whitley (1999). He builds up a set of fully sociological models of capitalism based on six types of business system (fragmented, coordinated industrial district, compartmentalized, state organized, collaborative, and highly coordinated), related to a number of different behavioural characteristics (ibid.: 42). He also presents five different ideal types of firms (opportunist, artisan, isolated hierarchy, collaborative hierarchy, allied hierarchy) (ibid.: 75), and a diversity of links between these types and certain fundamental institutional contexts (the state, financial system, skill development and control, trust and authority relations) (ibid.: 84). Significantly, Whitley's main fields of study are Japan, Korea, Taiwan, and other far-eastern economies, rather than either the US or the German cases, and he is therefore further removed from the obsession with neoliberalism and a contrast between it and a model of 'organized capitalism' that sometimes distorts the analysis of those who concentrate on western Europe and North America.

By far the best and most sophisticated approach to a 'post-dualist' typology of capitalism to date is that established by Amable (2003). He collected quantitative data on a vast range of characteristics of the national economies of most OECD countries: product markets, labour markets, financial systems, social protection. He uses literally dozens of individual indicators to assess each. He then allows a typology of groups of countries to be formed empirically by these data; he does not start from paradigm cases. This procedure gives him five groups, which, as with other authors, fall into familiar geo-cultural patterns: market-based (primarily anglophone), social democratic (Nordic), Asian (Japan and Korea), Mediterranean (southern European), and continental European (continental, western European less the Nordic and Mediterranean countries). He further finds (as have others, e.g. Crouch 1999) that this last group does not show much internal coherence, and for some purposes splits it further into two subgroups, one comprising the Netherlands and Switzerland, the other Austria, Belgium, France, and Germany. Further, Amable is not afraid to draw attention to further diversity for some of the characteristics, with the result that countries do not always figure within their normal group.

At times Amable lapses from his finely nuanced stance. For example, the book ends (2003: ch. 6) with a future- and policy-oriented dialectic between the market-based and a simplified and generalized continental European model. It seems that engaging in the rhetoric of debate about the future course of capitalism leads always to dualism, even when, as in Amable's case, the best strength of the author's position lies precisely in the demonstration of a far more differentiated world. He also depends necessarily for his data on sources like the OECD which are often constructed with in-built biases. For example, although at one point Amable (2003: 200) acknowledges the importance of military-related research and production in many of the high-tech sectors of the US economy, he follows the OECD in excluding all consideration of this from the indicators of the role of the state in the economy and of the regulation of external trade.

These minor criticisms apart, Amable has demonstrated that a genuinely scientific approach, using very extensive and diverse kinds of data, produces a useful and coherent typology comprising five or six types, at the same time enabling clear recognition of exceptions within types.

Dichotomizers will argue that they are applying the principle of parsimony and Occam's razor to complex schemes of Amable's or Whitley's kind. They will claim that, while there is clearly a loss of information if one collapses Whitley's 'coordinated industrial district, compartmentalized, state-organized, collaborative, and highly coordinated' mechanisms into the single idea of a CME, that idea seizes on the essential point that divides all these forms from the pure market one: coordination. But, as Scott (2001: ch. 9) and Hay (2002) have separately argued, parsimony must not become an excuse for inaccuracy and ignoring important diversity. Is coordination the fundamental attribute of all the types in Whitley's list? On what grounds could this quality be regarded as more fundamental than the other characteristics which divide them, especially since the coordination takes place at very different levels? Recent developments in the governance approach (Crouch et al. 2004) draw attention to the role of collective competition goods provided by various governance modes in local economies, without demonstrating anything remotely strong enough to be called national 'coordination'. This suggests the possibility of analyses more moderate than those addressed at the whole macroeconomy.

Meanwhile, Hage and Alter (1997) have convincingly demonstrated analytical distinctions among several institutional forms. In that case, to apply Occam's razor to reduce them all to one idea of coordination is to cut into serious theoretical and empirical flesh. An explanation becomes more parsimonious than another when it uses a smaller number of explanatory variables *while explaining at least as much* as its opponent. For example, it is more parsimonious to model the solar system as heliocentric than terracentric, because the former uses far simpler mathematics to account for at least as many planetary movements as the latter. We should be far less impressed with the heliocentrist if she had to say: 'Forget about the outer planets; this theory is more parsimonious because it just looks at the inner ones.' But contemporary social science often makes use of precisely this kind of argument, using the idea of parsimony as meaning a kind of rough, tough macho theory that concentrates on the big picture and ignores detail.

One explanation of this tendency is a technical methodological one. In the social sciences (outside psychology) it is rarely possible to achieve very high levels of accuracy in explanations. The variables are so diffuse; the number of cases so few (at least for cross-national comparativists); and our means of observation are so less precise than those available to natural scientists. We are therefore very happy to achieve coefficients of correlation (R^2) with values like 0.65, which means that we have explained about one-third of the variance. Natural scientists, for example chemists, are likely to insist on (and can in practice achieve) correlations of 0.99. A theory that claims parsimony when it has achieved an R^2 of 0.65 has a very different stature than one that claims it at 0.99.

As Whitley's formulations demonstrate, the relationships between different forms and different behavioural characteristics present a varied patchwork of similarities and differences, not a set of polar contrasts. This suggests in turn the fundamental point: *that individual empirical cases might well comprise more complex amalgams still of elements from two or more theoretical types.* Whitley (1999) himself treats a fragmented market model of economic organization separately from one dominated by large firms, and is therefore able to see the USA itself as a hybrid of two different forms of capitalism rather than a pure case (see also Jackson forthcoming).

This question has considerable practical implications. It is often recognized by authors who speak of 'hybrid' forms. For example, Schmidt (2002: ch. 4) suggests strongly that some changes in French institutions are making that case increasingly a hybrid, with borrowing from Germany as well as from neoliberal sources. Dees and Jackson (2007) suggest that hybridization, as opposed to simple imitation of the exogenous, is the usual outcome of attempts at 'borrowing' institutions, even under extreme periods of transition, such as Germany or Japan under post-war occupation. Other researches (Ferrera, Hemerijck, and Rhodes 2000; Hemerijck, and Schludi 2000) have shown the power of hybrid cases in achieving important reforms in welfare state organization – for example in recent changes in the Danish, Dutch, and Irish cases (Ferrera and Hemerijck 2003). Zeitlin (2003) discusses various national cases that have become exceptions to their 'types' as the result of mixing institutional forms at the initiative of what I would call institutional entrepreneurs. Considering an earlier period, Windolf (2002: 85) discusses how French family capitalism played an important part in the country's post-war modernization, merging with advanced financial means of control and the strong state to produce a dynamic new model.

'Hybridization' deals with only one way in which cases may deviate from types, and it is still very close to the idea of clear, macro-level types, because it sees these as the source of the hybridization. However, it does constitute an important challenge to simple equations of cases and types.

3. QUESTIONING THE CENTRALITY
OF THE NATION-STATE

The centrality of the nation state in most typologies of capitalist diversity also needs to be questioned. This centrality is found in most neo-institutionalist studies, including those on 'social [i.e. national] systems of innovation and production' (Amable 2000; Boyer and Didier 1998). It is also central to work from the parallel but distinct literature on 'national systems of innovation' (Freeman 1995; Lundvall 1992; Nelson 1993). At one level the case is well made. Very extensive elements of governance in the industrial and post-industrial societies of which we have knowledge do operate at the level of the nation-state: states have been the main sources of law, and most associations and organizations target themselves at the state (Crouch 2001). Given that markets are framed by law, this means that of the modes of governance usually discussed in governance theory, the state itself (obviously), markets, and various levels of associations are all heavily defined at national level, while community and informal association exist at a lower geographical level. Even research that explicitly works at comparisons between regional or other substate geographical levels often has to acknowledge the importance of the nation state as a major instance for the determination of socio-economic variables (Cotts Watkins 1991; Rodriguez-Pose 1998, 1999).

But many macro-level neo-institutionalists go further than this and postulate virtually hermetically sealed national institutions – often because they are concerned to address debates about economic and social policy, and these are mainly conducted at national levels. Radice (2000) argues that this has perhaps been particularly the case for left-of-centre analysts desiring to 'bring the state back in', leading to an exaggeration of the importance of national policy. More generally neo-institutionalists are led to stress the nation-state by their functionalist assumptions, which model discrete, autonomous systems, each equipped with their sets of institutions, like a body with its organs. There are also methodological advantages in being able to treat nation states as discrete units of analysis, as many economic data are produced at national levels. Theorists of the diversity of capitalism are therefore eager to play down the implications of globalization, and argue intelligently and forcefully against the naive assumptions of much other literature that globalization somehow abolishes the significance of national differences (Hall and Soskice 2001a: 54–60; Whitley 1999: ch. 5; Hirst and Thompson 1997).

However, the position of the nation-state as the definer of the boundaries of cases is not so fixed that it should be taken for granted *per definitionem*.

This is particularly obvious with respect to multinational corporations. As Beyer (2001) shows, large firms draw on resources from a range of different national bases; it is very difficult to identify them with particular national types and to see their institutional possibilities as being constrained by their country(ies) of location (see also Grant 1997). As Jackson (forthcoming) puts it, national models of capitalism are becoming 'institutionally incomplete'. This seems particularly true where international corporations are concerned, but even firms that are nationally owned and operate primarily within one nation-state have access to knowledge, links, and practices existing outside the national borders. Radice (1998: 278) similarly criticizes the national innovation system literature for a kind of mercantilism, arguing that it does not take adequate account of the fact that technology is always a public/private collaboration, and that the private actors are usually global firms. Something always 'leaks' abroad from national programmes; innovation is at once global and national. He also points out (ibid.: 274–5) the falsity of the dichotomy between the so-called globalizing and national forces, as though one could identify them and then establish their relative importance. The phenomena associated with globalization are brought about at the behest of domestic actors working to influence national governments. Keune (2004) has demonstrated this in relation to the former communist countries of central Europe. So the idea of national versus global collapses. As Helleiner (1994) earlier made the point: internationalization is not an independent variable, because it is an outcome of state policy.

Radice (1998: 273–4) demonstrates a different weakness of nation-state based analysis by pointing out that all states are not equal as units. The USA is able to borrow to fund its deficits in a way not available to others, which means that comparing the 'performance' of that economy with others is not a true comparison of institutional capacities. One can move from that observation to point out that nation-states cannot always be treated as a series of unit instances of the same phenomenon; they are also linked together in a hierarchical way to form an overall system, as Wallerstein and other world system analysts showed (Hopkins and Wallerstein 1982). For example, the units 'Portugal' and 'France' cannot be treated as equal units within which the effects of various independent variables can be independently and comparatively assessed, because they are partly defined by their relationship to each other. Scott (2001: 83 ff.) stresses the need to consider a range of levels: world system, society (nation-state), organizational field, organizational population, organization, and organizational subsystem. As he points out, different disciplines tend to look at different components of this. Hollingsworth and Boyer (1997: 4) are helpfully explicit that their scheme can be used at subnational and transnational, as well as national, levels (see also Coleman 1997).

We need always to be able to ask: are arguments about the characteristics of national economies limited to specific economic sectors and industrial branches, or do they claim to apply to all? And how far beyond the heartland of the economy does the theory claim to range? If the nation-state is at the heart of the analysis, are political institutions also to be covered by the characterization? Or does the theory apply even further, to structures like the welfare state, family, or religion, for example? As we develop thinking of this kind, we soon come to see that the clear division between endogenous and exogenous that is so fundamental to nation-state-based theories becomes replaced by *a continuum of accessibility* – an idea which is explored in *Capitalist Diversity and Change*.

4. CONCLUSION

The governance approach to institutional analysis both builds on sociological and political science concepts of action and departs strongly from dualism – though it is often still tied to the analysis of national systems. Because it looks principally at the way in which economic action is governed or regulated, the focus of this body of theory is on action rather than structures. Structures emerge from the encounter between the actions of maximizing agents and the rules that are framed both to facilitate and to restrain the maximizing search. It is important to note that, just because this approach deals with rule-making, it is not necessarily concerned solely with either formal rules or the restraint of economic actors. As the *régulationistes* have shown us, rules are more a means by which economic actors attain their goals than just constraints over them.

The action-centred as opposed to functionalist orientation of governance theorists enables them to deal with greater complexity at the theoretical level. The market is present as a type and often remains a starting point or even a limiting case, but contrasts between it and other forms are not the sole focus of the account; these latter can be compared with each other without necessarily relating back to the market. Significantly, and in contrast with the varieties of capitalism school, the governance approach identifies corporate hierarchy as a form distinct from that of the free market (Crouch 2005: ch. 5). Meanwhile, on the basis of the present chapter we have established the following unsatisfactory characteristics of much, though by no means all, neo-institutionalist analyses of capitalism:

1. There is confusion between ideal types and cases, with the latter being seen as exemplifiers of the former, rather than the former being seen as constituents of the latter.

2. Despite the claim to be firm-centred, the approach has been too concerned with the macro-level picture of whole economies, and the account of types has been too closely linked to the polemic between neoliberalism and social democracy.

3. Characteristics of economies have been bundled together as coherent wholes with inadequate attention being paid to the forces that produce the bundles.

The next stage in the development of neo-institutional theory has to be an attempt to surmount these defects.

NOTE

1. It has become routine to use the term 'Anglo-Saxon' here, but it is problematic. It was developed originally to group together the collection of peoples of English, German, and Scandinavian origin who inhabited England on the eve of the Norman invasion of 1066; it served to contrast them with both the French-speaking (though originally Scandinavian) invaders and the Celtic inhabitants of other parts of the British Isles. Such a term became useful over 800 years later to distinguish the British and other northern European (and by now primarily Protestant) inhabitants of the late nineteenth-century USA from more recent Latin-language-speaking and Irish immigrants, and by extension also from Poles and other Catholics as well as from Blacks and Jews. Its contemporary use by academic social scientists as well as international organizations like the OECD seems not only blithely ignorant of these connotations, but also commits the solipsism of using it mainly as a contrast with Germany—which includes the Saxon half of the mythical Anglo-Saxon identity. Its contemporary use also normally includes Ireland—a people explicitly excluded from both the original and subsequent US terms. It is in fact used entirely consistently to identify that group of countries where English is the dominant language and the majority population is white-skinned: the UK, Ireland, the USA, Canada, Australia, and New Zealand. The correct, unambiguous term, which precisely identifies this group of countries is 'anglophone', and one wonders why this clear and accurate term is not used instead of the more popular, exotic, but highly dubious, alternative. To insist on this point is not pedantry, but draws our attention to certain possible implications of the fact that the economics literature which finds it far easier to make sense of the anglophone economies than others is itself almost solely anglophone.

3

Institutional Change
in Advanced Political Economies

*Wolfgang Streeck and Kathleen Thelen**

Our volume *Beyond Continuity* (Streeck and Thelen 2005) was written as a collective contribution to the current debate in political science and sociology on institutional change. Instead of abstract theoretical reasoning, it offers in-depth empirical case studies. The underlying assumption, amply supported by recent literature, is that there is *a wide but not infinite variety* of modes of institutional change that can meaningfully be distinguished and analytically compared. It is also assumed that an empirically grounded typology of institutional change that does justice to the complexity and versatility of the subject can offer important insights on mechanisms of social and political stability and evolution generally.

Empirically the chapters of the book deal with current changes in selected political–economic institutions of rich, mostly Western democracies. To us the most prominent theoretical frameworks employed in the analysis of the welfare state and of contemporary political economy generally seem singularly ill-equipped to capture significant developments underway in many if not all of them. While we join with a large literature that rejects the notion that previously diverse political economies are all converging on a single model of capitalism, we notice that many arguments in support of the idea of distinctive and stable national models lack the analytic tools necessary to capture the changes that are indisputably going on in these countries. One consequence is a tendency in the literature to understate the extent of change, or alternatively to code all observed changes as minor adaptive adjustments to altered circumstances in the service of continuous reproduction of existing systems.

The conservative bias in much of this literature—the widespread propensity to explain what might seem to be new as just another version of the old—is at least partly a consequence of the impoverished state of theorizing on issues of

*We are grateful to the participants in *Beyond Continuity* for the ideas and insights they contributed, and to Suzanne Berger and Peter A. Hall, for their comments on this chapter.

institutional change. In the absence of analytic tools to characterize and explain modes of gradual change, much of the institutionalist literature relies—explicitly or implicitly—on a strong punctuated equilibrium model that draws an overly sharp distinction between long periods of institutional stasis periodically interrupted by some sort of exogenous shock that opens things up, allowing for more or less radical reorganization. As the problems of the literature on the political economies of advanced capitalism are symptomatic of broader theoretical deficits in the institutionalist literature as a whole, we submit that a close analysis of the processes through which they are currently changing can provide a particularly fertile terrain within which to explore frequently overlooked mechanisms and modes of change more generally.

The opening section of this chapter will address three general issues. It begins with a summary account of the *historical setting* of the cases of institutional change analyzed in subsequent chapters. In particular, it describes the secular process of *liberalization* that constitutes the common denominator of many of the changes presently occurring in advanced political economies. Second, it characterizes and places in context the *type* of institutional change associated with current processes of liberalization, change that is at the same time *incremental* and *transformative*. And third, a definition of the concept of institution is provided that is to allow for an adequate conceptualization, not only of institutional statics, but also of institutional change. In the second part, we review the lessons that the case studies in the volume hold for the theorization of institutional change. First we ask how we may distinguish 'real' change from 'superficial', merely adaptive change, and how to detect change in the absence of disruptive events leading to institutional breakdown. Then we explore the contribution of our cases to an empirical inventory and analytical typology of modes of *gradual transformative change* of modern political–economic institutions. *Beyond Continuity* ends with a concluding summary that returns to the substantive theme of *Beyond Continuity*, the current liberalization of advanced political economies.

1. INSTITUTIONAL CHANGE IN ADVANCED POLITICAL ECONOMIES

1.1. Institutional Change as Liberalization

In the 1980s and 1990s, the political economies of the second post-war settlement began to undergo major changes. What exactly these changes were – or rather, are – is far from being unanimously agreed upon. At a very general level, however, most observers describe a secular expansion of market relations inside and across the borders of national political – economic systems, significantly beyond the limits that the organized capitalism of the post-war 'mixed economy' had set for them. With due caution, it would therefore seem justified to characterize the prevailing trend in the advanced economies during the last two decades of the twentieth century and beyond as a broad process of *liberalization.*

Clearly, differences between countries are of importance, and we would be making a severe mistake if we were to belittle them. But commonalities also count and must be taken no less seriously. Major differences between them notwithstanding, the post-war political economies of the countries that after 1945 under American leadership came to form the 'Free World' of democratic capitalism shared a number of features that set them apart from the capitalism of the inter-war period and of the Great Depression. After the Second World War, governments accepted political responsibility for full employment, to be discharged by means of a Keynesian economic policy that, if necessary, placed the interests of workers above that of capitalist 'rentiers'. Trade unions were conceded constitutional or quasi-constitutional rights to free collective bargaining; large parts of industrial capacity were nationalized or in other ways controlled by the state, sometimes together with organized business and trade unions, in various ways exempting industries from market pressure and providing safe employment at good pay; economic growth was to a significant extent spent on an expanding welfare state that insured rising standards of mass consumption against the vagaries of the market while partly 'de-commodifying' the supply of labor; and sophisticated international arrangements enabled national governments democratically to respond to popular demands for social protection without upsetting an international free trade regime that made for ever increasing productivity and growing demand for mass-produced consumer goods.

Why the 'Golden Age' of post-war capitalism came to an end is the subject of an extensive debate that we cannot and need not summarize in this essay. First fissures began to show in the 1970s, in the aftermath of a worldwide wave of worker militancy that, among other things, reflected a new level of material and social aspirations after twenty years of peace, prosperity, and democracy. For a few years after, a new generation of workers and citizens used the institutions of democratic capitalism without being restrained by the cultural inhibitions and the historical traumas that had helped make economic democracy compatible with capitalist markets and hierarchies. Then the tide began to turn. In most Western countries heightened distributional conflict, reinforced by the welfare losses imparted on the rich industrialized world by the two oil crises, caused rising inflation and, subsequently, unemployment.

In some places earlier than in others, but ultimately throughout the countries of the second post-war settlement, governments gradually reneged on their promise to provide for full employment and began to return to the market growing segments of national economies that had become too politicized to be governable by democratic politics.

Again, time and pathways of liberalization differed greatly between countries. There is also no doubt that a number of factors were at work that had little if anything to do with the explosion of popular economic and political demands after the demise of the disciplining memories of war and depression. The new microelectronic technology comes to mind that revolutionized work, skill requirements, employment structures, products, and product markets. In addition there also was internationalization and globalization, in part unquestionably accelerated and indeed called upon by governments striving to defend themselves against ever more demanding constituents, but in part clearly not. Rising competition in world markets both forced and legitimated sometimes deep revisions of welfare state policies, and the same can be said of fundamental demographic changes especially in Europe that originated in the 1970s and seemed to hang together in complex ways with increased consumer prosperity and citizen equality. In the 1990s at the latest, tightening political and economic limits on public budgets, in part constructed by international agreement between national executives that were about to lose their room for fiscal maneuver, combined with intensified international and domestic competition to discredit collective solutions to economic and social problems, providing strong ideological support for privatization, deregulation, self-reliance, and a general opening-up of social and economic arrangements to the logic of 'free' competitive markets – not just in the traditionally 'liberal' but also in the so-called 'coordinated' market economies.

Liberalization, then, may be described both as an inevitable economic adjustment in organized political economies to growing internal and external market pressures, and as a political strategy of either governments overwhelmed by unsatisfiable political demands or of business extricating itself through internationalization from the profit squeeze imposed on it by labor at the height of its postwar power in the early 1970s. As already emphasized, the liberalization of the institutions of organized capitalism – their 'disorganization', as it was called by Offe (1985) and Lash and Urry (1987) – took different forms and proceeded at different speeds in different countries, due in part to the effects of different institutional endowments interacting with what may in shorthand be described as identical exogenous and, in part, endogenous challenges. Indeed as pointed out prominently by the economic historian, Karl Polanyi, liberalization always comes with, and is enveloped in, all sorts of countermeasures taken by 'society' – or by specific socie*ties* in line with their respective traditions – against the destructive effects of free, 'self-regulating' markets. This, however, must clearly not be read with the unquenchable optimism of much of functionalist reasoning, which seems to accept as a general premise that liberalization can never be destructive because ultimately it will always be balanced by newly invented institutions and methods of social regulation. Rather it puts us on alert that in studying liberalization as a direction of institutional change, we should expect also to observe changes in institutions intended to re-embed the very same market relations that liberalization sets free from traditional social constraints.

1.2. Transformation Without Disruption

The institutional change that we observe in the political economies of today's advanced capitalist societies is associated with a significant renegotiation of the politically regulated social market economy of the post-war period. Important qualifications notwithstanding, the current transformation of modern capitalism is making it more market-driven and market-accommodating as it releases ever more economic transactions from public–political control and turns them over to private contracts. One particularly intriguing aspect of this broad and multifaceted development is that it unfolds by and large incrementally, without dramatic disruptions like the wars and revolutions that were characteristic of the first half of the twentieth century. In fact, an essential and defining characteristic of the ongoing worldwide liberalization of advanced political economies is that it evolves in the form of gradual change that takes place within, and is conditioned and constrained by, the very same post-war institutions that it is reforming or even dissolving.

Clearly it is hard to determine with any degree of accuracy whether the difference between the capitalist political economies of today and of the early 1950s is greater or smaller than that between capitalism in the middle and at the beginning of the nineteenth century. Perhaps the convulsive transformations associated with the First and Second World Wars did in fact unsettle the societies of western Europe and, to a lesser extent, North America more deeply than the gradual changes that began to chisel away at the post-war mixed economy in the 1980s and 1990s. But to us this cannot mean that the changes we are observing today throughout the advanced capitalist world are only of minor significance, or are merely modifications on the surface of a fundamentally stable and self-reproductive social order. For a few years when one could still speak of a 'crisis' – usually in the expectation of a return to a stable state similar to what the world was like when its transformation began – this might have seemed plausible. But ongoing change and its accumulating results increasingly suggest that the current process of liberalization involves a major recasting of the system of democratic capitalism as we know it, issuing in a social order dissociated from fundamental assumptions of social integration and political–economic conflict resolution that underlay the construction of the post-war settlement after 1945.

In our view, central properties of the developments currently underway in the advanced political economies are not being adequately theorized, nor even fully recognized, in the most influential theoretical frameworks guiding research on political economy and the welfare state. For different reasons, contemporary scholarship both on 'varieties of capitalism' and on the welfare state seem to be producing analyses that understate the magnitude and significance of current changes. Hall and Soskice's highly influential work on varieties of capitalism is one example (Hall and Soskice 2001). The framework they propose is premised on a broad distinction between 'coordinated' and 'liberal' market economies based on the extent to which employers can coordinate among themselves to achieve joint gains. Differences between the two types of economies are expressed in different clusters of institutions – including particular kinds of financial arrangements, collective bargaining institutions, vocational training institutions, and welfare state institutions – that together support distinctive types of employer strategies in the market. Against popular convergence theories that see all systems bending toward the Anglo-Saxon model, Hall and Soskice's argument predicts continuing cross-national divergence. Specifically, and most directly at odds with convergence theories, Hall and Soskice argue that employers in coordinated market economies who have invested in and organized their strategies around indigenous institutions will not abandon these arrangements in the face of new market pressures. While providing a compelling account of observed institutional resiliency, the theory is much less suited to understanding contemporary changes. Emphasizing divergent employer preferences rooted in pre-existing institutional configurations, the theory, in fact, seems to regard almost all feedback within a system as positive and operating to maintain traditional structures (Thelen and van Wijnbergen 2003; Kume and Thelen 2004).

Similarly in the welfare state literature, the most influential theoretical frameworks stress continuity over change. Pierson's agenda-setting work on welfare state retrenchment paints a picture that emphasizes the obstacles and political risks of change. Contrary to previous accounts, Pierson argues that the politics involved in dismantling the welfare state are not simply the mirror image of the politics of constructing and expanding it. For instance, even if organized labor and Left political parties had been crucial to the construction of the welfare state, their declining political power does not necessarily imperil its continuity. The reason, Pierson argues, is that large-scale public welfare programs are subject to important feedback effects, as they create new constituencies and beneficiaries that develop vested interests in their maintenance. Following Pierson, conventional wisdom in the welfare state literature today largely focuses on the difficulties of retrenchment. As Hacker points out (2005), the dominant view is that while the welfare state is perhaps under greater strain than before 'social policy frameworks remain secure, anchored by their enduring popularity, powerful constituencies, and centrality within the post-war order'.

The prevailing emphasis on institutional stability even in the face of indisputable and important change points to a general problem in contemporary institutional analysis, which has always emphasized structural constraints and continuity. In the past, this involved a highly static conception of institutions as 'frozen' residues, or 'crystallizations', of previous political conflict. Presently a growing body of work has begun to conceive of institutional reproduction as a dynamic political process. Recent work on path dependence in particular has emphasized mechanisms of increasing returns and positive feedback that sustain and reinforce institutions through time. Still, however, increasing returns and positive feedback are more helpful in understanding institutional resiliency than institutional change (the following paragraphs draw on Thelen 2004: 27–30).

In fact, when it comes to the latter, the notion of path dependence seems to encourage scholars to think of change in one of two ways, *either* as very minor and more or less continuous (the more frequent type) *or* as very major but then abrupt and discontinuous (the much rarer type). This has yielded a strangely bifurcated literature that links path dependence as a concept to two completely different and in some ways diametrically opposed conceptions of change. Some scholars invoke the term to support the broad assertion that legacies of the past always weigh on choices and changes in the present (e.g. Sewell 1996). Especially studies of transitions to democracy and market economy in contemporary eastern Europe, for example, employ path dependence in this way, as in: 'Path-dependency suggests that the institutional legacies of the past limit the range of current possibilities and/or options in institutional innovation' (Nielson, Jessop, and Hausner 1995: 6). Invoked in this way, the concept is to stress the *limited degrees of freedom* that exist for innovation, even in moments of extreme upheaval. In many such cases, the characterization of change as 'path dependent' is meant as a refutation of and an alternative to voluntarist ('rational design') accounts that view institution-building as a matter of constructing efficient incentive structures on a more or less 'clean slate' (e.g. Stark 1995).

Others, however, and often those who insist on a more precise definition of path dependence, tend toward a very different view of change, one that is closer to a strong version of a punctuated equilibrium model that draws a sharp distinction between the dynamics of institutional innovation on the one hand and of institutional reproduction on the other (Krasner 1988). Mahoney, for instance, criticizes loose definitions of path dependence and argues that 'path-dependence characterizes specifically those historical sequences in which contingent events set in motion institutional patterns or event chains that have deterministic properties' (2000: 507). By emphasizing the very different logic of contingent institutional choice and deterministic institutional reproduction, this definition implies and encourages a strong distinction between 'critical juncture' moments in which institutions are originally formed, and long periods of stasis characterized by institutional continuity. Any number of examples could be given here but the idea is generally captured in what Pempel calls 'long continuities' periodically interrupted by 'radical shifts' (1998: 1). In his words: 'Path-dependent equilibrium is periodically ruptured by radical change, making for sudden bends in the path of history' (ibid.: 3).

Claims about relative contingency at historic choice points and relative determinism in trajectories once chosen are pervasive in the social science literature and they are by no means exclusively associated with scholars invoking the concept of path dependence.[1] In sociology, Ann Swidler has drawn a distinction between 'settled' and 'unsettled' times, in which the latter are seen as 'periods of social transformation' or 'historical junctures where new cultural complexes make possible new or reorganized strategies of action' (1986: 278, 283). Ira Katznelson adopts this formulation and links it to the age-old debate on the balance between agency and structure, arguing that structure figures heavily in the 'settled' while agency reigns in 'unsettled' times. He writes of 'multiple possibilities inside unsettled moments of uncommon choice', such moments being defined as periods in which the 'constraints on agency are broken or relaxed and opportunities expand so that purposive action may be especially consequential' (Katznelson 2003: 277, 283). This kind of perspective is reflected, among others, in Jowitt's work on eastern Europe, which sees post-Leninist societies as 'genesis environments' characterized by a new openness in which 'leaders will matter more than institutions, and charisma more than political economy' (quoted in Stark 1995: 68).

Rational-choice scholarship, too, has mostly gravitated to a model of discontinuous institutional change (Weingast 2002: 692), though from a different starting point. This is because some of the core premises underlying rational-choice theorizing – above all, the view of institutions as self-enforcing equilibria in which behavior is generated endogenously – suggest a sharp line between the logics and the analysis of institutional reproduction and change. Here again, there is a tendency to see change mostly in terms of dynamics unleashed by some exogenous shift or shock, ignoring the possibility of endogenously generated institutional change that is more than just adaptive (but see Greif and Laitin 2003: 2).[2] Moreover, similar to perspectives such as Katznelson's that stress agency and openness in 'critical junctures', the *direction* of change (i.e. the reason why a particular institutional equilibrium prevails over other possible ones) seems to be a function of factors exogenous to the institutions.[3] As Pierson points out, this perspective has little to say 'about what is likely to happen if a particular institutional equilibrium does give way', and in fact the implication often is that 'any new equilibrium may be as likely as any other' (2004: 143–4). In other words, where the problem of change is posed in terms of breakdown and replacement, there is often no sense of a 'path' at all.

The analyses offered in this chapter suggest that there are severe limits to models of change that draw a sharp line between institutional stability and institutional change and that see all major changes as exogenously generated. Sometimes institutional change *is* abrupt and sharp (e.g. see Beissinger 2002). However, it is not at all clear that this exhausts the possibilities, nor even that it captures the most important ways in which institutions evolve over time. Certainly, the cases examined in this volume do not conform to a strong punctuated equilibrium model. On the contrary, they suggest that we must avoid being caught in a conceptual schema that provides only for either incremental change supporting institutional continuity through reproductive adaptation, or disruptive change causing institutional breakdown and innovation and thereby resulting in discontinuity. In short, we argue that equating incremental with adaptive and reproductive *minor* change, and *major* change with, mostly exogenous, disruption of continuity, makes excessively high demands on 'real' change to be recognized as such and tends to reduce most or all observable changes to adjustment for the purpose of stability.

The biases inherent in existing conceptual frameworks are particularly limiting in a time, like ours, when incremental processes of change appear to cause gradual institutional transformations that add up to major historical discontinuities. As various authors have suggested, far-reaching change can be accomplished through the accumulation of small, often seemingly insignificant adjustments (e.g. Pierson 2004 and others on 'tipping points'). To be able to take due account of this, we suggest that we distinguish between *processes* of change, which may be incremental or abrupt, and *results* of change, which may amount to either continuity or discontinuity (Figure 3.1). From the perspective of a punctuated equilibrium model, 'real' change that results in discontinuity takes place through abrupt institutional breakdown and replacement (the cell on

		Result of change	
		Continuity	Discontinuity
Process of change	Incremental	Reproduction by adaptation	Gradual transformation
	Abrupt	Survival and return	Breakdown and replacement

Figure 3.1. Types of institutional change: processes and results

the lower right of Figure 3.1). Authors writing in this tradition do recognize that there is also incremental change; but they tend to conceive of this as fundamentally reactive and adaptive and serving to protect institutional continuity (upper left cell). In reality, however, there often is considerable continuity through and in spite of historical break points, as well as dramatic institutional reconfiguration beneath the surface of apparent stability or adaptive self-reproduction, as a result of an accumulation over longer periods of time of subtle incremental changes (see also Thelen 2004). The former, which we tentatively refer to as 'survival and return' (lower left cell), is of less interest to us in the present context than the latter, which we call *gradual transformation* and which stands for institutional discontinuity caused by incremental, 'creeping' change (upper right cell).

It is to the exploration of this type of change that *Beyond Continuity* is devoted—and, we believe, should be if we want to be able to conceptualize properly current developments in the political economy of modern capitalism. Rather than big changes in response to big shocks, we will be looking for *incremental change with transformative results*.[4] To move beyond the punctuated equilibrium models that are employed, almost by default, by most political scientists, sociologists, and economists working on institutional change, we invited contributions organized around a theoretically self-conscious investigation of empirical cases of institutional change in advanced industrial societies that do not fit received conceptualizations. As *Beyond Continuity* (Streeck and Thelen 2005) demonstrated, such cases are not just frequent but they are also found in core areas of contemporary political economies. Authors were asked to work toward general insights in the character and the mechanisms of the sort of change they observed within and across individual countries. Contributions were to draw on ongoing or completed empirical work and highlight the significance of its findings for an improved theoretical understanding of institutional change, in particular of the relationship between continuity and discontinuity, and between incremental and fundamental change.

1.3. Institutions as Regimes

Definitions of institutions abound. As none of them has yet become firmly institutionalized in the social and political sciences, a brief conceptual exercise cannot be avoided.[5] Very generally, institutions may be defined *as building-blocks of social order*: they represent socially sanctioned, that is, collectively enforced expectations with respect to the behavior of specific categories of actors or to the performance of certain activities. Typically they involve *mutually related rights and obligations* for actors, distinguishing between appropriate and inappropriate, 'right' and 'wrong', 'possible' and 'impossible' actions and thereby organizing behavior into predictable and reliable patterns.

In *Beyond Continuity* (Streeck and Thelen 2005) we focused on institutions that govern behavior in the political economies of advanced capitalism. As we believe in historically grounded concepts and theories, this relieves us of the need to define institutions so generally that all possible forms of normative regulation of social action are covered. For example, anthropologists might conceive of mores and customs, like shaking hands with everyone present in a certain order when one enters a meeting room, as institutions, provided there are strong enough sanctions against deviating from them. Indeed in more conservative social settings in Germany, like a business meeting, not shaking hands is very likely to reflect negatively on someone, and those present will in one way or other make the deviant feel that they disapprove of what is disrespectful and impolite behavior to them.

Mores and customs are no trivial matter. The sanctions that are applied to enforce them may be extremely painful – in the case above, they may mean that business is lost to the competition, or that an overdue promotion is refused. But what is important for us in the example is that the sanctions that are available to the group to enforce the norm are strictly *informal* in nature, as indeed is the 'institution' of the handshake that such sanctions are supposed to protect. Informal institutions exist by no means only in premodern societies; in fact informal norms enforced by community disapproval are universally present in social life. *They are, however, not the subject of our study.* This is because to the extent that modern economies are *political* economies – that is, governed by politics – they are mainly controlled by norms and sanctions that are *formalized*.[6]

Modern, formal, legal–political institutions differ in a variety of ways from informal, 'anthropological' ones, not least in how they change: the former by decision and the latter by cultural evolution. Still, they also have important properties in common. Foremost among these is their *obligatory character*. Actors may and frequently will voluntarily comply with the demands of an institutionalized social norm, either because they believe in its value or because they find compliance with it expedient. This, however, is not what *defines* an institution. Defining of an institution is, rather, that actors are *expected* to conform to it, regardless of what they would want to do on their own. Moreover, such expectations are held, not just by actors directly affected by the expected behavior, but by 'society' as a whole. Someone who does not know how to greet people properly in a meeting room and in what order will incur the disapproval of *all* well-socialized middle- or upper-class Germans, whether or not they themselves have been refused the opportunity to shake hands with him or her. And in a country with an institutionalized right to collective bargaining, an employer who turns his shop into a 'union-free environment' will not just be reproached by the unions he has locked out, but also by the courts that will remind him of the obligations the law of the land imposes on an employer of labor as a matter of legal duty.

In sum, the institutions in which we are interested here are formalized rules that may be enforced by calling upon a third party. Following Stinchcombe (1968), it is this possibility of third-party enforcement that indicates whether a rule has legitimacy. As long as the breach of a rule or the violation of an expectation, informal or formal, leads to no more than a strategic response by the actors directly affected, we are dealing, *not* with an institution, but with a more or less voluntarily agreed social convention.[7] We are dealing with an institution only if and to the extent that third parties predictably and reliably come to the support of actors whose institutionalized, and therefore *legitimate*, normative expectations have been disappointed. This they do not necessarily because they identify with the interests of such actors, although they may. Rather, they intervene as an expression of moral disapproval (in traditional societies, or on behalf of informal institutions) or because they are specifically charged by an organized modern society with ensuring the reliability of certain expectations of actors with respect to the behavior of others.

By emphasizing the obligatory character of institutions, and in particular of the formal institutions of modern political economies with which we are concerned, we exclude from our discussion empirical phenomena and dissociate ourselves from conceptual constructions that would make our subject too broad to be meaningful. Our definition shares with the more economistic treatments associated with 'rational choice' theory an emphasis on strategic behavior within institutional constraints, rejecting the shared cognitive templates that some sociologists associate with institutions (e.g. Meyer and Rowan 1991). But against the rational-choice view of institutions as coordinating mechanisms, we draw attention to relations of authority, obligation, and enforcement as opposed to voluntarism.[8] In this way we distinguish institutions from private pacts or conventions that lack third-party or societal support and with it, in our definition, legitimacy. Pacts or conventions, in other words, become institutions only when their stability ceases to depend exclusively on the self-interested behavior of those directly involved and rather becomes, in a strict sense, a matter of 'public interest'.[9]

Defining institutions in this way, we believe we gain at least three advantages. First, our emphasis on enforcement as a social process by which institutions are translated in behavior distinguishes our approach from the voluntaristic variety of 'rational choice' where institutions are seen in functional terms, as facilitating coordination for actors to achieve joint gains—which does not allow for the possibility of a gap between the institution as designed and the behavior under it. Similarly, at the other end of the spectrum, it sets us off against a view of institutions as shared scripts where also, by definition, there is no gap between institution and behavior, and therefore no conflict over competing interpretations that could be explored as a source of change.[10] Put otherwise, the way we include obligation and enforcement into our concept of institution, we can explicitly provide for a significant amount of 'play' in the rules actors are expected to follow, and thus for the possibility that institutional change may be generated *as a result of the normal, everyday implementation and enactment of an institution*. We will return to this theme shortly when we introduce the concept of an institutional 'regime'.

Second, especially when political scientists write about institutions, the question sometimes arises whether *policies*, like, for example, early retirement or the provision of state support to small- and medium-sized firms, should be included or not—and to what extent theories of institutional change may at the same time be theories of policy change. To us this depends on the character of the policy in question. If a government agrees or refuses to support the American occupation of Iraq by sending troops, this certainly is a policy but we would not consider it as an institution. There are policies, however, which stipulate rules that assign normatively backed rights and responsibilities to actors and provide for their 'public', that is, third-party enforcement. Thus early-retirement policies create expectations among workers and employers with respect to when people become entitled to draw a pension from the state, and to the extent that stipulated conditions are met, they can consider their expectations to be legitimate and indeed go to the courts to have them vindicated. Policies, that is to say, are institutions in our sense to the extent that they constitute rules for actors other than for the policy-makers themselves—rules that can and need to be implemented and that are legitimate in that they will if necessary be enforced by agents acting on behalf of the society as a whole.

Third, in colloquial language the word 'institution' is sometimes used for a specific category of actors, usually corporate actors or organizations, rather than for legitimate rules of behavior. The Federal Reserve Bank, for example, certainly falls in this category, and so does a state as a whole. Even private organizations are sometimes considered institutions, for example, trade unions in Scandinavian countries or the Deutsche Bank in the German post-war economy. To us this does not pose a big conceptual problem. We suggest that organizations come to be regarded as institutions to the extent that their existence and operation become in a specific way publicly guaranteed and privileged, by becoming backed up by societal norms and the enforcement capacities related to them. A central bank is considered an institution because its existence is an outflow of the strongly sanctioned state monopoly on issuing legal tender. It stands for the collectively enforced expectation that other actors will stay away from printing money and instead will accept for payment the money issued by the central bank. Also, as long as trade unions are mere organizations, they can be suppressed and may even be outlawed by a hostile government. In some societies, however, where their existence and their activities have become protected by collective values and politically enacted norms, they constitute a socially sanctioned constraint for economic actors. Similarly, a bank is just a bank as long as it is not performing semi-public functions in a country's industrial policy; if it is, however, the opportunities and constraints its decisions create for others can be disregarded only at the price of disapproval, not just by the bank, but also by other agents that represent the community as a whole.

Summing up so far, to us the closest general concept for the kind of institution in whose dynamics of change we are interested is that of a social *regime*. By regime we mean a set of rules stipulating expected behavior and 'ruling out' behavior deemed to be undesirable. A regime is legitimate in the sense and to the extent that the expectations it represents are enforced by the society in which it is embedded. Regimes involve rule-makers and rule-takers, the former setting and modifying, often in conflict and competition, the rules with which the latter are expected to comply. In the limiting case, rule-makers and rule-takers are identical; in any case, relations and interactions between the two are crucial for the content and the evolution of the regime as such. An institution conceived as a regime resembles what Weber calls a *Herrschaftsverband*, translated by Guenther Roth as a 'ruling organization' (Weber 1978 [1956] 53).[11] Conceiving of institutions as regimes not only makes them eminently accessible to empirical research as it translates institutional relations into relations between identifiable social actors. Even more importantly, as the analyses in *Beyond Continuity* confirm, it is only if we can distinguish analytically between the rules and their implementation or 'enactment' – and, by extension, if we can identify the gaps between the two that are due to or open up opportunities for strategic action on the part of actors – that we can capture important features of incremental endogenous change.

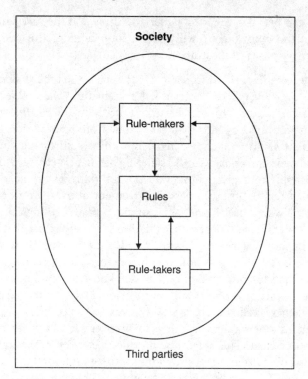

Figure 3.2. Institutions as regimes

In Figure 3.2 we have summarized the main properties of *institutions as regimes*. Embedded in a societal context of supportive third parties that makes for institutional legitimacy, we locate our ideal–typical distinction between rule-makers (or institutional designers) and rule-takers. Note that we provide for a direct feedback from the latter to the former, which we expect to be of relevance certainly in democratic societies. In order not to make our figure too confusing, we have decided not to indicate the relations between both rule-makers and rule-takers with the surrounding society and the values the latter enforces on them. Just as the surrounding society affects both parties through the constraints and opportunities it creates for socially backed rule-making and rule enforcement, it is itself affected by the social and political influence exercised by agents lobbying for their interpretation of social rules and norms. We will address this in more detail further below.

Defining institutions as regimes has the advantage for us that it directs attention to important sources of institutional change. They all have to do with the fact that the *enactment of a social rule is never perfect* and that there always is a gap between the *ideal pattern* of a rule and the *real pattern* of life under it. In the following we will address four facets of this complex relationship for purposes of illustration:

1. As we have learned from sociologists such as Reinhard Bendix (1974 [1956]), the meaning of a rule is never self-evident and always subject to and in need of interpretation. This is relevant especially in the relationship that is indicated in Figure 3.2 by the downward arrow from rules to rule-takers. Life in a social, that is, normatively ordered community requires ongoing efforts to develop and maintain a shared understanding of what exactly the rule says that one has to apply to a given situation. As ideal patterns are necessarily less complex than real patterns, honest disagreement over how a norm is to be applied may always arise. Rather than simply a matter of logical deduction, applying a general rule to a specific situation is a creative act that must take into account, not just the rule itself, but also the unique circumstances to which it is to be applied. This holds for highly formalized norms, like written law, no less than for informal ones. Lawyers know the complexities of subsuming the empirical properties of an individual case under a general rule. Recourse to what is called in some legal systems 'the will of the legislator' is for good reason just one way among others to discover what a rule really demands in a concrete context. This is because no rule-maker can be assumed to have been aware of the full variety of situations to which his law might in the future have to be applied. In fact he might find it difficult to remember with hindsight the complex variety of motives that may have driven his decision. Sociologists have pointed out that typically, clarification of the operative meaning of formal law presupposes a shared culturally based tacit understanding between the actors involved that may, however, either not really exist or change over time, in which case the rule *in effect* changes with it. Indeed often what a rule 'really means' can be established only by the rulings of a legitimate authority charged with adjudicating between different interpretations. Such rulings, too, can and are likely to change with time and circumstances, which may be entirely functional as they may provide a regime with the sort of ground flexibility that it may require for its reproduction.

2. A related issue is the cognitive limits of rule-makers, which become relevant in the downward relationship in our figure between rule-makers and rules. Even the honest application in good will of a rule to empirical conditions may cause unanticipated results that may differ from what was intended when the rule was written, which in turn may cause its corrective rewriting. On the other hand, that rules cannot be unambiguously and definitively stated facilitates their creative application in uncertain circumstances, keeping them valid in spite of the inevitably imperfect information of their designers

on the circumstances of their implementation. In fact regimes capable of survival in a complex environment are likely to have built-in feedbacks that inform rule-makers how their rules are working out in practice. (In Figure 3.2, these are indicated by the upward arrows from rule-takers to rule-makers.) Supported by intelligence of this sort rule-makers may then revise the rules, setting in motion another sequence of practical exploration of their real meaning, observation of their real consequences, and further revision in the light of the latter.

3. Questioning the true meaning of institutionalized rules happens of course not only in good will. Rule-takers do not just implement the rules made for them, but also try to revise them in the process of implementation, making use of their inherent openness and under-definition (see the upward arrow in Figure 3.2 from rule-takers to rules). One advantage of defining institutions as *Herrschaftsverbände* within which rule-makers and rule-takers interact is that this avoids an 'over-socialized' (Wrong 1961) conception of human actors as is often implied by purely normative, or cultural, concepts of institution. While sometimes rule-takers are socialized to follow a rule for its own sake, sometimes they clearly are not, and this seems to apply particularly in modern societies and economies. To the extent that rules impose uncomfortable and costly obligations, less than perfectly socialized rational actors may look for ways to circumvent them. Finding loopholes in a law is a specialty of lawyers, especially tax lawyers. Their continuous probing of the boundary between the legal and the illegal is part of the interpretative struggle that begins as soon as a rule is laid down: it is one mechanism by which the meaning of a rule is both clarified and modified ('worked out') in practice. Favorable discoveries made by adventurous interpretative entrepreneurs may spread fast among the subjects of a regime, forcing rule-makers to revise the law in order to restore it. Sometimes the only way this can happen is by more special rules being added to cover unforeseen cases. As this makes the regime more complex, it may further extend the opportunities for inventive opportunists to evade or subvert it to their advantage.

4. Finally, there are limits to the extent to which socially authorized agencies of social control can prevent and correct unintentional or subversive deviation from social rules. A case in point is the phenomenon of illegal employment, or more generally of the underground economy. Some labor market regimes are more likely than others to give rise to anomic behavior of this sort. In fact, underground employment seems to be most frequent in highly regulated economies. Mass deviant behavior in breach of a social or legal regime can often be ended only by changing the regime and making the behavior legal. Sometimes, however, rule-makers are willing to live with a great deal of anomie since the stability of a norm may, as famously pointed out by Durkheim, require that it be broken. For example, illegal employment

may furnish a modicum of flexibility to an economy that would otherwise be too rigidly regulated to perform well (what Berger and Piore (1980) have some time ago described as economic 'dualism').

What all this amounts to is that those who control social institutions, whoever they may be in a concrete case, are likely to have less than perfect control over the way in which their creations work in reality. What an institution *is* is defined by continuous interaction between rule-makers and rule-takers during which ever new interpretations of the rule will be discovered, invented, suggested, rejected, or, for the time being, adopted. The real meaning of an institution, that is to say, is inevitably and because of the very nature of social order subject to evolution driven, if by nothing else, by its necessarily imperfect enactment on the ground, in directions that are often unpredictable. Indeed the more sophisticated the makers of a regime are, the more they recognize that a good part of institutional and political life consists of unanticipated consequences of their 'institutional design' decisions, requiring that these are continuously adjusted and revised if they are to be made to stick.

We conclude this section by noting that, conceived as systems of social interaction under formalized normative control, institutions cease to appear as a rigid hardware of social life mechanistically relegating actors and action to narrowly circumscribed residual spaces for spontaneous voluntarism and rational calculation. Instead a grounded, 'realistic' concept of social institutions, as adopted in *Beyond Continuity*, emphasizes their being continuously created and recreated by a great number of actors with divergent interests, varying normative commitments, different powers, and limited cognition. This process no single actor fully controls; its outcomes are far from being standardized across different sites of enactment; and its results are contingent, often unpredictable, and may be fully understood only with hindsight.[12]

2. DYNAMICS OF INSTITUTIONAL CHANGE: LESSONS FROM *BEYOND CONTINUITY*

2.1. What Counts as Change? Or When is a Change a 'Real' Change?

As suggested above, the most influential frameworks for the study of the political economy of advanced countries exhibit a distinct if inadvertent conservative bias, in that the sophisticated analytic tools they provide for understanding stability are not matched by equally sophisticated tools for understanding change. As a consequence, whether such frameworks are premised on an equilibrium model (as in the varieties of capitalism literature) or not (as in much of the welfare state literature), current scholarship is prone to ignore or downplay observed changes, or to code all that appears to be new as a variation of the old.

The chapters in *Beyond Continuity* (Streeck and Thelen 2005) demonstrate how much is missed when contemporary trends are analyzed from the perspective of these theoretical frameworks. Jacob Hacker's chapter (Hacker 2005) on the US welfare state documents a trend toward the privatization of risk across a number of policy areas. The traditional literature on the welfare state rightly suggests that most large-scale social welfare policies have proven very resistant to overt cutback efforts. However, as Hacker argues, 'the conventional story about retrenchment appears only half right', for as he shows, risk coverage in the United States has narrowed significantly as policy-makers have failed to adapt welfare programs to cover new risks that have emerged outside the scope of existing policies. As Hacker puts it, in a context in which social risks are changing and where the gap between them and the 'reach' of social programs is growing, 'conservatives have not had to enact major policy reforms to move toward many of their favored ends' (2005: 46–7). Analyses that focus exclusively on the lock-in effects characteristic of large entitlement programs miss the story of a major de facto shrinkage of welfare state coverage in the United States over the past two decades.

The chapters by Jonah Levy (Levy 2005) and Steven Vogel (Vogel 2005), on the French and Japanese political economies, respectively, make a similar point. Anyone looking for evidence of the continued viability of the traditional French and Japanese political–economic 'models' will find a lot of it. France has traditionally been considered the classic example of a state-led political economy and as Levy points out, the French state still looms extremely large in the lives of its citizens. In fact, by many conventional measures, like spending and taxation, the state is bigger than ever, and certainly no less economically active. However, as Levy argues, if we focus on these continuities, we miss an enormous and highly consequential transformation: the abandonment of the traditional *dirigiste* strategy of directing capital while excluding labor, in favor of a strategy of aggressively promoting market liberalization while cushioning its social effects. Levy's account shows how existing state capacities, far from being dismantled, were 'redeployed' in a major way during the post *dirigiste* period.

Vogel's chapter on Japan describes a similar phenomenon. Despite the strains of prolonged economic crisis, traditional Japanese political–economic institutions have exhibited remarkable staying power. Much remains of the institutions that support and sustain Japan's version of a 'coordinated' market economy – like long-term employment in the area of labor relations, or corporate and financial networks. Vogel documents these continuities but notes that stability should not obscure change, particularly in the way in which old institutions and policies are being used in the service of new ends. Among other things, the corporate ties that are often seen as defining a distinctively 'coordinated' as opposed to a 'liberal' model of capitalism are being tapped as mechanisms through which to accomplish corporate down-sizing and a move toward more liberalized labor markets. Liberalization in Japan, that is to say, has unfolded above all by traditional institutions being deployed in novel and, indeed over the long run, transformative ways.

One thing the three cases have in common is that they illustrate, as suggested by our definition of institutions as regimes, that formal institutions do not fully determine the uses to which they may be put. This is one important reason why major change in institutional practice may be observed together with strong continuity in institutional structures. Gregory Jackson's (2005) analysis of German co-determination is a case in point, documenting as it does profound changes in the way co-determination has functioned over successive historical periods in the absence of major institutional discontinu-ity. At its inception, co-determination was partly intended as an independent, workplace-based counterweight to Germany's rather radical national labor movement at the time. By the 1950s, however, works councils had been fully though not formally incorporated into the strategies of, now moderate, trade unions. Now, not only did co-determination not detract from the strength of the unions, but it magnified their voice by providing them with a stable, legally anchored foothold in workplaces across the entire economy. Clearly this is change of a quite fundamental sort although it has taken place within an institutional form that has remained recognizably similar, or was recon-structed in recognizably similar forms, over a long period of time.

How can transformative change result from incremental change, in the absence of exogenous shocks? Institutional structures, the chapters in Streeck and Thelen (2005) suggest, may be stickier than what they do and what is done through them. If the latter changes significantly, however gradually, analytical frameworks that take the absence of disruption as sufficient evidence of insti-tutional continuity miss the point, given that *the practical enactment of an institution is as much part of its reality as its formal structure*. In this vein, Hacker rightly suggests including in institutional analysis the actual *conse-quences* of institutionalized behavior, while Jackson emphasizes the possibility of changing *meanings* and *functions* being attached to an otherwise stable institution. Similarly, Vogel and Levy point to the different purposes that may be pursued by means of a given institutional arrangement, and Deeg locates the beginning of a new 'path' where a new 'logic of action' is established. The latter he defines as a *general orientation* of actors that, one might add, operates like a 'meta-rule' governing the interpretation of a given structure of institutional constraints and opportunities – whose meaning, as we have argued, is never self-evident and therefore needs to be continuously constituted in practice.

Fundamental change, then, ensues when a multitude of actors switch from one logic of action to another. This may happen in a variety of ways, and it certainly can happen gradually and continuously. For example, given that logics and institutional structures are not one-to-one related, enterprising actors often have enough 'play' to test new behaviors inside old institutions, perhaps in response to new and as yet incompletely understood external conditions, and encourage other actors to behave correspondingly. We will return to the concept of logic of action below.

2.2. How Institutions Change

Contemporary theories of institutional development mostly locate significant change in convulsive historic ruptures or openings. This is not what the essays in *Beyond Continuity* do. Rather than abrupt and discontinuous, they find transformative change often to result from an accumulation of gradual and incremental change (see also Djelic and Quack 2003: 309–10). Moreover, rather than emanating on the outside, change is often endogenous and in some cases is produced by the very behavior an institution itself generates. Reminded of this by their empirical material, the analyses in *Beyond Continuity* provide an angle on institutional change that is different from dominant punctuated equilibrium models. In particular, they document from different perspectives how significant change can emanate from inherent ambiguities and 'gaps' that exist by design or emerge over time between formal institutions and their actual implementation or enforcement (see also Pierson 2004: ch. 4). These gaps may become key sites of political contestation over the form, functions, and salience of specific institutions whose outcome may be an important engine of institutional change (see also Thelen 2004).

'Agency' and 'structure', in other words, do not just matter sequentially – unlike in Katznelson (2003) where institutions mostly constrain and where change has to wait for those rare moments when agency defeats structure. Political institutions are not only periodically contested; they are the object of ongoing skirmishing as actors try to achieve advantage by interpreting or redirecting institutions in pursuit of their goals, or by subverting or circum-venting rules that clash with their interests. Instead of separating institutional development into periods in which agency matters more than structure or the other way around, the aim must be to understand, as Deeg puts it, the way actors cultivate change from within the context of existing opportunities and constraints – working around elements they cannot change while attempting to harness and utilize others in novel ways.

Our analysis suggests five broad modes of gradual but nevertheless trans-formative change that we will call *displacement, layering, drift, conversion,* and *exhaustion.* We discuss each of these modes briefly, drawing on a broader literature. After this we will close with a consideration of the lessons the essays assembled here can tell us, substantively, about current processes of liberal-ization in advanced industrial democracies.

Displacement From the perspective of whole systems (or what some sociolo-gists call 'organizational fields') change can occur through a process of displacement. In the 'new' institutionalism in sociology, displacement hap-pens as new models emerge and diffuse which call into question existing, previously taken-for-granted organizational forms and practices (Fligstein 1990, 1997; DiMaggio and Powell 1991; Dobbin 1994; Clemens 1997; Schneiberg n.d). In the political science literature, the emphasis is typically more on political than on cognitive or normative factors, with change eman-ating mostly from shifts in the societal balance of power (see, among others, Collier and Collier 1991; Skowronek 1995; Huber and Stephens 2001).

For our present purposes, the important point (associated above all with the works of Karen Orren and Stephen Skowronek) is that the institutional frameworks that exist in any particular society are never completely coherent. While some institutional arrangements may impose a dominant logic of action, these typically coexist with other arrangements, created at different points in time and under different historical circumstances, that embody conflicting and even contradictory logics (Orren and Skowronek 1994, 2004). Beyond this, and equally important, even within dominant frame-works there will normally remain possibilities of action that institutions neither prescribe nor eliminate. Where either of these is the case, institutional configurations are vulnerable to change through displacement as traditional arrangements are discredited or pushed to the side in favor of new institutions and associated behavioral logics. Such change often occurs through the rediscovery or activation – and, always, the cultivation – of alternative institutional forms. As growing numbers of actors defect to a new system, previously deviant, aberrant, anachronistic, or 'foreign' practices gain salience at the expense of traditional institutional forms and behaviors.[13]

Where the institutions and behaviors enacted by *displacement through defection* come from can vary widely. For example, an older literature in political science drew attention to the 'reactivation' or 'rediscovery' of what Barrington Moore once called 'suppressed historical alternatives' (Moore

1979: 376). Thus Michael Piore and Charles Sabel (1984) attributed the success of the German political economy in the 1980s in large part to the survival of institutional and organizational forms (among others a vibrant and flexible small business sector and a skill system that preserved and promoted the acquisition of traditional 'craft' skills) that had been declared anachronistic and irrelevant in the heyday of Fordist mass production. As the terms of competition shifted in the 1980s, these institutions could be tapped and activated to become the basis for alternative competitive strategies premised on what one of us has elsewhere called 'diversified quality production' (Streeck 1991).

Work by Colin Crouch and Maarten Keune (2005) suggests a similar logic. In the two cases they analyzed, change occurred as actors 'worked creatively with institutional materials that were at hand...[by virtue of their historic] legacies, but submerged by more dominant or more recent practices' (ibid: 84–5). In the case of the rejuvenation of the Hungarian region of Györ, this involved tapping into and cultivating the Western-oriented, market-countenancing practices that had developed alongside and under the dominant state-socialist economy. When the time came for the transition to capitalism, the ruling local elite needed merely to '[bring] to the fore the previously secondary development path of the region' (ibid: 99). Similarly in their analysis of Britain's transition to neoliberalism in the early 1980s, Crouch and Keune show how displacement was facilitated by the related facts that the foundations of Keynesianism had been precarious to begin with, and that they had coexisted with alternative institutions and practices firmly anchored in the country's financial sector. The point in both cases is that in critical moments or periods latent subsidiary ways of action can be rediscovered, and by switching over actors then promote them to dominance or move them from the periphery of the institutional system to its center.

Underlying Crouch and Keune's analysis is an image of social structure in which different institutions inside one and the same society may embody conflicting, mutually contradictory 'logics' – with one institution requiring or licensing behavior that is *in principle* incompatible with the behavior required or licensed by another institution. Human actors seem to be quite capable of operating simultaneously in different institutional contexts governed by different 'logics', moving back and forth between them, or playing them off against one another. Also, human societies appear to have enough slack and their causal texture usually seems to be loose enough (or cause takes enough time to turn into effect) to be tolerant of considerable friction between differently constructed institutions or action spaces. All societies, in other words, are in some way hybrids, some more and some less.[14]

Change through displacement can occur endogenously through the rediscovery or activation of previously suppressed or suspended possibilities. But it can also occur through what Castaldi and Dosi call 'invasion', in either a literal or metaphoric sense (Castaldi and Dosi n.d.: 24). Literally, invasion refers to the supplanting of indigenous institutions and practices with foreign ones, presumably those of the victor or occupying power – although we know from historical work that this is never complete and more typically produces hybrids of one variety or another (Herrigel 2000; also Quack and Djelic 2005). In a broader literature (e.g. the sociological literature on diffusion) and for our purposes, the more relevant version of invasion is the metaphorical one, which involves the importation and then cultivation by local actors of 'foreign' institutions and practices.

In all of the instances of displacement discussed above,[15] change occurred, not through explicit revision or amendment of existing arrangements, but rather through shifts in the relative salience of different institutional arrangements within a 'field' or 'system'. This type of change, as Deeg (2005) and Quack and Djelic (2005) emphasize, requires active cultivation by agents whose interests are better served by new arrangements. Deeg's analysis in particular hints, incidentally, at an important, often overlooked relationship between endogenous and exogenous change: for external shocks to bring about fundamental transformation, it helps if endogenous change has prepared the ground. Endogenous evolution of a social system may generate potentials that, when activated by interested parties in response to changing external conditions, can provide the foundation for a new logic of action (on this see also Schneiberg n.d.).

Layering Institutional change can also occur through a process that one of us has elsewhere, following Eric Schickler, called layering (Schickler 2001; Thelen 2002). Paul Pierson has convincingly argued that not just economic institutions but also political ones may be subject to increasing returns and lock-in effects. In his work on social security, he has demonstrated how each new client added to a pay-as-you-go pension system creates additional vested interests in the maintenance of that system. The older the system, therefore, the more costly it becomes both politically and fiscally to dismantle it (Pierson 1994; Myles and Pierson 2001). Many other kinds of institutional arrangements are subject to this sort of effect. However, as Schickler points out, this does not preclude change altogether provided reformers learn to work around those elements of an institution that have become unchangeable. Layering is the term he uses to characterize the nature of such reform. In his empirical work Schickler shows how, in the case of the US Congress, successive rounds of institutional reform produced a highly 'disjointed' pattern and a much higher degree of institutional incoherence than prevailing functionalist accounts of congressional institutions would predict.

For our purposes what is most interesting about change through layering is that it can set in motion path-altering dynamics through a mechanism of what we might think of as *differential growth*. The classic example from the welfare state literature is the layering of a voluntary private pension system onto an existing public system. While the established public system may well be unassailable, faster growth of the new private system can effect profound change, among other things by draining off political support for the public system.

Bo Rothstein has written of analogous reform efforts in the Swedish context in which customized private alternatives, for example, in schools or day care centers, are offered alongside the uniform public system (Rothstein 1998). As he points out, fundamental change can be – gradually – effected, not through a frontal attack on traditional institutions, but through differential growth of private and public sector institutions siphoning off the support of key constituencies for the latter, in particular the middle class which occupies the politically pivotal position. In cases like this, new dynamics are set in motion by political actors working on the margins by introducing amendments that can initially be 'sold' as refinements of or correctives to existing institutions. Since the new layers created in this way do not as such and directly undermine existing institutions, they typically do not provoke countermobilization by defenders of the status quo. To the extent, however, that they operate on a different logic and grow more quickly than the traditional system, over time they may fundamentally alter the overall trajectory of development as the old institutions stagnate or lose their grip and the new ones assume an ever more prominent role in governing individual behavior.

Bruno Palier (2005) provides an additional example of layering as a mode of institutional change. Palier describes the gradual transformation of French social policy over the past two decades. The backdrop to Palier's analysis is the liberalization of French economic policy, which for political reasons had to be embedded initially in an expanding conservative welfare state. This historical period and broader context is analyzed by Levy (2005). Palier examines the subsequent liberalization of the welfare state, which may have been an inevitable next step forced by the high costs to the state of full compensation and status maintenance for the losers of economic change. Welfare state liberalization, as Palier shows, departs from the logic of the traditional corporatist welfare state, and in particular entails increasing reliance on means-tested, minimum-level protection paid out of public funds. Importantly, it also involves 'activation' instead of decommodification or status maintenance outside employment. In Palier's account, liberalization policies were designed to avoid generating too much resistance, proceeding incrementally and without much rupture or fanfare, and avoiding a direct assault on existing institutions and policies. In fact, Palier notes that reformers introduced change mainly at the margins and 'as if their purpose were only to fix or complement the system' (2005: 131). New programs were introduced alongside the immovable and politically firmly established old ones, adding to the 'enduring realm of social insurance' based on contributions and on a traditional social-conservative logic a wholly new and thoroughly liberal welfare regime of targeted minimum benefits financed by taxes. Palier shows how, despite their incremental nature, and despite the fact that they were introduced as minor additions and repairs to make the existing system more stable, the reforms set in motion dynamics that produced a deep transformation of the French welfare state.[16]

Layering involves active sponsorship of amendments, additions, or revisions to an existing set of institutions. The actual mechanism for change is differential growth; the introduction of new elements setting in motion dynamics through which they, over time, actively crowd out or supplant by default the old system as the domain of the latter progressively shrinks relative to that of the former. Unlike Schickler, who mostly emphasizes the institutional incongruence that layering can produce, for us it is an important question to what extent the fringe and the core can peacefully coexist, or whether the fringe can attract enough defectors from the core eventually to displace it.

Drift There is nothing automatic about institutional stability – despite the language of stasis and stickiness often invoked in relation to institutions. Institutions do not survive by standing still, nor is their stable reproduction always simply a matter of positive feedback or increasing returns (Thelen 2004: ch. 1). Quite to the contrary institutions require active maintenance; to remain what they are they need to be reset and refocused, or sometimes more fundamentally recalibrated and renegotiated, in response to changes in the political and economic environment in which they are embedded. Without such 'tending', as Hacker's (2005) analysis of health care policy in the United States illustrates, they can be subject to erosion or atrophy through *drift*. As with layering, change through drift, while potentially fundamental, may be masked by stability on the surface. Indeed Hacker begins by noting that, as other analysts have shown, social programs in the United States have indeed 'resisted major retrenchment'. However, Hacker also observes that the American welfare system has failed to be adapted to cover a set of risks that have newly emerged or increased in salience. The result is a significant shrinkage in the social protections enjoyed by American citizens as a matter of right. Hacker's analysis suggests that in addition to the formal attributes of institutions, we must take account of their implementation, and especially of the gaps that may emerge between the two as a consequence of shifting contextual conditions. Analyses that focus only on the continuity of existing rules miss the potential slippage between these and the real world to which they are supposed to apply.

A disjuncture between social programs and changing profiles of social risk can result from 'natural' trends. For example, slow changes in family structures may alter the composition of risk and therefore also de facto welfare state coverage. In cases like this, drift occurs without explicit political maneuvering: the world surrounding an institution evolves in ways that alter its scope, meaning, and function. Drift can also be caused by gaps in rules allowing actors to abdicate previous responsibilities. In Hacker's analysis, changes in the incentives faced by employers (as important private sector welfare providers in the United States) caused many of them to scale back their efforts. Again, the result was declining welfare state coverage even without major retrenchment and indeed in the absence of any public debate or decision at all.

Parallels exist between Hacker's analysis of drift in US health care policy today and Skocpol's analysis of civil war benefits, which provides us with another, especially dramatic, example of change through drift (Skocpol 1992). Civil war pensions, Skocpol argues, could have become the core of a general public pension system had its supporters been able to forge the broader alliances needed to secure its political foundation. That they did not succeed in this was, by Skocpol's account, in large measure due to opponents of expansion being able to invoke a connection between civil war pensions on the one hand and the patronage politics and corruption of the Progressive Era on the other, 'as a reason for opposing or delaying any move toward more general old-age pensions' (Skocpol 1992: 59). Failure to extend benefits to new groups made the atrophy and ultimate demise of the original system a foregone conclusion: the program literally died out as civil war veterans and their spouses themselves passed away.

Conversion A fourth mode of change is what Thelen (2002, 2004) has elsewhere called conversion. Different from layering and drift, here institutions are not so much amended or allowed to decay as they are *redirected to new goals, functions, or purposes*. Such redirection may come about as a result of new environmental challenges, to which policy-makers respond by deploying existing institutional resources to new ends. Or it can come about through changes in power relations, such that actors who were not involved in the original design of an institution and whose participation in it may not have been reckoned with, take it over and turn it to new ends. Here, too, there are elements of stability and even lock-in. However, whereas conventional increasing-returns arguments point to a dynamic in which actors adapt their strategies to existing institutions, conversion works the other way around: existing institutions are adapted to serve new goals or fit the interests of new actors.[17]

The redirection of institutional resources that we associate with conversion may occur through political contestation over what functions and purposes an existing institution should serve. Political contestation driving change through conversion is made possible by the gaps that exist by design or emerge over time between institutionalized rules and their local enactment. Four sources of such gaps are of particular relevance in the present context (see also the discussion in Pierson 2004: ch. 4). The first is the cognitive limits of institutions' builders and associated problem of *unintended consequences*. As Elster (2003) and others have pointed out, designers of institutions are not all-seeing; they make mistakes and in any event they can 'never do just one thing' (Pierson 2004: 115). For Elster the point is to challenge the presumption, pervasive in the rational-choice literature, that institutions can be thought of as rational solutions to specific social problems. Elster's analysis, of successive waves of constitution writing in France, ends on the note that behavior in general and institutional design in particular are almost by definition irrational – the implication of which could be that they are not amenable to systematic analysis. Our conclusion here is somewhat less sweeping as we limit ourselves to noting that unintended consequences of institutional design may offer opportunities for political contestation that theoretical treatments that assume an identity between design and effect by definition cannot account for.

Second, institution-building, to the extent that it occurs through political negotiation, typically involves *compromise*. As Schickler has argued, new institutions often constitute 'common carriers' for coalitions of actors who support them for highly diverse reasons (Schickler 1999; Pierson 2004). The resulting *ambiguities* in the rules that define institutionalized behavior provide space for political contestation over how rules should be interpreted and applied. An example of this is given by Palier (2005). Welfare state reform in France was premised on highly ambiguous agreements, with all parties accepting the need for reform in general while consensus on any particular reform was based on widely different understandings of what the reform was to mean. Similar ambiguities seem to have made possible economic liberalization in France which, according to Levy, was embedded in the same rhetoric that was in the past used to legitimate state planning.

Similarly, as shown by Jackson (2005), the institutions and rules governing German co-determination were always characterized by deep ambiguities as rule-makers had in part to leave open their meaning lest they lose support from necessary allies. As a result, both the uncertainty that is inherent in all rules that need to be applied to varying conditions and the discretion rule-takers must inevitably exercise in following a rule are amplified considerably.

Third, and again echoing points made earlier in this chapter, actors are strategic and even those not involved in the design of an institution will do everything in their power to interpret its rules in their own interest (or *circumvent* or *subvert* rules that clash with their interests). Elizabeth Clemens' work, among others, has drawn attention to processes through which familiar organizational forms were redeployed by 'marginal' actors who had been blocked out of the system – in ways that subverted and undermined received behaviors and logics of action (Clemens 1997). An example of the strategic use of institutions not of their own making can be found in Quack and Djelic's (2005) discussion of multilevel governance systems like the European Union (EU). Lower-order institutions regulated from above in a multilevel institutional structure are not once and for all determined by the latter: like rule-takers in general, those in control of national institutions inevitably have some leeway to adjust the supranational rules that apply to them, and they can also try to change such rules by putting pressure on rule-makers or rule enforcers.

Fourth and as most forcefully argued by Pierson, *time matters* (Pierson 2004). Many institutions – and certainly some of those in which we are most likely to have an interest – have been around long enough to have outlived, not just their designers and the social coalition on which they were founded, but also the external conditions of the time of their foundation. Changes in the nature of the challenges actors face or in the balance of power allow for institutions created to serve certain interests to be redirected to very different and even diametrically opposed goals and ends. Time, in other words, and the changes it brings in actors and problems, opens gaps that entail possibilities for institutional conversion. An example explored elsewhere by one of us (Thelen 2004: chs 2 and 5) are the institutional arrangements comprising Germany's celebrated system for vocational training. The 'founding' legislation around which this system came to be constructed was passed in 1897 by an authoritarian government and was above all directed against the country's social democratic labor movement. A hundred years later, some of the central institutional pillars are still recognizable, even though the system has been turned completely on its head in political-distributional terms, serving now as a key source of strength for organized labor and a pillar of social partnership between labor and business. The process of conversion through which this occurred was not one of dramatic and sudden renegotiation in moments of historic rupture – of which Germany of course experienced several over the twentieth century. Rather, conversion was the result of ongoing political contestation and periodic incremental adjustment through which inherited institutions were adapted and fitted to changes in their social, economic, and political environment.

Jonah Levy (2005) provides another example of this mode of change. Levy characterizes the transformation he documents as an instance of 'redeployment', consisting of the formidable interventionist powers of the French state being diverted away from industrial to social policy, and in the process also from market-correcting to market-conforming ends. The failure of the old statist model precipitated the transition. However, rather than dismantling previous institutional capacities (and in the absence of societal actors to whom social policy could be handed – itself a consequence of statism as Levy's work has instructed us) political elites redirected them to new ends. For our purposes, the important message of Levy's analysis is not so much that state activism continues in France – although it does and this is in itself an outcome of considerable interest. Rather it is that the French state has managed to move gradually in a decidedly liberal direction, with policy-makers taking full advantage of the considerable institutional capacities at their disposal to make change appear less fundamental than it was, or to make fundamental change proceed gradually enough so that it was not recognized as such.

Exhaustion We call our fifth mode of change institutional exhaustion. We include it although, unlike the four others, the processes we have in mind here strictly speaking lead to institutional breakdown rather than change – although the collapse is gradual rather than abrupt. As argued most famously by Marx, social arrangements may set in motion dynamics that sow the seeds of their own destruction. Different from institutional drift, in which institutions may retain their formal integrity even as they increasingly lose their grip on social reality, institutional exhaustion is a process in which behaviors invoked or allowed under existing rules operate to undermine these.

Recent work by Avner Greif and David Laitin provides an example (Greif and Laitin 2003). Greif and Laitin begin, as we do, with a critique of theories of institutions in which change by definition must be generated exogenously. By examining the divergent fate of governing institutions in Venice and Genoa in the early modern period, they try to specify the conditions under which such arrangements either become self-reinforcing or self-undermining over time.[18] In both cases, political institutions were created that provided a foundation for cooperation among rival clans, generating returns for all. Institutional arrangements in Venice operated in ways that weakened the clan structure, however, whereas in Genoa they 'contained inter-clan rivalry, but did not eliminate it' (Greif and Laitin 2003: 18). In both cases cooperative arrangements led to economic prosperity. But in the Genoese case this heightened competition among rival elites, not least by raising the stakes. In this way the institution gave rise to dynamics that made it more and more vulnerable and, indeed, self-undermining over time.

Yet another facet of time-related exhaustion concerns the *age* of an institution, which may be much underrated as a subject of research. 'Young' institutions require elaboration of their meaning in practice, by a sequence of decisions on the part of rule-makers as well as rule-takers. The 'path' along which an institution is 'worked out' in this sense is shaped by exogenous circumstances as well as a myriad of strategic choices, deciding together which of the many possible meanings of a young institution are practically explored and which are foreclosed or left behind by the wayside. Institutions may, however, also age. For example, viz. Trampusch, they may meet 'limits to growth' where their further expansion destroys or uses up resources that they require for their continued operation. Or they may become ever more complex in a process by which, like in the decline of a Kuhnian 'paradigm', more and more exceptions and special provisions have to be added to a given set of institutionalized rules, thereby depriving it of its legitimacy or practicability or both.

In Table 3.1, we have summarized the main properties of the five types of gradual but nevertheless transformative institutional change that we have identified.

2.3. Liberalization as Gradual Transformation

The dominant trend in advanced political economies, we have stated early in this chapter, is liberalization: the steady expansion of market relations in areas that under the post-war settlement of democratic capitalism were reserved to collective political decision-making. Although liberalization amounts to a quite fundamental transformation, it proceeds gradually and continuously, apart from occasional but short-lived episodes of turmoil like in Britain under Thatcher when the Keynesian model of economic policy was replaced with a rediscovered neoliberal model.

Whatever its economic and political deserts – on which one can have different views – it cannot be doubted that the advance of liberalism in the countries of democratic capitalism is greatly supported by the fact that it mainly moves forward only slowly, through what we have called displacement, layering, drift, conversion, and the exhaustion of existing institutions and policies. This raises the question – which we can no more than raise here – whether liberalization under modern capitalism is in whatever way *a privileged direction of 'normal' institutional change* in the absence of historic ruptures. Notably, as Levy (2005) argues, the instruments of post-war state interventionism in France

Table 3.1. Institutional change: five types of gradual transformation

	Displacement	Layering	Drift	Conversion	Exhaustion
Definition	Slowly rising salience of subordinate relative to dominant institutions	New elements attached to existing institutions gradually change their status and structure	Neglect of institutional maintenance in spite of external change resulting in slippage in institutional practice on the ground	Redeployment of old institutions to new purposes; new purposes attached to old structures	Gradual breakdown (withering away) of institutions over time
Mechanism	Defection	Differential growth	Deliberate neglect	Redirection, reinterpretation	Depletion
Elaboration	Institutional incoherence opening space for deviant behavior Active cultivation of a new 'logic' of action inside an existing institutional setting Rediscovery and activation of dormant or latent institutional resources 'Invasion' and assimilation of foreign practices	Faster growth of new institutions created on the edges of old ones New fringe eats into old core New institutional layer siphons off support for old layer Presumed 'fix' destabilizing existing institutions Compromise between old and new slowly turning into defeat of the old	Change in institutional outcomes effected by (strategically) neglecting adaptation to changing circumstances Enactment of institution changed, not by reform of rules, but by rules remaining unchanged in the face of evolving external conditions	Gaps between rules and enactment due to: (1) Lack of foresight: limits to (unintended consequences of) institutional design (2) Intended ambiguity of institutional rules: institutions are compromises (3) Subversion: rules reinterpreted from below (4) Time: changing contextual conditions and coalitions open up space for redeployment	Self-consumption: the normal working of an institution undermines its external preconditions Decreasing returns: generalization changes cost-benefit relations Overextension: limits to growth

were available to promote liberalization in a way that a liberal state could hardly be used for non-liberal, corporatist, or even socialist purposes. Levy's account confirms that liberalization, as already Polanyi knew, tends to come together with a 'countermovement' that 're-embeds' emerging and expanding market relations. But the redeployment of French state capacities after 1983 to social policy was mainly designed to 'anaesthetize' society and 'demobilize' potential resistance. Indeed it did the job quite successfully, only to become afterward the subject of more reform, as described by Palier. Not only was that reform again presented in ambiguous ideological terms so as to be acceptable to actors with widely divergent world-views, but it was also introduced as a series of minor additions and repairs to fix the existing system to make it more stable, rather than to replace it.

Liberalization, our argument implies, can take many forms: not only can it be advanced by the state, like in France, but state functions can also, like in Germany, be delegated to civil society. The resettlement of German early retirement in the collective bargaining system amounts to a move back from the sphere of social rights, in Marshall's sense, to that of industrial rights. This may well be regarded as quite far-reaching change, in spite of the fact that it progressed more slowly and went less far than French social security reform. It also represents change towards liberalization: instead of 'de-commodifying' state legislation, it is now by collective contract negotiated under market constraints that early retirement is made possible and paid for. Collective contracts are concluded in the economic rather than in the political arena; moreover, they are by definition less universal than social rights based on legislation since they apply only to the core and no longer to the periphery. Internalizing the costs of early retirement in workers' pay helps in the consolidation of public budgets. But it also, again, brings in private insurance companies and employers with their company-based pension plans who can be relied upon further to promote liberalization out of their own interests.

Co-determination, too, is undergoing a process of liberalization, according to Jackson (2005), in that its practice is increasingly becoming enmeshed in and circumscribed by market relations. Just as changing capital markets manifest themselves in growing pressure by non-strategic shareholders, changing product markets intensify needs for corporate restructuring to defend and increase competitiveness. As workforce representatives cannot afford to overlook the changed external conditions, they become increasingly part of a joint comanagement of change for which the continued economic viability of the firm is the uppermost goal. While under German institutional conditions restructuring does not and cannot result in workplaces being turned into 'union-free environments', co-determination slowly mutates in practice toward the institutional base of a tight economic community of face between managers and core workforces.

How powerful and at the same time necessary the slow shift of functions between and within institutions is for the progress of liberalization is demonstrated by the Japanese case. In Japan there is no welfare state to relieve firms of the social obligations they entered into in the past, nor is there a collective bargaining system to relieve the state of functions it can no longer perform. This seems to be a main reason why liberalization in Japan proceeds even more slowly than in Europe. As Vogel (2005) argues, and as we have noted above, now small adjustments are being undertaken within firms themselves, with attempts to expand internal labor markets beyond company boundaries and, simultaneously, redefine on the margins traditional institutions such as long-term employment. In a world in which workers cannot distinguish between the social contract and their employment contract, liberalization has a higher threshold to cross and must take a different path than in Western social democracies.

Could it be that measures of liberalization are somehow particularly suited to being imposed gradually and without disruption? Is, in other words, the relationship we observe between gradual transformative change in institutions and liberalization more than historically contingent? Non-liberal reforms in a market economy seem to require 'political moments' in which strong governments create and enforce rules that individual actors have to follow, even if they would on their own prefer not to do so. Liberalization, by comparison, can often proceed without political mobilization, simply by encouraging or tolerating self-interested subversion of collective institutions from below, or by unleashing individual interests and the subversive intelligence of self-interested actors bent on maximizing their utilities. To this extent, liberalization within capitalism may face far fewer collective action problems than the organization of capitalism, and much more than the latter it may be achievable by default: by letting things happen that are happening anyway. All that may be needed for liberalization to progress in this case would be to give people a market alternative to an existing system based on collective solidarity, and then give free rein to the private insurance companies and their sales forces.

Put otherwise, if we follow Deeg (2005) and define a liberal regime as one in which exit is favored as a dominant logic of action over voice, individual actors may find it easier to start a movement toward liberalization than one toward constraining market relations by institutional obligations. This is because encouraging others to exit from a previously obligatory social relationship for self-regarding reasons may require no more than setting an example, while tightening normative controls would need collective rather than individual action followed, importantly, by collectively binding decisions. We conclude this chapter by speculating that it may not be by accident that it is predominantly through our five modes of gradual yet transformative change – displacement of dominant with dormant institutions, institutional layering and subsequent differential growth, tolerated drift of institutions away from social reality, slow conversion of existing institutions to new purposes, and exhaustion due to systemic incompatibility and erosion of resources – that the current liberalization of advanced political economies mainly proceeds.

NOTES

1. Nor, conversely, do all path dependence theorists subscribe to a strong punctuated equilibrium model of change.
2. As Barry Weingast has argued: 'Rational choice theory provides a variety of mechanisms that afford predictions of discontinuous change'. However, questions of 'endogenous emergence, choice and survival of institutions' he regards as 'frontier issues' (Weingast 2002: 692).
3. The difference is that, in the historical institutionalist version, 'new' arrangements are mostly assumed to be very different from the 'old' ones as a result. In the rational-choice version the distance between the new and the old equilibrium could in fact be small; the change, in other words, need not be particularly 'big'.
4. Djelic and Quack (2003: 309) have also drawn attention to the phenomenon of 'incremental but consequential change' and, for metaphorical illustration of the mechanism behind such change, propose a 'stalactite model of change'. See their contribution to *Beyond Continuity*.
5. For an excellent overview see Voss 2001.
6. We deliberately say 'mainly' as we do not generally preclude that informal sanctions may also be of importance. Typically, however, as Colin Crouch reminds us, these are today studied by lawyers as 'soft law', indicating that in modern societies even informal rules, like those governing certain production networks, may sometimes become legally enforceable.
7. We might also say: with a private contract. But this may be misleading since, as Durkheim has pointed out, 'in a contract not everything is contractual' (Durkheim 1984 [1893]: 158), meaning that *the contract as such* is a social institution precisely because individual contracts can be and are enforced by agencies of social control that are not parties to them.
8. A few rational-choice scholars have criticized the voluntaristic conception of institutions characteristic of their school (see, for example, Knight 1992; Moe 2003). But even in revisionist versions the treatment of power is sometimes thin, coming in mainly by virtue of the fact that some actors need an institution more than others, or that the opportunity costs of revising existing institutions are different for different actors. More on this below.

9. As a result their stability increases. 'Self-interest is, in fact, the least constant thing in the world. Today it is useful for me to unite with you; tomorrow the same reason will make me your enemy. Thus such a cause can give rise only to transitory links and associations of a fleeting kind' (Durkheim 1984 [1893]: 152).

10. By noting that institutions are always interpreted, and thus can be interpreted differently, we also reintroduce room for agency and political conflict that is eliminated when institutions are conceived either in purely functional terms or as shared cognitive frames (taken-for-granted understandings).

11. A *policy* may give rise to a *Herrschaftsverband* to the extent that it creates a distinction between policy-makers and policy-takers. Socially backed *corporate actors* may be *Herrschaftsverbände* themselves, or may be included in them at their center.

12. Constraint, of course, remains constraint. In fact as we have pointed out above in criticizing rational voluntaristic concepts of institutions, enforceable obligation is for us among the most important defining characteristics of social institutions. Our point is simply that obligations may be ambiguous and are in any event generally subject to interpretation and contestation.

13. See also Kuran (1991) for an analogous model of change, which however draws attention to changes in the revealed preferences of growing numbers of actors and relies more heavily on a tipping point logic. Another example, based more on what one could call a 'cascading logic', is Beissinger's analysis of the development and success of nationalist movements across the states of the former Soviet Union in the late 1980s and very early 1990s (Beissinger 2002). In this case, the impact of events and processes in a densely, temporally and spatially, connected context produced what Beissinger calls a 'tidal' dynamic, such that nationalism in countries lacking the structural prerequisites of success ('improbable nationalisms', as Beissinger calls them) nonetheless succeeded as a result of linkages to other unfolding nationalisms and the ability of politicians to 'ride nationalism's tidal force'.

14. Although it appears that the closeness of inter-institutional coupling, and the degree to which a society insists on congruence between its institutions, is a variable; see the image Vogel (2004) projects of the Japanese political economy.

15. See also the chapter by Trampusch (2004), which analyzes the migration of a particular policy from one institutional context to another – as it were, to a reserve system ready to take over as the primary system became overloaded.

16. It is perhaps important to underscore the subtle but important difference between displacement and layering. A central feature in both Deeg's account of displacement and Palier's and Hacker's examples of layering is differential growth of parallel systems – an expanding fringe that potentially crowds out a shrinking core. The difference is that in Deeg's case proponents of change are cultivating a wholly new set of institutions on the fringes of an existing system, thus setting up a competition between two alternative logics. In Hacker's and Palier's cases, by contrast, innovators are attaching new elements to existing institutions, effecting change gradually within the traditional arrangements themselves.

17. Building new institutions from scratch may take longer than the rise of new goals or purposes, so it often makes sense to try to accomplish new goals with old institutions. This is nicely illustrated by Levy (2005) who explains the conversion of French statism from industrial to social policy in part by the fact that institutions other than the state that could have carried the new social policies simply were not available – not least as a result of statism itself which by default, as it were, had to be converted instead of dismantled.

18. Where most rational-choice theories see change as emanating from a shift in an institution's parameters, Grief and Laitin pay attention to what they call 'quasi-parameters', which 'are assumed in the rules of the game but in reality are part of the broader context within which an institution is embedded' (Greif and Laitin 2003: 3). In the language that they employ, the question is whether the behavioral effects that an institution generates either expand or narrow the range of situations (quasi-parameters) in which the institution is self-reinforcing.

Part II

Debating Varieties of Capitalism

4

Varieties of Capitalism and Institutional Complementarities in the Political Economy: An Empirical Analysis

*Peter Hall and Daniel W. Gingerich**

The field of comparative political economy has been interested for many years in understanding how differences in the organization of national political economies condition aggregate economic performance. Behind such inquiries lies the intuition that more than one economic model can deliver economic success. But what are the central features that distinguish the operation of one political economy from another, and how should countries be categorized along these dimensions of difference?

For the developed economies, the answers usually given to these questions in each era have corresponded to the principal challenges confronting those economies. During the 1960s, when economic modernization was high on the agenda, efforts to identify distinctive types of capitalism emphasized variation in the character of state intervention into the economy.[1] When inflation rose to new heights during the 1970s, the emphasis shifted to the contributions of neo-corporatism to wage and price moderation.[2] In recent years, scholars have been seeking approaches salient to an era of globalization.[3]

The object of this analysis is to subject one of the most prominent of these new approaches to a set of empirical tests. We focus on the 'varieties of capitalism' perspective introduced in a volume edited by Hall and Soskice and now widely referenced in the literature.[4] Applying the new economics of organization to the macroeconomy, this approach distinguishes among capitalist economies by reference to the ways firms and other actors coordinate

* We are grateful to Alexander Kuo and Stanislav Markus for efficient research assistance and to the John D. and Catherine T. MacArthur Foundation for a grant to Hall for research and writing. For helpful comments, we thank James Alt, Bruno Amable, Moreno Bertoldi, Robert Boyer, Colin Crouch, Ekkehard Ernst, Peter Gourevitch, Torben Iversen, Bruce Kogut, Jonas Pontusson, Marino Regini, David Soskice, and Wolfgang Streeck.

their endeavours. It suggests that nations cluster into identifiable groups based on the extent to which firms rely on market or strategic modes of coordination. From these formulations follow many important contentions about variations in economic performance, comparative institutional advantage, national responses to globalization, and comparative public policy.

The varieties of capitalism approach is grounded in a rich set of comparative case-studies, but efforts to assess it using statistical analysis on larger numbers of cases are still at an early stage.[5] Those efforts have been limited partly because we do not yet have good measures for the character of coordination, the concept at the heart of the analysis. As a result, the position of many countries within those categories remains ambiguous. We seek indicators for coordination that will allow us to test some basic tenets of this approach and that others can use for subsequent assessments.

We are especially interested in one of the core contentions of the varieties of capitalism approach, namely, its theory of *institutional complementarities* in the macroeconomy.

One set of institutions is said to be complementary to another when its presence raises the returns available from the other. Economists have identified such complementarities at the level of the firm, where marketing strategies based on customized products, for instance, may be complementary to computer-controlled production processes.[6] However, Hall and Soskice argue that complementarities, with positive effects on aggregate economic performance, are embedded in institutions across sub-spheres of the political economy.[7] This is an important contention. If correct, it implies that efforts to reform one sphere of the political economy may yield negative economic results if unaccompanied by parallel reforms in other spheres. It predicts a particular politics of institutional defence.

By subjecting that contention to empirical assessment, we bring together issues typically treated by quite separate literatures. One considers the impact of institutional reform in labour markets, while another considers reform in corporate governance.[8] However, there is growing evidence of interactions across some spheres of the political economy.[9] We ask whether the interaction effects postulated by the varieties of capitalism approach can be found across the spheres of labour relations and corporate governance.

We begin by developing indices to measure the character of coordination in labour relations and corporate governance. We then use these measures to assess the plausibility of the logic used by varieties of capitalism analysts to differentiate among developed political economies and the appropriateness of its categories. Turning to the theory's core postulates about the presence of institutional complementarities in the macroeconomy, we ask whether the institutional arrangements it sees as complementary actually yield higher rates of economic growth. Finally, we inquire into the durability of the categories generated by the varieties of capitalism literature, by examining patterns of institutional change over the past two decades. Before taking up its core propositions, however, we open with an overview of the varieties of capitalism perspective.[10]

1. THE VARIETIES OF CAPITALISM APPROACH

In contrast to the literature focused on national labour movements, varieties of capitalism analyses assume that firms are the central actors in the economy whose behaviour aggregates into national economic performance. In order to prosper, firms must engage with other actors in multiple spheres of the political economy: to raise finance (on financial markets), to regulate wages and working conditions (industrial relations), to ensure workers have the requisite skills (education and training), to secure access to inputs and technology (via inter-firm relations), to compete for customers (in product markets), and to secure the cooperation of their workforce (firm–employee relations). Adopting a relational view of the firm, this perspective assumes that success in each of these endeavours depends on efficient coordination with other actors. The central problems facing firms are, therefore, coordination problems.

The varieties of capitalism approach draws a distinction between two modes of coordination. In one, firms coordinate with other actors primarily through competitive markets, characterized by arms-length relations and formal contracting. Here, equilibrium outcomes are dictated primarily by relative prices, market signals, and familiar marginalist considerations. In the second, firms coordinate with other actors through processes of strategic interaction of the kind typically modeled by game theory. Here, equilibrium outcomes depend on the institutional support available for the formation of credible commitments, including support for effective information sharing, monitoring, sanctioning, and deliberation.[11]

Although instances of market and strategic coordination occur in all capitalist economies, this approach contends that, in the spheres central to firm endeavour, the balance between these two types of coordination varies across political economies. At one end of the spectrum stand *liberal market economies* (LMEs) where relations between firms and other actors are coordinated primarily by competitive markets. At the other end are *coordinated market economies* (CMEs) where firms typically engage in more strategic interaction with trade unions, suppliers of finance, and other actors.[12]

Whether a firm coordinates its endeavours through market relations or strategic interaction is said to depend on the institutional setting. Where markets are imperfect and there is substantial institutional support for the formation of credible commitments, firms can be expected to rely more extensively on strategic coordination. Where markets are fluid and there is little support for such commitments, firms will rely more heavily on market coordination. Accordingly there should be a correspondence between the institutional configuration of each sphere of the economy and the character of coordination there.[13]

The distinction will be clearer if we describe a liberal and coordinated market economy. Market coordination is a familiar concept in neoclassical economics, and the United States is a typical liberal market economy. Here, firms face large equity markets marked by high levels of transparency and dispersed shareholding, where firms' access to external finance depends heavily on publicly assessable criteria such as market valuation. Regulatory regimes allow hostile takeovers that depend on share price, rendering managers sensitive to current profitability. Because trade unions are relatively weak and employment protection low, labour markets are fluid and wage-setting primarily a matter of contract between workers and individual employers. Because labour markets are fluid, workers have incentives to invest in general skills that can be taken to other jobs, and, because industry associations are weak, firms lack the capacity to mount the collaborative training programmes that confer industry-specific skills. Technology transfer is accomplished primarily by licensing or taking on expert personnel, and standards are usually set by market races. Top managers enjoy substantial authority over all aspects of firm strategy, including lay-offs. In such settings, many of the relationships firms form with other actors are mediated by competitive markets. Although there are variations among them, the United Kingdom, Ireland, Canada, Australia, and New Zealand are also generally identified as liberal market economies.

Germany provides a good example of a coordinated market economy. Its firms are closely connected by dense networks of cross-shareholding and influential employers associations. These networks provide for exchanges of private information, allowing firms to develop reputations that permit some access to capital on terms that depend more heavily on reputation than share value. Accordingly, managers are less sensitive to current profitability. In the presence of strong trade unions, powerful works councils, and high levels of employment protection, labour markets are less fluid and job tenures longer. In most industries, wage-setting is coordinated by trade unions and employers associations that also supervise collaborative training schemes, providing workers with industry-specific skills and assurances of positions if they invest in them. Industry associations play a major role in standard setting, and substantial amounts of technology transfer take place through inter-firm collaboration. Hemmed in by powerful workforce representatives and business networks, top managers have less scope for unilateral action, and firms typically adhere to more consensual styles of decision-making. It should be apparent that, in order to perform their core functions, firms in coordinated market economies like that of Germany must engage in strategic interaction in multiple spheres, although the institutions on which they rely and the quality of the outcomes may vary from one country to another. Austria, Japan, South Korea, Sweden, Norway, Finland, Denmark, Belgium, the Netherlands, and Switzerland are usually identified as coordinated market economies.

2. ESTABLISHING COORDINATION AS A CRUCIAL DIMENSION

We begin our analysis by examining the core contention of the varieties of capitalism approach: that the developed economies differ from one another according to the extent to which firms depend on market or strategic coordination to accomplish their endeavours. Of course, the character of coordination is difficult to measure directly. However, as Hall and Soskice point out, the nature of coordination depends on the type of institutions available to support it. Accordingly, a factor analysis designed to identify commonalities that may be unobservable in themselves but that correlate with a range of observable variables provides an appropriate technique for identifying the character of coordination.[14] By performing a factor analysis on a set of institutional measures that are commonly associated with one type of coordination or another, we can assess whether the dimensions of market and strategic coordination posited by varieties of capitalism theory exist and where they are present. Varieties of capitalism theory generates three hypotheses that can be tested using such an analysis:

H1: *The character of coordination constitutes a key dimension stretching across spheres of the political economy.*

If this is correct, a confirmatory factor analysis in which the latent variables are defined as the degree of coordination in each sphere of the political economy should do a good job in accounting for the observed covariance between a set of indicators representing the institutional conditions associated with different types of coordination in those spheres.

H2: *The underlying latent variables corresponding to each sphere of the economy should reflect variation along a spectrum running from market coordination to strategic coordination.*

If this is correct, the factor loadings produced by the confirmatory factor analysis should be consistent. This means that if an observable indicator of institutional support for strategic coordination loads positively (negatively) onto a given latent variable, other indicators of support for strategic coordination should also have positive (negative) factor loadings for this latent variable; whereas indicators of support for market coordination should have negative (positive) factor loadings.

H3: *It is possible to identify a distinctive set of liberal market economies that make extensive use of market coordination and another set of coordinated market economies that make extensive use of strategic coordination.*

If this is correct, when the factor loadings are used to construct scores for each nation, the nations identified by the case study literature as liberal market economies should be located toward the 'market' end of the dimension for each sphere, and those identified as coordinated market economies should be located closer to the 'strategic' end for each sphere.

The central obstacle to such an analysis is the paucity of relevant indicators available for more than a few countries. The measurement of coordination poses special difficulties. In principle, types of coordination are observable, but intense observation is required. In only one sphere has coordination been assessed in this way, namely that of wage-bargaining. Accordingly, we employ two independent assessments of coordination in wage-bargaining. The other variables used in the factor analysis are all indicators of institutional features of the political economy that can reasonably be said to reflect or provide support for one type of coordination or the other. We have identified variables that extend across two important spheres of the political economy, those pertinent to labour relations and corporate governance. The observations were drawn from the 1990–95 period, the latest for which comparable data is available.

The variables employed in the factor analysis are as follows:[15]

Shareholder Power reflects the legal protection and likely influence over firms of ordinary shareholders relative to managers or dominant shareholders. It is a composite measure of legal regulations covering six issues: the availability of proxy voting, deposit requirements for shares, the election of directors, the legal recourse available to minority shareholders, shareholders' rights to issues of new stock, and the calling of shareholder meetings. Regulations governing each issue are coded 0 or 1 and summed. Higher scores indicate that ordinary shareholders enjoy more rights vis-à-vis managers and dominant shareholders.[16]

Dispersion of Control indicates how many firms in the economy are widely held relative to the number with controlling shareholders. Taking the smallest ten firms with market capitalization of common equity of at least $500 million at the end of 1995 as a sample of firms, it reports the percentage that do not have a controlling shareholder, defined as one who controls, directly or indirectly, more than 10 per cent of the voting rights in the firm. Higher values indicate that larger proportions of firms in the economy are widely held.[17]

Size of Stock Market: the market valuation of equities on the stock exchanges of a nation as a percentage of its gross domestic product in 1993.[18]

Level of Wage Coordination: the level at which unions normally coordinate wage-claims and employers coordinate wage-offers where 3 represents the national level, 2 the intermediate level, and 1 firm level. Levels of coordination for unions and employers are assessed separately and averaged. Higher values indicate higher levels of coordination in wage setting.[19]

Degree of Wage Coordination reflects estimates by the OECD Secretariat of the degree to which wage-bargaining is (strategically) coordinated by unions and employers along a scale on which 3 indicates coordinated and 1 indicates uncoordinated. Observations are for 1994. Higher values indicate higher levels of wage coordination.[20]

Labour Turnover is an indicator of the fluidity of national labour markets and reports the number of employees who had held their jobs for less than one year as a percentage of all employees surveyed in 1995.[21]

The appropriateness of these variables for the analysis should be apparent from our description of liberal and coordinated market economies. The first three variables reflect institutional variation in the sphere of corporate governance of the sort highlighted by the varieties of capitalism approach. Where the balance of influence tilts toward dominant shareholders, ownership relatively concentrated, and equity markets small, securing access to external finance and negotiating corporate control is more likely to involve firms in strategic interaction within corporate networks. When these conditions are reversed, issues of finance and corporate control are determined by more competitive markets. The next three variables reflect relevant variation in the sphere of labour relations. Two assess the level and degree of strategic coordination in wage-bargaining. Labour turnover reflects the frequency with which workers move from one firm, a measure of the fluidity of labour markets.

Since the number of indicators available for such an analysis is limited and the likelihood of some measurement error high, we entered the analysis with low expectations. Given these constraints, the results are highly supportive of the terms the varieties of capitalism literature uses to characterize political economies. We performed the confirmatory factor analysis whose structure is presented in Figure 4.1.[22] Table 4.1 reports the estimates of the linear relationship between the latent and observable variables (factor loadings) as well as a set of indicators of the 'goodness of fit' of the overall model. All of the factor loadings were significant by conventional standards and signed in the

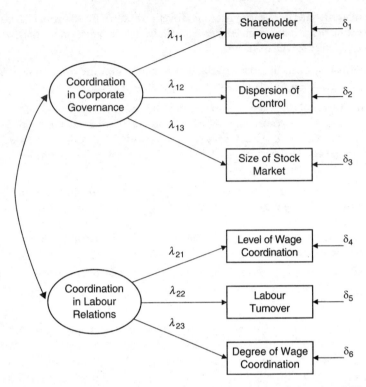

Figure 4.1. Path diagram of the two-factor model for the six observed variables

appropriate manner. The fit indicators suggest the model does a good job of explaining the covariance among the observed variables. As expected, the estimated correlation between the levels of coordination found in each sphere of the economy was high (−.81).[23] These results suggest that the first two hypotheses examined here should be accepted rather than rejected.

How well do these results conform to the cross-national patterns postulated by the varieties of capitalism literature? Using the factor loadings, we construct scores for each nation for each factor, normalized to lie between 0 and 1. These scores are reported in Table 4.2, and Figure 4.2 arrays each of the OECD nations for which we have scores in a two dimensional space where movement away from the origin along the X-axis reflects higher levels of strategic (vs market) coordination in corporate governance and movement up the Y-axis reflects higher levels of strategic coordination in labour relations. If the varieties of capitalism approach to understanding the institutional differences among developed political economies is correct, we should expect

Table 4.1. Parameter estimates of coordination in corporate governance and labour relations CFA (N=*20*)

Parameter	ML Estimate (standard errors in parentheses)
λ_{11}	.96
	(.31)
λ_{12}	.24
	(.05)
λ_{13}	21.58
	(6.46)
λ_{21}	.53
	(.15)
λ_{22}	−3.63
	(1.46)
λ_{23}	.63
	(.12)

$\chi^2 = 4.71$ (p-value = .79)
Normed Fit Index (NFI) = .95
Goodness of Fit Index (GFI) = .92
Adjusted Goodness of Fit Index (AGFI) = .80

	Correlation Matrix of Factors	
	Corp	Labour
Corp	1.00	
Labour	−.81	1.00
	(.12)	

to see a clustering pattern: liberal and coordinated market economies should be found primarily in the southwest and northeast quadrants, respectively.

The results are broadly supportive of the hypothesis. As the regression line indicates, there is a strong and statistically significant relationship in the predicted direction between coordination in labour relations and corporate governance. Nations cluster toward the southwest and northeast quadrants of the diagram, as the theory would lead us to expect. Six nations, all normally identified by varieties of capitalism theory as liberal market economies, cluster to the southwest, on or below the regression line. The economies of northern Europe generally identified as CMEs cluster toward the northeast in this two-dimensional space.

Japan and Switzerland are the two most obvious outliers. We view their position as the result of measurement error associated with the limitations of our measure for coordination in corporate governance. The latter attaches considerable weight to the size of the stock market and both nations have

Table 4.2. Coordination in labour relations and corporate governance

	Labour Relations	Corporate Governance
Australia	.29	.47
Austria	1	1
Belgium	.50	.77
Canada	.09	.23
Denmark	.58	.65
Finland	.66	.71
France	.60	.82
Germany	.92	.95
Ireland	.28	.35
Italy	.77	.99
Japan	.94	.72
Netherlands	.53	.74
New Zealand	.09	.27
Norway	.81	.74
Portugal	.62	.85
Spain	.54	.77
Sweden	.59	.71
Switzerland	.48	.44
United Kingdom	.04	.14
United States	0	0

Note: Factor scores were constructed using Thomson's regression method with correlated factors and then normalized to be between 0 and 1.[65]

large stock markets relative to their GDP. But there is also extensive cross-shareholding in these nations not picked-up by our measure of shareholder dispersion because many of the relevant holdings fall below our 10 per cent cut-off.[24] Nevertheless, these cross-shareholdings limit hostile takeovers and serve as vehicles for network monitoring. In short, we think an accurate assignment of these cases would put them into the northeast quadrant of the diagram. The coordination of labour relations in the Netherlands and Belgium may also be underestimated here, reflecting OECD figures that may underestimate coordination in labour relations. Given the potential for such measurement error in indices taken entirely from external sources, however, the correspondence between the location of economies in Figure 4.2 and the account of such economies given by the varieties of capitalism literature is striking.

The proximity of various nations to one another in this institutional space also facilitates more fine-grained assessment of variations among the OECD economies. Correcting for measurement error, there are four distinct clusters of nations. Among the liberal market economies, the United States and the United Kingdom appear as relatively 'pure' cases, while four other liberal

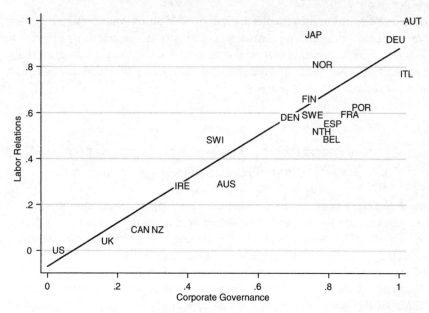

Figure 4.2. The balance between market and strategic coordination in labour relations and corporate governance in OECD countries

Note: On each axis, movement away from the origin indicates higher levels of strategic coordination in the relevant sphere of the political economy and movement toward the origin indicates higher levels of market coordination.

market economies stand slightly apart by virtue of systems of corporate governance in which market coordination is not as fully developed. On the other side of Figure 4.2, the nations most often identified as coordinated market economies lie near or above the regression line, indicating high levels of strategic coordination in both their labour and financial markets.

Six nations lie to the east in the Figure but clearly below the regression line (Sweden lies just slightly below). This is especially interesting because there has been some controversy about whether four of these nations (Spain, Portugal, France, and Italy) are coordinated market economies or examples of another distinctive type of capitalism often associated with high levels of state intervention.[25] Figure 4.2 clarifies some of the issues that render these ambiguous cases. These nations all have institutional capacities for strategic coordination in labour relations and corporate governance that are higher than those of LMEs. However, their capacities for strategic coordination in labour relations tend to be lower than those in northern Europe, probably because their union movements are still divided along what used to be called 'confessional' lines. Although strategic coordination is clearly more important in these nations than in liberal market economies, these findings suggest there may be systematic differences in the operation of southern, as compared to northern, European economies.[26]

3. CONGRUENCE ACROSS SPHERES OF THE POLITICAL ECONOMY

Although we have focused on corporate governance and labour relations because they are the two most important spheres of the economy, regulating the supply of labour and capital, the varieties of capitalism approach also expects systematic variation, between LMEs and CMEs, across other spheres of the political economy, including those concerned with product-market competition, social protection, vocational training, and inter-firm relations. Much of the force of the varieties of capitalism approach as a theory of comparative capitalism rests on its claim to be able to specify systematic variations across nations that extend to many spheres of the political economy. We turn now to assessment of that claim.

In some cases, the relevant variation is in institutionalized practices; in others, it is in the formal institutions or regulatory regimes that govern endeavours in each sphere. In the varieties of capitalism literature, the theoretical basis for expectations of institutional congruence lies in the contention that, where institutional complementarities are available across spheres, firms and governments will often (although not always) adapt their strategies to take advantage of these complementarities.[27] The relationships on which we focus are as follows.

Varieties of capitalism analysts argue that, where *labour relations* are based on high levels of job mobility and firm-level wage-setting, *training systems* that provide general skills through formal education will be more efficient than collaborative training schemes that confer industry-specific skills, because workers who must frequently shift jobs have strong incentives to acquire the general skills that qualify them for other positions. Conversely, where labour relations are based on strong unions and coordinated wage-bargaining, it will be efficient for firms to operate collaborative training schemes conferring high levels of industry-specific skills. High wages set at the industry level encourage workers to acquire industry-specific skills, and they make it more difficult for non-training firms to poach workers by offering wage premiums.

The organizations that coordinate wages can also be used to coordinate training systems.[28]

A similar set of arguments specifies the potential for institutional comple-mentarities between the character of *corporate governance* and the character of *inter-firm relations*. Firms are said to find it easier to enter into collaborative arrangements with other firms – for the purposes of research, product development, or technology transfer – where the institutions of corporate governance limit the demands on them to maximize current profitability or shareholder value, because they can then make more credible commitments to the incomplete contracts and co-specific investments that such collabor-ation requires. Conversely, where fluid capital markets facilitate the move-ment of funds from one endeavour to another, it will be more efficient for firms to access technology by acquiring other enterprises or new personnel rather than engage in long-term collaboration with other firms.[29]

Estevez et al. argue that *social policies* providing generous employment and unemployment protection will be complementary to *production strategies* based on the use of specific skills because they provide workers with incentives for acquiring those skills.[30] Hall and Soskice argue that high levels of *product-market regulation* may be complementary to *financial systems* based on network monitoring, to wage coordination, and to inter-firm collaboration in research and development because they limit the intensity of competition in product markets that might otherwise undermine cooperation in these other spheres.[31]

The varieties of capitalism perspective also identifies potential complemen-tarities between institutional arrangements in the broader political economy and the *strategy or structure of firms themselves*. This is the basis for an important set of claims that corporate structures and strategies are likely to vary systematically across nations. The theory suggests that, where fluid labour markets facilitate lay-offs and dispersed financial markets often demand them, it will be advantageous for firms to adopt hierarchies that vest management with extensive prerogatives over such matters. Conversely, where strong trade unions or regulatory regimes inhibit lay-offs, corporate structures that provide stakeholders with more influence over enterprise decision-making may offer efficiencies by strengthening the credibility of the commitments a firm can make to its employees and thus the levels of cooperation it can secure from them. On such reasoning, the approach contends that firm strategy will vary systematically across political economies in tandem with the institutional support provided there for different types of coordination. Firms are said to exploit this institutional support to derive competitive advantages that cumu-late into comparative institutional advantages at the national level.[32]

In short, the varieties of capitalism literature contends that systematic variation across nations is present not only in labour relations and corporate governance, but also across many other spheres of the political economy, extending to relevant regulatory regimes and firm practices. To assess this contention, we have sought indicators for the types of variation in institutions or practices that varieties of capitalism theory expects to find in a wide range of spheres of the political economy. Finding indicators for the relevant institutional dimensions is a major challenge if more than a handful of cases are to be considered and we are not to code them ourselves – a technique we have resisted in order to avoid biasing the tests. However, we have found indicators for the relevant types of institutional variation across seven spheres where the varieties of capitalism approach suggests major complementarities are available and some institutional congruence should be found.[33] For labour relations and corporate governance, we use the same indicators employed in the preceding analysis. The others are as follows:

Social Protection refers to the level of support provided to the unemployed and to limitations on the right of firms to lay-off workers. We measure it by combining the indices of 'unemployment protection' and 'employment protection' devised by Estevez et al. using the factor scores produced when an exploratory factor analysis is applied to the two indices. Higher values indicate higher levels of social protection.[34]

Product Market Regulation refers to the limits placed on competition in product markets by the regulatory restrictions that national governments impose on businesses. The measure is based on an OECD survey of many types of regulatory practices combined into a composite measure through multi-level factor analysis by Nicoletti et al.[35] Higher values indicate product market regulations more restrictive of competition.

Training Systems are assessed with a view to establishing the extent of institutional support a nation provides for the development of vocational skills in young workers beyond what they secure in formal secondary or university education. In general, this entails apprenticeship schemes or training programmes dependent on the collaborative involvement of firms. The measure is based on the factor scores produced by an exploratory factor analysis on two variables: the number of pupils at the upper secondary level in vocational or technical training programmes as a proportion of all students enrolled in educational programs and the mean scores on a literacy test secured by a sample of workers between the ages of 20 and 25 who left school before completing secondary education.[36] Higher values indicate higher levels of institutional support for this kind of vocational training.

Inter-Firm Relations refer to the institutionalized practices that link firms to other firms producing goods and services. Of particular relevance is the extent to which firms collaborate with others to secure access to new technology or markets relative to their reliance on competitive market relations for such purposes. Mergers and acquisitions are typical of the latter. Accordingly, the measure is based on the annual number of mergers and acquisitions in a nation during 1990–97 expressed as a ratio of its population.[37] We reverse the direction of the measure so that higher values indicate more inter-firm collaboration.

To assess the ancillary claim that systematic variation in the institutions of the political economy will be associated with distinctive types of firm structures and strategies, we have also sought measures for the latter, as follows:

Managerial Prerogative refers to the extent to which firms concentrate control over their operations in the hands of top management. On the premise that compensation will correspond to the level of responsibility they are assigned for the firm's operations, our measure is the average compensation of chief executive officers as a ratio of the compensation of average production workers in manufacturing in 1999.[38] Higher values indicate higher levels of managerial prerogative.

Employment Tenure is a measure of the length of time employees typically stay with the same firm, assessed here by median employer tenure in 1995.[39] This can be read as a reflection of the extent to which firm strategies turn on the development of close relations with a stable workforce rather than on production regimes that can be operated by more transient and potentially less-skilled labour.

Firm Strategy is a composite measure tapping many of the core practices of firms, including the use they make of multidivisional project teams, participatory work teams, alliances with other firms, close, voice-based relations with suppliers, long-term relations with investors, and cooperative labour–management relations built on employment guarantees. Each practice has been coded on a 3 point scale and combined via factor analysis by Hicks and Kenworthy.[40] Higher values indicate firm strategies that make more extensive use of these 'cooperative' practices.

Using these variables, we test the following hypothesis:

H4: *Institutionalized practices extending across the spheres of the political economy identified here, including those associated with firm strategies, vary systematically such that the practices associated with market coordination are present in multiple spheres of political economies classified as LMEs and practices associated with strategic coordination are present in multiple spheres of political economies classified as CMEs.*

If this is correct, there should be significant correlations across spheres at the national level among the variables representing the institutional practices the varieties of capitalism perspective identifies as important to coordination.

Figure 4.3 summarizes the results of this test. The boxes around 'firm strategy' represent the four spheres in which a firm coordinates with other actors to accomplish its principal endeavours. The two boxes at the top indicate policy regimes relevant to this coordination. The lines between the boxes correspond

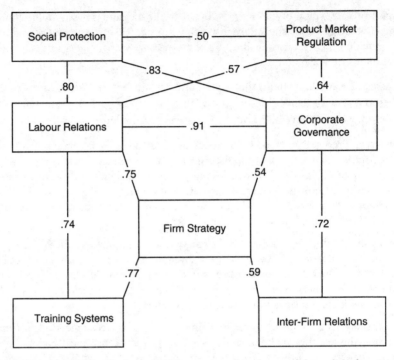

Figure 4.3. Potential complementarities across sub-spheres of the political economy

to hypotheses about complementarities generated by the varieties of capitalism literature. Using cross-national comparisons of all the cases for which we have relevant measures, we have calculated correlation coefficients indicating whether the presence of institutional practices of a particular type in one sphere are associated with institutional practices in adjacent spheres that correspond to those posited by a varieties of capitalism perspective. That perspective predicts positive coefficients across the diagram. The results are impressive. The coefficients in Figure 4.3 are uniformly positive and relatively large. All are statistically significant at the .05 level. The uniformity of the results is striking. They tend to confirm the varieties of capitalism contention that differences based on market-oriented or strategic coordination stretch systematically across multiple spheres of the political economy. The results on firm strategy indicated in Figure 4.3 are also notable: they confirm that corporate strategies tend to vary systematically with the institutional support available for different types of coordination in the political economy. Table 4.3 provides further evidence by comparing the relationship between two indicators for corporate strategy and national scores on the coordination indices.

Table 4.3. The relationship between institutional support for strategic coordination and corporate strategy

	Correlation with Coordination in Labour Relations	Correlation with Coordination in Corporate Governance
Employment Tenure	.686	.660
	(.002)	(.003)
Managerial Prerogative	−.764	−.664
	(.002)	(.013)

Note: Significance levels in parentheses.

In each case, there is a strong and statistically significant correlation in the direction posited by the theory.

4. THE EFFECT OF INSTITUTIONAL COMPLEMENTARITIES ON ECONOMIC GROWTH

These results indicate that the patterns of institutionalized practices the varieties of capitalism perspective expects to see across the developed economies are often present there. We turn now to one of the most important propositions linked to this observation, namely to the claim that there is, not only congruence among institutional practices in different spheres of the economy, but that some of these practices can be complementary to others. Institutional practices are said to be complementary when each raises the returns available from the other. We focus on one of the most fundamental sets of complementarities, namely those between institutional practices in the sphere of corporate governance and in labour relations.

Working from the formulations of Aoki, Hall and Soskice develop a theoretical rationale for why such complementarities might exist.[41] They argue that institutions in the sphere of corporate governance that encourage cross-shareholding and concentrate control in the hands of management, thereby limiting hostile takeovers and providing firms with access to sources of finance that turn on reputational monitoring, enhance the efficiency of institutional practices in the sphere of labour relations that provide high levels of employment security and long job-tenures as well as forms of wage-setting that depend on strategic interaction among employers associations and trade unions.[42] In the face of a fluctuating economy, firms that do not have to sustain current profitability are better placed to make long-term commitments to their employees about wages and jobs, and therefore to realize the gains available from deploying production regimes based on such commitments. This combination of institutions corresponds to the institutional patterns in CMEs.

Conversely, where firms are more dependent on dispersed equity markets, face the prospect of hostile takeovers, and confront regulations that give shareholders more power relative to stakeholders, the autonomy of the firm and its managers will be more dependent on current profitability. Here, labour markets allowing for high levels of labour turnover and competitive wage-setting will be more efficient, because they enable managers to reduce staffing levels quickly or to hold down wages in response to fluctuations in current profitability. This combination of institutional practices corresponds to the case of a LME. In summary terms, the efficiencies available to firms should be higher in settings where the spheres of labour relations and corporate governance are *both* dominated by the practices characteristic of either strategic or market coordination and, according to the varieties of capitalism analysis, these efficiencies should show up in improved aggregate economic performance.[43]

Our indicator for aggregate economic performance will be rates of economic growth per capita, widely accepted as the best measure of such performance and appropriate for testing postulates about the general efficiency of the economy. Moreover, this measure provides an exceptionally hard test for institutional analyses such as these. Because aggregate rates of growth depend on the efficiency of the entire economy, specific sets of institutions will have to make substantial contributions to efficiency to show up in aggregate rates of growth. To summarize the character of coordination in labour relations and corporate governance, we use the two indices developed here. Although time-variant measures would be preferable, the difficulties of measuring coordination and data limitations preclude them. However, we think the use of these two indices is appropriate because they capture differences across political economies widely seen as stable over time. As a check on this, we examined Kenworthy's measures for coordination in wage-setting, which do vary over time.[44] On his measure, only three of our eighteen countries evince much fluctuation on his measure over the 1971–97 period, and we assess the specific import of those cases for our results below. Our own examination of institutional change in the 1980s and 1990s also finds considerable stability in the cross-national differences relevant to coordination. Therefore, this approach to the measurement of coordination should be adequate for the purposes at hand.

We estimate the interaction effects between these two measures of coordination and their impact, with a range of appropriate controls standard in the growth literature, on annual rates of per capita economic growth for twenty

OECD nations from 1971 to 1997, taking two different econometric approaches to the panel data.[45] The two estimators we employed were pooled ordinary least squares regression with panel-corrected standard errors and the generalized least squares random effects estimator.[46] The former is traditionally employed for times-series cross-section data, that is, data sets in which the number of observations over time is large relative to the number of panels. The technique produces correct standard errors in the presence of an error term that is heteroskedastic and contemporaneously correlated across countries. The latter is traditionally employed for panel data, that is, data sets in which the number of panels is large relative to the observations over time. This technique produces consistent coefficient estimates and standard errors in the presence of a composite error term that consists of a (mean zero) time-invariant, country-specific disturbance (representing unmeasured features of a polity that remain fixed over time) and a traditional country-year disturbance. Since the number of panels and time periods in our dataset were roughly equivalent ($N = 20$, $T = 27$), we present the results for both estimators.[47]

For each econometric technique, we estimate two separate regression equations, one containing the coordination indices and their interaction effect along with a standard set of economic controls, and another containing the coordination indices and their interaction effect, the economic controls and a set of political institutional variables. The two equations estimated were the following:

$$Y_{it} = \beta_0 + \beta_1 C_i^{LR} + \beta_2 C_i^{CG} + \beta_3 C_i^{LR} \cdot C_i^{CG} + \beta_4 \ln GDP_i + \beta_5 Int_{it}$$
$$+ \beta_6 \pi_{it} + \beta_7 Exp_{it} + \beta_8 D_{it} + \varepsilon_{it}$$

$$Y_{it} = \beta_0 + \beta_1 C_i^{LR} + \beta_2 C_i^{CG} + \beta_3 C_i^{LR} \cdot C_i^{CG} + \beta_4 \ln GDP_i + \beta_5 Int_{it}$$
$$+ \beta_6 \pi_{it} + \beta_7 Exp_{it} + \beta_8 D_{it} \beta_9 PLU_{it} + \beta_{10} MAG_{it} + Leftcab_{it} + \varepsilon_{it}$$

where C_i^{LR} represents the character of coordination in labour relations in country i and C_i^{CG} represents the character of coordination in its sphere of corporate governance. Estimation of these models was used to test the following hypothesis derived from the varieties of capitalism perspective on institutional complementarities:

H5: *When there are higher levels of market (strategic) coordination in the sphere of labour relations or corporate governance, rates of economic growth increase as the level of market (strategic) coordination in the other sphere increases.*

If this is correct, the interaction term in the model, $C^{LR}i^* C^{CG}i$, should be statistically significant and positive. A significant coefficient indicates that the impact of coordination in one sphere is dependent on the character of coordination in the other sphere, and a positive coefficient indicates that analogous types of coordination in the two spheres raise rates of growth.

The controls employed here are standard for estimating rates of economic growth: $lnGDP_i$ is the log of gross domestic product per capita for country i at the beginning of the period controlling for 'catch up' effects that generate higher rates of growth in nations at lower levels of economic development. Int_{it} represents international demand conditions measured by the average rate of growth for all countries in our sample in period t except country i, weighted by the trade openness of country i. π_{it} is the country's rate of inflation measured by the rate of increase in its consumer price index. In the developed world, where rates of inflation are moderate, we expect them to be positively related to rates of growth. Exp_{it} is the percentage change in the income terms of trade for country i weighted by trade openness: adverse movements should lower rates of economic growth. D_{it} is the dependency ratio measured as the share of the population below the age of 15 or above the age of 65. A higher proportion of dependents is expected to lower rates of economic growth.

In recent years, political economists have evinced growing concern for the influence of electoral institutions on political rents, productivity, and economic growth.[48] Accordingly, in our second regression equation, we include two variables to capture the potential influence of the electoral-institutional environment: PLU_{it} is an indicator variable equal to 1 if a majority of representatives in lower house are elected by plurality voting and 0 otherwise; and MAG_{it} is the average district magnitude in the lower chamber. Based on the literature about political rents, we expect PLU_{it} to be associated with higher economic growth and, since low district magnitude is a proxy for barriers to entry in the political system, higher levels of MAG_{it} may be associated with greater economic growth. In addition, we include a variable designed to capture the influence of partisan preferences: $Leftcab_{it}$ reflects Left party cabinet portfolios as proportion of total cabinet portfolios. Detailed variable descriptions are provided in the appendix.

Table 4.4 reports the results of the estimations. The parameter estimates are broadly stable across the four models. In all, the coefficient on the interaction term is positive, of considerable magnitude, and statistically-significant. These results tend to confirm the presence of substantial complementarities between the spheres of labour relations and corporate governance of the sort postulated by varieties of capitalism theory.

Using model RE●1a for the purposes of simulation, Figure 4.4 depicts the impact of coordination in corporate governance on economic growth for

Table 4.4. The impact on rates of economic growth of interaction between coordination in labour relations and corporate governance

	Pooled OLS w/ Panel Corrected Standard Errors†		Random Effects	
	PCSE•1a	PCSE•1b	RE•1a	RE•1b
ln GDP_0 (i)	−1.85***	−1.54**	−2.02***	−1.74***
	(.637)	(.728)	(.484)	(.472)
International Demand	2.27***	2.35***	2.12***	2.17***
Conditions (it)	(.220)	(.178)	(.232)	(.235)
π (it)	−1.35	−1.06	−.119	−.558
	(2.41)	(1.95)	(2.21)	(2.23)
Dependency Ratio (it)	9.66	9.06	8.11	3.22
	(13.6)	(12.7)	(11.4)	(11.4)
Exports as capacity to	−.006	−.004	.019	.001
import (it)	(.051)	(.045)	(.060)	(.061)
Plurality voting (it)	–	.866**	–	.793***
		(.345)		(.296)
District magnitude (it)	–	.005	–	.004
		(.006)		(.004)
Left cabinet (it)	–	.582**	–	.654**
		(.302)		(.291)
Coordination in	−3.09**	−3.18***	−2.38**	−2.43**
Corporate Governance (i)	(1.26)	(1.19)	(1.13)	(1.08)
Coordination in Labour	−.747	.340	−1.78**	−.183
Relations (i)	(1.52)	(1.10)	(1.51)	(1.40)
Corporate*Labour (i)	3.18**	2.73**	4.00**	2.87*
	(1.29)	(1.19)	(1.63)	(1.50)
N	538	528	538	528
R^2	.27	.28	.21	.24
χ^2	176	308	141	160

Note: Standard errors in parentheses; (i) denotes panel-varying but time-invariant explanatory variable; (it) denotes panel-varying and time-varying explanatory variable; †model assumes panel-specific first-order autocorrelation; *** denotes significant at the .01 level; ** denotes significant at the .05 level; * denotes significant at the .1 level.

different levels of coordination in labour relations (holding control variables fixed at their mean values). Two trajectories are shown. In the first case, coordination in labour relations is held constant at its minimum value (0) and coordination in corporate governance is allowed to vary from minimum (0) to maximum (1). In this instance, the predicted growth rate declines from 2.99 per cent to .61 per cent. In the second case, coordination in labour relations is held constant at its maximum value (1) and coordination in corporate governance is allowed to vary from minimum to maximum. In this instance, the predicted growth rate increases from 1.21 per cent to 2.83 per cent.

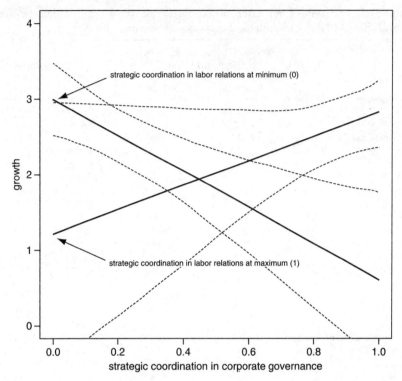

Figure 4.4. The effect on rates of economic growth of the interaction between types of coordination in labour relations and corporate governance

Note: Movement from the origin along the X-axis indicates that coordination in corporate governance becomes more strategic. Predicted values denoted by solid dark lines, 90% confidence intervals denoted by dashed lines; simulation based on model RE●1a.

The simulations show clear evidence of interaction effects between the character of coordination in the two spheres. Rates of growth are highest where competitive markets coordinate both spheres, or where strategic coordination is high in both. Where labour relations are strategically coordinated, substantial efficiencies seem to be available from strategic coordination in the sphere of corporate governance. Where corporate governance is dominated by fluid equity markets, however, rates of growth are substantially higher when labour markets are also fluid and competitive.

Although it is beyond the scope of this paper to test for the presence of specific complementarities across other spheres of the political economy, we conduct one other assessment of these contentions at the aggregate level. The varieties of capitalism approach implies that aggregate economic performance should be better in nations whose institutionalized practices correspond more closely to relatively pure types of LMEs or CMEs. Long-term rates of growth should be higher in countries where market or strategic coordination is more fully developed across multiple spheres of the political economy, compared to those where the type of coordination varies across spheres or where either type of coordination is secured but in less complete form. This implication yields the following hypothesis:

H6: *Rates of economic growth should be higher in nations where levels of market coordination or levels of strategic coordination are high across spheres of the political economy but lower in nations where neither type of coordination is so well-developed or market and strategic coordination are combined.*

If this is correct, estimates for rates of growth when other relevant factors are controlled should show higher rates of growth in nations where levels of market or strategic coordination are consistently high across spheres and lower rates in other nations.

In order to test this hypothesis, we created a single coordination index using the separate indices of coordination in corporate governance and labour relations. The coordination index measuring the balance of market and strategic coordination in the political economy for country i is equal to:

$$C_i = (CG_i + LR_i)/\max(CG_i + LR_i)$$

where CG_i and LR_i refer to the score of country i on the coordination in corporate governance and coordination in labour relations indices, respectively. We then estimated the effect of coordination on annual rates of per capita economic growth for OECD nations from 1971 to 1997 using regression models of the following form:

$$Y_{it} = \beta_0 + \beta_1 C_i + \beta_2 C_i^2 + \beta_3 \ln GDP_i + \beta_4 Int_{it} + \beta_5 \pi_{it} + \beta_6 Exp_{it} + \beta_7 D_{it} + \varepsilon_{it}$$

$$Y_{it} = \beta_0 + \beta_1 C_i + \beta_2 C_i^2 + \beta_3 \ln GDP_i + \beta_4 Int_{it} + \beta_5 \pi_{it} + \beta_6 Exp_{it} + \beta_7 D_{it} +$$
$$\beta_8 PLU_{it} + \beta_9 MAG_{it} + \beta_{10} Leftcab_{it} + \varepsilon_{it}$$

If the relationship between growth and coordination is U-shaped, β_1 should be negative and β_2 positive. The controls are the standard ones used previously and, once again, we estimated the model using two different types of econometric specifications.

Table 4.5 reports the results of these three estimations. In all, the coefficients on coordination are significant, of the same sign, and of similar magnitude, increasing our confidence in the results. The significance and signs of the coefficients on C_i and C_i^2 indicate that the relationship between coordination and economic growth is non-linear. Using model RE●2a for the simulation, Figure 4.5 shows the estimated relationship between coordination

Table 4.5. The relationship between coordination and rates of economic growth

	Pooled OLS w/ Panel Corrected Standard Errors†		Random Effects	
	PCSE•2a	PCSE•2b	RE•2a	RE•2b
ln GDP_0 (*i*)	−1.74***	−1.46**	−2.01***	−1.76***
	(.628)	(.718)	(.471)	(.471)
International Demand	2.27***	2.33***	2.10***	2.14***
Conditions (*it*)	(.221)	(.182)	(.231)	(.234)
Π (*it*)	−1.94	−1.91	−.294	−1.23
	(2.27)	(1.89)	(2.15)	(2.16)
Dependency Ratio (*it*)	11.4	11.4	8.36	4.49
	(13.6)	(12.7)	(11.3)	(11.3)
Exports as a capacity to	−.009	.002	−.020	−.002
import (*it*)	(.052)	(.045)	(.060)	(.061)
Plurality voting (*it*)	−	.827**	−	.747**
		(.349)		(.299)
District magnitude (*it*)	−	.004	−	.003
		(.006)		(.004)
Left cabinet (*it*)	−	.502*	−	.595**
		(.297)		(.286)
Coordination index (*i*)	−4.44***	−3.44**	−4.52***	−3.23**
	(1.39)	(1.44)	(1.60)	(1.60)
Coordination index	3.90***	3.53***	4.36***	3.51**
squared (*i*)	(1.29)	(1.27)	(1.55)	(1.47)
N	538	528	538	528
R^2	.27	.27	.21	.24
X^2	173	286	141	159

Note: Standard errors in parentheses; (*i*) denotes panel-varying but time-invariant explanatory variable; (*it*) denotes panel-varying and time-varying explanatory variable; † model assumes panel-specific first-order autocorrelation; *** denotes significant at the .01 level; ** denotes significant at the .05 level; * denotes significant at the .1 level.

and growth when the control variables are held at their means. The U-shaped relationship is apparent. Where the institutional structure of the political economy allows for either higher levels of market coordination or higher levels of strategic coordination, estimated growth rates are larger than they are when there is more variation in the types of coordination present in the political economy.

These results suggest that the varieties of capitalism approach to institutional complementarities, built on the distinction between market and strategic coordination, has real merit. When complementary institutions are present across spheres of the political economy, rates of economic growth are higher. The institutional complementarities identified by this perspective appear to offer general efficiencies.

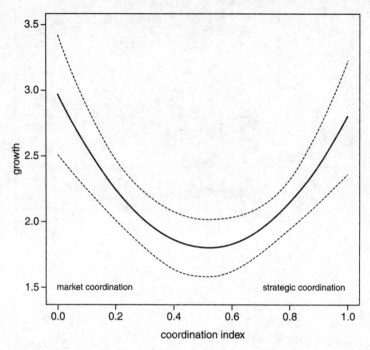

Figure 4.5. The estimated relationship between coordination and rates of economic growth

Note: Predicted values are denoted by solid dark lines, 90% confidence intervals denoted by dashed lines; simulation based on model RE●2a.

We conducted a number of robustness checks on these results, with particular attention to cases that might not be coded entirely accurately as noted above, namely Japan and Switzerland, and to cases where Kenworthy's index for coordination in wage-setting shows more than negligible movement over this time period, namely Denmark, Italy, and New Zealand, as well as the UK which showed some movement prior to 1980.[49] We asked whether the exclusion of any of these cases, singly or together, would affect our findings. Table 4.6 presents the results of these re-estimations. The table depicts the coefficient on the interaction between coordination in labour relations and coordination in corporate governance as well as the coefficients on the overall coordination index and its square for each combination of excluded cases. The table clearly suggests that our results do *not* depend on the inclusion of any one of these cases. Our findings are remarkably robust to the exclusion of particular cases, and even to the simultaneous exclusion of all potentially

Table 4.6. Robustness of regression results to the exclusion of specific cases

Excluded Cases	Coefficient on:							
	Corporate*Labour (i)				Coordination index (i), Coordination index squared (i)			
	Pooled OLS w/PCSE		Random Effects		Pooled OLS w/PCSE		Random Effects	
	Base model	Full model	Base model	Full model	Base model	Full model	Base model	Full model
Japan	3.60*** (1.38)	2.27* (1.29)	4.52*** (1.74)	2.79* (1.67)	-4.49***, 3.79*** (1.39), (1.27)	-3.77**, 3.60*** (1.58), (1.26)	-4.60***, 4.31*** (1.65), (1.60)	-3.60***, 3.66*** (1.69), (1.50)
Switzerland	2.55* (1.33)	3.13** (1.35)	3.36** (1.68)	3.00* (1.55)	-4.26***, 3.71*** (1.43), (1.41)	-3.62**, 4.10*** (1.45), (1.37)	-4.25***, 4.04*** (1.63), (1.60)	-3.10**, 3.64** (1.56), (1.45)
Japan & Switzerland	3.12** (1.57)	2.65* (1.40)	4.15** (1.87)	2.94* (1.75)	-4.31***, 3.61*** (1.43), (1.37)	-3.74**, 4.13*** (1.57), (1.34)	-4.32**, 3.99*** (1.70), (1.67)	-3.31**, 3.70** (1.65), (1.47)
Denmark	2.42** (1.23)	2.34** (1.14)	3.34** (1.69)	2.49 (1.60)	-3.60***, 3.14** (1.35), (1.25)	-3.11**, 3.17** (1.43), (1.26)	-3.92*, 3.81** (1.74), (1.67)	-2.99*, 3.24** (1.69), (1.55)

(Continued)

Table 4.6. (Continued)

Excluded Cases	Corporate*Labour (i)				Coordination index (i), Coordination index squared (i)			
	Pooled OLS w/PCSE		Random Effects		Pooled OLS w/PCSE		Random Effects	
	Base model	Full model	Base model	Full model	Base model	Full model	Base model	Full model
Italy	2.86** (1.34)	2.06** (1.03)	4.01** (1.79)	2.45 (1.59)	−4.57***, 3.99*** (1.37), (1.26)	−3.44**, 3.49*** (1.42), (1.22)	−4.65***, 4.48*** (1.66), (1.63)	−3.23**, 3.48*** (1.64), (1.52)
New Zealand (pre-1988)	3.15** (1.25)	2.71** (1.15)	3.81** (1.57)	2.80* (1.51)	−4.35***, 3.82*** (1.35), (1.17)	−3.45**, 3.50*** (1.45), (1.07)	−4.27***, 4.17*** (1.56), (1.50)	−3.16**, 3.45*** (1.62), (1.48)
UK (pre-1980)	3.44*** (1.27)	3.05** (1.22)	4.22*** (1.62)	3.21** (1.50)	−4.83***, 4.17*** (1.42), (1.25)	−3.94***, 3.90*** (1.39), (1.21)	−4.86***, 4.61*** (1.62), (1.55)	−3.75**, 3.88*** (1.63), (1.48)
Denmark, Italy, NZ (pre-1988) & UK (pre-1980)	2.14** (1.02)	1.59* (.920)	3.21* (1.82)	1.90 (1.73)	−3.65***, 3.18*** (1.21), (1.06)	−3.09**, 3.09*** (1.27), (.959)	−3.80**, 3.76** (1.77), (1.71)	−2.90*, 3.13* (1.75), (1.62)

Note: Standard errors in parentheses; *** denotes significant at the .01 level; ** denotes significant at the .05 level; * denotes significant at the .1 level.

problematic cases. Outliers and unmeasured changes in coordination over time do not appear to pose serious threats to our conclusions.

5. POLITICAL AND ECONOMIC ADJUSTMENT PATHS

We conclude by turning to issues of institutional change. Although the historical record is generally supportive of the varieties of capitalism approach to comparative capitalism, a number of scholars have raised questions about the persistence of the cross-national differences identified by this analysis in the face of international pressures associated with 'globalization'.[50] The varieties of capitalism literature addresses such issues. Some contributors to it explore the response of firms and governments to pressures for change, outlining how existing institutions structure processes of change.[51] These formulations generate a set of predictions about national adjustment paths that we now examine empirically with a view to establishing whether the categories generated by the varieties of capitalism perspective remain a relevant typology.

5.1. Economic Dynamics

There are both economic and political sides to this matter. The principal economic issue is whether institutions that appear to have been complementary in previous decades continue to be complementary as secular developments, such as the shift from manufacturing to services, technological change, and international liberalization, alter the economic challenges facing the developed democracies.[52] These developments might alter the efficiencies available from existing combinations of institutions. If productivity growth is lower in services, for instance, the growth of that sector may undercut the efficiency gains available from systems of coordinated wage-bargaining or of social protection that sustain high wage floors.[53] Conversely, in epochs of rapid technological advance that increase the opportunities for radical innovation, the market-oriented complementarities of liberal market economies that lend themselves to this type of innovation may offer even higher returns relative those found in coordinated market economies which are better at incremental innovation.[54] International integration could alter the value of an economy's comparative institutional advantages by improving access to production sites offering other kinds of complementarities.[55]

It is beyond the scope of this article to consider the effects of each of these developments on institutional complementarities. However, a summary impression can be formed by comparing the economic impact of particular combinations of institutions in more recent years with their impact in an earlier period. For this purpose, we re-estimate the models for the economic impact of coordination in labour relations and corporate governance, allowing the coefficient on the interaction of these variables to vary across two different time periods, 1971–84 and 1985–97. These estimations are used to test the following hypothesis:

H7: *Secular economic developments over the past two decades have not altered the efficiency of the institutional complementarities between labour relations and corporate governance posited by a varieties of capitalism perspective.*

If this hypothesis is correct, the coefficient on the interaction term between coordination in labour relations and corporate governance, $C_i^{LR} * C_i^{CG}$, should be positive, statistically significant, and of comparable magnitude across both periods. An F-test to evaluate the presence of structural change should fail to reject the null hypothesis of no difference across the two periods.

The results of the estimations are presented in Table 4.7. For both time periods, the coefficients on the interaction of coordination in corporate governance and labour relations are positive and statistically significant. Moreover, the difference in the magnitude of the coefficients across the time periods is miniscule, suggesting that the impact of institutional complementarities in these two spheres of the economy has not appreciably diminished with time. For both regressions, we performed an F-test, which indicates that we should not reject the null hypothesis of no difference across the two periods. This supports the hypothesis that secular economic developments in the 1980s and 1990s did not alter the basic complementarities identified by the varieties-of-capitalism perspective.

5.2. Political Dynamics

The varieties of capitalism literature also advances a particular view of the political dynamics associated with globalization. This view is built on the contention that the market-oriented institutions of liberal market economies encourage firms, holders of capital, and workers to invest in switchable assets, whereas institutional support for strategic interaction in coordinated market economies encourages higher levels of investment in specific assets.[56] Fluid markets that facilitate the transfer of resources among uses enhance the returns to switchable assets in LMEs. In CMEs, better institutional support

Table 4.7. The impact on economic growth of interaction between coordination in labour relations and corporate governance in 1971–84 and 1985–97

	Pooled OLS w/ Panel Corrected Standard Errors†	Random Effects
ln GDP_0 (*i*)	−1.97***	−2.21***
	(.626)	(.497)
International Demand Conditions (*it*)	2.50***	2.33***
	(.211)	(.214)
π (*it*)	−3.58	−1.70
	(2.39)	(2.42)
Dependency Ratio (*it*)	2.37	5.55
	(13.9)	(11.4)
Exports as capacity to import (*it*)	−.006	.004
	(.048)	(.056)
Coordination in Corporate Governance (*i*)	−1.49	−1.81
	(1.26)	(1.16)
Coordination in Labour Relations (*i*)	−3.23**	−3.20**
	(1.64)	(1.56)
Corporate*Labour(*i*) *I*[period 1971–1984]	3.91***	4.59***
	(1.23)	(1.70)
Corporate*Labour (*i*) *I*[period 1985–1997]	3.44***	4.07**
	(1.21)	(1.69)
N	538	538
R^2	.31	.25
Test of structural change in the effect of interaction between coordination in corporate governance and labour relations	H_0: β(interaction 1971–84) = β(interaction 1985–97) H_A: β(interaction 1971–84) ≠ β(interaction 1985–97) F-stat. = .443 Pr(1.52, v_1=1, v_2=527) = .506	H_0: β(interaction 1971–84) = β(interaction 1985–97) H_A: β(interaction 1971–84) ≠ β (interaction 1985–97) F-stat. = .505 Pr(.910, v_1=1, v_2=527) = .478

Note: Standard errors in parentheses; (*i*) denotes panel-varying but time-invariant explanatory variable; (*it*) denotes panel-varying and time-varying explanatory variable; † model assumes panel-specific first-order autocorrelation; *** denotes significant at the .01 level; ** denotes significant at the .05 level; * denotes significant at the .1 level.

for the formation of credible commitments reduces the risks of investing in co-specific assets whose value depends on the cooperation of other actors.

These patterns of investment are significant because each generates a different politics. In the face of an exogenous shock threatening returns to existing activities, holders of mobile assets will be tempted to 'exit' those activities to seek higher returns elsewhere, while holders of specific assets face higher incentives to exercise 'voice' in defence of existing activities.[57] The argument is analogous to the distinction drawn between a Hecksher–Ohlin world, where factors are mobile and shifts in relative prices (of the sort associated with increasing economic openness) generate conflict between the holders of basic factors, such as capital and labour, and a Ricardo–Viner world of sector-specific factors where shifts in relative prices inspire inter-sectoral conflicts that unite employers and workers in defence of sectoral interests.[58]

From this perspective, the varieties of capitalism literature argues that the political response to contemporary economic challenges will vary across liberal and coordinated market economies. In LMEs, the response will be market-oriented. When returns to existing activities are threatened, holders of mobile assets, such as workers with general skills or owners of capital on fluid equity markets, will move their assets to new activities. Many will be inter-ested, therefore, in rendering markets even more fluid and governments may be responsive to them. Moreover, where nations respond to shocks by relying on markets to adjust prices and wages, substantial shifts in the distribution of income are likely to occur, reflecting the advantages of those with market-power.

In coordinated market economies, by contrast, the varieties of capitalism perspective expects economic challenges to inspire a political response medi-ated by higher levels of asset specificity. When returns to existing activities are threatened, holders of specific assets, such as workers with industry-specific skills and owners of enterprises deeply invested in co-specific assets, will find it difficult to shift to new activities. As a result, they will be less inclined to favour deregulatory initiatives that increase market competition and more inclined to demand institutional support for existing activities. The result is likely to be a much slower process of liberalization and a politics that unites workers and employers in 'cross-class' coalitions of sectoral defence.[59]

These postulates about political dynamics suggest that economic shocks will produce different institutional outcomes in liberal and coordinated market economies. Although all capitalist economies use markets to adjust and international integration automatically renders some markets more com-petitive, this analysis anticipates more rapid deregulation in liberal market economies, where there should be more political support for it, compared to coordinated market economies, where cross-class coalitions support existing regulatory regimes. The perspective anticipates change in all countries, in-cluding some liberalization in CMEs, but institutional adjustment paths that diverge across different types of political economies.[60]

In order to assess whether that account accurately describes the response to recent challenges, we examine a number of indicators beginning with levels of inequality. If LMEs respond to economic challenges by relying more heavily

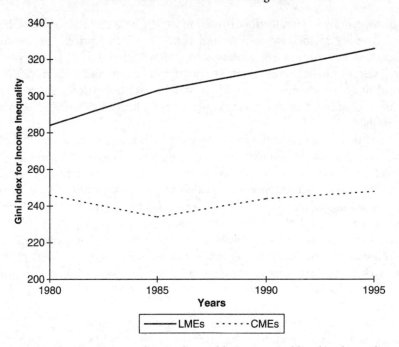

Figure 4.6. Changes in inequality in disposable income in liberal and coordinated market economies, 1980–1995

Source: Luxembourg Income Study.

on competitive markets to reset wages and prices, we should see more rapid increases in income inequality there in response to the recent experiences of globalization. Figure 4.6 show that this has indeed been the pattern.[61]

To what extent have the institutional differences that underpin different modes of coordination narrowed in the face of globalization? To form an assessment, we assembled indicators for the character of institutional practices in six spheres relevant to the varieties of capitalism arguments. The observations are drawn from the 1980s and the 1990s, including the early 2000s where data was available, and they are reported in Table 4.8. We distinguish among liberal market economies, coordinated market economies, and a third group of Southern European nations termed here 'mixed market economies' because they are not definitively classified into the other two categories by the varieties of capitalism literature and cluster distinctively in Figure 4.2.[62]

The figures presented in Table 4.8 display substantial differences between CMEs and LMEs during the 1980s of the sort associated with different types of coordination. Of most interest, however, are the changes taking place from

Table 4.8. Patterns of institutional practices in different types of political economies from the 1980s to the early 2000s

	CMEs			LMEs			MMEs		
	1980s	1990s	% Δ	1980s	1990s	% Δ	1980s	1990s	% Δ
Industrial Relations									
Trade Union Density	49	51	4	34	32	−6	30	32	7
Bargaining Coverage	76	75	−1	58	48	−17	78	84	8
Bargaining level	4.2	4.0	−5	1.9	1.8	−5	2.2	2.7	23
Social Protection									
Employment Protection	2.6	2.0	−23	0.7	0.7	0	3.6	3.3	−8
Benefit Entitlements	32.6	35.5	9	24.4	24.1	−1	19	28.4	50
Social Spending /GDP	21	25	19	15	18	20	16	24	50
Labour Market Flexibility									
Part-Time Emplyment	16	18	13	16	20	25	8	10	25
Average Hours Worked	1,722	1,553	−10	1,837	1,732	−6	1,943	1,705	−12
Income Inequality	.24	.26	8	.28	.33	18	.31	.32	1
Firm Structure									
Average Job Tenure	9.5	9.9	4	7.3	7.3	0	10.7	9.6	−11
CEO Compensation	8.5	9.8	15	10.3	17.6	29	9.7	15.3	37
Corporate Governance									
Stock Market Capitalization	28	69	146	47	79	68	8	37	363
Debt/Equity Ratio	2.8	1.9	−40	.60	.89	48	2.3	2.2	−4
Earnings and Employment									
Real Earnings	0.75	1.26	68	0.45	0.78	74	1.13	0.93	−18
Unit Labour Costs	73.4	99.4	44	67.6	97.4	35	54.4	101.8	87
Total Employment	69	70	1	65	64	−2	57	57	0

Note: The table compares average figures for 1980–89 with average figures for 1990–2002 or latest date available. For variable descriptions and sources, see Appendix 2. LMEs include: USA, UK, Canada, Australia, NZ, Ireland. CMEs include: Germany, Japan, Austria, Sweden, Norway, Denmark, Finland, Netherlands, Belgium, Switzerland. MMEs include: Portugal, Spain, France, Italy, Greece, but sample sizes vary with data availability.

1980 to the early 2000s. Did these differences between LMEs and CMEs narrow in ways that reflect convergence on a single economic model? Table 4.8 shows that the direction of institutional reform is often similar across the two types of political economies. But, when variation in the pace and extent of movement is considered, substantial differences in the institutional practices of CMEs and LMEs remain. Although the locus of wage-bargaining has moved downward in most of these economies, for instance, the proportion of workers covered by a collective agreement declined much more rapidly in liberal than in coordinated market economies. In the realm of social protection, social spending has crept upward and employment protection has declined, but differences between the two types of economies remain pronounced. While LMEs sharpened market mechanisms, many CMEs cushioned their citizens against the effects of market adjustment with increases in benefit entitlements.[63] In the labour market, increases in part-time employment indicate a general movement toward labour market flexibility, but LMEs increase income inequality and CMEs reduce hours of work faster than their counterparts.

Especially intriguing are indicators for the institutional practices associated with firm strategy and finance. Here, much has been made of changes in CMEs that seem to reflect convergence on the practices of LMEs. However, these figures tell a more nuanced story. In CMEs, the ratio of the compensation of chief executive officers to that of manufacturing workers and the size of stock markets increased, but the analogous increases in LMEs were also substantial, leaving large gaps in institutional practices between the two types of political economies, which is also apparent in the debt-to-equity ratios of non-financial enterprises. The figures for earnings and employment tell a classic story of different adjustment paths. Strategically coordinated wage bargaining pushed real earnings up in CMEs at rates that outpaced those in LMEs, but effective forms of coordination in the workplace and high levels of investment kept the increase in unit labour costs in CMEs roughly commensurate with that of LMEs.

On balance, we read these figures as suggesting that institutional practices did not converge dramatically in the decades after 1980. Modest efforts were made to improve the flexibility of coordinated market economies, including some liberalization of labour and capital markets, but the pace of movement was slow enough to leave significant differences in institutional practices across the two types of political economies. The absence of more convergence in the face of intense pressures during the 1980s and 1990s suggests that the distinctions drawn by the varieties of capitalism literature may be relevant for years to come.

6. CONCLUSION

We entered this project uncertain about whether we could find indicators for the relevant variables and what the tests of the hypotheses would reveal. We leave it impressed with the uniformity of the results. The weight of the evidence suggests that the varieties of capitalism literature captures important differences among political economies. The concepts of market-oriented and strategic coordination do seem to reflect an underlying dimension distinguishing practices across countries in the spheres of labour relations and corporate governance. The contention that institutional complementarities operate across these two spheres of the political economy is also borne out by the evidence. Persistent cross-national differences in institutional practices in the face of intense pressures for convergence, suggests that, despite some liberalization in coordinated market economies, the distinctions central to the varieties of capitalism perspective are likely to be of continuing value.

Our findings about complementarities have especially important implications for reform proposals now being considered in the developed world. The deregulation of labour markets is a popular cause. However, our evidence suggests that labour-market deregulation is likely to produce large economic gains only in nations where financial markets are correspondingly fluid (see Figure 4.4). Otherwise, the gains in growth may be relatively small. Many nations have come under pressure from international agencies or global enterprises to increase competition in markets for corporate governance. However, our estimates suggest that such steps may have positive effects only where labour markets are also highly fluid.

The broader lesson is that those seeking to understand the effects of institutional change should pay careful attention to the potential for institutional complementarities across spheres of the political economy. Most proposals to reform labour or capital markets are based on estimates of the effects of such reforms that consider data only for the sphere being reformed. If the distribution of institutions across national cases were random, estimates generated from cross-national data of this sort might produce accurate results. But our evidence indicates that this distribution is far from random: nations with particular types of institutions in one sphere tend to have particular types of institutions in other spheres. As a result, models that do not take interaction effects across institutional spheres into account may attribute to one set of institutions effects that are actually generated by interaction among several sets of institutions.

This is a research agenda rather than a counsel of despair that finds complementarities everywhere. Although there are undoubtedly other ones, the varieties of capitalism literature presents propositions about particular complementarities that can be examined more closely. The range of institutional indicators available for doing so is growing, as is the evidence that such analyses can be fruitful.[64] In broad terms, this analysis lends weight to the theoretical perspectives advanced in the varieties of capitalism literature. It suggests that the concepts of market-oriented and strategic coordination can illuminate the operation of many developed political economies and contribute important insights to understanding their politics and economic performance.

Appendix 4.1. Variable Descriptions for the Growth Regressions

Variable	Definition	Source
Y_{it}	Growth rate of real GDP per capita (constant prices: chain series)	Penn World Table 6.1
$lnGDP_i$	Log GDP per capita in 1971 calculated using real GDP per capita (constant prices: chain series)	Penn World Table 6.1
Int_{it}	Average rate of growth for the entire sample in each year weighted by a country's trade openness	Openness: OECD Statistical Compendium 2006, vol.1
π_{it}	Rate of growth of inflation (as measured by the CPI)	World Bank, World Development Indicators
Exp_{it}	Percentage change in exports as a capacity to import (constant LCU) weighted by trade openness. Exports as a capacity to import equals the current price value of exports of goods and services deflated by the import price index	World Bank, World Development Indicators
D_{it}	Percentage change in the dependency ratio (number of individuals under 15 and older than 65 as a percentage of working-age population)	World Bank, World Development Indicators
PLU_{it}	1 if majority of representatives in lower house are elected by plurality voting, 0 otherwise	Database of Political Institutions, World Bank Institute, http://www.worldbank.org/wbi
MAG_{it}	Average district magnitude in the lower chamber	Database of Political Institutions
$Leftcab_{it}$	Left party cabinet portfolios as proportion of total cabinet portfolios	Duane Swank's Comparative Parties Data Set (http://www.marquette.edu/polisci/Swank.htm)

Appendix 4.2. Variable Descriptions for Table 8

Variable	Description	Source
Trade Union Density	Union membership as percent of labour force: 1980–89 vs 1990–2002.	Comparative Welfare States Data Set 2004, OECD *Employment Outlook* 1997, European Industrial Relations Observatory On-line
Bargaining Coverage	Percentage of labour force covered by collective bargaining: 1980, 1985 vs 1990, 1994, 2000, 2001, 2002	OECD *Employment Outlook* 1994, 1997, European Industrial Relations Observatory On-line
Bargaining Level	Degree of centralization in wage bargaining: 1980–89 vs 1990–2000	Comparative Welfare States Data Set 2004, OECD *Employment Outlook* 1997, European Industrial Relations Observatory On-line
Employment Protection	Strictness of legislation for regular and temporary contracts: late 1980s vs late 1990s	OECD *Employment Outlook* 1997
Benefit Entitlements	Gross replacement rate for unemployment benefit averaged over earning levels and family situations: 1981, 83, 85, 87, 89 vs 1991, 93, 95, 97, 99	OECD Benefits and Wages Indicators 2002.
Social Spending/GDP	Public social expenditure as a percent of GDP: 1980 vs 2003	OECD *Factbook* 2007
Part-Time Employment	Percent of labour force employed less than 30 hours per week in their main job: 1980–89 vs 1990–2002	OECD *Labour Force Statistics* 2003.
Average Hours Worked	Hours per year worked per person in employment: 1980 vs 2005	OECD *Factbook* 2007.
Income Inequality	Gini Coefficient for disposable income: year closest to 1980 vs most recent available year	Luxembourg Income Data Study Key Figures.
Average Job Tenure	Average number of years employed with same firm: 1980, 85, 89 vs 1990, 91, 95	OECD, *Employment Outlook* 1993, 1997.
CEO Compensation	Ratio of total CEO compensation and benefits to that of manufacturing operatives: 1984 vs 1996	Abowd, John M. And David S. Kaplan, 'Executive Compensation, Six Questions that Need Answering.' National Bureau of Economic Research Working Paper No. 7124. May 1999.

(Continued)

Appendix 4.2. (*Continued*)

Variable	Description	Source
Stock Market Capitalization	Ratio of stock market capitalization to GDP: 1980–89 vs 1990–2001	World Bank Online Database.
Debt/Equity Ratio	Ratio of debt to equity for non-financial enterprises: 1980/85 vs 1992/3	OECD *Economies at a Glance: Structural Indicators* 1996.
Real Earnings	Year to year percent change in real hourly earnings in manufacturing: 1980–89 vs 1990–2000	OECD *Historical Statistics* 2001.
Unit Labour Costs	Wages, salaries employer contributions per unit of output: 1980–89 vs 1990–2000	OECD STAN Indicators database.
Total Employment	Total employment as percent of population aged 15 to 64: 1980–89 vs 1990–2000.	OECD *Historical Statistics* 2001.

NOTES

1. Andrew Shonfield, *Modern Capitalism* (Oxford: Oxford University Press, 1969), Chalmers Johnson, *MITI and the Japanese Miracle: The Growth of Industrial Policy 1925–75* (Stanford: Stanford University Press, 1982).
2. Fritz Scharpf, *Crisis and Choice in European Social Democracy* (Ithaca: Cornell University Press, 1991); Peter J. Katzenstein, *Small States in World Markets* (Ithaca, Cornell University Press, 1985); Lars Calmfors and John Driffill. 'Centralization of Wage Bargaining', *Economic Policy* 6 (1988), 13–61; David Cameron, 'Social Democracy, Corporatism, Labour Quiescence and the Representation of Economic Interest in Advanced Capitalist Society' in John H. Goldthorpe, ed, *Order and Conflict in Contemporary Capitalism* (New York: Oxford University Press, 1984), 143–78.
3. Bruno Amable, *The Diversity of Modern Capitalism.* (Oxford, Oxford University Press, 2004); Vivien Schmidt, *The Futures of European Capitalism* (New York: Oxford University Press, 2002); Colin Crouch and Wolfgang Streeck, eds, *The Political Economy of Modern Capitalism, Mapping Convergence and Diversity* (London: Sage, 1997); Suzanne Berger and Ronald Dore, eds, *National Diversity and Global Capitalism* (Ithaca, Cornell University Press, 1996); Michel Albert, *Capitalism Against Capitalism* (London, Whurr, 1992).

4. Peter A. Hall and David Soskice, eds, *Varieties of Capitalism, The Institutional Foundations of Comparative Advantage* (Oxford: Oxford University Press, 2001); Bob Hancké, Martin Rhodes and Mark Thatcher, eds, *Beyond Varieties of Capitalism, Conflict, Contradiction and Complementarities in the European Economy* (Oxford: Oxford University Press, 2007); John L. Campbell, John A. Hall, and Ove K. Pedersen, *National Identity and the Varieties of Capitalism, The Danish Experience,* (Montreal: McGill University Press, 2006); David Rueda and Jonas Pontusson, 'Wage Inequality and Varieties of Capitalism', *World Politics* 52 (2000), 350–83; Herbert Kitschelt, Peter Lange, Gary Marks, and John Stephens, eds, *Continuity and Change in Contemporary Capitalism.* (New York, Cambridge University Press, 1999).

5. For efforts to look at some of its propositions, see Mark Zachary Taylor, 'Empirical Evidence Against Variety of Capitalism's Theory of Technological Innovation', *International Organization* 58 (2004), 601–31; Lane Kenworthy, 'Institutional Coherence and Macroeconomic Performance', *Socio-Economic Review* 4 (2006), 69–91; Allen, Matthew, Lothar Funk, and Heinz Tüselman. 'Can Variation in Public Policies Account for Differences in Comparative Advantage?' *Journal of Public Policy* 26 (2006), 1–19.

6. R. Jaikumar, 'Postindustrial Manufacturing', *Harvard Business Review* (November–December 1986), 69–76; Paul Milgrom and John Roberts, 'The Economics of Modern Manufacturing, Technology, Strategy and Organization', *American Economic Review* 80 (1990), 511–28; Paul Milgrom and John Roberts, *Economics, Organization and Management.* (Englewood Cliffs: Prentice Hall, 1992).

7. See also Masahiko Aoki, 'The Japanese Firm as a System of Attributes, A Survey and Research Agenda, in Masahiko Aoki and Ronald Dore, eds, *The Japanese Firm, Sources of Competitive Strength* (Oxford, Clarendon Press, 1994), pp. 11–40; Martin Höpner, 'What Connects Industrial Relations and Corporate Governance? Explaining Institutional Complementarity', *Socio-Economic Review* 3 (2005), 331–58; Glenn Morgan, Richard Whitley, and Eli Moen, eds, *Changing Capitalisms, Internationalisation, Institutional Change and Systems of Economic Organization.* (Oxford: Oxford University Press, 2005).

8. Stephen Nickell, 'Unemployment and Labour Market Rigidities, Europe versus North America', *Journal of Economic Perspectives* 11 (1997), 55–74; Organization for Economic Cooperation and Development, *OECD Jobs Study, Evidence and Explanations III, The Adjustment Potential of the Labour Market* (Paris: OECD, 1994); Calmfors and Driffill. 'Centralization of Wage Bargaining'; Wendy Carlin and Colin Mayer, 'How Do Financial Systems Affect Economic Performance?' in Xavier Vives, ed., *Corporate Governance, Theoretical and Empirical Perspectives* (New York, Cambridge University Press, 2000), 137–68; Rafael LaPorta, Florencio Lopez-de-Silanes, Andrei Schleifer, and Robert W. Vishny, 'Law and Finance', *Journal of Political Economy* 106, 6 (1998), 1113–55.

9. Robert J. Franzese, Jr, *Macroeconomic Policies of Developed Democracies.* New York, Cambridge University Press, 2001); Bruno Amable, Ekkehard Ernst, and Stefano Palombarini, 'How do Financial Markets Affect Industrial Relations, An Institutional Complementarity Approach,' *Socio-Economic Review* 3 (2005),

311–30; Ekkehard Ernst, 'Financial Systems, Industrial Relations, and Industry Specialization, An Econometric Analysis of Institutional Complementarities', in H. Schubert, ed., *The Transformation of the European Financial System* (Vienna: 2004), pp. 60–95; Torben Iversen, 'Wage Bargaining, Central Bank Independence and the Real Effects of Money', *International Organization* (1998), 469–504; Peter A. Hall and Robert J. Franzese, Jr., 'Mixed Signals, Central Bank Independence, Coordinated Wage Bargaining, and European Monetary Union', *International Organization* (1998), 502–36; Michel Goyer 'Capital Mobility, Varieties of Institutional Investors and the Transforming Stability of Corporate Governance in France and Germany', in Hancké, Rhodes and Thatcher, eds, *Beyond Varieties of Capitalism*, pp. 195–222.

10. This approach originates in the early work of David Soskice and the account given of it here draws extensively on joint work with him. See David Soskice, 'Reinterpreting Corporatism and Explaining Unemployment, Coordinated and Non-coordinated Market Economies', in R. Brunetta and C. Dell'Aringa, eds, *Labour Relations and Economic Performance* (London: Macmillan, 1990), pp. 170–214; David Soskice, 'The Institutional Infrastructure for International Competitiveness, A Comparative Analysis of the UK and Germany', in A.B. Atkinson and R. Brunetta, eds, *The Economics of the New Europe* (London: Macmillan, 1991), pp. 45–66.

11. This list of the institutional correlates of effective strategic coordination is a familiar one that draws on the conventional literature plus the presence of a capacity for deliberation whose importance is outlined in Hall and Soskice, 'Introduction'. See Elinor Ostrom, *Governing the Commons: The Evolution of Institutions for Collective Action* (New York: Cambridge University Press, 1990).

12. The approach concentrates on cross-national variation because it examines spheres were national regulations and nation-specific institutions are especially important, but it acknowledges there can be additional variation across specific regions or sectors. See John L. Campbell, Rogers Hollingsworth, and Leon Lindberg, *Governance of the American Economy* (New York: Cambridge University Press, 1991); and Gary Herrigel, *Industrial Constructions: The Sourcs of German Industrial Power* (New York: Cambridge University Press, 1996).

13. Of course, the distinction between institutions and coordination is a narrow one, especially if coordination is construed as rule-patterned behaviour. Here, institutions are defined as rules and practices, more or less formal, that actors take into account when making decisions about what actions to undertake. These include the institutions generated by the organizational setting. See Hall and Soskice, 'Introduction', p. 9; Randall Calvert, 'The Rational Choice Theory of Social Institutions: Cooperation, Coordination and Communication' in J. Banks and E. Hanushek, eds, *Modern Political Economy* (New York: Cambridge University Press, 1995), pp. 216–67.

14. Kenneth A. Bollen, *Structural Equations with Latent Variables* (New York: Wiley, 1989).

15. Further details of the derivation and definition of these measures can be found in the original sources.

16. LaPorta, Lopez-de-Silanes, Schleifer, and Vishny, 'Law and Finance', 1130.
17. Rafael LaPorta, Florencio Lopez-de-Silanes, and Andrei Schleifer, 'Corporate Ownership Around the World', 1998, Mimeo, Table II, Panel B.
18. Oecd.org/corporate affairs.
19. Richard Layard, Stephen Nickell, and Richard Jackman, *Unemployment, Macroeconomic Performance and the Labour Market.* (Oxford: Oxford University Press, 1991), p. 52.
20. Organization for Economic Cooperation and Development, *Employment Outlook* (June 1997), 71.
21. Ibid., p. 138. The value for New Zealand on this variable is estimated using a multiple imputation technique.
22. The path diagram reflects the following assumptions. First, we assume that the covariance among our observed variables is a function of the presence of two latent (unobservable) variables: the balance between market-based and strategic coordination in the sphere of corporate governance and in the sphere of labour relations. Second, we assume that each latent variable is linearly related to the corresponding observable variables within its particular sphere of the economy. Coordination in one sphere of the economy does not exert a *direct* linear effect on the level of the observable variables found in the other sphere of the economy. Third, we assume that our two latent variables are correlated: given the presence of institutional complementarities, we would expect countries characterized by high levels of one type of coordination in one sphere to have high levels of coordination in the other sphere. Thus, the empirical model reflects our theoretical belief that variation in the observable variables found in one sphere of the economy is related to the level of coordination found in the other sphere of the economy only by way of the correlation between the levels of coordination in the two spheres, which in turn is a function of the presence of institutional complementarities. Our final assumption is that measurement error across our observable variables is uncorrelated.
23. The estimated correlation is negative because the latent factor driving the covariance between the corporate governance indicators is the degree of strategic coordination whereas the latent factor driving the covariance between the labour relations indicators is the degree of market coordination (i.e. strategic coordination in reverse).
24. Paul Windolf, *Corporate Networks in Europe and the United States* (New York: Oxford University Press, 2002); Mark J. Roe, 'Political Preconditions to Separating Ownership from Corporate Control', *Stanford Law Review* 53 (2000), 539–605.
25. Schmidt, *The Futures of European Capitalism;* Amable, *The Diversity of Modern Capitalism;* Hall and Soskice, *Varieties of Capitalism,* Martin Rhodes 'Globalisation, Labour Markets and Welfare States, A Future of "Competitive Corporatism"?' in Martin Rhodes and Yves Meny, eds, *The Future of European Welfare* (London: Macmillan, 1997), 178–203.

26. The varieties of capitalism literature acknowledges that such differences may exist. Those between the 'industry-coordinated' economies of northern Europe and 'group-coordinated' economies of Asia have been elaborated most fully. See David Soskice, 'National Patterns in Company Innovation Strategies: A Comparative Institutional Approach' WZB, 1996.

27. Note that our concern here is simply to assess whether the institutional patterns that the varieties of capitalism approach expects to find across nations actually occur and not to assess explanations for why these institutional patterns arise. Many causal processes may underlie such patterns and our analysis is not meant to imply that they arise for any specific set of functional reasons.

28. David Finegold and David Soskice, 'The Failure of Training in Britain, Analysis and Prescription', *Oxford Review of Economic Policy* 4 (1988), 21–53; Pepper Culpepper, *Creating Cooperation, How States Develop Human Capital in Europe.* (Ithaca: Cornell University Press, 2003).

29. Steven Casper, 'High Technology Governance and Institutional Adpativeness'. Discussion Paper 99–307, Wissenschaftszentrum, Berlin (1999); Peter A. Hall and David Soskice, 'An Introduction to Varieties of Capitalism', in Hall and Soskice, eds, *Varieties of Capitalism, The Institutional Foundations of Comparative Advantage* (Oxford, Oxford University Press, 2001), 1–70.

30. Margarita Estevez-Abe, Torben Iversen, and David Soskice, 'Social Protection and Skill Formation, A Reinterpretation of the Welfare State', in Hall and Soskice, eds, *Varieties of Capitalism,* pp. 145–83; cf. Isabela Mares, 'Firms and the Welfare State, When and How does Social Policy Matter to Employers', in Hall and Soskice, eds, *Varieties of Capitalism,* pp. 184–212.

31. See also David Soskice, 'Divergent Production Regimes, Coordinated and Uncoordinated Market Economies in the 1990s', in Herbert Kitschelt et al., eds, *Continuity and Change in Contemporary Capitalism* (New York: Cambridge University Press, 1999), pp. 101–34.

32. Hall and Soskice, 'Introduction' and Mark Lehrer, 'From Macro-Varieties of Capitalism to Micro-Varieties of Firm Strategy, Applying Comparative Institutional Analysis to Strategic Management', in Hall and Soskice, eds, *Varieties of Capitalism,* pp. 361–86.

33. Note that the sample sizes vary for some of these measures.

34. Estevez-Abe et al., 'Social Protection and Skill Formation, A Reinterpretation of the Welfare State'.

35. Giuseppe Nicoletti, Stefano Scarpetta, and Olivier Boylaud, 'Summary Indicators of Product Market Regulation with an Extension to Employment Protection Legislation'. OECD, Economics Department Working Papers No. 226, p. 80.

36. OECD on-line education database (http://www1.oecd.org/scripts/cde/members/linkpage.html; OECD, *Literacy in the Information Age* (Paris: OECD, 2000), p. 159.

37. Pagano, Marco and Paolo Volpin. 'The Political Economy of Corporate Governance'. Centro Stude in Economia e Finanza, Departimento di Scienze Economiche, Universitya degli Studi di Salerno, Working Paper No. 29 (2000), Table 4.4.

38. Economic Policy Institute, *The State of Working America 2000–01* (Washington, Economic Policy Institute, 2000).

39. OECD, *Employment Outlook* (June 1997), 138.

40. This measure uses the average 1960–89 scores for a factor that Hicks and Kenworthy label 'firm-level cooperation' which includes some further variables assigned low weights that we do not enumerate here; Alexander Hicks and Lane Kenworthy, 'Cooperation and Political Economic Performance in Affluent Democratic Capitalism', *American Journal of Sociology* 103 (1998), 649.

41. Masahiko Aoki, 'Toward an Economic Model of the Japanese Firm', *Journal of Economic Literature* 28 (1990), 1–27; Masahiko Aoki, 'The Japanese Firm as a System of Attributes, A Survey and Research Agenda'; Hall and Soskice, 'Introduction'.

42. When we say that one institutional practice enhances the efficiency of another, this means that its presence increases the returns available from using the other institutional practice.

43. The terms 'market' and 'strategic' coordination refer to broad patterns of firm behaviour that tend to be altered only by large-scale institutional changes: no one has suggested that any measure to introduce some competition into one of these spheres necessarily impairs strategic coordination in the other. Similarly, although these institutions also have distributive effects that increase the returns to particular actors, following the varieties of capitalism literature, we focus here on returns to the economy as a whole of the sort reflected in aggregate economic performance.

44. Lane Kenworthy, Wage Setting Coordination Scores. 2001. Available at http://www.u.arizona.edu/~lkenwor/WageCoorScores.pdf.

45. The countries included in the estimations consist of all those for which it was possible to calculate the coordination indices. See Table 4.2 for the complete list.

46. Nathaniel Beck and Jonathan Katz, 'What to Do (And Not to Do) with Time-Series Cross-Section Data', *American Political Science Review* 89 (1995), 634–48.

47. One of the more common approaches to statistical analysis with panel data, namely, fixed effects regression, was unavailable to us as a result of the time-invariant nature of our coordination indices.

48. T. Persson and G. Tabellini, *The Economic Effects of Constitutions.* (Cambridge, MA: MIT Press, 2003).

49. As a summary measure of variation over time, we calculated the percentage of years in which a country's wage coordination score was less than or equal to 1 point away from its modal score during the 1971–97 period. For all countries except for Denmark, Italy, and New Zealand, this was greater than 70 per cent.

50. Susanne Soederberg, Georg Menz, and Philip G. Cerny, eds, *Internalizing Globalization, The Rise of Neo-Liberalism and the Decline of National Varieties of Capitalism* (Houndsmills: Palgrave Macmillan, 2005); Jürgen Beyer Martin Höpner, 'The Disintegration of Organised Capitalism, German Corporate Governance in the 1990s', *West European Politics,* 26 (2003), 179–98; Berger and Dore, eds, *National Diversity and Global Capitalism;* cf. Peter A. Hall, 'The Evolution of

Varieties of Capitalism in Europe', in Hancké, Rhodes, and Thatcher, eds, *Beyond Varieties of Capitalism*, pp. 39–88.

51. Hall and Soskice, eds, *Varieties of Capitalism*.

52. Peter A. Hall, 'The Political Economy of Adjustment in Germany' in Frieder Naschold, David Soskice, Bob Hancké, and Ulrich Jurgens, eds, *Okonomische Leitstungsfahigkeit und Institutionelle Innovation* (Berlin: Sigma, 1997), 293–317; Peter A. Hall, 'The Political Economy of Europe in an Era of Interdependence', in Herbert Kitschelt et al., eds, *Change and Continuity in Contemporary Capitalism* (NY: Cambridge University Press, 1999), pp. 135–63.

53. Torben Iversen and Anne Wren, 'Equality, Employment and Budgetary Restraint', *World Politics* 50 (1998), 507–46; Viven Schmidt and Fritz Scharpf, *Welfare and Work in the Open Economy, From Vulnerability to Competitiveness*. (Oxford: Oxford University Press, 2002).

54. Hall and Soskice, 'Introduction'; Hall, 'The Political Economy of Adjustment in Germany'; David Soskice, 'Innovation Strategies of Companies, A Comparative Institutional Analysis of some Cross-Country Differences' in W. a M.D. Zapf, ed., *Institutionenvergliech und Institutionendynamik* (Berlin: WZB, 1994), 271–89. On this point, our thinking has been influenced by conversations with Robert Fannion and Gavyn Davies.

55. Jeffry A. Frieden and Ronald Rogowski, 'The Impact of the International Economy on National Policies, An Analytical Overview' in Robert Keohane and Helen Milner, eds, *Internationalization and Domestic Politics* (New York: Cambridge University Press, 1996), 25–47.

56. Hall and Soskice, 'Introduction'; Torben Iversen and David Soskice, 'An Asset Theory of Social Policy Preferences', *American Political Science Review* 95 (2001), 875–93.

57. Albert Hirschman, *Exit, Voice and Loyalty* (Cambridge, MA: Harvard University Press, 1964).

58. Michael J. Hiscox, 'Class versus Industry Cleavages, Inter-Industry Factor Mobility and the Politics of Trade', *International Organization* 55, 1 (2001), 1–46; Frieden and Rogowski, 'The Impact of the International Economy on National Policies, An Analytical Overview'; James Alt, Jeffry Frieden, Michael Gilligan, Dani Rodrik, and Ronald Rogowski, 'The Political Economy of International Trade – Enduring Puzzles and an Agenda for Inquiry', *Comparative Political Studies* 29 (1996), 689–717.

59. Peter Swenson, 'Bringing Capital Back In, or Social Democracy Reconsidered, Employer Power, Cross-Class Alliances and Centralization of Industrial Relations in Denmark and Sweden', *World Politics* 43 (1991), 513–44; Kathleen Thelen and Ikuo Kume, 'The Effects of Globalization on Labour Revisited, Lessons from Germany and Japan', *Politics and Society* 27 (1999), 477–505; Stewart Wood, 'Employer Preferences, State Power and Labour Market Policy and Germany and Britain' in Hall and Soskice, eds, *Varieties of Capitalism*, 247–74.

60. Hall, 'The Evolution of Varieties of Capitalism in Europe'.

61. For the empirical analysis in this section of the paper, we adopt the classification of political economies that Hall and Soskice use, terming those that they do not classify definitively as liberal or coordinated market economies, mixed market economies. Portugal, Spain, France, and Italy are in the latter category. See Hall and Soskice, 'Introduction'.

62. As labelled here, mixed market economies include those that fall clearly below the regression line on the right hand side of Figure 4.2, i.e. Spain, Portugal, Italy, and France.

63. However, some of these entitlements are being gradually reduced again. See Elmar Rieger and Stephan Leibfried, *Limits to Globalization, Welfare States and the World Economy* (Cambridge: Polity Press, 2003).

64. Amable et al., 'How do Financial Markets Affect Industrial Relations, An Institutional Complementarity Approach'; Ernst, 'Financial Systems, Industrial Relations, and Industry Specialization, An Econometric Analysis of Institutional Complementarities'; Nicoletti, Scarpetta and Boylaud, 'Summary Indicators of Product Market Regulation with an Extension to Employment Protection Legislation'; LaPorta, Lopez-de-Silanes, Schleifer, and Vishny, 'Law and Finance'; Lane Kenworthy, *In Search of National Economic Success* (Thousand Oaks, CA: Sage, 1995).

65. Derrick N. Lawley and Albert E. Maxwell, *Factor Analysis as a Statistical Method* (London: Butterworths, 1963).

5

Institutional Coherence and Macroeconomic Performance

Lane Kenworthy*

1. INTRODUCTION

In their 'Introduction' to *Varieties of Capitalism*, Peter Hall and David Soskice (2001) suggest that affluent capitalist economies can usefully be grouped into two types according to their institutional frameworks: 'coordinated market economies' and 'liberal market economies'. Neither of these types, according to Hall and Soskice, is inherently better at generating good macroeconomic outcomes. Instead, they posit that superior macroeconomic performance is a product of *institutional coherence*. Both coordinated market economies (such as Germany and Japan) and liberal market economies (such as the United States and the United Kingdom) can be coherent. Both within and across the two types of economies, countries with more coherent sets of institutions – that is, with consistently non-market-oriented or consistently market-oriented institutions – should perform better.

Hall and Gingerich (2004) have recently created a measure of institutional coherence. I use their measure, along with an alternative measure I develop here, to assess the impact of institutional coherence on variation in economic growth and employment growth across 18 affluent countries over the period 1974–2000. The results are not particularly supportive of the Hall–Soskice hypothesis.

*The data used in this paper and a set of supplementary charts are available at www.u.arizona. edu/~lkenwor. Earlier versions were presented at the 2002 American Political Science Association annual meeting and the 2002 Society for the Advancement of Socio-Economics annual meeting. I am grateful to participants in those sessions, to Peter Hall, and to the *Socio-Economic Review* reviewers for helpful comments.

2. VARIETIES OF CAPITALISM AND INSTITUTIONAL COHERENCE

Research on institutional variation across affluent nations differs in a number of respects, one of which is the choice about whether to focus on quantitative or qualitative variation in institutions. Many researchers prefer scales or country rankings for the institution(s) of interest. Most studies of the effects of Left government, wage-setting centralization/coordination, and central bank independence fall into this camp. Others focus on categorical differences. Early studies of corporatism (Crouch 1985) and research inspired by Esping-Andersen's (1990) 'three worlds' welfare-regime typology are illustrative.

The 'varieties of capitalism' perspective advanced by Hall and Soskice (2001) at first glance appears to fall squarely into the latter camp. Hall and Soskice focus on the distinction between economic coordination that is primarily market-based and coordination that occurs mainly via non-market institutions. They examine five economic 'spheres': (a) industrial relations (bargaining over wages and working conditions); (b) vocational training and education; (c) corporate governance (relations between firms and their investors); (d) inter-firm relations (between firms and their suppliers, clients, and competitors); (e) relations with employees (information-sharing, work-effort incentives). Their core thesis is that political economies tend to be characterized by 'institutional complementarities'. A complementarity exists when 'the presence (or efficiency) of one institution increases the returns from (or efficiency of) the other' (Hall and Soskice 2001: 17). For instance, 'long-term employment is more feasible where the financial system provides capital on terms that are not sensitive to current profitability. Conversely, fluid labour markets may be more effective at sustaining employment in the presence of financial markets that transfer resources readily among endeavors thereby maintaining a demand for labour' (Hall and Soskice 2001: 18). Because institutional complementarities generate beneficial returns, 'nations with a particular type of coordination in one sphere of the economy should tend to develop complementary practices in other spheres as well' (Hall and Soskice 2001: 18).

Hall and Soskice find that institutional complementarities do indeed tend to be present in the affluent Organization for Economic Cooperation and Development (OECD) economies, and they suggest that these economies fall into two groups. Coordination is market-based in six 'liberal market economies': Australia, Canada, Ireland, New Zealand, the United Kingdom, and the United States. Coordination is based largely on non-market or extramarket institutions in ten 'coordinated market economies': Austria, Belgium, Denmark, Finland, Germany, Japan, The Netherlands, Norway, Sweden, and Switzerland. These two labels are somewhat misleading. Hall and Soskice make it clear that economic processes are coordinated in both groups. The difference lies in the type of institutions doing the coordinating. A more accurate (if perhaps less elegant) set of labels would be 'market-coordinated economies' and 'non-market-coordinated economies'. France and Italy – also Greece, Portugal, Spain, and Turkey – are 'in more ambiguous positions' (Hall and Soskice 2001: 21). They do not fit into either group.

Hall and Soskice are not, of course, the first to assert that the institutional frameworks of affluent OECD nations consist of two principal types. Predecessors include Albert's (1993) notion of a 'Rhine model' of organized capitalism versus Anglo-Saxon free-market capitalism, Crouch and Streeck's (1997) reference to 'institutional capitalism' versus market-oriented capitalism, and Rueda and Pontusson's (2000) distinction between 'social market economies' and 'liberal market economies'. The Hall–Soskice formulation, however, is the most clearly specified.[1]

Hall and Soskice, and others who have used the varieties of capitalism approach, tend to be interested in it mainly as an explanatory device (rather than for merely descriptive purposes). That is my interest as well. Taken as an assertion of categorical difference, the varieties of capitalism perspective predicts that institutions, policies, or shocks will have different effects in the two groups of countries. A standard way to test this hypothesis in quantitative analysis is to interact a dichotomous 'coordination regime' variable with one or more other independent variables of interest. To my knowledge, only a few such tests have been conducted. Rueda and Pontusson (2000) find that the effect of wage-setting centralization on earnings inequality is more pronounced in social market economies than in liberal market economies. Kenworthy (2003) finds that the effect of earnings inequality on private-sector service employment growth is stronger in liberal market economies than in coordinated market economies. In a qualitative analysis, Thelen (2001) finds that globalization and heightened competition have had different effects on developments in labour relations in Germany, Sweden, and Italy than in the United Kingdom and the United States.

However, my aim in this paper is not to assess the merits of the Hall–Soskice classification. Instead, I want to suggest that the varieties of capitalism perspective also is in the camp of comparative political economy research that focuses on variation in degree – rather than in kind – across countries. With respect to performance outcomes, the key claim made by Hall and Soskice (2001) is not that there are two fundamentally distinct groups of countries, but rather that *successful macroeconomic performance is a function of institutional coherence*: 'When firms coordinate effectively, their performance will be better, and the result will be better overall economic performance' (Hall and Soskice 2001: 45).[2]

Hall and Soskice assert that institutional coherence, and thus effective coordination, can exist in both coordinated market economies and liberal market economies. Indeed, they refer to both Germany and the United States as examples of political economies that are highly coherent (Hall and Soskice 2001: 21–33). Both non-market-oriented and market-oriented institutions can work well, in this view, provided they are coupled with complementary institutions in other spheres: 'Although each type of capitalism has its partisans, we are not arguing here that one is superior to another. Despite some variation over specific periods, both liberal and coordinated market economies seem capable of providing satisfactory levels of long-run economic performance' (Hall and Soskice 2001: 21). Thus, for economic performance outcomes the decisive question for national economies is not 'Which group are you in?' but rather 'How coherent are your institutions?'.

Note that 'coherence' applies both within and across economic spheres. A country's institutional mix is deemed more coherent, and thus better coordinated, to the extent that (a) its institutions within each sphere are closer to one or the other of the two poles (liberal market or coordinated market) rather than in between and (b) its institutions are consistent across spheres. Incoherence can be a product either of being in the middle within each sphere or of having liberal market institutions in some spheres and coordinated market institutions in others.

There are several precedents in the comparative political economy literature for the notion that coherence affects national economic performance. Perhaps the best-known is Lange and Garrett's (1985) argument about the interaction between labour strength and government partisanship. Lange and Garrett suggested that strong unions and wage centralization generate rapid economic growth when coupled with leftist government, and that weak unions and decentralized wage-setting also generate fast growth when coupled with rightist government. 'Incoherent' arrangements – strong labour with rightist government, weak labour with leftist government – were predicted to yield slower growth. In contrast, the typical assertion, and empirical finding, in comparative political economy research has been that the effects of the particular institution (or group of institutions) of interest are linear. Thus, more corporatism, Left government, or central bank independence is thought to be better for rapid growth, low unemployment, or low inflation. And intermediate levels are presumed to be better than low levels.

3. MEASURING INSTITUTIONAL COHERENCE

To test the Hall–Soskice hypothesis, we need a measure of institutional coherence. In a recent paper that considerably advances empirical assessment of the varieties of capitalism perspective, Hall and Gingerich (2004) provide such a measure. They develop a 'coordination index' that attempts to gauge the degree to which countries rely on non-market economic institutions. (This label too is somewhat misleading; it would be better labeled a 'non-market coordination index' or 'strategic coordination index'.) The index is created via factor analysis of six indicators, each measured as of the early- or mid-1990s (Hall and Gingerich 2004: 11): (a) shareholder power ('legal protection and likely influence over firms of ordinary shareholders relative to managers or dominant shareholders'); (b) dispersion of control ('how many firms in the country are widely held relative to the number with controlling shareholders'); (c) size of the stock market ('market valuation of equities on the stock exchanges of a nation as a percentage of its gross domestic product'); (d) level of wage coordination ('level at which unions normally coordinate wage claims and employers coordinate wage offers'); (e) degree of wage coordination ('degree to which wage bargaining is (strategically) coordinated by unions and employers'); (f) labour turnover ('number of employees who had held their jobs for less than one year as a percentage of all employees'). The factor analysis yielded a single factor, which is highly correlated with each of these six indicators.

The country scores are shown here in Table 5.1. They are the factor scores, adjusted to vary between zero and one. Countries with a high or low score are those deemed to have the most coherent institutional framework. Hall and Gingerich enter this variable into economic growth regressions in curvilinear form—the variable itself and its square. They predict, and find, faster rates of growth over the period 1971–97 in countries with high or low levels of the variable (Hall and Gingerich 2004: 22–9).

Hall and Gingerich's attempt to utilize 'hard' indicators in measuring institutional coherence is laudable, as it reduces the influence of subjective judgement. And their factor analysis suggests strongly that types of corporate governance arrangements and industrial relations systems do tend to cohere in a number of countries (see also Höpner 2005). However, as a measure of institutional coherence their coordination index has several problematic features. One is that the six indicators are measured as of 1990–95, creating a potential time-ordering problem (the effect precedes the cause) in attempting to explain performance outcomes over the past several decades. More important, the six indicators used in the factor analysis cover only three of the

Table 5.1. Indexes of coordination/cooperation

Hall–Gingerich coordination index, 1990–95		Hicks–Kenworthy cooperation index, 1960–89	
Austria	1.00	Japan	0.82
Germany	0.95	Norway	0.75
Italy	0.87	Sweden	0.74
Norway	0.76	Austria	0.70
Belgium	0.74	Finland	0.68
Japan	0.74	Germany	0.66
Finland	0.72	Denmark	0.58
Denmark	0.70	Belgium	0.56
France	0.69	Switzerland	0.44
Sweden	0.69	The Netherlands	0.43
The Netherlands	0.66	Italy	0.42
Switzerland	0.51	France	0.28
Australia	0.36	Australia	0.14
Ireland	0.29	New Zealand	0.13
New Zealand	0.21	United Kingdom	0.10
Canada	0.13	Ireland	0.08
United Kingdom	0.07	United States	0.07
United States	0.00	Canada	0.06

Note: For data definitions and sources, see the Appendix section.

five spheres highlighted by Hall and Soskice (2001). The first three of Hall and Gingerich's indicators focus on corporate governance, the fourth and fifth on industrial relations, and the sixth on relations with employees. Two of the five Hall–Soskice spheres, vocational training/education and inter-firm relations, are not represented at all. And one of the five spheres, corporate governance, accounts for half of the six indicators. It is quite possible that, across countries, institutions in the other two spheres are relatively closely correlated with those in the spheres of corporate governance and industrial relations/wage-setting. If that is the case, the Hall–Gingerich index may be fairly accurate. Yet there certainly is room for skepticism.

Although the coordination index arrays countries more or less as the Hall–Soskice dichotomous classification would lead us to expect, there are several surprises. One is that Japan, which is frequently cited as an example of a highly coherent non-market-coordinated economy (e.g. Aoki 1988; Dore 1997), scores in the middle of the pack among the 'high coordination' countries. Another is that Italy and (to a lesser extent) France have relatively high scores. These two countries are classified as 'ambiguous' by Hall and Soskice (2001: 21), which suggests that their scores ought to be in the middle.

For purposes of comparison, I also include in Table 5.1 a 'cooperation index' calculated from data in Hicks and Kenworthy (1998). This is based on a scoring of the degree of cooperation in nine spheres: (a) relations among firms across industries; (b) relations among unions; (c) relations between the state and interest groups; (d) relations among firms and investors; (e) relations among firms and suppliers; (f) relations among competing firms; (g) relations between labour and management; (h) relations among workers; and (i) relations among functional departments within firms. For each sphere, in each year from 1960 to 1989, each nation was scored 0, 0.5, or 1 – representing weak, moderate, and strong cooperation, respectively. The scores were then averaged to form the index, which ranges from 0 to 1. These scores are subjective. They were created based on the authors' reading of secondary and primary sources.

The Hall–Gingerich and Hicks–Kenworthy indexes are relatively consistent with one another. Indeed, they correlate at 0.85. Among the Hall–Soskice coordinated market economies (what I refer to here as non-market-coordinated economies), the main differences are that Japan and Sweden score higher and Germany and Austria score lower on the Hicks–Kenworthy index than on the Hall–Gingerich index. Italy (and to a lesser degree France) scores in the middle on the Hicks–Kenworthy index, which is more consistent with the assessment of Hall and Soskice (2001: 21).

An alternative is to take a 'softer' – more subjective – approach to measuring institutional coherence. Doing so reduces the reliability of the measure, but may heighten its validity. I attempt to create a simple ranked grouping of countries in terms of their degree of institutional coherence. Because of the paucity of hard data and the lack of clarity regarding how to weight various indicators that do exist, I use just three groups: high coherence, intermediate coherence, and low coherence.

I focus on the five spheres identified by Hall and Soskice (2001) as critical in differentiating modern political economies. Other spheres could be added – for example, relations between divisions/departments within firms and relations between firms and the government. But the Hall–Soskice five are, in my view, reasonable enough. Like Hall and Gingerich (2004), I ignore changes in the degree of coherence within countries over time and focus on differences across countries. In order to make this simplification justifiable, I focus on the period since the mid-1970s. I include 18 OECD countries (abbreviations listed in parentheses): Australia (Asl), Austria (Aus), Belgium (Bel), Canada (Can), Denmark (Den), Finland (Fin), France (Fr), Germany (Ger), Ireland (Ire), Italy (It), Japan (Ja), the Netherlands (Nth), New Zealand (NZ), Norway (Nor), Sweden (Swe), Switzerland (Swi), the United Kingdom (UK) and the United States (US).

Table 5.2. Measures of institutional coherence

	Hall–Gingerich institutional coherence index	Kenworthy institutional coherence ranked grouping
Austria	1.00	High
United States	1.00	High
Germany	0.90	High
United Kingdom	0.86	High
Canada	0.74	High
Italy	0.74	Low
New Zealand	0.58	Intermediate
Norway	0.52	High
Belgium	0.48	Intermediate
Japan	0.48	High
Finland	0.44	Intermediate
Ireland	0.42	Low
Denmark	0.40	Intermediate
France	0.38	Low
Sweden	0.38	High
The Netherlands	0.32	Low
Australia	0.28	Intermediate
Switzerland	0.02	Low

Note: For data definitions and sources, see the Appendix section.

Table 5.2 shows two measures of institutional coherence. In the first column is a 'linearized' version of the Hall–Gingerich coordination index: the index is transformed so that more coherent countries have higher scores and less coherent countries have lower scores (see the Appendix section for details). I refer to this as the 'Hall–Gingerich institutional coherence index'.

My ranked grouping is shown in the second column. Surely Germany, Austria, Japan, the United States, and the (post-1979) United Kingdom *Thatcher* should be classified as highly coherent. Most observers would probably add Sweden, Norway, and Canada to this group. The only one of these eight countries that is scored significantly differently on the Hall–Gingerich institutional coherence index is Sweden, which is lower on that index than might have been expected. In contrast, on the Hicks–Kenworthy cooperation index (Table 5.1) Sweden scores near the top, behind only Japan and Norway.

France and Italy seem clearly to belong in the low-coherence group. As noted earlier, Hall and Soskice consider these to be 'ambiguous' cases, and I fully concur. Italy is less coherent than other affluent countries in terms of its deep divisions between north and south, between the formal and informal economies, and between large and small firms. The French economy has been characterized by a unique mix of close and stable relationships, short-term atomistic ties, and heavy-handed government intervention.

I include three other countries in the low-coherence group: the Netherlands, Switzerland, and Ireland. The Netherlands is in certain respects a
paradigmatic coordinated market economy. This applies in particular to its
tradition of relatively coordinated wage setting (formally centralized through
the 1970s, informally centralized since then). Yet investor–firm relationships
and relations among companies and their suppliers have tended to be comparatively short-term and arms-length (van Iterson and Olie 1992: 102–3,
109–10; Kurzer 1993: 50, 122, 146–7). With respect to relations with employees, median job tenure in the Netherlands is closer to the liberal market
economies than to the coordinated market economies (Estevez-Abe et al.,
2001: 170). Switzerland has a high level of wage coordination (Soskice 1990)
and close relationships between firms (Porter 1990: 319–24), but little employment protection and relatively short median job tenure (Blaas 1992: 369;
Estevez-Abe et al., 2001: 165, 170). The Hall–Gingerich institutional coherence
index scores the Netherlands and Switzerland as among the least coherent
countries (Table 5.2).

What about Ireland? In terms of corporate governance and interfirm relations, Ireland is a typical 'liberal market economy'. But beginning in the late
1980s and continuing throughout the 1990s, it has had a highly coordinated
system of wage setting (Baccaro and Simoni 2004). In addition, Ireland has a
higher level of employment protection than other liberal market economies
and longer median job tenure (Estevez-Abe et al., 2001: 165, 168, 170). Why,
then, does Ireland not score lower on the Hall–Gingerich institutional coherence index? The main reason is that the wage coordination indicators used in
Hall and Gingerich's factor analyses do not include the 1990s. One, from
Layard et al. (1991), is based on the 1980s and the other, from the OECD
(1997), provides no score at all for Ireland. Were the extensive Irish wage
coordination during the late 1980s and the 1990s taken into account, Ireland
would almost certainly move down on the Hall–Gingerich institutional coherence index to join Switzerland and the Netherlands at the bottom.

I score the remaining five countries – Belgium, Denmark, Finland, Australia, and New Zealand – as intermediate. The first three are classified by Hall
and Soskice (2001) as coordinated market economies and the latter two as
liberal market economies. However, these countries tend to be less coherent in
their institutional mix than nations such as Japan and the United States.
At the same time, they are less incoherent than France, Ireland, Italy, the
Netherlands, and Switzerland.

Plainly there is room for disagreement about the assignment of particular
countries. Yet I believe the ranked grouping shown in Table 5.2 is the one
most consistent with the discussion in Hall and Soskice (2001), with the
Hall–Gingerich (2004) and Hicks–Kenworthy (1998) indexes, and with my

reading of the comparative and case study literatures. The measurement approach pursued by Hall and Gingerich has considerable merit, in that they rely mainly on 'hard' indicators. This seems to me, however, to come at potentially considerable cost in terms of validity. One of the five spheres emphasized by Hall and Soskice, corporate governance, accounts for half of the indicators used to create the Hall–Gingerich factor analytical index; and two of the five Hall–Soskice spheres are not represented at all. Of course, there is no perfectly accurate measure of institutional coherence. But given the limited available data and the lack of clarity regarding how to properly weight indicators that do exist, a ranked grouping along the lines of that in Table 5.2 may be preferable.

4. THE IMPACT OF INSTITUTIONAL COHERENCE ON MACROECONOMIC PERFORMANCE

The three most common measures of macroeconomic performance are economic growth, employment (or unemployment), and inflation. Owing to financial globalization and the requirements for European monetary integration, there was relatively little cross-country variation in inflation rates in the 1990s. I therefore focus on growth and employment.

Economic growth can be measured in various ways, including growth of real gross domestic product (GDP), growth of real GDP per capita, and growth of real GDP per employed person. Hall and Gingerich use growth of nominal GDP per capita, but they control for inflation in their regressions, so in effect their measure is the second: growth of real GDP per capita. I focus on the third: growth of real GDP per employed person. Commonly referred to as 'productivity growth', it is perhaps the best macro-level indicator of efficiency. I also show (in Table 5.3) results for growth of real GDP per capita, which do not differ substantially.

Employment is measured as employed persons as a share of the population aged 15–64. I focus on growth of employment.

I examine the post-'golden age' period of 1974–2000. This covers three complete business cycles – 1974–79, 1980–89, and 1990–2000—which I also examine separately to see if there have been period-specific patterns. For the full 1974–2000 period I show the data in scatterplot form, in Figures 5.1–5.4. I also present regression results in Table 5.3. For the subperiods I show only the regression results. Scatterplots for the subperiods are available at www.u.arizona.edu/~lkenwor, as are all of the data used in the analyses.

Table 5.3. Regression results: estimated impact of institutional coherence on productivity growth, per capita GDP growth, and employment growth

	Hall–Gingerich institutional coherence index		Kenworthy institutional coherence ranked grouping	
	Coefficient	R^2	Coefficient	R^2
Economic growth				
Productivity growth				
1974–2000	0.15	0.00	0.01	0.00
1974–79	0.31	0.00	−0.35	0.01
1980–89	0.32	0.01	0.08	0.00
1990–2000	−0.15	0.00	0.09	0.00
Catch-up-adjusted productivity growth				
1974–2000	0.38	0.05	−0.18	0.03
1974–79	0.52	0.02	−0.51	0.04
1980–89	0.69	0.07	−0.15	0.01
1990–2000	0.23	0.01	−0.03	0.00
Per capita GDP growth				
1974–2000	0.42	0.02	−0.01	0.00
1974–79	1.56	0.12	0.53	0.03
1980–89	0.07	0.00	0.21	0.03
1990–2000	0.12	0.00	−0.49	0.03
Catch-up-adjusted per capita GDP growth				
1974–2000	−0.05	0.00	−0.02	0.00
1974–79	0.98	0.08	0.51	0.05
1980–89	0.03	0.00	0.27	0.05
1990–2000	0.05	0.00	−0.11	0.00
Employment growth				
Employment growth				
1974–2000	0.03	0.00	0.06	0.00
1974–79	0.97	0.12	0.94	0.28
1980–89	−0.28	0.02	0.26	0.03
1990–2000	−0.20	0.01	−0.71	0.05
Catch-up-adjusted employment growth				
1974–2000	−0.10	0.01	0.08	0.01
1974–79	0.91	0.10	0.97	0.02
1980–89	−0.20	0.01	0.10	0.01
1990–2000	−0.50	0.07	−0.24	0.04

Note: Unstandardized coefficients from bivariate OLS regressions. Both of the institutional coherence measures range from zero to one. For data definitions and sources, see the Appendix section.

Figure 5.1 shows two scatterplots, each with the average rate of productivity growth over 1974–2000 on the vertical axis and a measure of institutional coherence (from Table 5.2) on the horizontal axis. The first chart uses the Hall–Gingerich institutional coherence index. The institutional coherence hypothesis predicts a positive relationship: productivity growth should be higher in countries scoring high on the index. But there is no indication of a

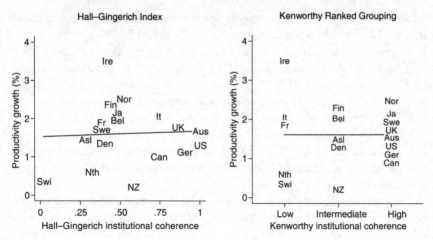

Figure 5.1. Institutional coherence and productivity growth, 1974–2000

Note: For data definitions and sources, see the Appendix section.

positive association. The regression line is essentially flat. And as reported in Table 5.3, the R^2 is 0.00. The second chart in Figure 5.1 substitutes my institutional coherence ranked grouping for the Hall–Gingerich index. Again there is no association. The regression coefficients in Table 5.3 indicate that in the 1974–79 period productivity growth is positively associated with the Hall–Gingerich measure but negatively associated with my measure. However, these associations are quite weak.

Hall and Gingerich's (2004) analysis is based on annual data rather than period averages. There are two advantages to using yearly data. One is that it permits a control for 'fixed effects' ('unobserved heterogeneity') – stable country-specific factors, such as culture or geography, which may be correlated with the independent variable of interest. But the fixed effects concern is that an apparent relationship between an independent variable and the outcome may be spurious. This is an issue only if the analyses do suggest a relationship between the independent variable and the outcome. The patterns in Figure 5.1 do not suggest a relationship, so there is no particular reason to worry about the lack of control for fixed effects.

The second advantage to yearly data is that it greatly increases the number of observations, allowing use of a larger number of control variables. Here, however, the number of observations is not a critical factor. Hall and Gingerich include five control variables in their regressions. Two of them – inflation and the share of the population younger than age 15 and older than age 64 – are unnecessary if we measure growth as change in real (inflation-adjusted) GDP per employed person. Their third control is the average growth rate among the group of countries as a whole weighted by the degree of trade openness in each nation. In an analysis with yearly data this is useful in order to control for business cycle effects, but it is unnecessary in an analysis that examines periods that correspond to business cycles. The fourth control variable is change in each country's terms of trade (export prices divided by import prices), weighted by the country's degree of trade openness. The expectation is that favourable price developments boost growth. However, this variable has the 'wrong' sign in almost all of the Hall–Gingerich regressions. The same was true in regressions I tried, and the variable's inclusion had no impact on the results for the institutional coherence measures (not shown here). Hence, this control seems unnecessary.

The fifth control variable used by Hall and Gingerich is each country's level of economic output in the initial year. Among the rich OECD nations there has been a strong 'catch-up' process operating since the Second World War, whereby less affluent nations tend to grow faster than richer ones because the former are able to benefit from technological developments and larger markets in the latter (Baumol et al., 1994). Thus, for instance, Ireland stands out in the charts in Figure 5.1 as having had by far the fastest productivity growth, but that could be due to the fact that as of the mid-1970s it was by far the poorest of these countries. Why might this affect the association between institutional coherence and productivity growth? Cross-country differences in institutional coherence have persisted over long periods of time; those with greater coherence today may also have had greater coherence half a century ago. If so, and if institutional coherence has in fact contributed to faster productivity growth, countries with greater institutional coherence may have had higher levels of productivity entering the 1970s than countries with less coherent institutions. The catch-up effect would permit countries with less institutional coherence and, therefore, lower 'initial' productivity levels to enjoy faster productivity growth during the ensuing decades than their level of institutional coherence would otherwise make possible. This catch-up boost might offset their otherwise less rapid growth rates, making it appear in the raw data as though institutional coherence had no impact on productivity growth.

Figure 5.2 shows another set of scatterplots with institutional coherence on the horizontal axis, but now the vertical axis measure is productivity growth adjusted for catch-up effects. The vertical-axis data are residuals from regressions of productivity growth on initial year level of productivity. (For the 1974–2000 period overall and for each business cycle the regression coefficient for the initial year level is negative and substantively strong, suggesting that catch-up effects were relevant.) The first chart uses the Hall–Gingerich index. Here there is some indication of the predicted positive relationship between institutional coherence and productivity growth. The magnitude of the estimated effect,

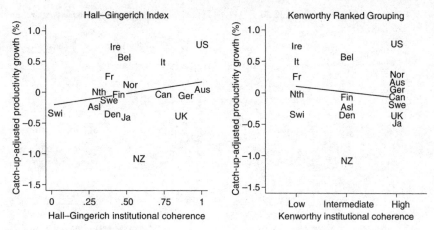

Figure 5.2. Institutional coherence and catch-up-adjusted productivity growth, 1974–2000

Note: For data definitions and sources, see the Appendix section.

while by no means large, is not inconsequential. In a regression of catch-up-adjusted productivity growth on the Hall–Gingerich institutional coherence index, the regression coefficient is 0.38 (Table 5.3), suggesting that, on average, a county scoring one on the index enjoyed a rate of productivity growth about four-tenths of a percentage point faster than a country scoring zero on the index. Over a long enough period of time this seemingly small difference can matter. In a country with an annual growth rate of 1.6 per cent, productivity will double in 45 years, whereas with a growth rate of 2.0 per cent it will double in 36 years. However, the association is confined to the 1970s and 1980s. More important, it is heavily dependent on the US case: if the United States is omitted, the regression coefficient drops to just 0.09 and the R^2 is 0.00 (not shown here).

The second chart in Figure 5.2 replaces the Hall–Gingerich institutional coherence index with my ranked grouping. Here there is no positive relationship. This is a product of the different scoring of particular countries. Several countries that had not-so-high rates of catch-up-adjusted productivity growth, such as Sweden and Japan, are scored intermediate on the Hall–Gingerich measure but high on my measure. And several countries that had comparatively high rates of catch-up-adjusted productivity growth, such as Ireland and Italy, are scored intermediate on the Hall–Gingerich measure but low on my measure. I leave it to others to decide which of the two measures of institutional coherence is preferable. The point is simply that the conclusion that institutional coherence is good for economic growth appears to hinge not only on the years examined and on the inclusion of the United States but also on the coding of particular countries.

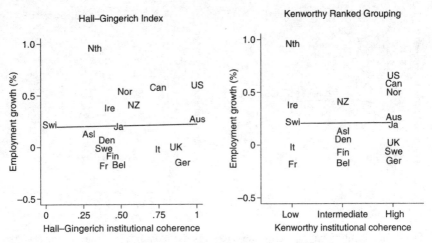

Figure 5.3. Institutional coherence and employment growth, 1974–2000

Note: For data definitions and sources, see the Appendix section.

Figure 5.3 performs the same exercise for employment growth. The first chart shows the average annual rate of growth in employment over 1974–2000 by the Hall–Gingerich institutional coherence index. Again the institutional coherence hypothesis predicts a positive relationship, but again it finds no support. As the regression coefficients in Table 5.3 indicate, in the 1974–79 period we do see the expected pattern. But the fit is poor: the R^2 for a regression of 1974–79 employment growth on the institutional coherence index is just 0.12, and it drops to 0.03 if Switzerland is removed (not shown here).

In the second chart in Figure 5.3 the Hall–Gingerich institutional coherence measure is replaced with my measure. Again there is no indication of an association in either direction. The regression coefficients reported in Table 5.3 suggest evidence of a positive association in the 1974–79 period, and here that association does not hinge on Switzerland's inclusion. However, this positive effect appears to have been offset by a similarly strong negative association between coherence and employment growth in the 1990–2000 period.

In Figure 5.4 employment growth is adjusted for initial levels of employment, since countries that began with low employment rates may have found it easier to achieve increases. This produces very little change in the patterns for either the Hall–Gingerich institutional coherence measure or my institutional coherence measure. The regression lines in the charts (and the coefficients in Table 5.3) suggest a possible negative relationship for the Hall–Gingerich measure and a possible positive relationship for my measure, but these associations, if genuine, are extremely weak.

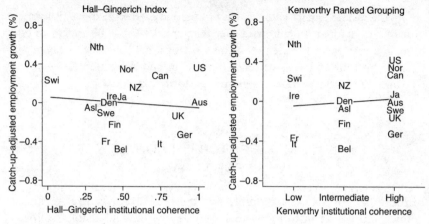

Figure 5.4. Institutional coherence and catch-up-adjusted employment growth, 1974–2000

Note: For data definitions and sources, see the Appendix section.

Aside from the initial level of productivity or employment, there are additional factors that should perhaps be controlled for in analyses of productivity growth and employment growth. But a number of them would be considered endogenous in the varieties of capitalism approach. For instance, educational attainment among the working-age population could well influence productivity growth, but in the varieties of capitalism framework this is likely to be affected by the type of economic coordination in the country: coordinated market economies tend to rely more on firm-specific skills acquired through on-the-job training, whereas liberal market economies rely more on general skills acquired through the school system (Hall and Soskice 2001). Employment protection regulations and the generosity of the unemployment benefit system may influence employment growth, but these too are expected to be a function of the type of coordination (Estevez-Abe et al., 2001).

I estimated a series of regressions with various combinations of four control variables that seem less likely to be endogenous and potentially likely to alter the association between institutional coherence and productivity growth or employment growth: trade-adjusted changes in terms of trade (discussed earlier), real interest rates, tax revenues (as a share of GDP) and left government. However, none of these variables is correlated with the Hall–Gingerich institutional coherence index ($r = 0.00, 0.10, -0.08, -0.17$ over 1974–2000), with my institutional coherence measure ($r = 0.14, 0.09, -0.01, 0.11$ over 1974–2000), or with the two macroeconomic performance measures. Hence, controlling for them did not substantively alter the regression results for either of the institutional coherence variables (not shown here; available on request).

On the whole, then, patterns of productivity growth and employment growth among these 18 countries over the period 1974–2000 appear to offer little, if any, support for the notion that institutional coherence – as conceptualized by Hall and Soskice (2001) and Hall and Gingerich (2004) – has contributed to healthy macroeconomic performance.[3]

5. FUTURE RESEARCH ON COHERENCE AND PERFORMANCE

Institutional coherence is certainly not the first broad, general feature of political–economic institutions to be posited as influential for macroeconomic performance outcomes in the world's most affluent countries. Others include free markets (Hayek 1960; Friedman 1962), distributional coalitions (Olson 1982), corporatism (Cameron 1984; Katzenstein 1985), flexible specialization (Piore and Sabel 1984), competition (Porter 1990), social capital (Putnam 1993), cooperation (Kenworthy 1995; Hicks and Kenworthy 1998) and policy coherence (Wilensky 2002), to mention but a few. However, there is reason to be skeptical about the veracity of empirical findings that appear to support linkages between aggregated concepts such as these and aggregated outcomes such as growth, employment, and inflation. Assessing such claims requires clear specification and testing of the purported causal mechanisms (Elster 1989: ch. 1; Hedström and Swedberg 1996; Goldthorpe 2001). Finding associations may or may not tell us something interesting. I am not suggesting that aggregate analyses are useless, but rather that they should be considered only a preliminary, partial step in the investigation of causal linkages.

This might be a useful route for further research on the influence of institutional coherence. If institutional coherence is good for macroeconomic performance, how exactly does the causal process work? Hall and Soskice (2001: 45) suggest that 'when firms coordinate effectively, their performance will be better'. Does this mean those firms will have higher productivity? If so, that presumably can be tested, at least for firms in certain sectors.[4] The evidence reviewed here suggests no aggregate-level association between coherence and successful macroeconomic performance. Yet if the causal pathways were investigated, it might turn out that there is a beneficial effect. Such an effect could be hidden in the analyses here due to the impact of some additional variable for which I have not controlled. Or it could be that institutional coherence has both positive and negative effects on productivity or employment, which offset each other.

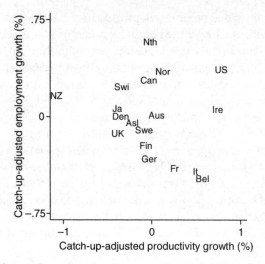

Figure 5.5. Catch-up-adjusted productivity growth and catch-up-adjusted employment growth, 1974–2000

Note: For data definitions and sources, see the Appendix section.

Another potentially fruitful avenue for empirical evaluation of the institutional coherence hypothesis is exploration of the US case. Notwithstanding its post-1999 stock market and employment declines, the American economy has experienced comparatively strong macroeconomic performance over the past several decades. Figure 5.5 shows rates of catch-up-adjusted productivity growth and catch-up-adjusted employment growth over 1974–2000. On the combination of these two measures, the position of the United States in the chart suggests that it had the best performance record among the 18 countries. (The United States also features well-known distributional maladies such as high poverty and inequality.) We lack a convincing account of recent US macroeconomic success. A host of factors surely have contributed, among them effective countercyclical monetary policy, robust demand owing to growing personal indebtedness along with the real estate and stock market booms, and first-mover advantages in various information technology industries. Advocates of the institutional coherence approach might emphasize growing marketization of the American economy since the late 1970s – most notably, deregulation of various industries, weakening of unions and reduced commitment to job security. As Hall and Soskice (2001: 49) suggest, 'because of the bluntness of the instruments available to states and the importance of markets to these economies, deregulation is often the most effective way to improve coordination in LMEs [liberal market economies]'.

Yet at the same time, other developments in the US economy during this period seemingly have heightened the importance of non-market institutional coordination. Many of these developments stem from the influence of Japanese practices on American management strategy in the 1980s and 1990s. They include greater reliance on stable long-term relationships between firms and suppliers, research and development alliances among competitors, and participatory work teams and multidivisional research-design-production teams within firms. Various accounts attribute some of the recent success of the US economy to these developments (e.g. Angel 1994; Applebaum and Batt 1994; Waterman 1994; Hollingsworth 1997). How does this fit in with the institutional coherence perspective? Are these developments in fact consistent with the accentuation of market-oriented coordination in the US economy? Are they of little or no relevance in explaining recent US macroeconomic success? Or is institutional coherence perhaps not so critical to that success?

NOTES

1. As always, questions can be raised about the classification of particular countries: Should the Nordic and/or Mediterranean countries be separated from those of northern continental Europe? Should Japan be distinguished from the European coordinated market economies? Should Australia and/or New Zealand be separated from other liberal market economies? See, e.g. Amable 2003.
2. In the terminology suggested by Höpner (2005), this is a claim that institutional coherence increases the benefits from institutional complementarity.
3. One other attempt to assess the impact of institutional coherence on economic performance outcomes is by Amable (2003: 213–24). Like Hall and Gingerich, Amable uses factor analysis to create country scores for the degree of non-market coordination in various economic spheres (product markets, the wage–labour nexus, financial systems, social protection, and education). Rather than using these coordination scores to create a measure of overall institutional coherence, Amable regresses macroeconomic performance indicators (economic growth, productivity growth, and unemployment) on interactions between the measures of sphere-specific coordination. He finds that some of these interactions have the expected positive sign, suggesting for instance that economic growth has been more rapid in countries in which product market regulation and labour market regulation are either both high or both low. However, it is not clear why we should expect only coherence between some spheres, rather than across all spheres, to boost macroeconomic performance. If overall coherence is what is predicted to matter, then the hypothesis is best tested using a measure of the overall degree of coherence, as in Hall and Gingerich (2004).

4. Ernst (2002) examines industry performance in three 'high-coherence' countries (Germany, Japan and the United States), but does not analyse differences across countries that have varying degrees of institutional coherence.

APPENDIX: VARIABLE DESCRIPTIONS
AND DATA SOURCES

Catch-up-adjusted employment growth. Residuals from a regression of employment growth on level of employment in the period's initial year.

Catch-up-adjusted productivity growth. Residuals from a regression of productivity growth on level of productivity in the period's initial year.

Employment growth. Average annual rate of change in employed persons as a share of the population aged 15–64. *Source:* Author's calculations from data in OECD (2004*a*).

Hall–Gingerich coordination index. Factor scores, adjusted to vary from zero to one, from a factor analysis of six indicators (see the text). Measured as of 1990–95. *Source:* Hall and Gingerich (2004: Table 2, p. 14).

Hall–Gingerich institutional coherence index. 'Linearized' version of the Hall–Gingerich coordination index. Calculated as follows: (absolute value of (0.50 minus the Hall–Gingerich coordination index score)) divided by 0.50. Ranges from zero to one.

Hicks–Kenworthy cooperation index. Average of scores on nine indicators of economic cooperation (see the text). Measured over 1960–89. *Source:* Hicks and Kenworthy (1998: Table 3, pp. 1642–3).

Kenworthy institutional coherence ranked grouping. See text and Table 2. Three categories: low coherence, intermediate coherence and high coherence. Scored as 0, 0.5 and 1 when used in regressions.

Left government. Left party cabinet portfolios as a share of all cabinet portfolios. *Source:* Author's calculations from data in Swank (2002, variable: LEFTC).

Per capita GDP growth. Average annual rate of change in inflation-adjusted gross domestic product per person. *Source:* Author's calculations from data in OECD (2004*b*).

Productivity growth. Average annual rate of change in inflation-adjusted gross domestic product per employed person. *Source:* Author's calculations from real GDP and consumer price data in OECD (2004*b*) and employment data in OECD (2004*a*).

Real long-term interest rates. Yield on long-term government bonds adjusted for inflation. *Source:* Author's calculations from data in OECD (2004*b*).

Tax revenues. Government tax revenues as a share of GDP. *Source:* Author's calculations from data in OECD (2004*c*: Table 3, pp. 67–8).

Trade-adjusted change in terms of trade. Average annual rate of change in the ratio of export prices to import prices, multiplied by exports plus imports as a proportion of GDP. *Source:* Author's calculations from data in OECD (2004*b*).

6

Can High-Technology Industries Prosper in Germany? Institutional Frameworks and the Evolution of the German Software and Biotechnology Industries

Steven Casper, Mark Lehrer, and David Soskice

The national institutional framework of the US economy has proven favourable to the expansion of high-technology industries. Since the early 1980s, the US political economy has evolved to support a dramatic expansion in biotechnology, software, and a variety of other fast-moving, high-tech activities with close links to basic science. In particular, the institutional framework of the US has evolved to provide large amounts of venture capital to high-risk start-up companies, to encourage new links between university scientists and companies, and to encourage, or at least not hinder, the reorganization of large companies for exploiting commercial opportunities in high-tech. In Germany firms and policy-makers are anxiously experimenting with their own institutional structures in an attempt to better support science-based high-tech innovation in their own country. This paper explores the influence of German institutional frameworks on the evolution of two of the most important 'new' industries, software and biotechnology.

German institutional patterns have long been thought to support the nation's comparative advantages in a range of medium-tech industries, typically complex process-oriented manufacturing industries. We review patent data on industry specialization for the years 1983–84 and 1993–94 from the European Patent Office (EPO) for Germany and the United States. These data reveal that Germany has tended to specialize in well-established but relatively complex products, involving complex production processes and extensive after-sales services with close, long-term customer links. These industries (machine tools, engineering elements, engines, materials processing, and so forth) clearly involve a lot of engineering and are characterized by a rather moderate rate of technological change and innovation. Germany does not patent extensively in many of the faster-paced, more radically innovative technologies such as biotechnology, telecommunications, or information technology. Firms located in the United States, by contrast, have developed a close to inversely related patenting profile, specializing heavily in a range of high-tech industries (biotechnology, information technology, telecommunications) but less in the spectrum of process and engineering industries dominated by German firms. These data further reveal a surprising intensification of this pattern during the 1990s; in virtually every category where German or US firms demonstrated a greater level of relative patenting specialization during 1983–84, this level of relative specialization had increased by 1993–94.

The German pattern of industry specialization has long been associated with a range of economic, social, and political institutions that favour what Streeck (1992) calls 'diversified quality production' (DQP). Notwithstanding the German post-war 'economic miracle' and the country's above-average economic performance during the shocks of the 1970s and 1980s (see Carlin and Soskice 1997), growing pessimism surrounds the German institutional model in the 1990s. Lack of national success in high-technology industries has been a major source of concern for German policy-makers. Seemingly squeezed by American competition in high-tech on the one hand and East Asian competition in traditional manufacturing industries on the other, many critics now see little room for traditional German product market strategies emphasizing incremental innovation in established technologies. Long standing institutions and policies for promoting innovation have come under attack. Critics argue that 'imitate and improve' innovation strategies are no longer adequate given shorter product life cycles (Jürgens and Naschold 1994). Streeck, long a leading proponent of the German model, now sees the declining relative importance of niche markets in manufacturing as an exacerbating factor in the 'exhaustion' of the German model (Streeck 1996).

Over the last two years Germany's 'innovation crisis' has spilled over into the public policy debate. The president of the German federation of industry (BDI) Henkel has repeatedly stated that 'nobody wants our model anymore' and called for a radical reworking of German company law and a deregulation of labour markets (*Die Zeit* 1997). While few political leaders on either the Left or the Right echo this sentiment, promoting high-technology innovation has emerged as a prominent theme in German policy debates. During its last years in power the Kohl government instigated a range of new technology policies aimed at promoting high-tech industries. In addition, substantial financial subsidies for many high-tech start-ups and new framework policies to support particular sectors have been developed at both the federal and state

(*Länder*) levels of government. The new German government pays at least lip service to high-tech and, if anything, programmes to bolster German high-technology will expand in future years.

German academics and policy-makers are increasingly dissatisfied with the country's narrow base of industrial strength, yet the patent data indicate that the country's traditional pattern of specialization has actually intensified during the 1990s. One goal of this chapter is to better explicate the process by which national social and economic institutions favour particular innovation strategies in Germany. We argue that Germany's pattern of industry specialization continues to be strongly influenced by an interlocking complex of national institutional patterns. Scholars working in the area of national innovation systems and comparative political economy have long suggested that differing institutional frameworks across countries contribute to cross-national variation in industrial organization, with implications for the ways in which different countries pursue innovation. We examine the impact of German institutions on developments in the areas of software and biotechnology, two of the most important high-technology industries that have been considered to be at a particular disadvantage due to unfavourable institutional conditions in Germany. Our analysis is structured in two parts. We first provide a general overview of the German institutional framework and its overall impact on patterns of commercial innovation in Germany. We then apply this theoretical lens to emerging patterns of commercial activity in German software and biotechnology.

To anticipate one of our key findings, our research in both software and biotechnology found that a multitude of different market niches are emerging in both industries. While German firms continue to be relatively unsuccessful in areas of these industries characterized by extreme financial risk and volatile technological trajectories, in other market segments German firms have prospered in recent years. We provide evidence suggesting that the types of company organizational structures and investment strategies needed to excel in these segments provide a close 'fit' with the incentives created by the German political economy. In fact, our analysis leads to the prediction that, in at least some segments of high-tech, German firms will develop comparative advantages in solving certain organizational and financial problems that are crucial to success. We suggest that while government policies in Germany are unlikely to alter the country's general pattern of industry specialization, framework policies can expedite the process by which German firms identify and enter favourable market segments within high-technology industries.

1. NATIONAL INSTITUTIONAL FRAMEWORKS AND NATIONAL SYSTEMS OF INNOVATION

The theoretical approach adopted here seeks institutional explanations of why incentive structures to undertake innovation differ across economies (see Soskice 1994). To innovate successfully, the management of companies must create and sustain relationships with a number of different groups: workers, technicians and scientists, owners, providers of finance, and other companies. The technologies needed to innovate rarely consist of specialized machines or codified knowledge that can simply be delivered to the doorstep of any organization and then 'turned on'. Rather, most technologies are dispersed across highly skilled experts embedded within complex organizational structures. Innovative capacity usually consists of tacit knowledge spread over networks of managers, scientists, and skilled workers acting within an institutionally structured environment (which often arches across several discrete firms, or, in science-based industries, firms and public research institutes). National institutional frameworks play a strong role by, among other things, influencing the relative cost of building the organizational competencies needed to pursue particular innovation strategies.

We begin by providing thumbnail sketches of institutional differences between Germany and the United States and then explain how the differing patterns of employment and ownership relations that evolve in relation to these institutions favour the innovation patterns commonly associated with each country.

Germany may be characterized as a 'coordinated market economy' (Soskice 1994) underpinned by a regulatory private law system. German business is organized in nature, primarily due to the embeddedness of large firms within networks of powerful trade and industry associations, as well as a similar, often legally mandated, organization of labour and other interest organizations within para-public institutions (Katzenstein 1987, 1989). Businesses engage these associations to solve a variety of incomplete contracting dilemmas and create important non-market collective goods. To discourage individual companies from exiting the collective business system, German public policy can rely on the legal system to regulate a wide variety of inter-firm and labour contracts as well as sustain neo-corporatist bargaining environments through the delegation of issue–area specific bargaining rights to unions and other stakeholders within firms. German courts use standardized business agreements produced through neo-corporatist arrangements as the basis to apply regulatory corporate laws throughout the broader economy.

Table 6.1. Institutional framework architectures in Germany and the United States

	Germany	United States
Labour law	Regulative (coordinated system of wage bargaining; competition clauses enforced); bias towards long-term employee careers in companies	Liberal (decentralized wage bargaining; competition clauses struck down by courts); few barriers to employee turnover
Company law	Stakeholder system (two-tier board system plus codetermination rights for employees)	Shareholder system (minimal legal constraints on company organization)
Skill formation	Organized apprenticeship system with substantial involvement from industry. Close links between industry and technical universities in designing curriculum and research	No systematized apprenticeship system for vocational skills. Links between most universities and firms almost exclusively limited to R&D activities and R&D personnel
Financial system	Primarily bank-based with close links to stakeholder system of corporate governance; no hostile market for corporate control	Primarily capital-market system, closely linked to market for corporate control and financial ownership and control of firms

The *United States* is characterized by a liberal market economy. Business organization depends primarily on market transactions and the use of a flexible, enabling private legal system to facilitate a variety of complex contracting situations. Because courts refuse to adjudicate incomplete contracts (see Schwarz 1992), market participants need to specify control rights in contracts to as full an extent as possible or, when this is not possible, to use extremely high-powered performance incentives to align interests within and across organizations (Easterbrook and Fischel 1991).

Differing patterns of market regulation and business coordination have led to substantial differences in institutional frameworks' structuring activity in different areas of the economy. Table 6.1 presents an overview of institutional patterns that most affect the organization of companies in technology-based industries.

This table highlights the conclusion that while most areas of economic activity in the United States are largely deregulated with market-based patterns of business coordination, in Germany both market regulation and non-market patterns of firm-level coordination are pervasive. Differing national institutional framework architectures allow firms in Germany to make different types of commitments to employees and other stakeholders than those that are possible in the United States. Systematic differences in the organization of careers, in patterns of company organization, and in relationships between firms and owners/investors exist across the two countries which can be ultimately linked to the broader patterns of industry specialization and innovation observed in Germany and the United States. We will examine the German case in some detail, and then highlight the strong role institutions play in shaping innovation patterns through a brief comparison with the United States.

First, how are *careers* for scientists and managers organized within the German economy? In Germany most employees spend most of their careers within one firm, often after a formal apprenticeship or, in the case of many engineers and scientists, an internship arranged in conjunction with their university degree (see Mason and Wagner 1999). While there exist no formal laws stipulating long-term employment, German labour has used its power on supervisory boards as well as its formal consultative rights under co-determination law over training, work-organization, and hiring to obtain unlimited employment contracts (Streeck 1984). Once the long-term employment norm for skilled workers was established, it spread to virtually all mid-level managers and technical employees. In particular, the migration of scientists and highly skilled technical employees across firms is limited, reinforced by the willingness of German courts to uphold clauses in employment contracts that forbid an employee to take a job at a different firm with the same skill classification for one year after leaving the original firm (see Keller 1991). Thus, the active labour market for mid-career scientists and technicians is limited.

Second, long-term employment and the 'stakeholder' model of corporate governance have important repercussions for patterns of *company organization* (Charkham 1995; Vitols et al. 1997). Long-term employment and limited codetermination rights for employees create incentives for management to create a broad consensus across the firm when major decisions will be made. As unilateral decision-making is limited, it is difficult for German firms to create strong performance incentives for individual employees. As a result, performance rewards tend to be targeted at groups rather than individuals within German firms, and individual performance assessments and bonus schemes are limited. Until early 1998 stock options, one of the most common incentive instruments used in American firms, were illegal in Germany. Though now allowed, they are still uncommon in Germany and typically, when used below top management levels, are distributed across large groups of employees to ensure that group rather than individual incentives are maintained. Finally, most career structures are well defined in German firms and based on broad education and experience within the firm rather than on short-term performance.

Third, *ownership and financial relationships* in Germany are strongly influenced by corporate governance rules. Despite the recent expansion of equity markets, Germany remains a bank-centred financial system. According to 1996 data, while market capitalization as a percentage of gross domestic product was 152 per cent in the United Kingdom and 122 per cent in the United States, in Germany it was only 27 per cent (Deutsche Bundesbank 1996). Banks and other large financial actors (e.g. insurance companies) have a strong oversight role on firms through seats on supervisory boards and through continuing ownership or proxy-voting ties with most large German industrial enterprises (Vitols 1995). Most German firms still rely on banks or retained earnings to finance investments. Banks are generally willing to offer long-term financing for capital investments, but not for research and development. German banks usually only offer financing for investments in which collateral exists, for example, fixed investments such as property or long-term capital investments. Banks can adopt a longer-term focus in part because they know that German firms are able to offer long-term commitments to employees and other stakeholders to the firm, and can often closely monitor the status of their investments through seats on the supervisory board or other direct contacts.

These patterns of company organization are ideally suited to the incremental innovation patterns long associated with successful German industrial firms. Incremental innovation patterns generally involve the systematic exploitation of particular technologies to a wide variety of niche markets. While high-volume 'blockbuster' products are uncommon, German engineering companies and, we will see below, software and biotechnology firms have successfully competed in a number of high-value-added market niches. Doing so requires a long-term dedication to particular markets and the building of firm-specific knowledge among highly trained employees. Such an approach is risky for firms in many countries, but particularly viable in Germany because of lifetime employment (see Soskice 1997). In addition, consensus decision-making ensures that, once new initiatives are agreed upon, they will not be 'held-up' by disgruntled units which feel their interests were not taken into account, so that while business policy formulation is not always rapid, its implementation is smooth and swift. Finally, incremental innovation patterns are well suited to Germany's bank-centred financial system. Most engineering firms have high capital-equipment costs that require long-term, but relatively low-risk financing of the sort which German banks have traditionally specialized in.

On the other hand, German institutional arrangements appear less suited to higher-risk innovation strategies in many newly emerging technologies. High-risk, high-return 'blockbuster' products are unlikely to be created from the German pattern of industrial and financial organization. It is difficult for German firms to quickly move in and out of markets characterized by rapidly evolving technologies. Since most employment contracts are unlimited, top managers of German firms must think twice before creating new competencies in high-risk areas, for cutting assets is difficult. Similarly, it is difficult for German firms to create the high-powered performance incentives that often characterize very high-risk technology companies. Large firms avoid creating high-powered incentives for managers, unilateral decision-making structures, and opportunities for rapid career advancement because these organizational structures go against the logic of the established institutional framework and would risk alienating important long-term stakeholders from the firm. Sharper incentives might be created within smaller entrepreneurial firms which, we will see below, have begun to appear in larger numbers within Germany. However, many of the traditional institutional constraints as well as the small labour market for mid-career scientists and technicians continue to hamper the efforts of German high-tech start-ups. These constraints limit the ability of start-up companies to move quickly into new fields as these firms start to grow.

Similar difficulties have plagued financial markets as well. While long-term but relatively low-risk financing is available from banks, high-risk short-term financing in Germany generally has not been available. As pointed out by Tylecote (1999), banks in 'insider' dominated corporate governance systems tend to have excellent knowledge of particular firms, but usually do not have the detailed *industry* knowledge that is necessary for investors to channel money into higher-risk technologies. Rather, financing for higher-risk activities is generally provided by venture capitalists, often in conjunction with industry 'angels' that have detailed technical and market expertise within particular industries. The growth in venture capital has been limited in Germany, in part by tax *dis*incentives for firm founder-owners to float shares of their successful ventures on the stock market. The lack of a viable 'exit option' has limited the development of refinancing mechanisms for venture capital funds.[1]

To provide a brief comparison, the institutional framework in the United States encourages few, if any of the company organizational and financial structures needed to pursue long-term incremental innovation strategies, but is ideally suited to the competitive requirements for radical innovation on a short time horizon. Labour markets are deregulated in the United States. Most firms offer limited employment contracts and, since courts in most US states refuse to uphold 'competition' clauses, poaching is widespread and an extensive 'headhunting' industry has emerged alongside most regional agglomerations of high-technology firms (see Saxenian 1994). This allows firms to quickly build or shed competencies as they move in and out of different technology markets.

Compared to the 'social' construction of German firms, the property rights structure of most US firms is financial in nature (Roe 1994). No legally stipulated co-determination rights for employees or other stakeholders exist. This allows owners to create high-powered incentive structures for top management (i.e. very high salaries often paid in company shares or share options), who are then given large discretion in shaping organizational structures within the firm. The top management of most US technology firms attempts to create similarly high-powered incentive structures within the firm. These structures include large bonus systems, opportunities for star performers to quickly advance through the firm, and much unilateral decision-control. These organizational structures tend to facilitate quickly shifting constellations of firm competencies that are often needed to innovate in rapidly changing technologies; they likewise facilitate the short-term dedication of employees to particular assignments. In contrast, the more long-term commitments and consultation rights prevalent within German firms are difficult to foster within America's decentralized and incentive-laden corporate environment.

Finally, a similar German–US contrast holds concerning finance. Most spectacularly through NASDAQ, large capital markets in the US fund technology firms which appear to have promising potential. This financing tends to be short term in nature, meaning that funds will dry up if firms fail to meet development goals or if products fail to live up to expectations in the marketplace. However, so long as the possibilities for high, often multiple returns on investment exist, a large market of venture capitalists and, at later stages of company development, more remote portfolio investors stand ready to invest in technology firms. The broad institutional structure of the US largely explains why this is the case. First, given the deregulated nature of labour markets, high quality managers and scientists can be found to fuel the growth of highly successful firms. Second, investors know that performance incentives can be managerially designed to 'align' the risk/return preferences of investors with rewards for top management and employees of particular firms. Once more, neither of these conditions holds in Germany.

This overview has provided a general framework for understanding why German institutional frameworks tend to favour 'DQP' industries more than fast-moving high-tech ones. We now apply this framework to understand recent developments in the software and biotechnology segments of Germany's high-tech sector.

2. CASE STUDIES FROM SOFTWARE AND BIOTECHNOLOGY

The 1980s and 1990s witnessed fundamental technological changes in both the pharmaceuticals and software industries. In pharmaceuticals, the emergence of new genetic-engineering-based techniques for drug discovery and design have created scientific and organizational challenges that exceeded the capabilities of traditional large pharmaceutical companies. Leading-edge research in biotech required the inputs of smaller more dynamic biotech firms along with an extensive reorganization of the in-house R&D activities of large pharmaceutical firms. In software, the emergence of personal computers, client/server architectures, and open systems enabled customized application software – formerly developed in-house by most user companies–to be replaced by highly complex standard software products that could be installed and maintained by external providers of software services. Large- and medium-sized user firms have increasingly reduced their dependence on in-house developed software in favour of software solutions that can be purchased on external markets.

At first glance, the German innovation system failed in reacting to these challenges. German biotech lagged far behind that of the USA and UK, while much of the German computer industry was overwhelmed by the magnitude and pace of technological and market change. Yet a few years after the alleged failure of German institutions, it is time for a reassessment. In biotechnology, activist government intervention has helped create a more active biotech industry within German borders. Meanwhile, in software, with much less government support, endogenous adjustments in the software industry shed a different light on the capacity of the German economy to cope with the technological upheavals in software. The sprouting of many new German biotech firms, the emergence of large German software service providers, and signs of strength in the standardized software segment all give rise to the need to reassess the strengths and weaknesses of Germany's national institutional framework in high-tech industries.

One evident question raised by developments in biotech and software is the following: how does the German institutional framework apply to these new high-tech industries encompassing activities that were formerly conducted within firms but are now increasingly organized by market forces? First, large German firms have started to reorganize their R&D activities to make better use of external alliances. While this was initially done through international alliances with American and other foreign technology firms, more recently this is occurring within Germany itself (see Cantwell and Harding 1998). Second, as each new industry developed it became increasingly differentiated, opening up new market opportunities for German companies to specialize in. For example, while the initial US biotechnology firms concentrated almost exclusively on the creation of new drugs to fight disease (therapeutics), today many successful German biotech firms have specialized in a number of broad, enabling or 'platform technologies'. Similarly, while the popular media tend to focus on software firms that design popular mass-market software products (an American specialty), there is also a vast market for business software in which German software houses have competed quite successfully, both in highly complex standard software and in software services.

Within both biotechnology and software it is possible to identify multiple market niches having widely contrasting technological characteristics. For example, therapeutics and standard software products each depend on *discrete technologies*, that is, technologies with a highly focused range of application and a short time window of opportunity. The value of these discrete technologies decays rapidly over time, for they are quickly outmoded by other technological substitutes. In contrast, platform technologies in biotech and the service segment of software are characterized by more *cumulative technologies* whose value remains more stable over time. These differing technological characteristics result in important differences in the type of competencies firms must build in order to successfully innovate. Firms in therapeutics and standard software require large amounts of high-risk finance due to the market uncertainty and high failure rate within their industry segments. The financial risk involved in platform technologies and software services is considerably less severe; on the other hand, because the technologies in these industry segments tend to develop in a cumulative fashion, firms and the employees who work for them must often be willing to invest in firm-specific skills with a fairly long-term time horizon. These technological characteristics are summarized in Table 6.2.

These contrasting market and technology profiles will be used to help explain patterns of intra-industry specialization within our case studies. Our empirical findings indicate that in both software and biotechnology German firms have selected the market segments that best 'fit' their inherited institutional environment: software services in software and platform technology in biotechnology. We now examine the two cases in more detail.

2.1. Software

The German software industry is sometimes depicted as strong in the production of technically sophisticated customized software and weak in more standardized software products. A publication of Germany's Federal Ministry of Education and Research on *Innovation in the Knowledge Society* declared: 'In the Federal Republic of Germany the strong point and competence of software development lies in the area of application software, especially of customer-specific customised software and software-based services' (BMBF

Table 6.2. Market segments of entrepreneurial ventures in biotech and software industries

	Therapeutics, standard software products	Platform technologies, software services
Market characteristics	Develop new products to meet specific mass-market needs	Create enabling competencies with broad application
Technological characteristics	Discrete technologies	Cumulative technologies
Firm-specific knowledge	Low	High
Financial risk	High (technological or market risk; high R&D costs)	Low to medium (markets and technologies well defined, lower R&D costs)
General risk profile	High	Low

1998). This conviction spills over into the nature of government support policy for software, which has focused on stimulating the development of software competence at the level of universities and research institutes and on making this competence available to commercial users. This is in contrast to the 'mission-oriented' policies of France, Britain, and Japan that aimed at improving their national software industries through targeted government support either for specific firms (France) or specific high-visibility projects (Britain, Japan) (Mowery 1996).

Instead of 'picking winners', German software-support programmes have reflected the institutional and historical features of German public policy: decentralized reliance on structured consultation and cascading initiatives, emphasis on education and human capital, and tying the distribution of public resources to co-operation among organizations on specific research projects. The Federal Ministry of Education and Research (BMBF) has granted financial support of approximately DM400 million since 1980 (figure extrapolated from BMBF/DLR 1996). The most recent BMBF-sponsored programme in software was the Sponsorship Initiative for Software Technologies in the Economy, Science, and Technology (*Initiative zur Förderung der Softwaretechnologie in Wirtschaft, Wissenschaft und Technik*). In the years 1995–98, a set of 27 software projects aiming at developing new software techniques for application software was sponsored (BMBF/DLR 1996). These projects involved 95 partner firms (including many small- to medium-sized ones) and research institutes (including universities and technical colleges). The programme's explicit goal was to transfer into commercial practice some of the extensive basic scientific research that had been conducted in academia, with three main areas of endeavour:

- New techniques for modelling organizational and technical systems and processes.
- Methods and tools for the update and reuse of pre-existing user applications.
- Development of methods for improving the security and reliability of complex software systems.

As a sign of commitment to technology transfer, the participating user firms rather than the scientific partners were charged with the writing of the final reports (BMBF/DLR 1998).

Such state policies implicitly consider software to be a *technology* but not a real *industry*. In fact, Germany's software *industry*, hardly influenced by government programmes, has changed dramatically in the last ten years. In Germany (as in the rest of the world) the leading producers of computer hardware were also the leading producers of software up to the mid-1980s. The advent of PCs, the switch to client/server architectures and the move to open operating systems have created an entirely new market for software products and services. While mainframe manufacturers lost market share in hardware and thus also in software, an enlarged market for standardized software and software modules (componentware) has arisen, including SAP's best-selling business application suite R/3. This was accompanied by an enlarged market for IT (information technology) services for the integration of the different hardware and software products offered on the market. So-called systems integrators help with the selection, integration, and adaptation of standardized software. Thus, software and software-related services form an increasingly autonomous – and global – industry, of which SAP, now the world's fourth-largest software company, is clearly Germany's most successful and well-known firm.

The software *industry* in Germany is highly fragmented, encompassing some 5,000 firms of various sizes, of which the vast majority employ less than ten employees. As in biotechnology, the software industry consists of rather heterogeneous sub-segments. For the sake of analysis we distinguish between the product segment of the software industry on the one hand and the service segment on the other. This distinction is admittedly artificial, since the activities of many IT firms involve both IT services and software products. Still, it is useful to conceive of IT firms in areas like systems integration (such as Debis Systemhaus or Andersen Consulting) as belonging to the IT service segment, while software houses who sell mass-produced 'products' (such as SAP's R/3 business application suite or Software AG's ADABAS database) can be considered to constitute the product segment of the software industry.

The standardized product segment of the software industry in Germany is weak compared to the USA, though it appears to be the highest of any country in Europe. In a list of the 20 largest standardized software vendors, two come from Germany (SAP and Software AG), all others are American (source: Broadway Associates, cited in *The Economist* 25 May 1996). Applications domains in which German software firms actively produce and export standardized software products include enterprise resource planning (ERP), computer-assisted software engineering (CASE) tools, production planning and workflow, architectural graphics, encryption, electronic commerce, and document management.

Whereas Germany's software industry has always had at least some strength in the area of standardized products, the services segment has historically been far less developed. German companies have traditionally revealed an above-average propensity to perform their computing activities in-house rather than to rely on external providers. Until very recently, therefore, Germany has lacked the large internationally operating IT service companies that one finds in the US and France. As recently as the early 1990s German IT companies were weakly represented in the lucrative business of systems integration.

Nonetheless, outsourcing in Germany has made headway in recent years, while large corporations like Debis (of Daimler-Benz) and Siemens have discovered that IT service provision can be successfully developed as a business by large industrial conglomerates. The IT service business of both companies has grown dramatically in recent years, to the point that they are now among the largest European IT service firms (Table 6.3).

While the 1990s created substantial turbulence for the German computer industry, leading many to view the relative decline of Siemens and Nixdorf as indicative of *Standort* deficiency, statistics on industry leadership present a more nuanced picture. Of the top 50 software and software services companies in Europe, the number of German-owned firms has held steady in the 1990s,

Table 6.3. Largest IT service providers in Europe, 1997

Rank	Company	Revenues (M Euro)	Nationality
1	IBM	5,500	US
2	EDS	3,230	US
3	Cap Gemini Sogeti	2,530	French
4	Andersen Consulting	2,040	US
5	Debis Systemhaus	1,600	German
6	Computer Sciences	1,560	US
7	Siemens Nixdorf	1,490	German
8	Sema Group	1,410	French
9	Bull	1,280	French
10	Compaq/Digital	1,050	US

Source: Pierre Audoin Conseil (1998): 1998 Survey: Software and I.T. Services in Europe.

whereas other European firms have generally faltered: for example, the number of French companies in the top 50 has fallen from 13 to 7 (source: Pierre Audoin Conseil 1998 survey). Meanwhile, 20 of the top software companies in Europe are today American owned, compared with 12 only a few years ago. Once again, the performance of German software companies is poor only in comparison with the USA, but is above average by any other standard.

The institutional requirements of the IT service segment of the software industry is quite compatible with the traditional national institutional framework of Germany. The technology is cumulative: as service providers carry out their projects and gain experience, they accumulate competence and are able to re-use many of the solutions, algorithms, and even code employed in earlier projects. The financial risk in the service segment is quite low. The firm-specific knowledge of employees is very high, for almost the entire capital of the firm is composed of human capital consisting of the knowledge, experience, and cooperation of the firm's employees. For these reasons, there is little reason to doubt that software services can thrive within the traditional institutional framework of the German economy and even within the corporate structures of large companies.

In contrast to IT service providers, producers of standardized software clearly do not prosper in a large-firm environment. Siemens Nixdorf, for precisely this reason, recently sold the bulk of its software business to Baan, a Dutch software company.[2] Successful software companies in the standardized product segment of the industry, in Germany as well as in the USA, generally have the following characteristics:

1. They begin as small start-up companies.
2. They focus their energies on a very small product niche.
3. They grow very rapidly once they create a blockbuster product.
4. Further growth usually revolves around improvements of this one product.

Standardized software development usually follows a hit-and-miss pattern of market success requiring a high level of risk, speed, and product focus. Such requirements are best met by small start-up firms guided by 'high-powered' market incentives.[3] Here the basic technology is discrete and the financial risk is high – conditions that do not correspond to Germany's traditional institutional framework.

Recent government initiatives have, however, been introduced to encourage a greater number of university graduates to start their own business, especially in the high-tech area. One example is the BMBF's recent initiative EXIST – *Existenzgründer aus Hochschulen* – launched in December 1997. The EXIST competition sought applications for the establishment of university-based regional networks to foster entrepreneurial ventures, particularly in high-tech. The response was overwhelming: 109 proposals involving about 200 of Germany's 326 universities and colleges. Of 12 finalists, five proposals were funded with DM45 million. Although software was not specifically mentioned, it is self-evident that the software sector represents one of the most attractive areas for entrepreneurial endeavour.

In summary, there exist two main types of government policy for supporting the software sector. The more traditional form of policy aims at strengthening the basic scientific competence of software development in a decentralized, cascading way. In contrast, the more recent supplementary approach seeks to encourage entrepreneurship and start-up ventures. Both approaches to software support revolve around universities and research institutes (decentralized diffusion-oriented policies) rather than around national strategic goals or national champion firms (centralized missions-oriented policies). In light of the high market uncertainty and rapid rate of technological evolution in the software industry, the thinking behind these kinds of policies appears to be fundamentally sound.

2.2. Biotechnology

During the 1980s very little start-up activity in biotechnology existed in Germany and most large pharmaceutical firms, after initial experiments in Germany, quickly invested in biotech research networks located in the United States. In the past two years the climate for biotechnology in Germany has improved dramatically. Large German pharmaceutical firms are investing in new German-based biotechnology labs and forming alliances with German biotech start-ups. The climate for founding entrepreneurial start-up firms has also improved dramatically. Recent surveys by Ernst and Young identified over 440 small biotechnology firms active in life-science fields, most of which were founded in the last two years (Ernst and Young 1998b: 10).

In Germany the recent upswing in biotechnology is commonly attributed to the introduction of extensive government programmes in support of biotechnology-based start-ups. Under the guise of federally orchestrated 'Bio-Regio' programmes and extensive subsidies granted by regional *Länder* governments, 17 regional biotechnology centres have been organized in the last three years. These centres typically are located in proximity to established university medical centres or Max Planck institutes working in different areas of molecular biology. The aim of the BioRegio programmes is effectively to create public surrogates for missing market activities needed for innovation, that is, to construct public programmes in Germany that supply those 'missing links' in the innovation chain linking public research to commercial biotech ventures – links well established in the United States but traditionally lacking in Germany.

Programmes typically include free consulting services for business-plan development and market scanning, subsidies to help scientists pay most patenting costs, the provision of low-cost lab space for fledgling start-ups in 'incubator labs' built in close proximity to university labs, and the provision of subsidized commercial space in nearby life-science-oriented technology parks once new firms start to grow. Most biotechnology start-ups also receive financial subsidies in the form of 'silent partnerships' through a new federal risk capital programme organized by the Deutsche Ausgleichbank as well as regional financial programmes (*Handelsblatt* 1998). While it is hard to estimate the total costs of Germany's BioRegio programmes, well over DM2 billion have been spent on the Munich *Genezentrum* alone, and similar projects of somewhat smaller size exist in several parts of Baden-Württemberg, as well as the Cologne and Berlin areas.

While financial subsidies and infrastructure programmes initiated in conjunction with the 'BioRegio' competition have played an undeniable role, the recent success of the German biotechnology industry has also been influenced by favourable industry factors which have shaped market segments that are compatible with incentives created by Germany's broader system of national institutional frameworks.

Although more than 20 years old, the biotechnology industry continues to favour the entry of new entrepreneurial start-up firms (Powell 1996). Scientific knowledge surrounding virtually all aspects of the drug discovery process remains highly specialized and fragmented with extremely close linkages to basic research (Penan 1996). Because the link between basic and applied research remains close, there are numerous opportunities for university researchers to become involved in commercial bio-medical activities, primarily through employment or consulting within small entrepreneurial biomedical firms. In order to keep track of developments in different research areas, large pharmaceutical firms have continued strategies of supporting large amounts of external research through alliances with small biotechnology firms. Pharmaceutical firms also sponsor extensive external research because they continue to hold specialized, expensive assets in drug development and marketing which ensure that they (and not the biotech research companies) will appropriate much of the commercial gains from innovation.

Multiple market segments exist within biotechnology. In addition to a very few highly publicized firms active in drug discovery research (therapeutics), German firms are particularly active and numerous in a more recently developed segment, platform technology. While therapeutics firms apply a variety of genetic manipulation technologies to the discovery or design of chemical compounds for use in the treatment of disease, platform-technology firms create the research tools used in therapeutics. Besides providing an assortment of consumables for use in lab processes, platform-technology endeavours include highly publicized commercial ventures in genetic sequencing and engineering as well as the application of information technology and automation techniques to drug screening (combinatorial chemistry).

While German firms can be found in both market sub-segments, the largest number of German biotechnology firms have chosen to specialize in the platform-technology segment, as substantiated by a July 1998 survey of over 300 German firms active in biotechnology activities. While a similar survey of UK biotech firms found that therapeutics was the most common area of specialization, in Germany contract research and platform technologies were the most favoured market segments, while therapeutics was only ranked fifth (Ernst and Young 1998a). Germany's most successful biotech firm, Qiagen, is a platform-technology firm that holds a near monopoly position in the provision of cheap consumable kits used to replace labour-intensive processes of DNA filtration. This firm is currently one of the world's most profitable small dedicated biotechnology firms, and has in the last few years seen its staff grow from a few dozen in the early 1990s to over 700 employees today. While Qiagen is the only German biotechnology firm to take a public stock listing (on both NASDAQ and the German Neuer Markt), four additional firms announced intended IPOs during the summer of 1998. Of these firms, three are platform-technology providers (*Wirtschaftswoche* 1998).

Platform technologies and therapeutics research have differing underlying technological characteristics. Our research suggests that German firms tend to specialize in platform technology because it is this segment that best 'fits' the broader constellation of incentives and constraints generated by Germany's national institutional framework. Therapeutics are characterized by a relatively 'discrete' technology, meaning that particular research programmes have a rather short time-span of market viability and thus demand frequent reorientation. As a result, therapeutics firms are often forced to quickly move out of particular research programmes to develop new areas. This entails frequent employee turnover that is difficult to manage within Germany's system of fairly regulated labour markets and system of company law (both of which push firms towards offering employees long-term contracts). The financial risk within therapeutics research is high, resulting from the high failure rate of particular research programmes, a long time to market (often 7–10 years due to regulatory testing and approval requirements), and the high percentage of costs devoted to R&D. Large public R&D subsidies along with the creation of the Neuer Markt and entry of substantial foreign venture capital have improved the situation. Nevertheless, it is uncertain whether market-based incentives to fund and nurture high-risk therapeutics ventures can be sustained within the present structure of German institutions.

Most platform-technology firms, on the other hand, rely on cumulative rather than discrete technologies. As a result, employees of platform-technology firms can afford to invest in much more firm-specific knowledge than those within therapeutics firms. Because long-term employment contracts are commonly used, employees of German platform-technology firms should even be more willing to invest in firm-specific skills than those working in US firms, where employment contracts are usually limited in nature. The financial risks of investing within most platform technologies are lower than those for therapeutics. Research and development costs are generally lower at platform-technology firms. This is generally due to a lower technological failure rate and the existence of fewer regulatory approval or testing requirements. Through continued research and development and intense interaction with users, key inventions are reliably leveraged into new markets. Because the financial risks are lower, these firms can find steady financing for most capital investments through existing German financial channels. Most German platform-technology companies have relied on state subsidies to invest in initial R&D, then hope to finance subsequent R&D through retained earnings.

3. CONCLUSION

Our empirical findings from the software and biotechnology industries indicate that German firms can successfully enter high-technology industries. However, they must do so within constraints created by the broader institutional logic of market regulation in Germany. German social and economic institutional patterns encourage incremental innovation, long-term relations between firms and their stakeholders, and the accumulation of knowledge and experience. Both the platform-technology segment of biotechnology and the services segment of software fit the inherited institutional framework of Germany better than many other segments of high-tech. For example, the therapeutics segment of biotechnology and standardized segment of software are characterized generally by more radical innovation, shorter time horizons on the market, and the exploitation of highly novel knowledge. This does not mean that Germany cannot field successful competitors in these segments of hightech industries; for example, Germany clearly has a couple of very successful standard software houses along with many recent promising start-ups in software products. But it does mean that nurturing German high-tech ventures in segments characterized by more risky, discrete technologies are likely to require special effort, whereas segments characterized by less risky, cumulative technologies represent a more natural market area for national specialization.

What role does this leave for government initiatives? There can be no doubt that the large-scale 'BioRegio' programmes have hastened the development of biotechnology in Germany. However, despite conscious efforts to replicate the American innovation chain, our evidence indicates that the market profile of most German biotechnology firms differs from the activities commonly chosen by American firms. We also found indications that a similar pattern of market specialization has developed in the software industry, but with far less government intervention. German firms might well have developed similar competencies in platform technologies with or without the large-scale assistance provided through the BioRegio programmes.

That being said, there is undoubtedly a strong need for broad framework programmes to support high-technology industries in Germany. Much high-tech activity in Germany has traditionally taken place outside the realm of market transactions, for example through in-house research of large firms or through projects orchestrated by para-public institutions such as trade associations or Fraunhofer institutes (see Abramson et al. 1997). Yet both software services and the platform-technology segment of biotechnology aim to provide technology infrastructure services through market mechanisms. For public policy-makers this means that support measures for this sector will increasingly have to take market processes into account.

While it is worth maintaining the traditional diffusion-oriented bent of government policy, it is not just a matter of sponsoring *innovation*, but of encouraging the formation of stronger *innovation markets* in Germany. Henceforth, much high-technology innovation in Germany will not only take place in academia and through the cooperation of the research world and industry, but will be driven by dynamic market processes, by new product and service offerings, and by the heat of competitive pressures. A key aspect of the BMBF-organized framework programmes for software as well as of most of the local BioRegio programmes has centred on mechanisms to diffuse basic university research into commercial activities. This focus should be continued.

NOTES

1. In recent years the German government has attempted to lesson the 'risk capital' problem in Germany by organizing extensive 'silent partnerships' for most technology-centred firms that can obtain some private financing. In addition,

the recently organized 'New Market' aims to create a NASDAQ style capital market for technology firms in Germany. While still tiny in terms of market capitalization, interest in this market is strong, hinting that a viable market for the public listing of technology firms is slowly developing in Germany.

2. According to the former General Manager of Siemens Nixdorf, Gerhard Schulmeyer, 'the working habits of programmers are simply too creative and unstructured to thrive in the rigid environment of an industrial company. These guys are only really productive if they have a deadline hanging over their heads. Just having them show up on a normal working day with 9-5 hours doesn't guarantee they will accomplish anything.' (personal conversation).

3. José Encarnacao, Director of the Fraunhofer Institute for Computer Graphics (Darmstadt), put it this way: 'The pattern of successful firms in packaged software firms has been small firms that grow large very fast. It is small firms that have the ability to learn fast in the marketplace' (personal conversation).

7

Empirical Evidence Against Varieties of Capitalism's Theory of Technological Innovation

*Mark Z. Taylor**

How can one explain cross-national differences in innovative activity across the industrialized democracies? Politics appear to play a strong causal role here, with case study after case study showing the clear influence of politics and political institutions on technological innovation.[1] However, this phenomenon is only sparsely studied by political scientists. Rather, this area has largely become the purview of a small number of economists and sociologists who often ignore important political variables in their analysis. Thus great interest has recently been generated by a new 'varieties of capitalism' (VoC) theory of innovation which holds that variance in political institutions is the primary cause of differences in national innovative behavior. In brief, the central claim of VoC's innovation theory is that the more a polity allows the market to structure its economic relationships, the more the polity will direct its inventive activity toward industries typified by 'radical' technological change. Conversely, the more a polity chooses to coordinate economic relationships via nonmarket mechanisms, the more it will direct its inventive activity toward 'incremental' technological change.

This question, of why some countries are more technologically innovative than others, should interest scholars of international political economy for several reasons. For example, even among otherwise friendly nations, economic rivalries between states can often come to resemble military ones,

*For their excellent insights, critiques, and encouragement I gratefully thank Thomas Cusack, Tracy Gabridge, Michael Brewster Hawes, Derek Hill, Daniel K. Johnson, Chappel Lawson, Mark Lewis, Benedicta Marzinotto, Andrew Miller, Michael Piore, Jonathan Rodden, Herman Schwartz, James Snyder, David Soskice, Edward Steinfeld, Scott Stern, Dan Winship, the editors at *International Organization*, and two anonymous reviewers.

with competition over trade, jobs, and markets leading to interstate disputes and strained relations.[2] In this competitive environment, technological innovation is a means not just for wealth creation but also for economic security; innovation provides the new products, new processes, and increased efficiencies that are the driving force behind modern economic growth, relative industrial power, and competitive advantage.[3] In recognition of this, almost every industrialized society expends a considerable share of its resources on the pursuit of technological advance. Yet, despite the random nature of innovation, and the seemingly clear fiscal and policy requirements for promoting innovative behavior, some countries are consistently more successful than others at technological progress, even among the industrialized democracies. This presents an increasingly nettlesome puzzle for social scientists.

Furthermore, VoC scholars see innovation theory as a key to resolving current problems in understanding global trade flows and production patterns. Classic trade theory holds that free trade will not deplete national wealth by impelling production abroad but will instead enhance economic performance and increase each trader's consumption possibilities. In this basic model, societies specialize production in their most efficient sectors and then trade the surplus for more goods than they otherwise could have produced locally. The Heckscher–Ohlin model improves on this basic theory by arguing that nations' relative endowments of basic economic factors (land, labor, capital) should determine the general lines along which international production and trade are structured. However, VoC proponents point to the rise of intra-industry trade during the past thirty years that has contradicted the inter-industry trading patterns predicted by the Ricardian or Heckscher–Ohlin models. Instead of specializing in particular sectors of production, the industrialized nations have maintained a broad spectrum of general economic activity and instead have concentrated their sectoral productive efforts geographically. Recent attempts to explain these phenomena posit an initially random distribution of productive activity that is then followed by agglomeration because of either increasing returns to scale or network externalities.[4] VoC scholars generally accept these agglomeration arguments, but they identify certain non-random patterns of international production and trade that are neither explained nor predicted by current agglomeration theories.[5]

VoC's innovation theory offers a resolution to both of the anomalies above, suggesting that domestic institutional structures can account for the different degrees of innovative effort and achievement between nations, and the production and trade relationships that subsequently develop. If VoC theory is correct, it would explain why nations maintain their innovative profiles in spite of strong pressures to change them, and why certain kinds of innovation-dependent production might tend to be concentrated in particular countries. However, the central claim made by VoC's innovation theory has yet to be proven. The purpose of this article is to use new data on patents and scholarly publications to test VoC theory's central assumptions and predictions and to see whether VoC theory properly describes the empirical world of technological innovation. I demonstrate that VoC theory does not accurately predict innovative behavior over time and space, and that VoC's existing empirical support strongly depends on the inclusion of a major outlier, the United States, in the set of radically innovative countries. I also find that some industries are more radically innovative than others in the short run, as assumed by VoC theory, but that this characterization cannot be confirmed in the long run as industries age and mature technologically.

1. POLITICS, ECONOMICS, AND INNOVATION THEORY

For much of the history of political economy, questions about the causes of national differences in technological innovation have remained at the periphery of the field.[6] One of the major reasons for this was the apparently random, or at least inexplicable, nature of innovation itself; even those social scientists who attempted to deal systematically with technological change (including Marx, Schumpeter, and Solow) generally regarded it, and the underlying body of scientific knowledge on which it drew, as a 'black box' proceeding according to its internal processes largely independently of political or economic forces.[7] This attitude changed gradually during the Cold War, as vast expenditures by the US government and industry on research and development (R&D) made it increasingly clear that technological innovation could be made responsive to economic and political needs, a fact further punctuated by the Soviet launch of Sputnik and later by the Japanese and German economic 'miracles'. In response, economists during the 1960s began to investigate whether certain supply-side or demand-side variables could explain why even developed nations followed different technological trajectories.[8] This somewhat inconclusive debate was followed in the late 1970s and 1980s by a plethora of case and country studies that tended to emphasize the importance of this or that policy, these or those historical conditions, but failed to produce any generalizable theory about the rate or direction of national innovation.

A recurring problem encountered in these debates was the contradiction between empirical observation and certain fundamental tenets of the economics of science. Specifically, Arrow had shown that much productive knowledge takes the form of unpatentable laws of nature and advances in basic science, and is therefore a non-excludable public good available to everyone without charge.[9] While patents and trade secrets act as temporary solutions to this appropriability problem in the area of applied knowledge, history has shown that the original inventors of technology often do not capture most of the benefits of their innovations when these inventions are transferred across borders, and that these transfers take place even in spite of considerable efforts to stop them. Theoretically speaking then, in the long run, developed nations should not display significant variation in either per capita innovation rates or in the type of innovative activities that they pursue. Yet differences appear to abound.

One possible solution to this paradox focuses on institutions. Institutions are perhaps the only variables that both influence the incentives for innovative behavior and differ across nations. Indeed, political scientists and economists have long recognized the capacity of government, labor, regulatory, and legal institutions to inhibit free market exchange and thereby hamper innovation. But it was not until Romer endogenized technological change that social scientists began to take seriously the ability of institutions to actively enhance aggregate economic performance through their effects on the rate and direction of technological progress.[10] To date though, beyond the broadest brush-strokes of political–economic theory, social scientists have yet to pinpoint the specific mechanisms by which institutions cause countries to differ technologically.

It is into this environment that VoC theory makes its foray, taking a radical new approach to explaining cross-national differences in the direction of technological progress.[11] VoC theory is broad and foundational; it touches on multiple aspects of political and economic life, of which innovation is but one part. At its most basic level, it is a theory of capitalism by gradation: some countries use markets more than others to coordinate economic actors and this variation is used to explain a myriad of comparative and international political–economic behavior. However, when fully articulated, VoC theory does not divide the world into 'freetrade versus protectionist' or 'state-owned versus privatized' systems of political economy as is traditionally done. This approach would focus attention on the state, which VoC scholars wish to avoid. Rather, they view the firm as the locus of trade and production in the capitalist economy and, therefore, take the firm, not the state, as their primary unit of analysis. Nor is the firm a lone or independent actor in VoC's analysis; successful operation of the firm depends heavily on its relationships with labor, investors, and other firms. It is these crucial relationships that, in turn, explain patterns of economic activity and policymaking. Therefore, the central claims of VoC theory focus on how a given political–economic institutional structure determines the conduct of these crucial relationships and how economic actors organize to solve the classic coordination problems that afflict such relations. At one end of this relationship spectrum lie the 'liberal market economies' (LMEs), such as the United States, in which firms tend to coordinate their relations and activities in the manner described by Williamson: through internal corporate hierarchies and external competitive market arrangements.[12] At the other end of the spectrum sit the 'coordinated market economies' (CMEs), such as Germany, in which firms tend to coordinate via nonmarket relationships, with greater dependency on relational and incomplete contracting, exchanges of private information within enduring networks, and a high degree of actor collaboration (as opposed to competition or confrontation). As I show in the next section, these distinctions have important implications for explaining and predicting national differences in innovation.

2. VARIETIES OF CAPITALISM'S THEORY OF TECHNOLOGICAL INNOVATION

According to VoC theory, technological innovation comes in two types, radical and incremental, each of which forms the basis for a different mode of production. While an exact definition is elusive, VoC scholars describe radical innovation as that which 'entails substantial shifts in product lines, the development of entirely new goods, or major changes to the production processes'.[13] They argue that radical innovation is therefore vital to production in high-technology sectors that require rapid and significant product changes (biotechnology, semiconductors, software) or in the manufacture of complex systems-based products (telecommunications, defense, airlines). Incremental innovation, on the other hand, is that which is 'marked by continuous but small-scale improvements to existing product lines and production processes'.[14] Unlike production based on radical innovation where speed and flexibility are crucial, production based on incremental innovation prioritizes the maintenance of high quality in established goods. This approach to innovation involves constant improvements in manufacturing processes to bring down costs and prices, but only occasional minor improvements in the product line. Incremental innovation is therefore essential for competitiveness in capital goods production (machine tools, factory equipment, consumer durables, engines).

VoC theory further predicts that LMEs and CMEs will tend to exert greater effort toward, and be successful in, different types of technological innovation.

VoC theory interprets innovation as just another productive activity; therefore, innovation should be sensitive to the firm's crucial relationships described above and the institutions that structure them. This does not mean that a given political–economic structure will result in only one kind of innovation, but that different institutions will create different types of comparative advantage for innovators. For example, incremental innovation requires a workforce that is skilled enough to come up with innovation, secure enough to risk suggesting it, and autonomous enough to see it as a part of their job. This in turn requires that firms provide workers with secure environments, autonomy in the workplace, opportunities to influence firm decisions, education and training beyond just task-specific skills (preferably industry-specific technical skills), and close interfirm collaboration that encourages clients and suppliers to suggest innovations as well. These are exactly the kinds of apparatus provided by CME institutions. In fact, CMEs are defined by the very institutions that provide a comparative advantage for incremental innovation. These institutions include highly coordinated industrial-relations systems; corporate structures characterized by works councils and consensus-style decision making; a dense network of intercorporate linkages (such as interlocking corporate directorates and cross-shareholding); systems of corporate governance that insulate against hostile takeovers and reduce sensitivity to current profits; and appropriate laws for relationship-based, incomplete contracting between firms. VoC scholars argue that this combination of institutions results in long employment tenures, corporate strategies based on product differentiation rather than intense product competition, and formal training systems for employees that focus on high skills and a mix of company-specific and industry-specific skills: in other words, the very factors that combine to foster incremental innovation.

On the other hand, VoC scholars argue that these same CME institutions that provide comparative advantages for incremental innovation also serve as obstacles to radical innovation. For instance, worker representation in the corporate leadership combines with consensus-style decision making to make radical change and reorganization difficult. Also, long employment tenures make the acquisition of new skills and rebalancing a company's labor mix difficult. Dense intercorporate networks also make the diffusion of disruptive innovations slow and arduous, and technological acquisition by mergers and acquisitions or takeovers hard. All of these act against, or reduce the potential rewards of, radical innovation.

In LMEs, the situation is reversed. LMEs are defined by institutions that provide a comparative advantage for radical innovation, while creating obstacles to incremental innovation. LMEs have flexible labor markets with few restrictions on layoffs, which means that companies can drastically change their product lines and still acquire the proper labor mix. LMEs also support extensive equity markets with dispersed shareholders providing innovators of all sizes with relatively unfettered access to capital. Also, inter-firm relations in LMEs allow for a variety of aggressive asset exchanges with few restrictions on mergers and acquisition, buyouts, personnel poaching, licensing, and so on, which permits firms to easily acquire scientific expertise and new technology. Concentration of power at the top of LME-based firms augments these institutions, allowing management to force major change quickly on complex organizations. All of these factors combine to create large incentives for, and an environment accommodative to, radical innovation. Conversely, LMEs' capacity for incremental innovation is limited because of financial arrangements that emphasize current profitability, corporate structures that concentrate unilateral control at the top and eliminate workforce security, and antitrust and contract laws that discourage inter-firm collaboration in incremental innovation. Meanwhile, fluid labor markets and short job tenures motivate workers to pursue selfish career goals and to acquire mobile general skills rather than firm-specific or industry-specific skills. Hence, in VoC's analysis, neither workers nor firms in LMEs tend to have the incentives or the resources for sustained incremental innovation.

3. TESTING THE VARIETIES OF CAPITALISM CLAIMS

The purpose of the remainder of this article is not to evaluate the accuracy of the LME–CME classification system or test a specific causal mechanism involved in VoC's theory of innovation. Rather, the question I ask here is whether the international patterns of innovation that VoC theory predicts actually exist. The VoC causal story outlined above is both theoretically appealing and dovetails with some widely held stereotypes about national differences in innovation; however, little empirical data has yet been produced to support its central claim. The evidence offered by Hall and Soskice consists of four years of patent data from the European Patent Office (EPO) that shows that Germany and the United States concentrate their patents according to the LME versus CME model discussed above. Specifically, Hall and Soskice examine patenting activity by Germany and the United States in thirty technology classes during 1983–84 and 1993–94. Overall, they found that Germany's patent specialization was almost equal and opposite that of the United States in both time periods.[15] More specifically, the Germans were found to be more active innovators in industries that Hall and Soskice characterize as dominated by incremental innovation (such as mechanical engineering, product handling, transport, consumer durables, and machine tools); meanwhile, firms in the United States innovated disproportionately in industries that the authors perceive as more radically innovative (including medical engineering, biotechnology, semiconductors, and telecommunications).

I have identified several possible problems with this approach. First, VoC theory implicitly assumes that some industries are inherently characterized by radical innovation, others by incremental innovation, and that these industries have been correctly identified. Second, in supporting their claims, Hall and Soskice use only four years' worth of patent data from only two countries, one of which, the United States, is an outlier by almost any measure. Third, Hall and Soskice use only simple patent counts as their measure of innovation, hence frivolous patents are counted the same as highly innovative ones; nor do Hall and Soskice use any non-patent measures of innovation.

In the following sections, I will address these issues in turn. In some instances, I use Hall and Soskice's data and methods to test the generality of their claims. In others, I take advantage of a new data set compiled at the National Bureau of Economic Research (NBER) of more than 2.9 million utility patents granted by the US Patent and Trademark Office (USPTO) to applicants from the United States and 162 other countries during 1963–99, and the sixteen million citations made to these patents between 1975 and 1999.[16] This new data set allows one to go beyond Hall and Soskice's empirical investigation to consider some 36 years of patenting activity for all of the LME and CME countries and to use patents weighted by forward citations in an attempt to control for the quality of the innovations being patented. Later, I consider data from the Institute for Scientific Information (ISI) on scholarly and professional journal publications, also weighted by forward citations, as an additional measure of innovation.

3.1. Independent Variable: LME Versus CME

According to VoC theory, the primary independent variable for predicting innovation characteristics is the type of national political–economic institutional structure (LME or CME) within which innovators operate. The LMEs include Australia, Canada, Great Britain, Ireland, New Zealand, and the United States. The CMEs include Austria, Belgium, Denmark, Finland, Germany, Japan, Netherlands, Norway, Sweden, and Switzerland. In between these two ideal types, and of less importance to VoC scholars, are a handful of hybrids denoted as 'Mediterranean market economies' (MMEs) that have mixed CME and LME characteristics. These countries include France, Greece, Italy, Portugal, Spain, and Turkey.[17] For the remainder of this article, references to the set of

'LME', 'CME', or 'MME' countries should be understood to mean only those states listed above, as these are the only ones explicitly mentioned in the VoC claims tested here. Later, in the multivariate regressions, 'LMEx' will be used to refer to the set of all LME countries except the United States.

Some critics might question the 'LME-ness' or 'CME-ness' of certain states classified above, for example the Oceanic countries during much of the Cold War. However, I employ the existing VoC classifications for several reasons. First, in VoC theory, it is not the amount of protectionism or regulatory burden that defines an LME or CME and determines its innovative profile, but whether markets or hierarchies form the context within which economic actors organize, conduct their relationships, and solve coordination problems. Therefore when accepting the VoC country classifications, I privilege the relational aspects of the LME–CME distinction as discussed by Hall and Soskice, rather than protectionist or state-interventionist behavior, because the former are the most relevant and active mechanisms in VoC's theory of innovation. Second, recall that the LME-CME dichotomy is not definitive but rather 'constitute[s] ideal types at the poles of a spectrum'.[18] All states have some degree of tariff and non-tariff barriers to trade, and no nation is free from regulation. Therefore, there are shades of LME and CME in every economy, and these qualities change over time. Hence when accepting particular classifications, I pay attention not to absolute qualities but to relative ones. Finally, all classification systems have debatable aspects, and their acceptance is often based more on their usefulness rather than their exactitude. Part of the goal of this article is to test VoC theory as stated, which includes the usefulness of their typology.[19]

3.2. Dependent Variable: Innovation

The most frequently used measure of innovation is patents. The debate over the proper use of patent data has proceeded vigorously and with increasing sophistication over the past several decades. The current consensus holds that patent data are acceptable measures of innovation when used in the aggregate (for example, as a rough measure of national levels of innovation across long periods of time), but are not appropriate when used as a measure of micro-level innovation (to compare the innovativeness of individual firms or specific industries from year to year). While this debate is ongoing and is better recounted elsewhere, this section will address some of the more pressing issues surrounding patent measures and their use in testing VoC theory.[20]

Strictly speaking, a patent is a temporary legal monopoly granted by the government to an inventor for the commercial use of his or her invention, where the invention can take the form of a process, machine, article of manufacture, or compositions of matters, or any new useful improvement thereof (USPTO).[21] A patent is a specific property right that is granted only after formal examination of the invention has revealed it to be non-trivial (that is, it would not appear obvious to a skilled user of the relevant technology), useful (that is, it has potential commercial value), and novel (that is, it is significantly different than existing technology). As such, patents have characteristics that make them a potentially useful tool for the quantification of inventive activity. First, patents are by definition related to innovation, each representing a 'quantum of invention' that has passed the scrutiny of a trained specialist and gained the support of investors and researchers who must dedicate time, effort, and often significant resources for its physical development and subsequent legal protection. Second, patent data are widely available and are perhaps the only observable result of inventive activity that covers almost every field of invention in most developed countries over long periods of time. Third, the granting of patents is based on relatively objective and slowly changing standards. Finally, the USPTO and the European Patent Office provide researchers with centralized patenting institutions for the two largest markets for new technology. In practical terms, this allows researchers to get around the issue of national differences in patenting laws as well as providing two separate and fairly independent data pools.

Given these qualities, patents have been used as a basis for the economic analysis of innovative activity for more than thirty-five years. Current use began with the pioneering work of Scherer and Schmookler who used patent statistics to investigate the demand-side determinants of innovation.[22] However, the labor intensive nature of patent analysis, which used to involve the manual location and coding of thousands of patent documents, severely limited the extent (or at least the appeal) of their use in political and economic research. These limitations were eased somewhat during the 1970s when the advent of machine-readable patent data sparked a wave of econometric analysis.[23] In the late 1980s, the use of patent data was further facilitated by computerization, which increased the practical size of patent data sets into millions of observations. Most recently, Hall, Jaffe, and Trajtenberg at the NBER have compiled a statistical database of several million patents complete with geographic, industry, and citation information, which I use later to test the VoC claims.[24]

However, patents do have significant drawbacks that somewhat restrict, but by no means eliminate, their usage as an index of innovation. First, there is the classification problem, in that it is difficult to assign a particular industry to a patent, especially because the industry of invention may not be the industry of eventual production or the industry of use or benefit. I address this issue, where possible, by using two different patent data sets with assorted systems and levels of patent classification. Second, it is not yet clear what fraction of the universe of innovation is represented by patents, because not all inventions are patentable and not all patentable inventions are patented. This problem is exacerbated when attempting comparative research because different industries and different countries may exhibit significant variance in their propensity to patent. I address these concerns by using publications data in addition to patents. In addition, although patents and publications both may be imprecise measures of innovation, as long as this measurement error is random and uncorrelated with the explanatory variables, then regressions using this data should produce unbiased estimates of the coefficients (and generally with inflated standard errors).

Finally, some critics point out that patents vary widely in their technical and economic significance: most are for minor inventions, while a few represent extremely valuable and far-reaching innovations. Moreover, it has been found that simple patent counts do not provide a good measure of the radicalness, importance, or 'size' of an innovation. Simple patents counts correlate well with innovation inputs such as R&D outlays, but they are too noisy to serve as anything but a very rough measure of innovation output.[25] Therefore, I use patent counts that have been weighted by forward citations. Forward citations on patents have been found to be a good indicator of the importance or value of an innovation, just as scholarly journal articles are often valuated by the number of times they are cited. The idea here is that minor or incremental innovations receive few if any citations, and revolutionary innovations receive tens or hundreds. Empirical support for this interpretation has arisen in various quarters: citation-weighted patents have been found to correlate well with market value of the corporate patent holder, the likelihood of patent renewal and litigation, inventor perception of value, and other measures of innovation outputs.[26]

3.3. Testing the VoC Industry Assumption

Armed with a better understanding of patents, I now use them to test some of the more controversial claims made by VoC scholars. One such controversy resides in their implicit assumption about the innovative characteristics of particular industries. VoC theory assumes that some industries are inherently and statically more radically innovative, and other industries inherently and statically more incrementally innovative. However, this assumption is contradicted by a vast empirical literature that shows that the innovative characteristics of any given industry are not static but dynamic and depend not so much on industry type but on the industry's technological maturity.[27] More specifically, studies have found that most industries are typified by two successive waves of innovation: first a flurry of radical product innovations that eventually converge on a dominant product design, followed by a flurry of process innovations in manufacturing the product at lower cost. In each wave, earlier innovations tend to be more revolutionary than subsequent ones that build on them. For example, during the first thirty years of automobile production, more than 100 US firms produced competing models of automobiles with tremendous variance in features and operability. During this period, innovation focused on radical product changes: introduction of enclosed bodies, wheel-based steering, electrical systems, gasoline-based fuel and engine systems, and so on. These innovations tended to be revolutionary and dramatically affected the look and performance of successive versions of the automobile, such that cars from this period bear little resemblance to the cars of today. However, as the market converged on a dominant design for automobiles, product innovations became gradually more incremental, and the focus of radical innovation shifted to production processes. This type of innovation dynamic has been observed in almost every industry that produces assembled products.

If the innovative character of industry changes over time, then Hall and Soskice's use of snapshots of patent activity in particular industries may not properly test VoC theory. That is, for the two brief time periods covered by Hall and Soskice's patent data, do the researchers correctly identify which industries were more radically or incrementally innovative? In order to answer this question I rely on the ability of forward citations to serve as a measure of 'degree' or 'value' of an innovation. For my empirical evidence, I make use of the newly compiled NBER patent data set described above. Using the USPTO patent classifications, the NBER scholars have grouped their data into six industry categories, each consisting of four to seven subcategories (for a total of thirty-six subcategories), which allows comparison of the average patent citation rates across different industries.

Table 7.1 shows the means of the forward citations per patent by industry category. The industries generally rank as assumed by VoC theory: information technology and telecommunications patents receive on average the most forward citations, followed by drugs and medical, electronic, chemical, others, and finally mechanical. T-tests reveal that the differences between these means are significant beyond the 99 percent confidence level. Even if one sharpens the level of analysis by further subdividing the industry categories into their smaller subcategories, patent citations would again behave more or less as assumed by VoC theory.[28]

Of course, analyzing the data in this manner introduces a potential truncation problem: older patents have had more time to be cited than younger patents. This problem is exacerbated in the NBER data set because it only includes citations data from 1975 onwards.[29] Therefore, patents granted

Table 7.1. Patents and forward citations by industry, 1963–99

Industry category	Number of patents	Mean (forward cites per patent)	Standard deviation (forward cites per patent)	Minimum (forward cites per patent)	Maximum (forward cites per patent)
IT/Telecom	290, 337	6.44	10.60	0	779
Drugs/Medical	204, 199	5.99	11.20	0	631
Electric	499, 741	4.75	6.70	0	251
Chemicals	606, 934	4.62	7.14	0	401
Others	641, 333	4.46	5.90	0	286
Mechanical	681, 378	4.17	5.71	0	411
Total	2,923, 922	4.78	7.35	0	779

Note: IT = information technology.

Source: National Bureau of Economic Research 2001.

before 1975 will suffer from further truncation in that a 1969 patent will contain the citations received from patents granted during 1975–99, but not from patents granted in 1969–74. I control for the overall truncation problem by excluding pre-1975 patents from consideration and by using multivariate regression analysis with a control for patent age.[30] The results of these regressions are reported in Table 7.2. First, the table shows in all of the regressions that the coefficient for patent age is significant and generally positive; note also that the age coefficient increases in strength when pre-1975 patents are omitted from the data set, and consistently hugs 0.3 in all regressions conducted using the 1975–99 patent data (see also Tables 7.5 to 7.7 below). This is suggestive of the truncation effects described above. One can interpret this coefficient as indicating the number of additional citations received per patent for each year of its existence. The age coefficient does turn negative in Model 5, where only the very oldest patents are used. This suggests that patented innovations may have a 'lifespan' of usefulness, generating much subsequent innovation while young, then slowly fading into obsolescence as either new innovations come to replace them or their capacity to serve as the foundation for new innovations is exhausted. Second, Models 1 and 2 show that, even when controlling for patent age (and with the added understanding that classification errors may exist), the industry coefficients generally line up as assumed by VoC theory: information technology and telecommunications (IT/Telecom) patents receive the most forward citations, followed by drugs and medical, electronic, chemical, others, and finally mechanical. The coefficients here can be interpreted as the additional number of citations received per patent for patents granted to innovations in a particular industry (relative to the omitted category 'Other'[31]). The mean

Table 7.2. OLS testing of VoC's industry-innovation assumption

Data used	Model 1 1963–99	Model 2 1975–99	Model 3 1975–99 (excluding US)	Model 4 1975–99	Model 5 1975–80	Model 6 1990–95
IT/Telecom	2.48	3.43	2.70	3.52	3.39	5.17
	(0.02)*	(0.02)*	(0.02)*	(0.02)*	(0.06)*	(0.03)*
Drugs/Medical	2.07	2.29	0.93	2.29	2.83	3.02
	(0.02)*	(0.02)*	(0.03)*	(0.02)*	(0.06)*	(0.04)*
Electric	0.42	0.95	0.92	1.07	0.59	1.42
	(0.01)*	(0.02)*	(0.02)*	(0.02)*	(0.04)*	(0.03)*
Chemicals	0.16	0.14	0.18	0.24	0.02	0.15
	(0.01)*	(0.02)*	(0.02)*	(0.02)*	(0.04)*	(0.03)*
Mechanical	−0.31	−0.22	0.13	−0.08	−0.61	0.016
	(0.01)*	(0.02)*	(0.02)*	(0.02)*	(0.04)*	(0.03)*
Other						
US				1.05		
				(0.01)*		
Patent age (years)	0.08	0.31	0.29	0.31	−0.04	0.65
	(0.000)*	(0.001)*	(0.001)*	(0.001)*	(0.008)*	(0.005)*
Constant	3.07	1.03	0.82	−0.40	−7.29	−0.42
	(0.01)*	(0.01)*	(0.01)*	(0.01)*	(0.17)*	(0.04)*
R^2	0.02	0.10	0.10	0.10	0.02	0.08
Observations	2,923,922	2,139,314	939,037	2,139,314	384,270	585,758

Note: Dependent variable = citations received per patent. Analysis is by ordinary least squares (OLS). Huber–White estimates of standard errors reported in parentheses. IT = information technology. $*p < .001$.

Source: National Bureau of Economic Research 2001.

citations received per patent in the 1975–99 data set is 4.9 (with a standard deviation of 7.8); therefore, the size of the innovative differences between industries suggested by the coefficients is significant, but not immense.

As my findings in subsequent sections indicate that VoC's evidence is sensitive to the United States outlier, I run two regressions to consider its effects on the industry rankings. In Model 3, I omit the US data entirely, which drastically reduces the coefficient for the IT/Telecom and drugs/medical categories and increases the coefficients for the Chemicals and Mechanical categories. When I instead use a US dummy (Model 4), the coefficients change significantly for only chemicals and mechanical patenting. The first thing to note in both these regressions is that the rankings do not change in the areas of most concern to VoC theory: chemicals, mechanical, and 'other' patents receive fewer citations than those in VoC's radically innovative sectors. Second, these regressions suggest that the United States is in fact a powerful outlier that affects the nature of global innovation, especially in frontier sectors.

Given the time dynamics of innovation, it is also important to confirm that the findings above are not an artifact of averaging across a long time period. Models 5 and 6 address this concern, revealing that VoC's industry assumption generally holds even when I limit the data set to either the earliest or latest five years of patenting activity. In these regressions, information technology and telecommunications patents consistently received the most citations, again followed by drugs and medical and electronics patents. There is however some shuffling among the remaining categories, especially mechanical patents that may suggest a recent small surge in innovation there. But these minor shifts do not create any major problems for the VoC assumptions. Also, though not shown here, if one were to further subdivide the six categories above into their thirty-six subcategories, patent citations would behave more or less as they do at the category level.[32] Finally, given the non-constant variance in forward citations across industries (and later, countries), I correct for heteroscedasticity using Huber–White estimators of standard errors in all regressions but find no significant differences from the results generated by the traditional estimator. In sum, patent data generally support the VoC assumption about industry innovation characteristics.

3.4. Testing VoC's Predictions About National Innovative Character: Simple Patent Counts

Having confirmed the industry-based innovation assumption above, I now reconsider the evidence on patent counts offered by Hall and Soskice. Again, this evidence is based on EPO patent data for the United States and Germany in 30 industries during two separate two-year periods. For each industry in each time period, Hall and Soskice calculated a patent specialization index (I) that simply subtracts a country's fraction of its total patents in a particular field from the world's fraction of total global patents in the same field.[33] Hence a positive index score means greater specialization in innovation in that particular type of technology. The chart shows that the United States specializes its patenting in industries typified by radical innovation, while Germany's patent specialization is in industries typified by incremental innovation. The question then is whether this finding holds true across time and space, or have Hall and Soskice inadvertently selected outlying countries or years? To test this possibility, I use the same EPO data set and computational formula used by Hall and Soskice, but instead I calculate the patent specialization indices across a much longer time-span (1978–95) and compare the innovative activities of the entire set of LME and CME countries.

The results of this exercise are summarized in Table 7.3. Note that rather than requiring an exact quantitative match, I apply a more lenient qualitative standard for VoC theory to pass, only testing which country (or set of countries) has a higher patent specialization index in each of the 30 industries. Using Hall and Soskice's data and methodology, I was able to closely reproduce their findings for Germany and the United States in 1983–84 and 1993–94. However, when I extend the time period to 1978–95, German and US patenting fails to meet VoC predictions in polymers, new materials, and nuclear engineering. Even more discrepancies arise when the data set is expanded to compare patent specialization by the set of all LME countries versus the set of all CME countries. For example, in the 1983–84 period, the set of LMEs had higher patent specialization indices than the set of CMEs in three industries that Hall and Soskice describe as incremental (mechanical elements, basic materials, polymers), while CME patenting had higher specialization scores in two radical industries (new materials, audiovisual technology). But the most striking disparity occurs when the United States is excluded from the set of LME countries; under these conditions VoC theory has only marginally more predictive power than random chance.

The NBER patent data provides a second data set with which to test the patent specialization indices devised by Hall and Soskice. Such a test adds value in that the NBER data set not only spans over twice the time period (1963–99) as the EPO data used by Hall and Soskice, but the NBER data set also consists of USPTO patents and is therefore completely independent. The NBER data also uses a completely independent classification scheme that provides controls for some of the potential classification problems and idiosyncrasies discussed above. Yet, despite these differences, my test results are generally the same as those found using Hall and Soskice's EPO data. I omit a graphic depiction of the results and instead explain the major findings. Of the 18 categories of innovation that I was able to map from Hall and Soskice to the NBER data, VoC's predictions were borne out relatively well (approximately 70 to 80 percent of the time, depending on the time period) when applied to the United States and Germany.[34] However, expanding the data set to test all LME countries versus all CME countries, I find that VoC theory loses a considerable amount of its predictive power, with a 72 percent success rate in 1983–84, but only 50 percent in 1993–94, and 56 percent over the entire 1963–99 period. Omitting the United States from the set of LMEs results in further deterioration, with VoC's success rate ranging from 44–56 percent. Thus, after analyzing two different data sets and competing classification methods, it appears that the success of VoC theory strongly depends on the inclusion of the United States as an LME.

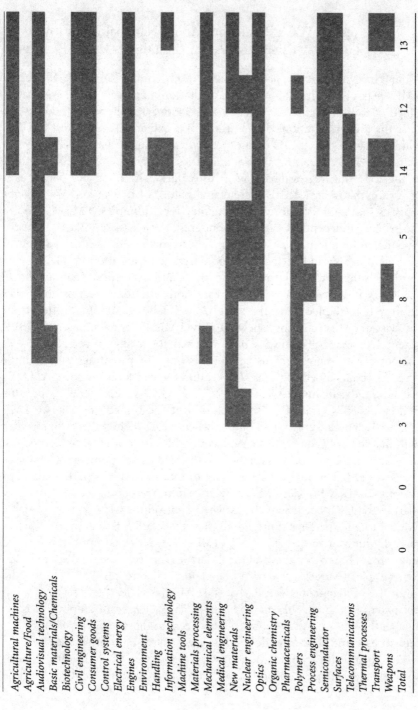

Note: Shaded squares indicate violations. Patent specialization indices (I) for the set of LMEs, CMEs, and LMEs (excluding United States) are calculated by treating each set of countries as a single 'country'. A violation in one of these columns indicates that the difference in aggregate patent specialization indices was opposite that found by Hall and Soskice (2001) in their German versus US comparison.

Source: European Patent Office (Hall and Soskice 2001).

3.5. Testing VoC's Predictions About National Innovative Character: Patent Citations

So far I have used simple patents counts in my comparisons of LMEs versus CMEs, yet as I explained above, forward citations of patents are an even better gauge of radical versus incremental innovation. Therefore, in this section, I use the forward citations data in the NBER patent data set to test the VoC country claims directly, retaining the same techniques that I used above in testing the VoC assumptions about industries. As my dependent variable in all of the following regressions I again use citations-received per patent as a proxy for the radical versus incremental nature of innovation. VoC theory suggests that country dummies or country-type dummies (LME, CME) are the primary independent variables of interest, as well as controls for industry type (again I use industry category or subcategory), and, of course, a control for patent age should be included to address the truncation problem. Since the US outlier proved important in the simple statistical analysis above, I address it in two ways in the regressions. In some regressions a US dummy is introduced, in others the United States is simply omitted from the class of LMEs (creating a new dummy: LMEx). For data, I use the NBER patent data set for all countries' patenting activity during the period 1975–99.

I begin with regressions using controls only for patent age and country type, the results of which (Table 7.4) reinforce what I found previously: LMEs are more radically innovative than CMEs (Model 1 versus Model 2), but this finding depends entirely on the inclusion of the United States as an LME (Model 3). This effect is apparent even when the CME dummy is run together with that for LMEs or LMEx's (Models 4 and 5). In each of these regressions, the coefficients can be interpreted as the additional number of citations received per patent for patents granted to innovations in a particular set of nations (LMEs, CMEs, or LMEx's) relative to the rest of the world. Note how sharply the LME coefficient drops when I introduce a US dummy variable (Model 6) and, perhaps more interesting, that the LMEx's appear to be less radically innovative than the CMEs (Model 7). Of equal importance is the small size of the coefficients and the differences between them. These indicate, for example in Model 4, that even when I do not control for the US outlier, the innovative difference between LMEs and CMEs is smaller than a single citation per patent. Although this may be a statistically significant amount, it is far smaller than the innovative difference between the most versus least innovative industries found above and does not suggest a large innovation gap.

VoC theory also includes industry type as a factor in determining innovative behavior. Hence a second set of regressions are run, identical to those

Table 7.4. OLS testing of VoC innovation theory, by country type (1975–99)

	Model 1	Model 2	Model 3	Model 4	Model 5	Model 6	Model 7
LME	0.95			1.71		0.65	
	(0.011)*			(0.02)*		(0.03)*	
CME		−0.59		0.93	−0.67	0.93	0.93
		(0.011)*		(0.02)*	(0.01)*	(0.02)*	(0.02)*
LMEx			−0.74		−0.95		0.65
			(0.022)*		(0.02)*		(0.03)*
Patent age (years)	0.28	0.28	0.29	0.28	0.28	0.28	0.28
	(0.001)*	(0.001)*	(0.001)*	(0.001)*	(0.001)*	(0.001)*	(0.001)*
U.S.						1.16	1.81
						(0.02)*	(0.02)*
Constant	1.51	2.26	2.09	0.76	2.33	0.76	0.76
	(0.01)*	(0.01)*	(0.009)*	(0.02)*	(0.01)*	(0.02)*	(0.02)*
R^2	0.076	0.074	0.073	0.077	0.074	0.08	0.078
Observations	2,139,314	2,139,314	2,139,314	2,139,314	2,139,314	2,139,314	2,139,314

Note: Dependent variable = citations received per patent. Analysis is by ordinary least squares (OLS). Huber–White estimates of standard errors reported in parentheses. *$p < .001$.

Source: National Bureau of Economic Research 2001.

reported in Table 7.4 but with the addition of controls for industry (Table 7.5). Yet I find no significant differences when the industry controls are added to the regression models. Again, the LME countries appear at first to be more radically innovative than the CMEs (Model 1 versus Model 2), but not when the United States is excluded from the group of LMEs (Model 3). Note also that the industry coefficients in this regression match those found when I tested the VoC industry-innovation assumption above (Table 7.2). To test this finding more directly, I add a US dummy, which again severely affects the coefficient of the LME dummy (Models 6 and 7). Regressions run at a finer level of analysis using industry subcategories (not shown) produce similar results.[35]

Given the broad nature of VoC theory and the complex array of causal mechanisms it hypothesizes, a fixed-effects model is perhaps the most efficient way to conduct a statistical test of its central predictions. While the NBER data set affords enough degrees of freedom to use country dummies for all 162 nations, computer memory does not. I therefore ran a final set of regressions in which I include dummies for 23 countries with the highest patenting activity.[36] These countries include the aforementioned LME and CME states in addition to France, Italy, Spain, Israel, Taiwan, Singapore, and South Korea. Using only country dummies, controlling for age, and correcting for heteroscedasticity, I find that the relative strengths of the coefficients for the remaining dummies do not quite line up along the lines predicted by VoC theory

Table 7.5. OLS testing of VoC innovation theory, by country type and industry (1975–99)

	Model 1	Model 2	Model 3	Model 4	Model 5	Model 6	Model 7
LME	0.94			1.66		0.66	
	(0.01)*			(0.02)*		(0.03)*	
CME		−0.59		0.89	−0.66	0.89	0.89
		(0.01)*		(0.02)*	(0.01)*	(0.02)*	(0.02)*
LMEx			−0.68		−0.90		0.66
			(0.02)*		(0.02)*		(0.03)*
US						1.10	1.76
						(0.02)*	(0.02)*
Patent age (years)	0.31	0.31	0.31	0.31	0.31	0.31	0.31
	(0.001)*	(0.001)*	(0.001)*	(0.001)*	(0.001)*	(0.001)*	(0.001)*
IT/Telecom	3.53	3.50	3.42	3.49	3.49	3.48	3.48
	(0.02)*	(0.02)*	(0.02)*	(0.02)*	(0.02)*	(0.02)*	(0.02)*
Drugs/Medical	2.28	2.28	2.29	2.29	2.29	2.29	2.29
	(0.02)*	(0.02)*	(0.02)*	(0.02)*	(0.02)*	(0.02)*	(0.02)*
Electrical	1.07	1.02	0.94	1.06	1.02	1.05	1.05
	(0.02)*	(0.02)*	(0.02)*	(0.02)*	(0.02)*	(0.02)*	(0.02)*
Chemicals	0.24	0.21	0.13	0.22	0.20	0.22	0.22
	(0.02)*	(0.02)*	(0.02)*	(0.02)*	(0.02)*	(0.02)*	(0.02)*
Mechanical	−0.09	−0.14	−0.22	−0.11	−0.13	−0.11	−0.11
	(0.02)*	(0.02)*	(0.02)*	(0.02)*	(0.02)*	(0.02)*	(0.02)*
Other Constant	0.41	1.28	1.07	−0.29	1.25	−0.29	−0.29
	(0.02)*	(0.01)*	(0.01)*	(0.02)*	(0.01)*	(0.02)*	(0.02)*
R^2	0.10	0.10	0.10	0.10	0.10	0.10	0.10
Observations	2,139,314	2,139,314	2,139,314	2,139,314	2,139,314	2,139,314	2,139,314

Note: Analysis is by ordinary least squares (OLS). Huber–White estimates of standard errors reported in parentheses. IT = information technology. *$p < .001$.

Source: National Bureau of Economic Research 2001.

(Table 7.6). Here the coefficients can be interpreted as the additional number of citations received per patent for patents granted to innovations in a particular nation relative to those granted to the rest of the world (ROW). Though not astronomical, the size of the coefficients do indicate significant innovative differences between states, and that these innovative differences are comparable to those across different industries. All of the coefficients are positive, indicating that patents from the rest of the world generally receive fewer forward citations than patents from these chosen countries. Patents from the United States receive the most forward citations, those from Spain, Austria, and New Zealand consistently receive the least. Interestingly, Australia and New Zealand appear to deserve a place among the CMEs, while Japan seems to be one of the most radical innovators (Model 1). While I am not immediately concerned with Hall

Table 7.6. OLS testing of VoC innovation theory, by country and industry (1975–99)

Model	Patent age (years)	LMEs					
		US	Ireland	Canada	UK	Australia	New Zealand
1	0.29	2.74	2.23	1.74	1.55	1.14	0.55
	(0.001)**	(0.03)**	(0.22)**	(0.05)**	(0.04)**	(0.06)**	(0.13)**
2	0.32	2.59	1.93	1.76	1.35	1.21	0.68
	(0.001)**	(0.03)**	(0.22)**	(0.04)**	(0.04)**	(0.06)**	(0.13)**

	CMEs									
	Japan	Netherlands	Belgium	Denmark	Sweden	Finland	Germany	Switzerland	Norway	Austria
1	2.52	1.34	1.27	1.07	1.07	1.05	0.92	0.77	0.61	0.42
	(0.04)**	(0.05)**	(0.07)**	(0.09)**	(0.05)**	(0.07)**	(0.04)**	(0.05)**	(0.10)**	(0.06)**
2	2.24	1.09	1.28	0.98	1.02	1.01	1.00	0.81	0.69	0.64
	(0.04)**	(0.05)**	(0.07)**	(0.09)**	(0.05)**	(0.07)**	(0.04)**	(0.05)**	(0.10)**	(0.06)**

	Others							
	Israel	Singapore	Taiwan	S. Korea	France	Italy	Spain	ROW
1	2.25	1.90	1.34	1.21	1.06	0.69	0.07	
	(0.09)**	(0.17)**	(0.04)**	(0.04)**	(0.04)**	(0.07)**	(0.08)	
2	1.79	1.54	1.56	0.78	0.86	0.72	0.18	
	(0.09)**	(0.17)**	(0.04)**	(0.04)**	(0.04)**	(0.05)**	(0.08)*	

	Industries						Constant	R²	Observations
	IT/Telecom	Drugs/Med	Electrical	Chemical	Mechanical	Other			
1							−0.25	0.08	2,139,314
							(0.03)**		
2	3.36	2.33	0.98	0.23	−0.14		−1.14	0.10	2,139,314
	(0.02)**	(0.03)**	(0.01)**	(0.01)**	(0.01)**		(0.04)**		

Note: Analysis is by ordinary least squares (OLS). Huber–White estimates of standard errors reported in parentheses. ROW = Rest of world. $**p < .001$, $*p < .05$.

Source: National Bureau of Economic Research 2001.

and Soskice's hybrid MMEs, the three MMEs that appear in the regressions (France, Italy, Spain) have major differences between them and do not appear to form a cohesive group. Also, the high placement of Israel (arguably a pre-1970s CME, increasingly MME thereafter) and Taiwan (arguably an MME), not mentioned in VoC theory, further suggest that there may be more to radical innovation than the variables captured by Hall and Soskice. Adding controls for industry does not have a significant impact on the rankings, except for some minor shuffling (Model 2).

Finally, if one believes that both quality and quantity of patents matter, that Ireland with its relative trickle of few but highly cited patents should not necessarily be considered more radically innovative than Germany with its slightly less cited ocean of patents, then one must instead look at total citations received over time. This data is charted in Figure 7.1. Here I have merely multiplied the mean citations received per patent by the total number of patents for each country. This captures both the number and value of patents in one measure. The plots are split horizontally into three groups (LMEs, CMEs, and other countries) for comparison. Again the figure shows the US outlier, but no strong general differences in total citations between the different VoC country types.

In sum, the VoC theory does not appear to explain innovation as measured by patenting activity. Rather, the success of VoC theory in predicting innovation appears to depend on the inclusion of the United States, a major outlier, in the set of liberal market economies. I find this fact repeated regardless of

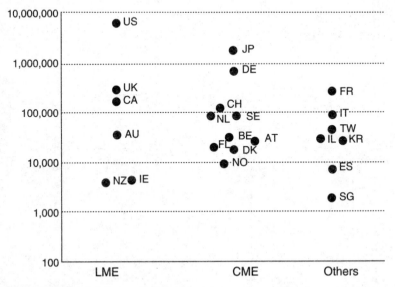

Figure 7.1. Total forward citations, 1975–99

the source of the patent data, the type of the industry classification system used, or whether simple patents or forward citations are used. However, one caveat that bears repeating is that this finding depends on an assumption of random error in using patents as a measure of innovation. Social scientists cannot yet completely describe the correlation between patents (an innovation output) and total innovation, nor do social scientists fully understand how propensity to patent varies across industry, across country, and over time.

4. CONCLUSIONS

In this article I have demonstrated that the predictions made by varieties of capitalism theory regarding national differences in technological innovation are not supported by the empirical data, and that the existing evidence depends heavily on the inclusion of a major outlier, the United States, in the class of liberal market economies. My empirical investigation included simple patent counts, patents weighted by forward citations, and scholarly publications (both simple counts and weighted). I investigated data covering all of the VoC countries over the course of several decades, little of which revealed the patterns predicted by VoC scholars.

These findings carry significant repercussions for both VoC and innovation theory. First, insofar as patents and scholarly publications are good indices of innovation, VoC theory clearly fails to provide an accurate picture of the innovation process, and hence the trade and production patterns that follow. Whether this is a problem with the LME–CME classification system or VoC's assumptions and causal mechanisms is not clear from the evidence presented here. However, I would suggest that while the firm may be the key actor in capitalist economies, and the primary producer of goods and services, it is difficult to ignore the role of the state in innovation as strongly as VoC's theory and classification system do. Throughout the world, much useful innovation is the result of state-sponsored and state-managed R&D, often originating in concerns with national security. Another stream of innovative R&D in many countries comes from the public university system, or private universities benefiting from significant state support. In still other states, innovation takes the form of incremental improvements on imported technologies, where the government has had a heavy hand in deciding which technologies will get imported. Often, the government also plays a key role as a market-maker for, and main diffuser of, new innovations. However, VoC's innovation theory omits these causal mechanisms entirely. This does not mean that VoC scholars are wrong to bring the firm onto the center stage of political economy, but rather that in trying to get away from a hackneyed focus on government protectionism and state ownership, they may have overcompensated. Future theorists must find a synthesis between the corporate-centered relationships emphasized by VoC and the state-centered mechanisms employed in traditional political economy.

Second, the statistical analyses above consistently point to the United States as an important factor in explaining global patterns of innovation. Further-more, the fixed-effects regressions reported in Table 7.6 reveal that many of the world's most innovative countries are those that also tend to have the strongest military and economic ties with the United States, including Japan, Canada, the United Kingdom, Israel, and Taiwan. Together, these observa-tions suggest that to better understand the political economy of comparative rates of innovation, future research should perhaps focus less on domestic institutions and more on international relations. This is not to argue that domestic institutions are insignificant, but rather that the scope and depth of a country's relationship with the lead innovator may also carry significant weight in determining its technological profile. There are theoretical grounds for this supposition in that while the basic laws of science may be public goods, the tacit knowledge required to apply these laws to proper use and development of new technology is relatively excludable. Therefore, factors such as foreign direct investment, educational exchanges, military assistance, and international flows of science and engineering labor between the lead innovator and other countries should be explored for their effects on innov-ation and the agglomeration patterns that interest VoC and trade theorists.

Of course, the research reported above, while suggestive, does not neces-sarily shut the door on a VoC approach to technological innovation. Innov-ation is a notoriously difficult phenomenon to measure quantitatively, and existing measures carry with them considerable noise, hence further progress needs to be made on method as well as theory. Nor does the critique here necessarily apply to other aspects of VoC theory. VoC is a broad approach to social behavior, consisting of myriad hypotheses regarding almost the whole spectrum of political economy including corporate governance, monetary policy, welfare programs, and labor reform. These hypotheses are not neces-sarily interdependent and need to be considered and tested each on its own merits. Finally, as social scientists increasingly turn to institutions and inter-national relationships to explain various phenomena related to cross-national variance in innovation, VoC scholars should be applauded for inserting political science into an area of research from which it has been all but absent.[37] While economists and sociologists have produced excellent studies of the role of these variables in international technological performance, the comparative advantage that political scientists bring to the field in terms of methods and theory make this an area deserving far greater attention by students of politics. VoC scholars have therefore provided a valuable and useful starting point for such an endeavor.

NOTES

1. See Edwards 1996; Bauer 1995; Samuels 1994; Mokyr 1990; Beasley 1988; Rosenberg and Birdzell 1986.
2. Scholars of security studies will also appreciate the importance of civilian technological innovation and its role in production and the general economy as complementary, if not foundational, to relative military power. See Samuels 1994.
3. See Tyson 1993; Mokyr 1990; Krugman 1986; Solow 1957.
4. See Saxenian 1994; Krugman 1991; Helpman 1984.
5. Hall and Soskice 2001: 36–7.
6. *Technology* is defined as a physical product, or a process of handling physical materials, which is used as an aid in problem solving. More precisely, technology is a product or process that allows social agents to perform entirely new activities or to perform established activities with increased efficiency. *Innovation* is the discovery, introduction, or development of new technology, or the adaptation of established technology to a new use or to a new physical or social environment.
7. For an alternative view of Marx, see Bimber 1994.
8. Summarized in Mowrey and Rosenberg 1979.
9. Arrow 1962.
10. Romer 1990.
11. I am concerned here specifically with those aspects of VoC theory discussed in Hall and Soskice 2001: 1–44.
12. Williamson 1985, 1975.
13. Hall and Soskice 2001: 38–9.
14. Ibid., 39.
15. Hall and Soskice's methodology will be discussed in greater detail below.
16. Hall, Jaffe, and Trajtenberg 2001; database available at (www.nber.org/patents). Accessed 24 March 2004.
17. Countries such as Luxembourg and Iceland are eliminated from the VoC typology because of their small size, while others, such as Mexico, are disqualified because they are developing nations.
18. Hall and Soskice 2001: 8.
19. Also, although country size, wealth, and other factors may be important to innovation theorists, there is no explicit motivation within VoC theory itself

for including these as separate independent variables other than restricting the data to the advanced capitalist democracies.

20. For a review of the debate see Griliches 1990; Trajtenberg 1990; Archibugi and Pianta 1996; Harhoff, Narin, Scherer, and Vopel 1999; Eaton and Kortum 1999; Jaffe, Trajtenberg, and Fogarty 2000; Hall, Jaffe, and Trajtenberg 2000, 2001.

21. Designs and plant life can also be patented; however, most econometric analysis of patent data is confined to utility patents granted for inventions such as those listed above. For a fuller description of patents and patent laws, classifications, and the application process see <http://www.uspto.gov/main/patents.htm>. Accessed 24 March 2004.

22. See Scherer 1965; Schmookler 1966.

23. Summaries of which can be found in Griliches 1984; Pakes 1986; Griliches, Hall, and Pakes 1987.

24. Hall, Jaffe, and Trajtenberg 2001.

25. Griliches 1984.

26. See Trajtenberg 1990; Hall, Jaffe, and Trajtenberg 2000; Lanjouw and Shankerman 1997, 1999; Jaffe, Trajtenberg, and Fogarty 2000.

27. Summarized in Utterback 1994.

28. Exceptions include patents in the drugs, biotechnology, food, and organic compounds subcategories that appear to be relatively poorly cited despite the fact that these are among VoC's 'radically innovative' industries; in the 'incremental' subcategories, patents related to gas, power systems, resins, and coatings appear to be more highly cited than VoC theory might assume. These might be partially explained by classification problems or by differences in the legal or technical need to cite in these industries.

29. This is because the citations data were not computerized before 1975.

30. All regressions reported here use a patent age based on grant year. Regressions performed using a patent age based on application year produced similar results.

31. 'Other' includes innovations in miscellaneous areas such as house fixtures, furniture, pipes and joints, jewelry, cutlery, receptacles, undertaking, and amusement devices.

32. With the same exceptions at the subcategory level as those found with the citations averages. See note 28 above.

33. For example, in biotechnology: $I_{US\ biotech} = US_{biotech}/US_{total} - World_{biotech}/World_{total}$.

34. Agricultural machines (a particularly difficult category to define in NBER terms) is the only category that persistently defies the VoC predictions in all time periods; while patenting in optics, pharmaceuticals, transport, organic chemistry, weapons, electrical energy, and nuclear engineering (narrowly measured) each contradicted VoC theory in different time periods.

35. An alternate interpretation of VoC theory suggests that in place of LME/CME/LMEx controls, one might include interaction terms (LME*industry,

CME*industry, and LMEx*industry). I experimented with such interaction terms but produced the same general results as those reported above.

36. As before, all pre-1975 patents are eliminated to control for truncation effects.

37. Notable exceptions include Edquist 1997; Samuels 1994; Nelson 1993; Lundvall 1992.

Part III

Rethinking Varieties of Capitalism

8

Institutional Change in Varieties
of Capitalism

Peter Hall and Kathleen Thelen*

1. INTRODUCTION

Comparative political economists have become deeply interested in processes of institutional change, especially those taking place in response to the opening of world markets associated with 'globalization' (Pierson 2001; Djelic and Quack 2003; Rieger and Leibfried 2003; Campbell 2004). They are asking a number of questions. When do the institutions of the political economy change? What factors drive the change? Are the changes in the international economy enforcing institutional convergence on the developed economies?

We take up these issues with reference to one of the more influential frameworks devised to explain national differences in economic performance and policy, namely the 'varieties of capitalism' perspective now employed by a substantial number of scholars (see Hall and Soskice 2001). Building on the literatures of neo-corporatism and the 'regulation school', this approach applies the new economics of organization to the macroeconomy (Boyer 1990; Schmitter and Streeck 1985; Milgrom and Roberts 1992). It focuses on firms, as actors central to the process of economic adjustment with core competencies that depend on the quality of the relations that they develop with other actors, including producer groups, employees, and other firms. Those relationships depend, in turn, on the institutional support provided for them in the political economy. Although the perspective acknowledges that these relationships can take on a wide range of forms, it emphasizes the distinction between liberal market economies, where firms rely heavily on competitive markets to coordinate their endeavours, and coordinated market economies, where more endeavours are coordinated strategically. These different modes of coordination are said to confer comparative institutional

* The authors are grateful to Sabina Avdagic, JohnCampbell, Richard Deeg, Henry Farrell, Martin Höpner, and Jonathan Zeitlin for their comments on earlier versions of this chapter.

advantages that mediate national responses to globalization. They rest on institutional complementarities that allow arrangements in one sphere of the political economy to enhance the results secured in others. The framework provides distinctive perspectives on many of the issues raised by globalization.

However, questions have been raised about the adequacy of the varieties of capitalism perspective for understanding institutional change. Some argue that this approach is overly static and its distinction between liberal and coordinated market economies outmoded by the liberalization of the world's economies. Others read into it an overweening functionalism that explains institutional change by reference to its macroeconomic effects, and suggest that the approach neglects the social or political dimensions of institutional change.[1] These critiques raise important issues that go well beyond the Hall and Soskice (2001) volume. The varieties of capitalism approach offers fresh and intriguing insights into differences among the developed economies, but it can hardly be considered viable if it cannot also comprehend processes of institutional change. Many of the criticisms suggest that the equilibrium elements of the new economics of organization analysis are inimical to dynamic analysis and that rationalist approaches understate the chaotic quality of institutional change or the contribution unintended consequences make to it. These concerns have significance for the analysis of institutional change more generally.

The objective of this paper is to address these issues by elaborating an account of institutional change more extended than the one provided in the study by Hall and Soskice (2001), but congruent with its varieties of capitalism perspective. Our claim is that this perspective embodies a sophisticated understanding of institutional change that is eminently political and useful for analysing the contemporary developments in the advanced political economies. We show that the equilibrium aspects of this approach are not incompatible with dynamic views of the political economy and explain why rationalist approaches to the political economy need not imply a barren functionalism.

We begin by reviewing some basic tenets of the varieties of capitalism approach that underpin cross-national comparisons in order to show that they can inform the analysis of change as well. Based on them, we develop a series of propositions concerning the sources of institutional stability, which we subsequently use to develop contentions about institutional change. Although our principal objective is to outline a theoretical perspective, we provide some preliminary substantiation for its propositions with reference to recent developments in Germany and other coordinated economies, since these are key cases for analysts of change in the political economy. We close by drawing some general conclusions about the trajectory of the European economies today.

2. THE INSTITUTIONAL AND THEORETICAL TERRAIN

In this paper, we conceptualize institutions as a set of regularized practices with a rule-like quality in the sense that the actors expect the practices to be observed and which, in some but not all, cases are supported by formal sanctions. They can range from regulations backed by the force of law or organizational procedure, such as the rules that apply when a worker is laid off, to more informal practices that have a conventional character, such as the expectation that firms will offer a certain number of apprenticeships.[2] In some cases, macro-institutions, such as the 'vocational training system', are composed of many component rules and practices that are themselves institutions.

Compared with alternative perspectives, several features of the varieties of capitalism approach to institutions are distinctive. First, as a firm-centric and broadly rationalist approach, it conceptualizes the political economy as a terrain peopled with entrepreneurial actors seeking to advance their interests as they construe them, constrained by the existing rules and institutions but also looking for ways to make institutions work for them. Although some institutions rely on sanctions for their operation, the varieties of capitalism approach moves away from a view of institutions purely as factors that constrain action towards one that sees them also as resources, providing opportunities for particular types of action, and especially for collective action (see Hall 1998).

Second, the varieties of capitalism framework emphasizes that the political economy is replete with a multiplicity of institutions, many nested inside others. Some can serve as functional substitutes for other institutions, at least for some purposes.[3] Thus, any strategy adopted by a firm or other actor is likely to be conditioned, not by one, but by a number of institutions. Emphasizing institutional interaction effects, the varieties of capitalism approach argues that firm strategies are conditioned simultaneously by multiple institutions, often in different spheres of the political economy (Hall and Soskice 2001: 21–36).

There are important points of tangency between this perspective and some other well-known approaches to institutions. From the 'logic of appropriateness' approach favoured by some new institutionalists, this perspective accepts the point that institutions may sometimes influence action because they define behaviour seen as appropriate to the endeavour at hand from the perspective of a particular cultural worldview (March and Olsen 1989; Dobbin 2000). From the 'institutions as equilibrium' approach advanced by Calvert (1995a, 1995b) and others, it accepts the observation that the stability of a particular pattern of strategic interaction often rests on the absence of

Pareto-improving alternatives apparent to the actors under current conditions. Although often presented as polar opposites, we do not regard these perspectives as mutually exclusive in a real world that contains many motives for and patterns of behaviour.

However, neither of these approaches fully conveys the 'institutions as resources' element of our perspective and, if carried to extremes, both overstate the degree to which any one institution determines the action. To say that an institution specifies patterns of behaviour seen as appropriate to the culture should not be taken to imply that all or even most in that culture adhere slavishly to it. There is always room, and often reason, to be critical of what is deemed 'appropriate'. Similarly, although the mutual benefits of strategic interaction may render an institution more stable, this observation says only a little about how institutions are sustained, because it ignores the omnipresent processes of search and negotiation whereby entrepreneurial actors look for alternative ways in which to advance their interests (Knight 1995). There is more intrinsic openness to the institutional arena than these two perspectives imply.

3. INSTITUTIONAL STABILITY AS A POLITICAL PROBLEM

Any analysis of how institutions change should begin from a conception of how institutions are sustained during periods when they remain stable. As noted above, the core theoretical pillars that distinguish the varieties of capitalism framework from many alternatives are (i) it puts employer interests at the centre of analysis, and (ii) it draws attention specifically to the institutions that support either market or strategic coordination among firms and between them and other actors. These two theoretical claims generate a specific set of propositions about institutional stability.

First, while the emphasis on employer interests does not imply that other actors (labour, governments) are unimportant, it underscores a crucial assumption, namely, that the institutions and practices of capitalist political economies can rarely be sustained over time without the active support of at least some powerful segments of capital (see, especially, Swenson 2002). Moreover, as we have noted, the varieties of capitalism framework holds that most institutions in the political economy rest not on practices of passive rule-following by firms, but on a more active process in which entrepreneurial actors seek to advance their interests, including in contexts of strategic interaction where institutions can improve the well-being of those who participate in them by resolving collective action dilemmas. Such a view belies any simple notions of 'institutional inertia' and implies a relatively loose coupling between self-interest and institutions.

This loose coupling means that a good deal of politics surrounds institutional stability. From the broadly rationalist perspective we adopt here, the durability of an institution can rest substantially, if rarely wholly, on how well it serves the interests of the relevant actors. Where an institution fails to serve those interests well, it becomes fragile and susceptible to defection from its rules. But actors' calculations about whether an institutional practice serves their interests are complex ones, dependent on a range of considerations. They entail balancing the multiple interests that one single actor has in a potential course of action, along with time discounts and competing evaluations about the effects of one's actions (Hall 2005).

In the context of this politics, the varieties of capitalism perspective draws attention to several factors that can militate in favour of the stability of institutions. One is the presence of institutional interaction. As we have noted, the strategies followed by an actor, such as a firm, and the benefits to be expected from the use of these strategies are usually conditional on the presence of a number of other institutions. Many German firms would perhaps be more willing to withdraw from the institutions that coordinate wage bargaining if they did not also face powerful German unions or operate particular types of production regimes.[4] Where the benefits of changing one institution are likely to be realized only when a substantial number of other institutions are also transformed, that institution should be more stable. Conversely, where there are alternative institutional means available for accomplishing a task, a firm's interests may bind it less tightly to one institution.

Considerations about the ease with which alternative institutions can be constructed also condition the judgements actors make about whether to adhere to an existing institution. Because institutions are collective constructs, it can be difficult to replace one with another. In a few cases, an alternative can be secured by fiat: the Swedish government shifted drivers from the left- to the right-hand side of the road in one fell swoop. But, in many instances, as Culpepper (2003) shows, it can be difficult to persuade actors to coordinate on new ways of doing things, even when there are reasons to think they might be Pareto-improving. Before a new institution is established, one cannot prove it will deliver benefits, and the relevant actors cannot be sure of the behaviour of others on whom its efficacy may depend. The presence of such uncertainties is a crucial factor underpinning institutional stability (Shepsle 1986).

Thus, the availability of meta-institutions for deliberation and rule-making can be crucial to the stability of existing institutions and to the prospects for reform (Hall and Soskice 2001: 10–12). When the world throws up shocks that unsettle the benefits flowing from the existing institutions, deliberative forums facilitate the re-equilibration of cooperative endeavour, by allowing for (i) 'diagnosis', where the issue is to agree on the cause-and-effect relations generating the problem and pertinent to the solution, and for (ii) 'agreement on distributive justice', where the issue is to apportion the risks and benefits that can flow unequally from cooperation.

However, if daunted, actors are not altogether deterred by uncertainty. The result is a *politics* of institutional stability. Actors are generally engaged in a continuous reassessment of their own scope for action and the intentions of those with whom they are interacting. They need to be reassured that existing institutions continue to serve their interests and that better alternatives are not available. While some actors probe the outer limits of existing arrangements, others try to defend these institutions by assuring others that they are better than the available alternatives. One feature of this politics is continuous experimentation, as the relevant actors test the bounds of what others will deem acceptable behaviour; seek new information about their partners; assess the effects of alternative courses of action; and consider how severely defection from institutionally sanctioned patterns of behaviour will be punished. For some actors at some times, of course, institutional stability might depend on habit. But, in the political economy, it more often depends on a stream of action that is political in the sense that it entails conflict designed to test the limits of cooperative arrangements and of the processes of mobilization that bring other actors in line with those arrangements (Thelen 2001: 73 ff.).

This brings us to the second pillar of the varieties of capitalism approach and its implications for the analysis of stability and change. The approach emphasizes two distinctive ideal-typical patterns of *coordination* among firms and other actors in the political economy (market coordination and strategic coordination). However, it follows from what we have just said that our perspective calls for some revision in the way in which 'coordination' is construed. In game-theoretic analyses, 'coordination' is sometimes seen as a pattern of behaviour that arises relatively spontaneously, when the opportunity appears among actors who are viewed as contractors.[5] Coordination is said to follow directly from the presence of supportive institutions. In contrast, from our perspective, the achievement of coordination appears as a political problem. Coordination is not easily secured and rarely follows automatically from the presence of certain institutions. Instead, active support for a specific mode of coordination must be mobilized on a relatively continuous basis from actors who are conscious of the limitations as well as the advantages of any particular course of action. Achieving and maintaining coordination usually also involves the exercise of power, because forging and maintaining particular institutional arrangements creates winners and losers, notably on both sides of the class divide (Moe 2005; Swenson 2002; Gruber 2000).

Here again, some factors militate in favour of continuity in the institutional landscape. If institutions do not simply resolve collective action dilemmas, but also contribute to the balance of power found in many parts of the political economy, then we can expect the feedback effects of existing institutions to work to the disadvantage of an institution's challengers (Pierson 1993, 1994). If power relations in a cooperative context turn, in part, on the relative opportunity costs to each side of failing to cooperate, as Knight (1992) has argued, those costs depend on other institutional practices in which the actors are imbricated that may not be immediately susceptible to change. When deciding whether to bargain cooperatively with unions, for instance, employers are influenced by other institutions, such as the works councils they face, the work practices and production regimes they have evolved, and a range of institutions affecting the costs a strike or lock-out would impose on them.

This outline of the politics of stability speaks to one of the principal criticisms levelled at the varieties of capitalism perspective, namely, that it adopts an overly functionalist approach to the problem of institutional change (cf. Crouch 2005; Streeck 2005). We can see what it borrows from functionalist approaches and where it rejects them. Our perspective shares the functionalist premise that the support that groups provide for an institution is motivated, to some extent, by the benefits the institution provides, flowing from the functions it performs. However, the perspective differs from functionalist accounts in two key respects.

First, we do not assume that support for an institution derives primarily from the contribution it makes to aggregate economic welfare. Varieties-of-capitalism analysts devote a good deal of attention to explaining how the institutions of the political economy contribute to national well-being. But they do not generally claim that the existence of an institution depends on that contribution. Institutional politics as we understand it turns not on the issues of aggregate welfare, but on the actions of self-interested actors seeking better outcomes for themselves or the groups they represent (Hall and Soskice 2001: 57–8).

Second, in contrast to some functionalist analyses, we think it dangerous to assume that the institutions of the political economy were originally created to serve the interests they advance at much later periods of time. German employers, for instance, expressed vociferous opposition to the 1950s legislation that enhanced labour's rights on the shop floor (Höpner 2003). However, once those institutions were in place, employers organized production strategies and a range of ancillary practices around them, aiming at high-priced, high-quality production (Streeck 1992). As a result, most large manufacturing firms support works councils, because their market and production strategies rely on them. In this as in many other such instances, the institutions of the political economy are instruments that actors gradually adapt to their purposes and in which they become invested only after they have accommodated their practices to them (Thelen 2004).[6] Thus, the current effects of an institution may help to explain contemporary support for it but can explain the origins of an institution only rarely.

In sum, although some see the varieties of capitalism approach as insufficiently political because it focuses on the ways firms coordinate their endeavours construed in equilibrium terms, it deploys an understanding of institutions that anticipates a lively politics, marked by experimentation, negotiation and conflict, even in cases of institutional stability. As Thelen (2001) argued, this approach has always rejected the notion that institutions are automatically stable, even when they are Pareto-improving, and it associates the maintenance of equilibrium outcomes with important political dynamics.

4. INSTITUTIONAL CHANGE IN THE POLITICAL ECONOMY

Our understanding of institutional change follows directly from this perspective on institutional stability. Because political economies are full of entrepreneurial actors interested in improving their position, existing institutions are bound to come under pressure. Institutional equilibria change, as developments shift the material situation, power and self-understandings of the actors. Thus, Hall and Soskice (2001: 54) argued that institutional change will be a regular feature of both liberal and coordinated market economies. The key issues are: what precipitates change, which actors are central to it, how will it occur, and how should we interpret the results?

4.1. The Impetus for Institutional Change

There is no doubt that events in the international political economy are important stimuli for contemporary institutional change. Among the OECD countries, such developments include the growing weight of the service sector in employment and falling barriers to trade or communication that intensify international competition and open up opportunities for sales or production elsewhere in the world. The liberalizing initiatives of the European Union, the collapse of Communism and the reunification of Germany have been of special importance to Europe. These developments have shifted the opportunity structures and returns to existing institutions for many firms and workers, inspiring institutional ferment in Europe, and some analyses treat the problem of institutional change as if the impetus were invariably exogenous to the institutions themselves (cf. Frieden and Rogowski 1996).

As others have noted, however, many institutional changes in the political economies of Europe have been inspired by unanticipated effects flowing from existing institutions (Thelen 2004; Thelen and van Wijnbergen 2004; Greif and Laitin 2005). The case of solidaristic wage bargaining in Sweden is a well-known example (see, especially, Pontusson and Swenson 1996). In the 1930s, Swedish employers pressed for centralized bargaining arrangements in order to link wages in the sheltered sectors to those bargained for the export sectors. But they did not anticipate that centralized bargaining would also become a vehicle for compressing differentials between the wages of skilled and unskilled workers. Over time, centralized bargaining strengthened the position of unskilled workers, whose interests could be pooled across all industries in a way that had not been possible under sectoral bargaining, and became the vehicle for political exchange with a strong social democratic government. As Sweden's unskilled workers used their strength to narrow differentials with skilled workers, however, they undermined the capacity of employers to recruit and deploy skilled labour. By the 1980s, concerns about this issue were grave enough to lead the export sectors to pull out of centralized bargaining arrangements, thereby modifying the institution they had originally created.

We see a similar dynamic of endogenously generated change in the German economy, where firms in declining industries, such as coal and steel, took advantage of early retirement policies to resolve structural crises during the 1950s and 1960s. As these strategies proliferated in unanticipated ways in the 1970s and beyond, they fuelled massive increases in non-wage labour costs (Manow and Seils 2000). Although effective at facilitating orderly workforce reductions in the 1980s and 1990s, these retirement practices had a deadening effect on job creation and imposed heavy burdens on social insurance funds. The effect was to spark not only revisions to the early retirement regime, but also broader pressures for labour market reform.

In short, the history of change in the European political economies should not be written as if it were entirely a series of responses to external shocks. The challenge facing analysts is to see it as a process partly endogenous to the character of the institutions developed in each nation and driven by the unintended consequences that flow from those institutions.

4.2. Multiple Agents of Adjustment

One of the notable features of the varieties of capitalism approach is its insistence that there are multiple agents of adjustment in the political economy. Globalization is often presented as a contest between states and market forces (cf. Cable 1995), and there is no denying that the decisions governments take in response to international challenges play a key role in the institutional development of the political economy. In such contexts, as Streeck (2004) has observed, governments come closest to being architectonic actors: on the regulations they promulgate depend many other institutions. However, the varieties of capitalism perspective insists that firms can be equally important agents of national adjustment. They cannot always construct new collective institutions without help from governments, but shifts in firm strategy can erode the viability of some institutions and strengthen others. Moreover, firms are even more sensitive than governments to shifts in the economy, because their survival is at stake. A good deal of the process of institutional adjustment in the developed economies can be understood as a *pas de deux* between firms and governments in which each responds to different pressures but has to cope with the moves made by the other side.

Recent analyses by Culpepper (2006) and O'Sullivan (2007) reveal the changes in the structure of French financial markets. Although those shifts began with government initiatives to privatize national enterprises and expand the ambit of French equity markets, the traditional networks binding French business to the state were unwound only when key firms took the initiative to dissolve their core shareholdings in the newly privatized enterprises and to seek foreign acquisitions and investors. Much of the impetus for their strategies derived from the opening of international markets made possible by agreements the French governments signed, but those strategies were driven by new market pressures and opportunities. Large French firms realized they would prosper only if they secured global market share, and higher stock prices became a major asset in the stock swaps used to secure new acquisitions. Thus, French companies took a series of initiatives to solidify their market positions, and the government obliged with congenial regulatory reforms (Tiberghien 2002).

As important as state policy is to how markets are structured and operate, governments typically do not have the luxury of responding to economic developments on a *tabula rasa*. In many cases, they have to react to corporate strategies that are shifting even more rapidly in response to those developments. Changes in rules often follow the accumulation of 'deviant' behaviour, with a view to bringing formal rules or legal regimes back into alignment with behaviour (Streeck and Thelen 2005: 15–16). By placing employers at the centre of analysis, the varieties of capitalism framework contextualizes the analysis of government reform, drawing attention to the transformative potential of shifting firm strategies.[7]

4.3. Institutional Change and the Politics of Coordination

As William Sewell has emphasized recently, tumult is a permanent feature of capitalism—as fortunes are made and lost, firms are founded and fail, workers are hired, trained, or fired, as technology transforms production, and as whole industries, regions, and countries prosper or decline (Sewell 2008). In a context whose defining feature is change, we need a theory to tell us *which changes exactly* we should be noting – in other words, which changes are likely to be *consequential* for the efficacy of the economy and related social outcomes.

The varieties of capitalism framework provides an answer, suggesting that the changes that should command our attention are those affecting the capacities of firms to coordinate strategically. As noted above, the varieties of capitalism perspective takes a broad view of institutions that does not fixate on formal 'parchment' rules. Indeed, this perspective insists that it is essential to distinguish between the formal institutional arrangements and the economic equilibria those institutions support through their impact on the incentives and strategies of actors, such as firms and workers. Many formal institutional changes – even quite dramatic ones – are largely inconsequential with respect to the extent and type of employer coordination achieved under them, and stability in formal institutional arrangements does not in itself imply the absence of potentially consequential shifts in coordination in the political economy. Let us pursue each of these somewhat counterintuitive points.

First, as an empirical matter, it is clear that specific types of coordination (whether market or strategic) can be sustained throughout many changes in the formal institutional infrastructure governing a political economy. The two broad families of political economies identified by the varieties of capitalism approach have deep roots in history (Iversen and Soskice 2007). Over the past century, for example, strategic coordination in Sweden has survived massive changes in the social and political context, including democratization and the transition from agriculture to industry to services. Thelen (2004) documents many significant revisions to the rules governing Germany's system of coordinated training, as it was adapted over a 100-year time period to incorporate new actors and address new technological and market conditions. A major message of her study was that significant revisions to formal institutional arrangements may not only be consistent with continued coord-ination, but are often necessary to sustain it (see also Hacker 2005).

Conversely, formal institutional stability is no guarantee of continued coordination. While many analysts of institutional change focus their atten-tion on major legislative initiatives, such as Margaret Thatcher's reforms to industrial relations or Gerhard Schröder's reform of corporate taxation, the framework we have outlined suggests that equally significant changes may transpire in more subtle ways, under the surface of formal institutional stability. In such cases, stability in formal institutional arrangements masks important shifts in the extent and type of coordination achieved under them. Among the developments that may be most consequential for coordination, we draw attention to processes of defection and reinterpretation.[8]

We borrow the term 'defection' from game theory, where it refers to strategies that deviate from the behaviours associated with a cooperative outcome, and use it for cases in which actors who have been following the practices prescribed by an institution stop doing so. Although less eye-catching than legislative reform, this is an important route to institutional change in the political economy. Recent developments in the German metal-working sector provide a good example (see Kume and Thelen 1999; Thelen 2000). For the past 50 years, German collective bargaining has taken the form of pattern bargaining led informally by the metalworking sector. Over the course of the 1970s and 1980s, however, growing numbers of small firms opted out of membership in the employer associations that organize this industry. Since collective bargaining coverage relies, not on union member-ship, but on whether a firm is a member of the employers associations, these defections have reduced bargaining coverage. The resulting erosion in bar-gaining has seriously compromised coordination in industrial relations des-pite the fact that the formal institutional apparatus for negotiation itself remains intact.

Another route to institutional change that often lies beneath the radar of many other analytic approaches is based on what we call 'reinterpretation'. In these instances, the actors associated with an institution gradually change their interpretation of its rules, and thus its practices, without defecting from or dismantling the formal institution itself. In some cases, this occurs when the courts reinterpret a legal or regulatory regime. In others, it involves the gradual acceptance of practices that would not formerly have been seen as congruent with the formal institution. In comparison with overt efforts to revise or abolish that institution, the process of reinterpretation shifts the existing practices in piecemeal fashion from below (Aoki 2001; Streeck and Thelen 2005).

Recent developments in German collective bargaining comprehend many instances of reinterpretation, as employers and workers attempt to bend the existing practices to suit their interests, without formally abolishing them. A good example lies in skirmishes over the meaning of a core provision in German labour law known as the 'favourability principle' (*Günstigkeitsprinzip*; Rehder 2004). This principle stipulates that certain issues normally reserved for collective bargaining at the industry level can be decided at the local level, in bargaining between works councils and individual employers, provided that the outcome operates 'to the advantage of the worker'. Thus, firms can pay wages in excess of the industry rate, but they cannot demand concession bargaining. In recent years, however, employers began to try to take advantage of an ambiguity in the meaning of 'favourability' (*Günstigkeit*) to justify local employment pacts that offer workers greater job security in return for lower wages. Their argument was that anything offering greater job security in a context of high unemployment operates 'in favour of the worker' ('*zu Gunsten des Arbeitnehmers*'). Although that particular practice has so far been deemed illegal by the courts, these sorts of efforts to reinterpret the rules that enshrine a particular division of labour in collective bargaining have been a regular feature of German industrial relations. In 1984, such efforts led to plant-level agreements on working time, and others continue to extend the space for work council bargaining on a range of issues (Thelen 1991; Hassel and Williamson 2004).

Processes such as these can act as shock absorbers in the face of new economic developments, bringing an elasticity to the institutions of the political economy that analyses focused on formal rules sometimes miss. A significant flexibilization of the German bargaining system has been accomplished without much rewriting of the formal rules, through successive (and successively expansive) interpretations of the scope for bargaining at the local level in response to the market conditions faced by individual firms. These are cases in which the 'rules' conventionally associated with an institution are reinterpreted, often informally, to accommodate new diversities in the interests of the actors associated with it. Moreover, this avenue poses fewer obstacles than might confront reformers if they were to launch a frontal assault on the formal arrangements. Changes can be sought quietly, for example, through the courts, avoiding noisy legislative battles that are sure to mobilize the opposition.[9] They can be sold as a way to 'fix' problems with the existing arrangements sustaining coordination, thereby offering opportunities to forge coalitions with those who might resist an institution's dismantling but be more than happy to cooperate in 'clarifying' its rules. In short, these forms of elasticity may be important to the survival of strategic coordination, even though they entail changes to the practices associated with a formal set of institutions and some of their substantive outcomes.

4.4. Governmental Reform and the Politics of Coordination

Of course, the more visible route to institutional change is through processes of reform, which we define as institutional change explicitly mandated or endorsed by governments. We see this form of institutional change as a process built on coalitional politics, in which segments of capital are usually pivotal. The principal challenge facing analysts, therefore, is to identify the coalitions of social or political actors that provide the support for a change in regulations or policy regimes and the factors motivating their support. The implication of this perspective is that institutional reform originates in political compromises among actors, whether producer groups or political parties, diversely motivated in contexts of distributive conflict (Palier 2005). Thus, there are no guarantees that the process of institutional reform will advance national well-being. If firms decide to support the regulatory regimes that sustain the comparative institutional advantages of the nation, it is because they also underpin the competitive advantages of the firm. Behind many reform debates lie other conflicts of interest, such as those that divide capital and labour or different types of firms and workers. Institutional change is a process of continuous mutual adjustment inflected by distributive concerns.

However, the varieties of capitalism perspective reminds us that the alignments central to these conflicts can be influenced by the character of existing institutions. Firms and other actors do not judge proposals for reform as if the new institutions will operate on a blank slate but in the context of institutions in other spheres of the political economy. Actors' assessments of the costs or benefits of a new set of institutions will turn on how those institutions fit with strategies into which they have been drawn by virtue of the presence of supportive institutions elsewhere in the economy. Therefore, institutional arrangements in one sphere of the political economy condition the positions that actors take on institutional reform in other spheres.

Swenson's (2001) comparison of pension politics in Sweden and the USA provides a nice example of this point. He shows how institutions developed in the arena of industrial relations during the 1930s conditioned the types of pension policies employers were willing to support in the 1950s. Because Sweden's centralized bargaining system kept wage competition in check, it inspired new forms of competition for skilled workers based on the provision of company pensions. As the costs of the latter rose under conditions of full employment, however, employers found this type of competition overly costly and were willing to support a social democratic initiative to institute generous public pensions. In contrast, the Wagner Act of 1935 left wage bargaining in the United States at the company level, fostering a segmentation between low-skill firms operating with low non-wage costs and high-skill firms that used generous company pensions to attract skilled labour. Because each type of firm had interests in the existing pension regime, in the context of segmental industrial relations, there was no broad business constituency for generous public pensions in the United States.

Goyer's (2005, 2006) comparison of reforms to corporate governance in France and Germany identifies a similar dynamic. In response to international economic developments, there was pressure for reform in both countries. But the character of the reforms firms were willing to support in the sphere of corporate governance was influenced, in each country, by the character of institutional arrangements in the sphere of labour relations. Many French firms were willing to accept measures that made hostile takeovers more feasible and corporate restructuring focused on share prices more urgent because they faced works councils and trade unions that were too weak to mount much opposition to restructuring. There, management's room for manoeuvre is substantial. In Germany, in contrast, where powerful works councils and trade unions are institutionally entrenched, managers were receptive to the adoption of international accounting standards and measures to strengthen the position of minority shareholders, but resisted efforts to expose firms to hostile takeovers, because industrial relations institutions made it more difficult for them to restructure quickly in response to demands for 'shareholder value'.

5. THE IMPLICATIONS FOR VARIETIES OF CAPITALISM

What does this analysis imply about the survival of distinctive varieties of capitalism in Europe and the trajectories of change in its political economies? The magnitude of the challenges should not be minimized. Over the past decade, Europe's largest economies have suffered from low rates of growth and high levels of unemployment. Aging populations burden many welfare states, and the rise of the service sector has called into question economic models attuned to the demands of industrial capitalism (Iversen and Wren 1998). In such contexts, there is bound to be institutional change.

5.1. Beyond Liberalization

However, the terms of contemporary debate about institutional change are manifestly inadequate for the task of assessing the impact of such changes.

Many analysts (e.g. Streeck 2008; Glyn 2004; Howell 2003; Coates 2005) ask whether the developed economies are 'liberalizing' and subsume under that label a wide spectrum of initiatives, including efforts to decentralize collective bargaining, neutralize unions, dismantle tripartism, privatize industry, cut back social benefits, reduce employment protection, promote equity invest-ments, encourage part-time employment, and lower minimum wages. Many of these measures reinforce the role of markets in the allocation of resources. But, for those interested in the impact of institutional reform on broad patterns of coordination, the crudeness of this category—'liberalization'—obscures more than it illuminates. It suffers from three prominent limitations.

First, liberalization is a multidimensional process. The types of initiatives we have just listed need not accompany one another and often do not. Denmark has made major cuts to unemployment benefits even as it shored up tripartism and strengthened unions. France has encouraged part-time work without cutting its minimum wage or reducing employment protections for regular full-time workers. To what extent these measures tend to occur together is an object for inquiry but, for that kind of inquiry to be possible, we need to disaggregate the concept of 'liberalization' and explore each of its dimensions.

Second, even measures to 'liberalize' a single sphere of the political econ-omy do not all have the same effects. Consider the reform of corporate governance. Steps to protect minority shareholders, to encourage inter-national accounting standards, to promote independent directors, to unwind cross-shareholdings and to allow hostile mergers and acquisitions are all often described as elements of a single 'liberalization' process that is undermining 'coordinated market economies'. But the impact of each of these measures on the ways firms coordinate is different. Some analysts seem to assume that any step in this direction will substantially enhance the power of shareholders vis-à-vis stakeholders and corrode the potential for strategic coordination. However, we see few reasons why the adoption of international accounting standards, independent directors and better protection for minority share-holders should damage the corporate networks that condition the provision of capital in such nations, let alone dictate changes in labour relations. Conversely, if hostile takeovers were to become a prominent feature of such economies, investors would have a way of enforcing their concerns about 'shareholder value' on managers, who might be impelled to unwind some of the cooperative arrangements with other stakeholders on which modes of strategic coordination depend. To treat all of these measures as part of a single process of 'liberalization' inadvertently disguises differences in their impact.

Third, if our analysis is correct, the economic impact of many institutional reforms should be dependent on the structure of other institutional arrange-ments in that economy. There is evidence, for instance, that the economic effects of reforms to corporate governance depend on the character of labour relations (Hall and Gingerich 2004). A number of studies have suggested that the impact of making the central bank more independent of political control will turn on the character of the national wage bargaining system (Iversen 1999; Hall and Franzese 1998). Even when identical institutional reforms are being examined, to assume they will have identical effects in all nations is a mistake. Because of institutional interaction effects, the impact may vary dramatically.

Without denying that the concept of 'liberalization' has an important political reality associated with the 'move to the market' begun in the era of Reagan and Thatcher, we question its value for diagnosing the impact of institutional reform on the developed political economies. Britain and Sweden both experienced what can be called significant 'liberalization' of industrial relations during the 1980s and 1990s (Wallerstein and Golden 1997). But liberalization in Britain was associated with the decline of unions and employers associations, effectively dismantling some kinds of coordinating capacities. In Sweden, in contrast, liberalization involved a movement away from national-level wage coordination, accompanied by a cross-class realignment that brought much closer coordination between blue and white collar bargaining within the export sector, while leaving the public sector to bargain separately (Thelen and Kume 2005). Not all changes grouped together under the rubric of 'liberalization' produce meaningful 'convergence' between coordinated and liberal market economies. To make sense of such developments, we need alternative categories with which to secure more fine-grained assessments of the impact of institutional change.

To frame the debate in terms of an undifferentiated view of 'liberalization' squanders one of the principal advances offered by the varieties of capitalism framework. The corporatist literature of the 1970s and 1980s often arrayed countries along a single continuum, portraying differences between them as differences in degree (i.e. as 'more' versus 'less' corporatist; Thelen 1994). In contrast, the varieties of capitalism framework recasts the debate, organizing the analysis of political economies around ideal-typical models that operate according to different logics. In other words, the differences among them are in kind rather than degree. Many current analyses of liberalization effectively resituate countries on a single continuum, thereby reducing the issue of change to one about movement along that single continuum.

By now an impressive body of research demonstrates that, even after two decades of liberalization, a substantial gap remains between the coordinated and liberal market economies (Hall and Gingerich 2004: Table 8). Despite increases in part-time and/or temporary employment, and declines in unemployment benefits, employment protection and union membership, the most generous welfare states remain the most generous (Garfinkel et al. 2007). Countries where firms have traditionally relied on specific, as opposed to general, skills continue to do so (Campbell et al. 2006; Estevez-Abe et al. 2001). Although wages are now rarely coordinated at the peak level and sectoral wage coordination is looser than 20 years ago, there is still extensive wage coordination in coordinated market economies (Hassel and Williamson 2004). More dramatic changes are visible in the areas of corporate governance and finance, although, even there, moves to liberalize have provoked resistance (Callaghan 2004; Guillen 2000).

5.2. The Nature and Direction of Change

The observation that contemporary changes have not erased the core distinction between liberal market economies and coordinated market economies does not imply, however, that the changes currently underway are insignificant. As a first step towards assessing that significance, we need to distinguish between particular sets of institutional arrangements present in the political economy and the type of coordination they sustain. Critics of varieties of capitalism sometimes view any changes in formal institutions as a sign of changes in coordinating capacities. As we have indicated, however, some institutional changes erode those capacities, while others may simply shore them up.

However, the breadth of the categories of 'market' and 'strategic' coordination *can* mask changes in the quality of the equilibria secured under each modality. This suggests the need to build out from the core dichotomy on which the original varieties of capitalism framework rests to more nuanced analyses of what might be described as non-trivial movement within the broad categories of 'coordinated' and 'liberal' market economies (see e.g. Höpner, 2007; Amable 2003; Swank et al. 2008). In Germany, for example, the reforms made in a number of realms, including industrial relations, vocational training and social policy, do not signal a shift to the Anglo-Saxon model so much as they point to the development of new forms of dualism and labour market segmentation. These are characteristics associated in the past with what the original varieties of capitalism volume identified as an alternative version of 'group-based' coordination, present, for example, in Japan (Hall and Soskice 2001: 33–6). The narrowing of collective bargaining coverage, the closure of internal labour markets especially in large companies, the trend towards more enterprise-oriented modes of in-plant training, and welfare state reforms that sharpen the divide between labour market insiders and outsiders represent important developments in the mode of coordination, even if they do not signal its collapse (Thelen and Kume 2006).

The emphasis of the varieties of capitalism framework on the systemic features of the political economy provides crucial tools for understanding the impact and direction of change. It draws our attention, for instance, to the relationship between cooperation involving labour and capital at the firm level (as between works councils and employers in large firms) and the state of coordination at the national-political level (Thelen and van Wijnbergen 2003). Developments in this relationship are not well captured on a simple liberalization continuum, although it is also clear that analysing their causes and consequences will require the development of more differentiated categories than the simple but powerful dichotomy between strategic and market coordination.

In developing such categories, our perspective suggests promise in focusing on the political coalitions that support the institutional arrangements under-pinning the coordination. Influenced by the varieties of capitalism perspective, a promising literature in comparative political economy is beginning to link institutional analysis to coalitional analysis (Iversen and Soskice 2007; Gourevitch and Shinn 2005; Thelen 2004; Mares 2003; Huber and Stephens 2001; Swenson 2002). Much of it traces the genesis of important institutional configurations to specific sets of coalitions, formed either among producer groups or within the electoral arena, many of them cross-class coalitions.[10]

A related set of analyses explains changes in the form or function of institutions over time by reference to shifts in coalitional politics on which they rest (Iversen 1999; Thelen 2004). These analyses suggest that important distinctions among liberal and coordinated market economies, bearing on the resilience of coordination in each and on the distribution of its benefits, can be based on variation in the sources of political support for the types of coordination they display (see also Pontusson 2005). Such studies have also begun to explain the resiliency of more solidaristic forms of coordination, even as they provide insights into why other countries drift towards more decentralized, segmentalist forms of coordination (Martin and Thelen 2007; Palier and Thelen 2008). In sum, the kind of coalitional analysis that has been so important for explaining the origins of many institutions in coordinated market economies also provides the basis for a dynamic account of how shifting alignments of interests bring about the reconfiguration of institutions and forms of coordination in both liberal and coordinated market economies.

Not all of the important changes in Europe, however, reflect renegotiations of coordination: it is also possible for strategic coordination to give way to market coordination. The 'mixed market economies' of southern Europe provide a set of cases, where this kind of outcome is in prospect, against which our perspectives can be assessed (Hall and Gingerich 2004). Historically, these political economies have been characterized by high levels of strategic coordination in corporate governance and labour relations, but coordination secured largely by the actions of relatively interventionist states (Schmidt 2002). Therefore, they are hard cases, in particular, for our proposition that institutional change is led as often 'from below' as 'from above'.

France is the paradigmatic case. There, large-scale change in the political economy was initiated by a series of governmental decisions to forsake *dirigiste* policies in favour of market-oriented coordination, beginning in 1983 (Hall 1987). By virtue of the prominent role its state played in strategic coordination, France was peculiarly vulnerable to the disillusionment with state intervention that followed the economic crises of the 1970s and the institutional transformation of its political economy more profound than elsewhere in Europe. As Culpepper (2006) has observed, however, once given a freer hand, French firms led the movement that was to move corporate governance and industrial relations in the private sector in market-oriented directions. Large firms took responsibility for devising new modes of inter-corporate coordination to replace those that had once been operated by the state (Hancké 2002). In short, although the endpoint was more dramatic, on close inspection, France displays a politics of institutional change involving initiatives from above and below, marked by various kinds of mobilization and experimentation, that corresponds to the model presented here (Culpepper et al. 2006).

6. CONCLUSION

The objective of this paper is to elaborate the perspective on institutional change we associate with a varieties of capitalism approach to the political economy. We have tried to show that an approach that understands institutions at least partly in equilibrium terms can accommodate an analysis of institutional change, and that a broadly rationalist approach can comprehend many of the subtle features of such processes of change. We have emphasized that, even when institutions are Pareto-improving in the context of strategic interaction, their stability should not be taken for granted because it rests on a highly political process of mobilization marked by conflict and experimentation through which informational issues are resolved and distributional issues contested.

We have portrayed the political economy as an institutional ecology in which the strategies of the actors are simultaneously conditioned by multiple institutions, and the process of institutional change is one of the mutual adjustments, inflected by distributive concerns, with incremental impacts on the strategies of firms and other actors. The model we propose acknowledges more change than analyses focused entirely on regulatory regimes or public policy normally recognize. Because we see firms as initiators of institutional change, virtually as important as the state and highly responsive to shifts in the economic environment, we observe a widespread transformation of the European political economies that is only partly reflected in policy regimes. Alongside familiar processes of reform, we see processes of defection and reinterpretation that are shifting institutional practices 'from below'. In some respects, these are simply extensions of the processes of institutional experimentation that are a regular feature of political economies, though we have also noted how incremental changes of this sort can result in major transformations over the medium and long run (Streeck and Thelen 2005).

We have elaborated several ways of moving beyond the current fixation on the 'liberalization' of the European political economies and suggest that the most promising way to extend the varieties of capitalism perspective is to devote more attention to the types of political coalitions supporting the principal institutions of the political economy, with a view to exploring how institutional arrangements in one sphere of the political economy condition perceptions of interest and the coalitions that form around institutional reform in other spheres. That yields an account of institutional change that is eminently political.

Moreover, precisely because we see institutions in equilibrium terms, we see institutional change as more than a matter of producer group politics. Although the interests of firms and workers are crucial to particular modes of coordination, capacities for coordination also depend on a sociological underlay, subsumed in many analyses under the rubric of 'common knowledge'. As a set of shared understandings about how other actors will behave under a variety of circumstances, this common knowledge extends to conceptions of social justice, about what one can reasonably expect from others, which are crucial to resolving the distributive conflicts that arise when actors try to coordinate (Rothstein 2005; Streeck 1997; Goldthorpe 1978).

Such conceptions are features of the polity as a whole and potentially the Achilles heel of the European political economies. If workers no longer believe that the industrial relations system or social regimes within which they labour will deliver a just set of rewards, a nation's capacities for coordination may be threatened, even if its institutions remain intact; and it is here that the most serious question marks hang over the European political economies. In the face of a changing economy, as firms and governments decide how to reallocate work, benefits, and leisure, and what to demand of those who receive them, the settled expectations of the post-war decades are being called into question. These issues render developments in the realm of electoral politics salient to the effectiveness of coordination in the political economy, and they too will have to figure in on-going analyses of institutional change.

NOTES

1.　For relevant critiques see Howell 2003; Goodin 2003; Watson 2003; Blyth 2003, as well as those collected in Coates 2005 and *Stato e Mercato*, 69 (December 2003).

2.　While analytically distinct, it is worth noting that the more formal and the more informal or conventional dimensions of institutions are often linked. For example, the convention that large firms supply apprenticeship slots is supported, albeit at slight remove, by a number of formal institutions–e.g. compulsory membership in employer chambers, strong unions pushing firms up-market, and relatively centralized wage-bargaining institutions that compress wages and allow firms to earn rents on training.

3.　In a powerful analysis, Streeck (1991) has described this last feature as one that supplies 'redundant capacities' to actors. As he notes, some of these capacities are more available in some places and for some purposes than others.

4.　This is confirmed by studies that show a strong correlation between membership in employers associations and union present in Germany.

5.　Bates (1988) and Knight (1992) have drawn attention to this problem.

6.　As Streeck (2004) notes, even institutional complementarities are therefore often 'discovered' rather than designed.

7.　Organized labor is another actor whose strategies, including those aimed at maintaining coordination across a diverse membership, is obviously important.

8.　These are not exhaustive of the modes of change that can be observed in contemporary political economies, and a somewhat broader (though, again, not exhaustive) inventory is discussed by Streeck and Thelen (2005). Defection is the mechanism that defines the mode of change that Streeck and Thelen call institutional 'displacement', and their mode of 'conversion' features reinterpretation as the main mechanism of change (p. 31).

9.　We thank Terry Halliday for emphasizing this point to us.

10.　For a review of the co-evolution of the literatures on varieties of capitalism and cross-class alliances, see Thelen 2002.

9

Beyond Varieties of Capitalism

Bob Hancké, Martin Rhodes, and Mark Thatcher

1. INTRODUCTION

The European political economy is facing a host of entirely new challenges, arising from both external forces and internal conflicts and contradictions. These include a novel macroeconomic regime under Economic and Monetary Union (EMU), supranational regulation under the Single Market of economies traditionally dominated by national governments and national champions, the accession to the European Union (EU) of central and eastern European nations still struggling with the transition to democratic market capitalism, the impact of globalization (the internationalization of production and finance), and a series of destabilizing domestic, demographic, and economic pressures.

How should we understand these developments and their effects? Recent advances in political economy and the 'varieties of capitalism' (henceforth VoC) school of analysis in particular, have given us new tools for analysing and comparing national political economies. The notions of 'complementarities' and 'system coordination' define the core of the VoC approach. Institutional subsystems (which govern capital, labour, and product markets) shape the evolution of political economies and often mutually reinforce each other. The presence of several 'correctly calibrated' subsystems increases the performance of the system as a whole, while producing specific adjustment paths in response to pressures for change.

But broad economic shifts and shocks may have important consequences for each of these subsystems and for the broader institutional framework that supports them. Thus, in their orthodox interpretations, EMU imposes pressures for adjustment on labour markets, the Single Market Programme frees up product and financial markets, eastern European enlargement raises questions about the viability of different development models within one economic zone, and high-unemployment levels and pension systems crises demand a rethinking of welfare state priorities. All may disrupt the existing equilibria of national subsystems, generating conflict and contradiction within and between them.

This chapter confronts the VoC framework with these shocks and explores its capacity to build research agendas and answer questions related to them. Our aim is to pay particular attention to four areas in which the VoC approach has proven most vulnerable to criticism. First, through an analysis of the role of political and distributive struggles in generating change and adjustment. Second, by reconsidering the nature and function of complementarities in shaping and constraining institutional change. Third, by extending the VoC approach to a broader range of political economies than traditionally receives attention, from southern Europe to central and eastern Europe and Russia. And fourth, by restoring the role of the state in VoC analysis, not just where that role is most but as an important factor in the construction everywhere of what Hall (in *Beyond Varieties of Capitalism*) refers to as 'institutional ecologies'.

2. 'VARIETIES OF CAPITALISM' — A *CRITIQUE RAISONNÉE*

Recent contributions from the VoC school (e.g. Hall and Soskice 2001a; Amable 2003) have reinvigorated a long analytical tradition that dates back at least to the work of Alexander Gerschenkron (1962) and Andrew Shonfield (1969) and includes more recent landmark publications such as Zysman (1983) and Gourevitch (1986). Like its predecessors, VoC is concerned with the macro-characteristics of national political economies. But one of its most important contributions has been to give micro-foundations to a more general theory of cross-national capitalist organization and adjustment. By placing the firm at the centre of the analysis, and adopting a 'relational view' of its role as an exploiter of the core competencies and capabilities in its environment, VoC demonstrates the links between the competitiveness of the firm and the 'comparative institutional advantage' of national economies.

The architecture of 'comparative advantage' is portrayed in terms of key institutional complementarities – between labour relations and corporate governance, labour relations and the national training system, and corporate governance and inter-firm relations. These relationships determine the degree to which a political economy is, or is not, 'coordinated'. The 'coordinated market economy' (CME) is characterized by non-market relations, collaboration, credible commitments, and the 'deliberative calculation' of firms. The essence of its 'liberal market economy' (LME) antithesis is one of arm's length, competitive relations, formal contracting, and supply-and-demand price signalling (Hall and Soskice 2001b; Hall and Gingerich 2004). VoC argues that institutional complementarities deliver different kinds of firm behaviour and investment patterns. In LMEs, fluid labour markets fit well with easy access to stock market capital, producing 'radical-innovator' firms in sectors ranging from biotechnology, semiconductors, software, and advertising to corporate finance. In CMEs, long-term employment strategies, rule-bound behaviour, and the durable ties between firms and banks that underpin patient capital provision predispose firms to 'incremental innovation' in capital goods industries, machine tools, and equipment of all kinds. While the logic of LME dynamics is centred on mobile 'switchable assets' whose value can be realized when diverted to multiple purposes, CME logic derives from 'specific or co-specific assets' whose value depends on the active cooperation of others (Hall and Soskice 2001b; Hall and Gingerich 2004).

If the centrality of the firm is one key innovation, contrary to the claims of many of its critics VoC also has a strong understanding of both domestic change in political economies and the impact of exogenous pressures. VoC attributes the persistence of capitalist diversity to 'positive feedbacks', whereby the different logics of LMEs and CMEs create different incentives for economic actors, generating in turn a differential politics of adjustment. As Hall and Gingerich (2004: 32) characterize this process: 'in the face of an exogenous shock threatening returns to existing activities, holders of mobile assets will be tempted to "exit" those activities to seek higher returns elsewhere, while holders of specific assets have higher incentives to exercise "voice" in defence of existing activities'. In LMEs, holders of mobile assets (workers with general skills, investors in fluid capital markets) will seek to make markets still more fluid and accept further deregulatory policies. In CMEs, holders of specific assets (workers with industry-specific skills and investors in co-specific assets) will more often oppose greater market competition and form status quo supporting cross-class coalitions (Hall and Gingerich 2004: 28–9).

This logic of adjustment and diversity is reinforced rather than undermined by globalization (Hall and Soskice 2001b; Gourevitch and Hawes 2002). Globalization will often reinforce comparative institutional advantage, for foreign direct investment (FDI) will flow to locations rich in either specific or co-specific assets, depending on investors' sector or firm-specific requirements. CMEs and LMEs will be located at different points in international production chains, again reflecting their respective institutional advantages: high value-added, high skill-dependent, high-productivity production will tend to remain in the core CMEs; lower value-added, lower-skill, price-oriented production will relocate to lower-cost jurisdictions. But the globalization of finance may prove to be more problematic (though not necessarily destructive) for CMEs. International capital flows could disrupt long-standing relations and cross-shareholdings between banks and firms, and bring the notion of 'shareholder value' and demands for higher rates of return into formerly closed and collaborative environments.

While Hall and Soskice (2001b: 61–2) imagine that this 'could engender shifts in strategy all the way down to production regimes', this is considered unlikely: rational owners and stakeholders in CMEs will not demand a wholesale adoption of Anglo-American management practices if it would endanger their comparative institutional advantage. Although an economic shock may trigger changes to existing institutions and practices, and may even entail a period of conflict and suboptimal outcomes, a new equilibrium will be induced by the incentives for renewed coordination imparted by existing deliberative institutions (Hall and Soskice 2001b: 63–5). Change, therefore, is most likely to be path-dependent, and significant path-shifting or equilibrium-breaking behaviour on the part of actors – producing a fully fledged shift from a CME to an LME, for example – is very unlikely to occur due to the 'general efficiencies' for distinctive political economies created by 'complementarities'. As Hall and Gingerich (2004: 27) put it, 'rates of economic growth should be higher in nations where levels of market coordination or levels of strategic coordination are high across spheres of the political economy but lower in nations where neither type of coordination is well developed or market and strategic coordination are combined'. There is no 'one best way', as in arguments for neoliberal convergence, but 'two', on which middle-spectrum countries (with muddled institutional architectures) may 'divergently converge'.

A salvo of criticism provoked by the Hall–Soskice approach to VoC theory has raised many points of contention:

- that it is too static and focused on permanency and path-dependence, missing important dynamic elements of economic change (Crouch and Farrell 2004; Crouch 2005a; Hancké and Goyer 2005; Streeck and Thelen 2005; Jackson and Deeg 2006);
- that it is functionalist (Howell 2003; Allen 2004; Boyer 2005a);
- that it ignores the endogenous sources of national system transformation and 'within-system' diversity (Coates 2005; Boyer 2005b; Crouch 2005a; Panitch and Gindin 2005);
- that it has a propensity to 'institutional determinism' in its mechanistic conception of institutional complementarities and neglect of underlying power structures, including social class (Thelen 2003; Crouch and Farrell 2004; Coates 2005; Pontusson 2005; Jackson and Deeg 2006);

- that it has a truncated conception of the firm as an 'institution-taker' rather than an autonomous, creative, or disruptive actor and neglects variation among firms within national models (Allen 2003; Crouch and Farrell 2004; Crouch 2005a; Martin 2005);
- that it divides the world into reified notions of LME and CME archetypes and lacks the tools for moving beyond this bifurcation (Schmidt 2002, 2003; Watson 2003; Hay 2005; Pontusson 2005; Boyer 2005b);
- that VoC theory is not built deductively, to create Weberian 'ideal types' that could be used for the construction of hypotheses, but rather creates 'types' by reading back empirical information from the countries it seeks to make its paradigm cases – the USA and Germany (Crouch 2005a);
- that it has a manufacturing bias and cannot deal with the presence of sizeable service sectors in CMEs (Blyth 2003);
- that it treats nation-states as 'hermetically sealed' and neglects the linkages between them and the forces of convergence and globalization (Crouch and Farrell 2004; Martin 2005; Panitch and Gindin 2005; Pontusson 2005);
- that it is 'apolitical', equilibrium-biased and downplays conflict (Howell 2003; Watson 2003; Kinderman 2005; Pontusson 2005);
- that it is 'sex-blind' and has problems understanding class inequalities among women and class differences in the nature and patterns of gender inequality (Estévez-Abe 2005; McCall and Orloff 2005a);
- and that it neglects the role of the state (Schmidt 2002, 2003; Regini 2003; Watson 2003).

However, many critics caricature rather than fully explore the VoC approach. Regardless of its formulation by Hall and Soskice (2001b: 1–3, 68) as an agenda for future research rather than 'settled wisdom', there is a general tendency for critics to treat it as if it were a 'unified theory of everything', attribute to it claims that it has never made, and consequently to fall wide of the mark in their attacks (see, e.g., the rebuttal to several critics in Hall and Soskice 2003). Even from the brief synopsis above, it is clear that, far from being static, VoC has a strong, non-deterministic understanding of change, given its appreciation that the institutions that underpin coordination are subject to constant renegotiation. The accusation that it is reductive and limited to LME and CME 'paradigm types' is belied by the attention paid (e.g. by Hall and Gingerich 2004) to economies – characterized as 'mixed-market economies', or MMEs – that fall outside this analytical dichotomy, even if that seam of analysis has yet to be fully exploited. The notion that the firm in VoC lacks the power to innovate in its environment is quite inconsistent with the complexity of its interactions with labour, finance, and other economic agents, as explored in multiple studies inspired by the VoC approach. The claim that the nation state in VoC is 'hermetically sealed' is unsustainable, given its focus on the nature and dynamics of comparative institutional advantage.

More acute and clearly focused criticisms (such as that concerned with 'sex-blindness') have already produced new and highly productive realms of scientific enquiry (on gender see, e.g., Estévez-Abe 2005; Iversen, Rosenbluth, and Soskice 2005; Soskice 2005). VoC allows us to understand the conflict generated by political–economic change, analyse economies beyond the LME–CME archetypes, and provides insights into the inter-sectoral dynamics and tensions generated by the rise of the post-industrial economy and labour market 'dualism'. This chapter seeks to mine the rich VoC seam as much as possible in an attempt to understand contemporary European developments. Yet we also want to build on its foundations in ways that make it less vulnerable to charges of determinism, functionalism, and over-concern with institutional equilibria. We seek to reveal its capacity for accommodating and understanding the centrality of conflict (class-based and otherwise) in political economies and the reconfiguration of long-standing coalitions; the consequent challenges these coalitional shifts may pose to complementarities and coordination; and the centrality and changing role of the state in all political economies – LMEs, CMEs, MMEs, and others.

We therefore focus in this chapter on four key dimensions that are ripe for development and exploration – conflict and coalitions, complementarities and institutional change, the nature of 'mixed market' (and other) political economies, and the role of the state – and answer the more serious criticisms made of VoC.

2.1. Conflict and Coalitions

First, regarding *conflict*, questions arise for VoC from numerous directions. Two important challenges that strike at the core of what are presumed to be deeply engrained preferences and structural characteristics in CMEs are, first, the apparent willingness of employers in certain key countries to break with long-established commitments to coordination, and second, the potentially disruptive consequences for system stability of company internationalization. According to VoC, one would expect CME businesses to hesitate in liberalizing their main factor markets. But while this was true of the 1980s (Wood 2001), today businesses are pushing a competitive, 'deregulatory' agenda in both labour and financial markets. In Germany, these changes appear to complicate coordination on both the employer and union sides and threaten the longterm stability of the system (Thelen and van Wijnbergen 2003; Kinderman 2005).

Several of these developments are related to internationalization. VoC argues that globalization will confirm rather than subvert the comparative institutional advantage of nations. Competition and the spread of global production networks will reward difference and drive divergence. Evidence suggests that production networks do extend globally in this fashion. But a subversion of institutional structures and relations in *home* locations may also result. A range of studies (Berger et al. 1999, 2001; Berger 2000; Lane 2003; Herrigel and Wittke 2005) demonstrates, for example, that national manufacturers who create diversified cross-border, producer–supplier linkages (spanning western and central and eastern Europe) often use them to change institutional incentive structures, both inside and outside the firm, in their own economies.

Some critics suggest that VoC is unable to accommodate the kind of conflict and change associated with these developments (Regini 2003; Watson 2003). For Howell (2003: 122), this is because it renders 'invisible the exercise of class power that underlies coordination and equilibrium in the political economy'; for Allen (2003) and Crouch (2005a), it is because VoC tends to interpret the strategic preferences of firms, mistakenly, as endogenous – or complementary – to their environments. Whilst business obviously can be competitive while its location is not or becomes decreasingly so, thus creating a source of incongruity and pressures for eventual change from disruptive firms (Siebert 2003), it is not clear that Howell, Allen, and Crouch are correct in claiming that VoC is unable to accommodate this relatively uncontroversial fact. Their argument does raise a number of questions, however, about the role of class power and the notion of 'complementarities' in VoC theory. We return to these issues below.

Conflict often leads to, or stems from, a reconfiguration of coalitions and alliances. This process may include new alliances with external actors, as economies become more open to foreign capital, including multinationals and pension funds (Rhodes and van Apeldoorn 1998). Hall and Soskice (2001b: 64) argue that actors in LMEs will react to globalization by calling for more deregulation, while cross-class coalitions in CMEs will defend strategic interaction and coordination. But there is evidence that a new politics of coalitions in CMEs may be disrupting rather than strengthening existing alliances. Deeg (2005b) argues that a domestic coalition for reforming the German financial system has allied with external investors to achieve its goals. Höpner (2001) argues that conflicts over shareholder value in Germany have shifted long-standing coalitions between shareholders, management, and employees. Berndt (2000) portrays an alliance of German small- and medium-sized firms in favour of breaking industrial relations bargains favoured by larger firms. Kinderman (2005) examines the coalition of firms within the large German business associations that is opposing the wage-bargaining status quo.

One way to innovate in VoC theory to accommodate such developments is to specify more clearly the circumstances in which firms will exercise 'exit', 'voice', or 'loyalty' and the extent to which exit and voice will imperil or be shaped by existing systems of coordination and complementarities. Another is to identify conditions under which firms will behave *creatively* in ways that challenge the prevailing institutional environment and begin to transform it (Hancké and Goyer 2005: 5). Explaining such developments requires a more dynamic conception of firm interests according to sector or market circumstances than VoC has traditionally provided and leads us to look at how complementarities affect institutional change.

2.2. Complementarities and Institutional Change

Can a literature that has largely focused on system coherence and complementarities accommodate contradiction and disjunction? The notion of complementarity has been central to VoC, and its continued relevance is strongly advocated by its main proponents (e.g. Hall 2005: 376). Building on Aoki (1994) and North (1990), Hall and Soskice (2001b: 17–18) argue that 'nations with a particular type of coordination in one sphere of the economy should tend to develop complementary practices in other spheres as well' (2000a: 18). This notion of institutional reinforcement explains VoC's arguments for path-dependent change in line with certain system logics. Crouch and Farrell (2004: 8–9) counter that a focus on the 'coherent logics of ordering' prevents an understanding of 'incongruencies, incoherence, and within system diversities'. In one of the most thoughtful recent critiques, Streeck and Thelen (2005) contrast VoC's over-emphasis on system stability with other approaches (including their own) that are more open to the dynamics of institutional innovation and punctuated equilibria.

This debate indicates a divide in the literature between the complementarity-based VoC form of analysis and a looser, power/interest-based perspective. Deeg (2005d) refers to these, respectively, as the 'equilibrium–functionalist' and 'historical–political' approaches. But such methodological distinctions may be less important than at first glance. The commonalities rather than contrasts are highlighted if we place the notion of institutions as flexible, subject to defection and always demanding a renewal of support alongside Streeck and Thelen's conception (2005: 12ff.) of institutions as a 'regime continuously created and recreated by a great number of actors with divergent interests, varying normative commitments, different powers, and limited cognition'. The critical difference seems to be the role for rational calculation in the Hall–Soskice view of strategic interaction versus the importance of agency and open-ended (though power-driven) outcomes in the analysis by Streeck and Thelen (Deeg 2005d).

We wish to retain the notion of complementarities as used in VoC but chart a path between its more functionalist interpretations and the dangers of a more open-ended, unstructured voluntarism. The direction of that path is signalled by recent analyses of European political economies that reveal several competing interpretations of the relationship between complementarities and change, whether generated endogenously, by external pressures, or by a combination of the two. The first interpretation is that *change can occur in a given institutional architecture without changing the nature of core complementarities.* This is because actors will seek institutional and functional equivalents to pre-existing forms of coordination. Such action, we argue, reveals strategic calculation as well as power-driven agency–suggesting there is little analytical merit in trying to divorce the two.

A second interpretation is that *change may be limited to one sub-sector of the economy, which may be significantly transformed, without spilling over, or snowballing into others.* We argue that compartmentalized change can occur without threatening coordination as such, as CMEs open up, for example, to 'alien' forms of organization such as growing service sectors.

A third interpretation argues, by contrast, that under certain circumstances *spillovers, snow-balling and contagion can occur, spreading change from one subsystem to another, precisely because complementarities in the purer CMEs are so tightly coupled.* Vitols (2004) notes that path-shifting change *could* occur in German finance, altering the centrality of banks, in the event of an increase in income inequality and a further pensions reform encouraging more private retirement savings.

But will coordination erode to the point of collapse, auguring a transition in Germany towards a capital market-based system? Or will firms retain the critical aspects of coordination that have served them well in the past? Although there is much speculation regarding the former (e.g. Hackethal, Schmidt, and Tyrell 2005), most evidence points to the latter.

2.3. The Nature of Mixed (and Emerging) Market Economies

A further set of questions concerning the nature, function, and future of complementarities are raised by developments in what Hall and Gingerich (2004) portray as 'mid-spectrum', mixed-market political economies, or MMEs. Although they focus on the purer CMEs and LMEs, Hall and Soskice

(2001b: 35–6) claim that VoC can also be useful for understanding political economies beyond these ideal types and that each economy displays capacities for coordination that condition how its firms and governments behave. This begs the question, though, of how pertinent the core concept of complementarities is for analysing such countries and how one should understand their dynamics of change.

The evidence shows that 'mid-spectrum' MMEs (and what we refer to as Emerging Market Economies (EMEs) in central and eastern Europe) mix market regulation with some elements of coordinated regulation as well as state-compensating coordination, sustaining subsystems that are far from 'correctly calibrated' over time. But does the absence of CME- or LME-type complementaries, and the lower degree of 'general efficiency' they generate, compel actors in these economies to create them, and move in a CME or an LME direction? Will they remain in their suboptimal institutional locations because strong actors – including state actors – wish to retain their stakes in the status quo (Bebchuk and Roe 2004; Pontusson 2005)? Will they derive only diminishing returns from the absence of ideal-type complementarities in their systems unless they can achieve some kind of systemic recalibration? Hall and Gingerich (2004) argue that this will indeed be the case: that 'hybrid' systems— such as those of southern Europe and the emerging market economies of central and eastern Europe – will *ceteris paribus* underperform against 'purer' types.

But others (Boyer 2005a, 2005b; Crouch 2005a) have warned against what they call the 'functional assumptions' underpinning this form of reasoning, pointing to the operation of complementarities across policy domains with different rationales and the potentially positive effects of hybridization when national architectures are heterogeneous and loose. If we accept institutional heterogeneity as a valid – and logically possible – source of institutional complementarities, then it may also be possible, in theory, for mixed economies to find their own forms of coordination in line with the needs of their respective production systems. Nevertheless, as evidence from analyses of MMEs and EMEs in this volume and elsewhere reveals (e.g. European Commission 2003; Radosevic 2005; Jones and Rhodes 2006), the core Hall–Gingerich insight that economies with mixed or poorly calibrated modes of coordination will be outperformed by more coherent systems remains a valuable one.

2.4. The Role of the State

Given its concern with the micro-foundations of the political economy and specific focus on the firm, macro-*political* as opposed to macroeconomic structures have not played a prominent role in the Hall–Soskice approach to VoC. This has led critics to either stress the role that the state (still) plays in coordinating and shaping the political economies of many countries or to develop alternative typologies in which the state is a major determining variable.

Differentiating himself from the basic Hall–Soskice approach, Whitley (2005) argues that the state plays a critical role in determining the characteristics of the business system and how employers behave associationally. He also argues that where the state adopts an active role in economic development (the 'developmental state') by directly intervening in certain sectors of the economy, the result is a greater diversity in employment policies, bargaining procedures, corporate governance, systems of skills formation, and so on, between firms of different size within the same sector. Other authors go further, identifying separate models of capitalism in which the state plays a predominant organizing role. Schmidt (2002) creates her own typology of capitalist models, separating 'state capitalism' (France) from 'managed' and 'market capitalisms' (Germany and Britain, respectively). Amable (2003) introduces a grouping of countries in his analysis of the diversity of modern capitalism in which the state plays a determining role – the European-integration/public social system of innovation and production (SSIP) – alongside three other European SSIPs (market-based, meso-corporatist, and social-democratic) and goes on to propose five international models of capitalism: market-based, social-democratic, Asian, continental European, and south European. Boyer (2005b) favours a similar categorization.

In the following, we share the VoC focus on coordination as the distinguishing feature of comparative political economies and suggest that the state can be accommodated within the basic VoC framework. This is because we view the state as one element among others of coordination and one that is present everywhere – in different forms, with different functions, and to varying degrees. There is too little analytical value-added to be derived from adding a separate variety of capitalism defined exclusively by the role of the state – especially given the transformation and diminution of that role wherever it may have been strong in the past. An approach that focuses on state mediation, control, and direction derived from the empirical case of pre-1990s France (Schmidt 2002) also fails to illuminate the still central though quite different role of the state, for example, in the southern European economies which we refer to below as predominantly 'compensatory'. The basic (and uncontroversial) insight that the state is important across a diverse range of political economies also inspires Amable's search for even more capitalist varieties, based on a wide range of indicators and characteristics, including not just the state and public intervention but science, technology, labour markets, competition, finance, and more. But the dangers in this approach (cf. Crouch 2005a) are that analytical power and parsimony are sacrificed in favour of a greater capacity for detailed description; and that in an effort to account for the entirety of national political economies, the quantity of variables proliferates but the number of core insights is reduced.

3. INTERESTS, COALITIONS, AND INSTITUTIONAL FRAMEWORKS

The questions raised by the preceding discussion can only be resolved by empirical analysis; however, that discussion does help us appreciate the ways in which the concept of complementarities can be nuanced and rendered less rigid than it is often thought to be, thereby enriching the VoC approach. It can also lead us via further theoretical development to a more complete under-standing of the dynamics of change in different kinds of political economies. We believe, as stated earlier, that achieving that goal demands paying closer attention to class, coalitions, and the role of the state than is the case in either conventional VoC analysis or in most of the literature that has criticized it for its alleged functionalism.

Streeck (2005a: 583–4) has argued strongly that what are often regarded as institutional complementarities in political economies today were born from class and industrial conflict in the past and the solutions that were found to them 'in the interstices of functionally interdependent institutions built with distrib-uted power and in pursuit of particularistic sectoral interests'. We are broadly sympathetic with that claim, and its core insight helps inform our discussion of networks and class- and sector-based coalitions below. There we make institu-tions the dependent rather than the independent variable, as they frequently are in much recent analysis. Specifically, we focus on the ways in which networks and class coalitions evolve (and potentially also *devolve*) around 'friction points' in relations between institutional subsystems. By raising the profiles of networks, class coalitions, and the state in the VoC framework, we argue that many of the problems and weaknesses frequently attributed to it can be resolved without detracting from the power and parsimony of its core insights.

3.1. Business Interests and Networks

Many of the contributions in Hancké et al. (2007) suggest an understanding of coordination and complementarities that builds on a set of prerequisites associated with networks of actors with broadly similar interests. Hall and Soskice (2001b) repeatedly refer to different modes of coordination in these terms, but give less attention to the ways in which such networks emerge. However, at least since Olson (1965) we have been aware that a confluence of interests is an insufficient condition for collective action to ensue. But while Olson locates the capacity for collective action in the distribution of sanctions and rewards, we emphasize the historical emergence and reproduction of networks. We make three broad points: that different modes of economic governance reflect a politically constructed institutional matrix, built in large part on elite networks; that these elite networks sought to control the strategic levers of the economy and state at politically opportune moments; and that the mechanisms that reproduce network structures provide for different levels of coordinating capacity.

As for the character of the institutional matrices, in LMEs strong networks do not emerge easily because their competition regimes preclude trusts and 'collusion'. In the UK, moreover, business networks have in any case been fractured by historical divisions between banking and industrial capital. By contrast, the origins of post-war German 'organized' capitalism can be found in the networks that tied many large firms and banks together in powerful industrial–financial groups before the Second World War (Hilferding 1910; Gerschenkron 1962; Herrigel 1996). Even after the break-up of large cartels by the Allies, it took little time for these groups to be reconstituted (Berghahn 1996).

Different modes of economic governance thus reflect a matrix that is frequently politically constructed. All share networks as the basis for their country's prevailing mode of business governance. This matrix socializes economic elites and provides a central building block for the rest of the political economy, since the broad orientations developed by these leading groups also influence the choices that other actors can make.

Second, elite networks achieved their centrality because they sought to control the strategic levers of the economy and state at politically opportune moments: the post-war governments led by De Gaulle in France did just that; the reconstruction of the post-war German economy along 'ordo-liberal' lines provided the ideological framework for the social market economy; the large public sector under IRI in Italy merged and modernized a scattered small-and medium-sized industrial sector; and the political and economic chaos of the post-Communist transition was exploited by some networks better than others. The role and function of the state is important in all three instances and contributes to both the structural coherence of economic governance and the potential for functional complementarities.

Third, the mechanisms that reproduce network structures provide for quite different levels of coordinating capacity. For networks to become and remain building blocks for coordination, they require both *external* reproduction (the recruitment of new members into the network) and *internal* reproduction (the development of sanctioning mechanisms that secure compliance). But whether functional compatibility and complementarity result will depend on the extent to which markets and their actors are *freely coordinated* (high in Germany's bank–firm–labour complex, medium in France's state-business system, and low – at least outside the industrial districts – in highly politicized Italy), rather than coerced and suppressed (as in the command economies of the former Soviet bloc).

Business networks are therefore to be found at the basis of coordination via three mechanisms: the institutional architecture of business, a set of short-term and long-term reproduction mechanisms, and a political opportunity for the groups that make up the networks to secure influence over the economy and, if necessary, the state. If they are all present, we claim, together they will help create a form of institutional coordination that will be structurally coherent and functionally complementary; if they are absent or only partially present, then core complementarities are unlikely to develop and an economy may even take an LME-type path.

If networks are at the basis of business coordination, what does this imply for the construction of broader institutional frameworks? One answer to this question, which is implicit in the VoC framework, is that institutions reflect the needs of business. This conception has, correctly in our view, come under criticism for its unnecessarily functionalist assumptions: capital may indeed be crucial in capitalist economies, but, paraphrasing Marx, it does not choose the conditions under which it operates. We therefore introduce the two other central actors in capitalist economies that influence these conditions: labour (and its relationship with capital) and the state.

3.2. Labour, Capital, and Cross-Class Coalitions

Labour constrains business in two ways: directly, because business needs workers and their skills to produce goods and services, and indirectly, via the constraints of collective organization. National 'settlements' between capital and labour reflect their relative positions of power. While VoC analysis typically focuses on companies rather than labour, we argue these settlements result from a confluence of equilibrium strategies on both sides (see also Iversen 2005; Iversen and Soskice 2006a).

Regarding labour, if skills are predominantly industry- or firm-specific, it will prefer CME-type institutions and policies. Employees in CME countries who have a high proportion of specific skills will also prefer a higher level of social insurance (and hence redistributive spending) than employees in LME nations where the proportion of general skills is higher. But when skill profiles are more general, as they predominantly are in LMEs, the choices are more complex. Employees in the primary segments of the labour market (lawyers, consultants, investment bankers, etc.) are likely to prefer liberal market institutions and individual rather than collective action. The rest may then be forced to fall in line and develop strategies that increase their survival in highly competitive labour markets. As for capital, two equilibrium strategies are available, since the nature of skills is tightly linked to other labour market institutions. Specific skills, plant- and firm-level workers' participation, and coordinated wage-bargaining all help safeguard the high value-added product market strategies of large CME firms, while general skills, unilateral management, and decentralized wage-setting allow for quite different company strategies in LMEs. Cross-class coalitions in CMEs can be understood as the point where the strategies of labour and capital meet: both have strong preferences for thick, inclusive, and well-institutionalized frameworks. In LMEs, the interests of both employers and highly skilled employees tend to converge on a less well-regulated institutional framework.

Introducing class into the standard VoC framework allows us to explore several points of criticism levelled against it. One is that institutional frameworks are not simply reflections of the strategic needs of firms, or the functional needs of 'systems', but express underlying cross-class coalitions, which in turn reflect the relative power – and agency – of important sections of capital and labour. While rendering the VoC framework and arguments more dynamic and realistic, this does not alter their basic logic.

Equally important, an emphasis on cross-class coalitions allows us to respond to criticisms of VoC's alleged conception of the firm as an 'institution taker' rather than an autonomous, creative, or disruptive actor (cf. Allen 2003; Crouch and Farrell 2004; Crouch 2005a). As suggested above, coordination is not constructed by the business class *as a whole*, but by its dominant sections, primarily those that are found in the large firms in CMEs and in the labour markets surrounding the leading sectors in LMEs – and often only after protracted struggles for control of the class agenda. Interest cleavages, for instance between large and small firms, mean that cross-class coalitions in CMEs are fundamentally unstable and require permanent reaffirmation. However, if they are intrinsically unstable, why do we not witness more defections from the system as a whole?

One important part of the answer to this question is obviously related to intra-class politics, and the codification of institutional arrangements in favour of the winners who lay down the rules for others – an example of the ways in which institutions can develop complementary forms of intensive interaction from a cross-class settlement of conflict. Swenson (1989) showed how in interwar Sweden the export sector and the metalworkers union forged a coalition against the interests of firms and their workers in the sheltered sector to impose a centralized wage bargaining system. The post-war settlements in most of Europe primarily reflected the interests of business and workers in large, mass-producing firms (Piore and Sabel 1984). And even today, collective bargaining systems frequently use large firms as their main point of reference. Yet these struggles were not settled by power alone: side-payments made the settlement acceptable to those who lost out.

On the workers' side, institutionalized subservience has come with an important benefit: in most (non-LME) European economies, wages for workers outside the core sectors of the economy are usually set following the prevailing rules in large industrial firms. Wages for these workers thus acquired a level of protection, predictability, and standardization that they would not have had otherwise. Even small firms gain from the arrangement, since they are allowed to exploit the benefits of coordination (such as well-developed skill provision and technology transfer systems, standardized wage grids, and social peace) without incurring all the costs.

Throughout this analysis of the nature of class coalitions runs a question that has been addressed to VoC since its inception. How can we differentiate between (*a*) an institutionalized compromise that worked well in the past (irrespective of why it existed in the first place) and which persists because of the potential and actuality of strategic, functional complementarity and (*b*) an institutional arrangement that was consciously designed, in part as a result of strategic inter-actions between socio-economic actors, and whose complementarities stem from distributive settlements whose *raison d'être* may erode and decline (Streeck 2005b)? This issue goes to the heart of the debates on the neo-institutionalist approach to political economy: in the first case, actors have internalized the constraints of the institutional framework, while the second case leaves more room for contingencies. The difference between the two is clear in how they account for change: if institutions are indeed constitutive of actors, then actors permanently reproduce the institutional framework, and change can therefore only occur when it is exogenous and sudden. In the other view, change in the institutional framework can occur in several ways: shifts in the existing cross-class coalitions, in the intra-class politics underlying coordination (e.g. when public sector trade unions dominate), or in the sociological conditions underlying the reproduction of business networks. In such cases, as Hall and Thelen (2009) have argued, the likely result is a shift in the mode of coordination. While VoC's critics maintain that the approach is imprisoned in the first perspective, we see no reason for that assumption if the agency of cross- and inter-class settlements are given their full and rightful place in VoC analysis.

Recapitulating our argument thus far, the causal chain that we have developed has the following three steps: (*a*) business networks are translated, to varying degrees, into modes of coordination; (*b*) the dominant sections of labour and capital enter a cross-class coalition, coercing and bribing others to follow; (*c*) this cross-class coalition then sets mutually agreed rules that strengthen the internal reproduction of the network and, by extension, the mode of coordination and its specific national manifestations. But only in certain circumstances – when markets and their actors are freely coordinated – do synergistic or strategic forms of complementarity emerge.

3.3. The State

This brings us to the third neglected issue regarding the nature and origins of coordination in VoC: the state. The dual equilibrium strategies and stable class coalitions examined above are obviously ideal types, closely resembling LMEs and CMEs. However, most empirical instances will differ in one way or another. For example, business coordination may be underdeveloped, and/or labour representation may be far from unitary and based on ideological divisions. Under those conditions, strategic interaction may only occur sporadically and infrequently produces stable institutional arrangements. As suggested by Hall and Gingerich (2004), in 'mid-spectrum' economies, CME-type strategic complementarities, positive spillovers, and public goods provision are inhibited by power asymmetries, organizational fragmentation, and class conflict, as (for the same reasons) are the complementarities that derive from the less visible market discipline found in LMEs. Yet instead of facing permanent and destructive economic dysfunctionality, in economies that exhibit such patterns – for example, France, Italy, or Spain – stability appears to prevail as well (as too does strong economic performance), and often the state provides that element of stability (if not fully fledged coordination) by compensating for weaknesses elsewhere in the political economy.

The main problem with the state in VoC analysis is that it is too often regarded as a reflection of the existing mode of coordination with no autonomous role to play. In its simplest form, the assumption seems to be that where the state attempts to push through reforms that contradict the basic interests of a well-organized business class – even if that implied substantial deregulation (see Wood 2001 on Germany) – the outcome would be the status quo, barely modified. Conversely, where business had a clear interest in deregulation, but was too weak to pursue this, as in the UK (and perhaps in a different way in France), government policies were simply aligned with the interests of business. The Thatcher and Reagan reforms were, in this view, nothing more than the state waging class war by proxy. Government policies will only work if they are *incentive compatible*, that is if they reflect the underlying mode of competitive or cooperative business coordination (Rhodes 2000; Wood 2001). In other words, politics follows economics: the nature of the state reflects the interests of business.

In many nations, however, the state is considerably more activist (Evans and Rueschemeyer 1985). The diversity in state–economy relations that persists until today suggests that there is a benefit in establishing the state and the mode of business coordination as analytically independent properties of any given model of capitalism.

3.4. A Revised Typology of Capitalist Varieties

Let us begin with the two basic forms that relations between the state and the (supply side of the) economy can take in advanced capitalism: either the state has close direct influence over the economy (e.g. as the owner of industries and/or main provider of industrial credit) or the state is primarily a regulator operating at arm's length. Post-war France and to some extent post-war Italy, as well as some central European economies, fall into the first category, while the UK, Sweden, and Germany fall into the second. Class-based interest organization, in turn, can run from being highly structured to being highly fragmented. In most countries, the levels of business and labour organization tend to mirror one another in this respect. In the first (highly structured) category, individual companies and industry associations or industrial groups balance their respective strategies and are able to strike bargains with organized labour. In the second (fragmented) category, collective interest definition above the company level is more or less absent, either among firms or between their representatives and (similarly fractured) trade union organizations. Dichotomizing these two continuums into a matrix (Figure 9.1) leads to four ideal types of coordination.

We want to stress that we are hereby creating logical categories for analysis, to which particular countries will broadly (though never precisely) conform, rather than constructing a typology by 'reading back' from empirical examples which we consider paradigmatic – a charge that has been levelled (though wrongly, we believe) at the original Hall–Soskice formulation of the LME–CME ideal-types (Crouch 2005a). Note also that we do not identify EMEs as a separate variety of capitalism of equivalent analytical status to the rest: we simply wish to indicate by this term their transitional character and that their respective mixes of modes of coordination (market and non-market) are embryonic in some cases, more developed in others, but in all cases still in a process of institutional construction.

Interest Organization	State–Economy Relations: **Close**	State–Economy Relations: **Arm's-length**
Fragmented	*Étatisme* France pre-1990s	*LMEs* UK, Baltics
Organized	*Compensating state* Italy, Spain some EMEs	*CMEs* Germany Slovenia

Figure 9.1. State–economy relations, interest organization, and modes of coordination

The first 'type' or mode of coordination, *étatisme*, has traditionally been associated with post-war France, where the state controlled the strategic levers of the economy through outright ownership of many companies and control of industrial credit (Hall 1986: 204). Partly as a result of the state's dominance and partly due to the deep interpenetration of the state and the economic elites, business organization in France has been weak. Similarly, unions have been weakened by ideological fragmentation, their weak roots in the workplace (outside the public sector), and an absence of vertical integration. As a result, the French model was built on the state (Levy 2000). Strategic complementarities, to the extent that they have existed at all, could be found in state–business linkages in the large-firm sector, based in the credit-allocation system, and predominantly in traditional manufacturing and public utilities State-protected markets and business in high-technology sectors have, by contrast, been highly dysfunctional (Rhodes 1985). In industrial relations, atomized business finds a parallel in the weak and ideologically divided labour movement. The result is less a class compromise or coalition than a permanently contested truce that frequently breaks down into conflict.

A different constellation can be found where the state is important as an actor in industrial policy, but where business is also relatively well-organized, more as a result of the type of ownership structures than associational capacity. Italy exemplifies this type although Rhodes and van Apeldoorn (1997) embed it in a broader Mediterranean family. There the compensatory state organized a large state-controlled business sector that has provided key basic industrial inputs and compensated for the absence of autonomous arrangements for capital and labour. Business and labour tend to be better organized and wage-bargaining more coordinated than in France. But the scope for synergistic, VoC-type complementarities is limited. Interest organizations are strong enough to make demands on the state but insufficiently cohesive to provide it with dependable bargaining partners. Attempts to build more effective coordination also run up against prisoners' dilemma type collective action problems.

The third type of state–business relations, and form of coordination, is the one we usually associate with LMEs in VoC. The state sets detailed legal frameworks, leaving business to operate within them, and guards the integrity of market operations by closely monitoring ownership arrangements and market concentration. In part resulting from its history and ownership structures business is weakly organized, and the regulatory frameworks set by the state reinforce this by precluding most forms of deep cooperation. The labour movement, in turn, is decentralized and poorly coordinated, contributing to a conflict-ridden form of industrial relations and strong, endemic weaknesses in employer–employee relations In LMEs, the political strategies of business are primarily oriented towards influencing the regulatory framework, and considerably less towards finding a compromise with labour (Wood 2001). Some CEE emerging market economies (e.g. the Baltics) have also rapidly moved towards this model.

The fourth and final type of coordination is conventionally associated with the north-west European economies (CMEs in VoC), of which Germany is the prime example. The state plays a small direct role in the economy (but organizes a large and robust welfare state) and offers broad frameworks for companies to operate within. Business is highly organized and relies on strong industry and employer associations for the provision of collective goods. The high level of economic regulation is less the result of state intervention, but rather follows from voluntary agreements by associations (including labour unions) to set limits on the behaviour of individual companies. Here too, as in the LME model, the coherence of economic governance is reinforced by functional complementarities. Yet if the class settlement between capital and labour in the LMEs has been fully settled in favour of the former, in the CMEs, the class settlement, based on a much more equal balance of power, is now subject to significant strains.

This typology allows us to explore several dimensions of the state's role in contemporary capitalism and to correct its absence in VoC. In the original iteration of VoC theory (Hall and Soskice 2001b), the underdevelopment of the state as a factor in economic organization was largely the consequence of the heuristic focus on two types of capitalism in which the state played a relatively distant role. But there is nothing in the approach as such that prevents a fuller accommodation of the state as an actor – architectural or otherwise (see the discussions in Streeck 2005b; Hall 2005). The state plays an important role everywhere, but in different ways. In some forms of capitalism, the state is a central actor in the sense that it provides both a framework for business activities and a means for pursuing them. In other forms of capitalism, the state is less a promoter of economic activity than a compensator for coordination deficits and provider of political consensus and legitimacy. In still others, the state allows markets to operate within a broad set of regulatory frameworks and refrains from direct interference.

'Bringing the state back in' thus provides us with a typology in which LMEs, CMEs, MMEs, and some EMEs can be accommodated. We believe that this approach is superior to attempts to produce a third model or variety of capitalism alongside 'market' and 'managed' types (Schmidt 2002), in which the state is architectonic (because it is, but to different degrees, in all systems), and to other approaches (e.g. Amable 2003; Boyer 2005b) which multiply the number of capitalisms in line with a large number of variables or characteristics. While the former conflates a distinctive mode of coordination with a different model of capitalism, the latter accommodates greater empirical complexity, but excessively dilutes the analytical strength of the VoC approach. The typology above also allows us to think about the institutional substructures of these systems, especially the capacity for coalition building and collective goods provision, given contrasting organizational characteristics of capital and labour, different modes of state involvement, distinctive forms of coordination, and the extent and importance of positive complementarities.

4. EXOGENOUS SHOCKS AND DOMESTIC CHANGE IN VARIETIES OF EUROPEAN CAPITALISM

A central question for VoC is its ability to deal with change. How have European political economies and their policy-makers coped with a series of dramatic exogenous shocks over the past decades, specifically trade liberalization, EMU, and economic transition (the CEE countries)? One argument, popular with economic liberals, is that 'continental' Western economies have failed to adjust, maintaining 'rigid' labour markets, 'excessive' state ownership and regulation, and 'bloated' government spending; in contrast, LMEs, such as Britain and eastern European nations, have moved swiftly to become more competitive. Our view, by contrast, is closer to the basic VoC insight that distinctive forms of economies – those close to the LME and CME ideal-types – derive their competitiveness from distinctive sources of comparative institutional advantage and will respond to exogenous shocks in quite different, but perhaps equally effective ways. Those economies that diverge from these types and contain mixes of coordinating modes of varying degrees of coherence will struggle to recalibrate their systems. Past forms of coordination between labour, the state, and firms, based on pre-existing coalitions and institutionally shaped interests, will condition national responses to exogenous shocks. But we depart from a functionalist reading of VoC in a critical respect in arguing that not all institutional arrangements that underpinned successful cross-class coalitions and were positive for competitiveness in the past will continue to succeed under altered economic circumstances.

We compare four different types of nation in Europe: countries that lie closest to the CME type, such as Germany and Switzerland; MMEs such as France, Italy, and Spain in which the state has played a more active role, as promoter, regulator, or compensator in processes of change; central and eastern European nations (which we refer to as EMEs) that have rapidly evolved from state-socialist to capitalist economies; and Britain as Europe's most fully developed LME. The British LME had already liberalized labour markets, retrenched the welfare state, and altered macroeconomic policy in response to the crises of the 1970s and 1980s (Rhodes 2000), and more recent exogenous shocks would seem to have had little impact on coordination in an economy that removed most vestiges of cross-class institutional compromise under Thatcherism. This is not to say that these shocks have no economic effects: there are repercussions, especially in the rapid redeployment of employees across sectors and the creative destruction and rebuilding, in particular of the services sector, that has accommodated so many former industrial workers as well as immigrant labour. Many of Europe's CMEs weathered the storms of thirty years ago with less dramatic consequences. But more recent international shocks seem to threaten the very essence of the cross-class settlements on which these economies have long been based. A host of challenges are regularly cited: high wages, strong employment protection rights, and coordinated national bargaining systems appear threatened by the loss of national control over interest rates and exchange rates, rising cross-national capital mobility, and increasing product-market competition. The social insurance foundations of their generous welfare states are undermined by heightened labour-cost competition, while the state's revenue base is threatened by tax competition. Exogenous forces also pose serious challenges for MMEs such as France, Italy, or Spain.

Both CME- and MME-type nations have responded to these challenges by introducing sweeping reforms over the last decade or so. Take welfare and labour policies. Faced with EMU, greater international competition, and greater sectoral differentiation in productivity gains, national wage-bargaining in Germany has been supplemented since the early 1990s by firm-level bargaining that can utilize opt-outs from national-level agreements. German companies have responded by becoming evermore concentrated in high value-added sectors. At the same time, with the creation of badly paid jobs that are not covered by collective agreements and have little security, a dual labour market has emerged. Low wages have been partially offset by increases in government spending on transfer payments. MMEs too have attempted to undertake major reforms that have altered the role of the state and the benefits it traditionally provides to large groups of citizens.

Similar patterns of rapid change can be found in the regulation of markets and firms. Surprisingly, perhaps, Germany and France often supported EU regulation that ended national monopolies in strategic markets such as telecommunications or energy. Domestically, they radically transformed regulatory institutions by privatizing public utilities, allowing competition and creating new independent regulatory authorities (Schmidt 1996, 2002; Thatcher 2004a, 2005). Some CMEs, such as Switzerland, but also Germany, and MMEs, such as France, have also greatly encouraged stock market development and shareholding, though both remain underdeveloped in Italy and to a lesser extent Spain (Lane 2005; Deeg 2005b). CMEs and MMEs differ from each other and from LMEs in the extent to which networks, varieties of coordination and complementary institutions have facilitated, obstructed, or otherwise shaped these changes and how cross-class coalitions have been sustained or fragmented. Four examples of coordination mechanisms that shape change can be given here: the structure of business and union associations, informal networks that link public policymakers and suppliers, intra-firm relations, and collective bargaining over training, skills, and wages. Even the transition to capitalism of the countries of eastern Europe has been shaped by the nature of pre-existing networks.

As discussed earlier, the nature of class settlements has produced quite different sets of relationships between capital and labour, both inside and outside the firm. When firm-level capital–labour arrangements are weak, management can restructure and switch product market strategies rapidly. In LMEs, this involves relatively low risks for managers; but in MMEs, it is either pursued with limited transparency, or remains contested, as workers may seek to respond, either at firm or company level or by pressuring the state to claw back management autonomy. In CMEs, managers have less autonomy but can offer higher levels of transparency to and enjoy higher levels of cooperation with employees. Inherited coordination mechanisms based on cross-class coalitions, also affect national responses to EMU, increased international competition, and liberalized European markets. A central choice for firms is whether to follow a high-value, high-quality product strategy or a low-price, low-cost strategy. The former requires a highly skilled and cooperative workforce, whereas the latter depends on management autonomy to reduce costs. In CMEs such as Germany and Switzerland, powerful coordination mechanisms have allowed cross-class cooperation and associated complementarities to persist. Firms in export sectors have built on the traditional model of high skills and high wages by using inherited coordinating arrangements and complementarities that link bargaining over wages, conditions, and employment with high levels of training and specialization in skills, in order to specialize further in high-value sectors.

One of the consequences of the latter strategy is that higher productivity gains and greater skills specialization will be labour-saving, compounding the problems of rising long-term unemployment in CMEs such as Germany, and in MMEs with large, highly competitive manufacturing sectors such as France and Italy. The combination of strong vocational training (and hence specific skills), an associated risk-aversion to loss of jobs and income, and proportional representation (PR) has led to profound problems in Germany and possibly elsewhere. Governments in the proportional electoral systems that typically characterize CMEs are facing strong demands to maintain the protection of unemployed workers through high transfer payments–ultimately contributing to higher labour costs and adding to, rather than alleviating, the CME service-sector trilemma (Iversen 2005: ch. 6). In contrast, in the UK, 'deregulated' labour markets and the absence of labour as a countervailing force make a lower-cost, lower-price strategy, underpinning service-sector expansion more realistic than in the high-value, high-skill approach of the CMEs that continues to serve their manufacturing companies well.

High-value, high-skill strategies in LMEs are concentrated instead in high-tech companies, advertising, corporate finance, and consulting, while service-sector development (both high- and low-value added) in the CMEs is more restricted. Moreover, the majoritarian political system discourages a redistributive coalition between the middle and working classes to pay for high social spending, while the high level of general skills reduces the fear of income loss from unemployment and hence demands for such spending These factors figure prominently among those that have shaped the distinctive ways in which Germany, Britain, Sweden, and France have dealt with wage, work, and total factor productivity challenges over the past several decades. Economic strategies (and government policies) remain differentiated, and in some respects increasingly so, thus supporting the core VoC insight that LMEs and CMEs will evolve in different directions, depending on their respective strengths in mobile versus specific and co-specific assets.

On the other hand, both LMEs and CMEs are subject to an increasingly fragmented labour market and rising income inequality. These developments have important implications for the cross-class settlement, which has become more fragile, and for the sectoral interests that underpin it, which have become more diverse. The small firm/large firm, sheltered sector/exposed sector divisions that have always been important (and destabilizing) in MMEs such as Italy and Spain are now becoming an increasingly important feature of the CMEs such as Germany as well. While this does not necessarily mean the demise of CME-type institutional complementarities, it does mean that the nature of the coordinated economy has become more contested and its reaffirmation and renegotiation less amenable to consensus-based solutions as 'insider–outsider' divisions grow (Rueda 2005). The structure of private interests is important for the policy options that can be implemented by the state, especially when the role of the state is pervasive. Thus, while in MMEs the state is much more directly involved in leading responses to exogenous forces for change than in CMEs (cf. Levy 2005), its actions are conditioned by its ability to coordinate decisions with interests such as business and labour. When those other actors have been fragmented and weakened, governments have been able to introduce liberal market reforms. But responses requiring coordination have been much more difficult. In contrast, when other interests have been stronger, the opposite pattern has been seen.

Our earlier discussion claimed that the role of the state vis-à-vis business coordination is important, though to varying degrees, in the different forms of capitalism that we identify. As our 2×2 matrix demonstrated, that role will differ in terms of the relationship between strategic and arm's-length state intervention, and atomized or organized business and labour interests. Consider utility privitization. An arm's-length state and atomized business and labour organizations, as in the UK, produce weak networks and facilitate market competition. When links between policy-makers and national suppliers are traditionally strong, as in France, they can aid a state-led form of privatization and re-regulation. But when business organization (in this case horizontal supplier networks) is stronger, and the role of the state is less central, as in Germany, industry led strategies have resulted.

The transition countries of central and eastern Europe provide fascinating laboratory cases of how the state and business interact to create different forms of economic coordination. These countries have all witnessed extensive institutional and political rupture over the last decade or so from which two broadly different types of coordination have emerged – one more market oriented and LME-like, the other a form of MME, but one in which a powerful though atomized business class dominates and the state is weak. If the old nomenclature is defeated, and patchwork forms of economic control can be established through an alliance between an organized, technocrat-led state and a mixture of foreign and domestic firms, then 'liberal dependent' systems, with open economic relations and high levels of FDI result, as in the Czech Republic, Hungary, and Poland. Trade unions are weak, but the state provides a range of public goods (pensions and other social transfers) for the economy and has modest steering capacity. In contrast, if the nomenclature retains power, as in Russia, Ukraine, or Romania, it uses its offices to acquire private property, giving rise to 'patrimonial' systems in which economic control (coordination would be much too strong a term) is exercised by the nomenclature and domestic producers through patron–client ownership networks. Foreign direct ownership is weak, and the state is also weak and unable to provide adequate public goods.

Complementarities and coordination as understood in VoC theory cannot be said to exist in these countries (whereas 'a-complementarities' abound). For instance, the Polish and Ukranian economies are currently characterized by rather unstable and largely incoherent mixes of labour-market institutions, financial intermediation, and corporate governance. Their evolutionary trajectories are as yet unclear, even if the former bears some resemblance to a Mediterranean MME, and the latter to a continental CME, though with neither its coherence of governance nor its productive interplay of complementarities. But some clearer and more coherent forms of incipient coordination have emerged in other, smaller transition economies. These have taken on a CME-type character in Slovenia but are closer to the LME archetype in the Baltic states, as revealed in their contrasting institutional characteristics, including levels of unionization, the presence or not of works councils, and the relative strength of business organizations. Thus, overall, and in the face of strong exogenous pressures, major institutional reforms have been undertaken in all of Europe's capitalist varieties. But change is particularly arduous in the CMEs and MMEs: it involves visible (re)distributive decisions which question the cross-class settlements that underpin coordination mechanisms, and requires the assent of powerful actors with key positions in those arrangements.

5. CONCLUSIONS

There is little doubt that VoC has revolutionized the study of contemporary political economy. Core VoC concepts, such as comparative institutional advantage and complementarities, the (soft) rationalist method that underpinned it, the attention to institutions as building blocks for coordination, and the CME–LME typology that resulted, have become the stock in trade of political economists everywhere, either used approvingly for building research agendas or critically as a foil for developing alternative approaches. The extraordinary range of critiques and debates of the VoC framework is perhaps the best indication of its impact on the field. Even though we have argued that many of those criticisms are unwarranted, many others raise important issues of analysis and logic in VoC, and have led us in this introduction to reconsider some of its basic tenets.

As we have tried to show, an extended VoC framework offers several ways of addressing these critiques. Three avenues of research in particular appear to be promising to us and have underpinned our argument above. The first is to consider the origins of different forms of coordination and different models of capitalism. The political–economic laboratory opened up in central Europe and a brief comparison of some core European countries suggested that elite networks played a critical role in determining the type of coordination that emerged. The second introduced a more dynamic interpretation of VoC by examining the cross-class coalitions that underpin the different modes of coordination. Finally, we explored the nature of the state and suggested that its relative absence in the original iterations of VoC theory was more related to its heuristic emphasis on CMEs and LMEs and less to intrinsic deficiencies in the framework. We then tied these insights to the broad empirical themes of this volume and showed how they helped us shed new light on the process of political–economic adjustment in Europe.

Our general verdict is that VoC provides a remarkably flexible framework for analysis which, in both its more and less orthodox versions, allows for the development of a highly innovative research agenda. Drawing on both the chapters in Hancké et al. (2007) and on broader debates, we have demonstrated that VoC can accommodate relatively easily the most important critiques levelled against it. The framework can be extended to incorporate cases that fall outside the standard CME–LME typology without losing the analytical sharpness that came with the original Hall–Soskice formulation. Focusing on cross-class coalitions allows us to explore how coordination is sustained but also how it can be threatened, demonstrating that models of capitalism are not simply class compromises, as Amable (2003) argues, but are as much the products of struggles within as between classes. And the state clearly matters, but in different ways in different models of capitalism. LMEs and CMEs share an arm's-length state–economy relationship, while in other types of capitalism the state is either a central coordinating mechanism (as in France) or compensates for weaknesses in the organization of capital and labour (as in Italy).

As a result of these conceptual extensions, a dynamic picture of capitalism emerges which can take account of change and the political–economic dynamics underpinning change, while keeping us aware of the continuities in the frameworks and in the strategies of the central actors in the different models. The interaction between the role of the state, shifting cross-class coalitions, and the ability of the latter to dominate political–economic agendas may be especially fruitful in analysing changes in modes of coordination. For as long as large manufacturing firms in the export sectors (and their workers) dominate these class agendas – a function of their high degree of collective organization and interest definition – national economies are likely to continue to follow existing patterns. However, when new cross-class coalitions emerge, perhaps furthered or instrumentalized by the state, and if these coalitions come to dominate domestic agendas, modes of coordination may shift.

If we place the analyses in this volume alongside others found in a burgeoning literature that the VoC framework has inspired, we can begin to grasp its power. In recent years, the framework has been usefully extended to include such diverse areas as gender politics (McCall and Orloff 2005b), emerging models of capitalism in central Europe (Bohle and Greskovits 2004; Innes 2005), links between macroeconomic frameworks and microeconomic adjustment (Hancké and Rhodes 2005; Carlin and Soskice 2006), electoral politics (Iversen and Soskice 2006b), and the political economy of liberalization and privatization in OECD countries (Thatcher 2004b). A very rich harvest indeed, and one which has significantly enriched our understanding of the world. If only ten years ago, we thought that we probably knew less than ten years earlier,[1] we can now say with certainty that we currently know more, and that VoC helped us get there.

Ultimately, however, an analytical framework such as VoC is only as good as its ability to make sense of what is going on in the world around us. And that world is changing quickly. We have tried to show that VoC is a useful tool to make sense of many of these changes, but others may disagree. We can therefore only emphasize the closing words of Hall and Soskice in their introduction to VoC (2001b: 68). They claimed, and the essays in Hancké et al. (2007) along with many others prove, that their volume was not an end point but a start – an invitation to a 'fruitful interchange among scholars interested in many kinds of issues in economics, industrial relations, social policymaking, political science, business, and the law'. Hancké et al. (2007), we hope, will become part of that ongoing discussion.

NOTE

1. The words in the text are John Zysman's, who echoed and inverted the phrase of Bob Dylan's 'My Back Pages' – 'but I was so much older then, I'm younger than that now' – at one of the founding conferences of the project that led to VoC.

References

Abramson, H. N., Encarnação, J., Reid, P., and Schmoch, U. (eds.) (1997). *Technology Transfer Systems in the United States and Germany*. Washington, DC: National Academy Press.

Albert, M. (1991). *Capitalisme contre capitalisme*. Paris: Seuil.

—— (1993). *Capitalism Against Capitalism*. London: Whurr.

Amable, B. (2000). 'Institutional Complementarity and Diversity of Social Systems of Innovation and Production'. *Review of International Political Economy* 7/4: 645–87.

—— (2003). *The Diversity of Modern Capitalism*. Oxford: Oxford University Press.

—— (2005). 'Dialogue on Institutional Complementarity and Political Economy'. *Socio-Economic Review* 3/2: 359–82.

—— Barré, R., and Boyer, R. (1997). *Les systèmes d'innovation à l'ère de la globalization*. Paris: Economica.

Anderlini, L., and Ianni, A. (1993). 'Path Dependence and Learning from Neighbours'. Economic Theory Discussion Paper 186. Cambridge: University of Cambridge Department of Applied Economics.

Angel, D. P. (1994). *Restructuring for Innovation: The Remaking of the U.S. Semiconductor Industry*. New York: The Guilford Press.

Aoki, M. (1988). *Information, Incentives, and Bargaining in the Japanese Economy*. Cambridge: Cambridge University Press.

—— (1994). 'The Contingent Governance of Teams: Analysis of Institutional Complementarity'. *International Economic Review* 35/3: 657–76.

—— (2001). *Toward a Comparative Institutional Analysis*. Cambridge, MA: MIT Press.

Applebaum, E., and Batt, R. (1994). *The New American Workplace*. Ithaca, NY: ILR Press.

Archibugi, D., and Pianta, M. (1996). 'Measuring Technological Change Through Patents and Innovation Surveys'. *Technovation* 16/9: 451–68.

Arrow, K. (1962). 'Economic Welfare and the Allocation of Resources for Invention'. In R. R. Nelson (ed.), *The Rate and Direction of Inventive Activity*. Princeton, NJ: Princeton University Press, 609–26.

—— (2000). 'Increasing Returns: Historiographical Issues and Path Dependence'. *European Journal of the History of Economic Thought* 7/2: 171–80.

Arthur, B. (1990). 'Positive Feedbacks in the Economy'. *Scientific American*. February: 92–9.

—— (1994). *Increasing Returns and Path Dependence in the Economy*. Ann Arbor, MI: University of Michigan Press.

—— Ermoliev, Y. M., and Kaniovski, Y. M. (1987). 'Path–Dependent Processes and the Emergence of Macrostructure'. *European Journal of Operational Research* 30: 294–303.

Baccaro, L., and Simoni, M. (2004). 'The Irish Social Partnership and the "Celtic Tiger" Phenomenon'. International Institute for Labour Studies, Discussion Paper 154/2004. Geneva: International Labour Organization (ILO). Available at <www.ilo.org/inst>.

Bagnasco, A. (1977). *Tre Italie: la problematica territoriale dello sviluppo Italiano.* Bologna: Il Mulino.

Baker, W. (1984). 'The Social Structure of a National Securities Market'. *American Journal of Sociology* 89: 775–811.

—— (1990). 'Market Networks and Corporate Behaviour'. *American Journal of Sociology* 96: 589–625.

Banks, J. S., and Hanuschek, E. A. (eds.) (1995). *Modern Political Economy.* New York: Cambridge University Press.

Barreto, H. (1989). *The Entrepreneur in Micro–Economic Theory: Disappearance and Explanation.* London: Routledge.

Bates, R. (1988). 'Contra Contractarianism: Some Reflections on the New Institutionalism'. *Politics and Society* 16: 387–401.

Bauer, M. (ed.) (1995). *Resistance to New Technology: Nuclear Power, Information Technology, Biotechnology.* New York: Cambridge University Press.

Baumann, A. (2002). 'Convergence Versus Path-Dependency: Vocational Training in the Media Production Industries in Germany and the UK'. Ph.D. thesis: European University Institute, Florence.

Baumol, W. J., Nelson, R. R., and Wolff, E. N. (eds.) (1994). *Convergence of Productivity.* Oxford: Oxford University Press.

Beasley, D. (1988). *The Suppression of the Automobile: Skulduggery at the Crossroads.* New York: Greenwood Press.

Becattini, G., and Burroni, L. (2004). 'Il distretto industriale come strumento di ricomposizione del sapere sociale'. *Sociologia del Lavoro* 92: 67–84.

Beer, S. H. (1982). *Britain against Itself.* London: Faber and Faber.

Beissinger, M. R. (2002). *Nationalist Mobilization and the Collapse of the Soviet State.* New York: Cambridge University Press.

Bendix, R. (1974 [1956]). *Work and Authority in Industry: Ideologies of Management in the Course of Industrialization.* Berkeley, CA: University of California Press.

Berger, S., and Dore, R. (eds.) (1996). *National Diversity and Global Capitalism.* Ithaca, NY: Cornell University Press.

—— and Piore, M. (1980). *Dualism and Discontinuity in Industrial Societies.* Cambridge: Cambridge University Press.

Berggren, C., and Laestadius, S. (2000). *The Embeddedness of Industrial Clusters: The Strength of the Path in the Nordic Telecom System.* Stockholm: Kungl. Tekniska Högskolan.

Bermeo, N. (ed.) (2000). *Context and Consequence: The Effects of Unemployment in the New Europe.* New York, Cambridge University Press.

Bertoldi, M. (2003). 'Varietà e dinamiche del capitalismo'. *Stato e Mercato* 69: 365–83.

Beyer, J. (2001). *'One best way' oder Varietät? Strategischer und organisatorischer Wandel von Grossunternehmen im Prozess der Internationalisierung.* MPIfG Discussion Paper 01/2. Cologne: Max Planck Institut für Gesellschaftsforschung.

Biagiotti, A., and Burroni, L. (2004). 'Between Cities and Districts: Local Software Systems in Italy'. In Crouch et al. (eds.).

Bimber, B. (1994). 'Three Faces of Technological Determinism'. In Smith and Marx (eds.).

Blaas, W. (1992). 'The Swiss Model: Corporatism or Liberal Capitalism?'. In Pekkarinen et al. (eds.).

Blanchard, O. J. (2004). *The Economic Future of Europe*. MIT Economics Working Paper 04–04. Cambridge, MA: Massachusetts Institute of Technology.

Blyth, M. (2003). 'Same as It Never Was: Temporality and Typology in the Varieties of Capitalism'. *Comparative European Politics* 1: 215–25.

BMBF (1998): *Innovation für die Wissensgesellschaft*. Bonn: BMBF.

BMBF/DLR (1996): *Statusseminar des BMBF: Softwaretechnologie, März 1996*. Berlin: Deutsche Forschungsanstalt für Luft-und Raumfahrt.

—— (1998): *Statusseminar des BMBF: Softwaretechnologie, März 1998*. Berlin: Deutsches Zentrum für Luft- und Raumfahrt.

Borrus, M., and Zysman, J. (1998). 'Globalization with Borders: The Rise of 'Wintelism' as the Future of Industrial Competition' In Schwartz and Zysman (eds.).

Börsch, A. (2007). 'Institutional Variation and Coordination Patterns in CMEs: Swiss and German Corporate Governance in Comparison'. In Hancké, Rhodes, and Thatcher (eds.).

Bourdieu, P., Chamboredon, J.-C., and Passeron, J.-C. (1973). *Le métier de sociologue: préalables epistémologiques*. Paris: Mouton.

Bourke, P., and Butler, L. (1996). 'Publication Types, Citation Rates, and Evaluation'. *Scientometrics* 37/3: 473–94.

Boyer, R. (1990). *The Regulation School: A Critical Introduction*. New York: Columbia University Press.

—— (1996). 'The Convergence Hypothesis Revisited: Globalization but still the Century of Nations?'. In Berger and Dore (eds.).

—— (1997). 'The Variety and Unequal Performances of Really Existing Markets: Farewell to Doctor Pangloss?'. In Hollingsworth and Boyer (eds.).

—— (2004*a*). 'New Growth Regimes, But still Institutional Diversity'. *Socio-Economic Review* 2/1: 1–32.

—— (2004*b*). *The Future of Economic Growth: As New Becomes Old*. Cheltenham: Edward Elgar.

—— (2005). Dialogue on 'Institutional Complementarity and Political Economy'. *Socio-Economic Review*. 3/2: 359–382.

—— and Didier, M. (1998). *Innovation et Croissance*. Paris: La Documentation Française.

—— and Saillard, Y. (eds.) (1995). *Théorie de la régulation: L'état des savoirs*. Paris: La Découverte.

Braczyk, H.-J., and Schienstock, G. (eds.) (1996). *Kurswechsel in der Industrie. Lean Production in Baden-Württemberg*. Berlin and Cologne: Kohlhammer.

Breen, R. (2000). 'Beliefs, Rational Choice and Bayesian Learning'. *Rationality and Society* 11/4: 463–79.

Burroni, L., and Trigilia, C. (2001). 'Italy: Economic Development through Local Economies'. In Crouch et al. (eds.).

Burt, R. (1988). 'The Stability of American Markets'. *American Journal of Sociology* 94: 356–95.

Butzbach, O. (2005). 'Varieties within Capitalism? A Comparative Study of French and Italian Savings Banks'. Ph.D. thesis: European University Institute, Florence.

Cable, V. (1995). 'The Diminished Nation-State: A Study in the Loss of Economic Power'. *Daedalus* 124: 23–54.

Callaghan, H. (2004). 'The Domestic Politics of EU Legislation: British, French and German Attitudes towards Takeover Regulation, 1985–2003'. Paper presented to the Conference of Europeanists, Chicago, 11–13 March.

Calmfors, L., and Driffill, J. (1988). 'Bargaining Structure, Corporatism and Macro-economic Performance'. *Economic Policy* 6: 13–61.

Calvert, R. (1995a). 'Rational Actors, Equilibrium and Institutions'. In Knight and Sened (eds) 1995: 57–94.

—— (1995b). 'The Rational Choice Theory of Institutions: Cooperation, Coordination and Communication'. In Banks and Hanuschek (eds).

Cameron, D. R. (1984). 'Social Democracy, Corporatism, Labour Quiescence and the Representation of Economic Interest in Advanced Capitalist Society'. In Goldthorpe (ed.).

Campbell, J. L. (2001). 'Institutional Analysis and the Role of Ideas in Political Economy'. In Campbell and Pedersen (eds.).

—— (2004). *Institutional Change and Globalization.* Princeton, NJ: Princeton University Press.

—— and Pedersen, O. (2001a). 'The Rise of Neoliberalism and Institutional Analysis'. In Campbell and Pedersen (eds.).

—— —— (2001b). 'The Second Movement in Institutional Analysis'. In Campbell and Pedersen (eds.) 2001: 249–82.

—— —— (eds.) (2001). *The Rise of Neoliberalism and Institutional Analysis.* Princeton, NJ: Princeton University Press.

—— Hall, J. A., and Pedersen, O. K. (2006). *The State of Denmark.* Montreal: McGill University Press.

—— and Pedersen, O., Hollingsworth, J. R., and Lindberg, L. N. (eds.) (1991). *Governance of the American Economy.* New York: Cambridge University Press.

Cantwell, J., and Harding, R. (1998). 'The Internationalisation of German Companies' R and D'. *National Institute Economic Review* 163: 99–115.

Carlin, W., and Soskice, D. (1997). 'Shocks to the System: The German Political Economy under Stress'. *National Institute Economic Review* 159: 57–66.

—— Glyn, A., and van Reenen, J. (2001). 'Export Market Performance of OECD Countries: An Empirical Examination of the Role of Cost Competitiveness.' *Economic Journal* 111/468: 128–62.

Carlsson, B., and Eliasson, G. (2003). 'Industrial Dynamics and Endogenous Growth'. *Industry and Innovation* 10/4: 435–56.

Carruthers, B. G., Babb, S. L., and Halliday, T. C. (2001). 'Institutionalizing Markets, or the Market for Institutions? Central Banks, Bankruptcy Law, and the Globalization of Financial Markets'. In Campbell and Pedersen (eds.).

Casper, S. (1999). 'National Institutional Frameworks and High Technology Innovation in Germany. The Case of Biotechnology'. Discussion Paper FS I 99–306. Berlin: WZB.

—— (2001). 'The Legal Framework for Corporate Governance: The Influence of Contract Law on Company Strategies in Germany and the United States'. In Hall and Soskice (eds.).

—— (2002). 'National Institutional Frameworks and High-Technology Innovation in Germany: The Case of Biotechnology'. In Hollingsworth et al (eds.).

—— and Kettler, H. (2001). 'National Institutional Frameworks and the Hybridization of Entrepreneurial Business Models: The German and UK Biotechnology Sectors'. *Industry and Innovation* 8/1: 5–30.

—— Lehrer, M., and Soskice, D. (1999). 'Can High-Technology Industries Prosper in Germany? Institutional Frameworks and the Evolution of the German Software and Biotechnology Industries'. *Industry and Innovation* 6/1: 5–24.

Castaldi, C., and Dosi, G. (n.d.). 'The Grip of History and the Scope for Novelty: Some Results and Open Questions on Path Dependence in Economic Processes'. Unpublished manuscript.

Castles, F. G., and Mitchell, D. (1991). *Three Worlds of Welfare Capitalism or Four?* Working Paper 63. Luxembourg: Luxembourg Income Study.

Chandler, A. D., Amatori, F., and Hikino, T. (eds.) (1997). *Big Business and the Wealth of Nations.* Cambridge: Cambridge University Press.

Charkham, J. (1995). *Keeping Good Company: A Study of Corporate Governance in Five Countries.* Oxford: Oxford University Press.

Clemens, E. (1997). *The People's Lobby: Organizational Innovation and the Rise of Interest Group Politics in the United States.* Chicago: University of Chicago Press.

Coase, R. (1937). 'The Nature of the Firm'. *Economica* 4: 386–405.

Coates, D. (ed.) (2005). *Varieties of Capitalism, Varieties of Approaches.* Basingstoke: Palgrave-Macmillan.

Coleman, W. (1997). 'Associational Governance in a Globalizing Era: Weathering the Storm'. In Hollingsworth and Boyer (eds.).

Collier, R. B., and Collier, D. (1991). *Shaping the Political Arena.* Princeton, NJ: Princeton University Press.

Considine, M. and Lewis, J. (2003). 'Working with Networks: Exploring Service Delivery Strategies in Public and Private Organizations as Networking Effects'. *Journal of European Public Policy* 10/1: 46–58.

Corbett, J., and Jenkinson, T. (1996). The Financing of Industry, 1970–1989: An International Comparison'. *Journal of the Japanese and International Economies* 10/71: 71–96.

Coriat, B., Orsi, F., and Weinstein, O. (2003), 'Does Biotech Reflect a New Science-Based Innovation Regime?'. *Industry and Innovation* 10/3: 231–54.

Cotts Watkins, S. (1991). *From Provinces into Nations: Demographic Integration in Western Europe 1870–1960.* Princeton, NJ: Princeton University Press.

Crane, D. (ed.) (1994). *The Sociology of Culture.* Oxford: Blackwell.

Crouch, C. (1977). *Class Conflict and the Industrial Relations Crisis.* London: Heinemann.

Crouch, C. (1985). 'Conditions for Trade Union Wage Restraint'. In L. N. Lindberg and C. S. Maier (eds.), *The Politics of Inflation and Economic Stagnation*. Washington DC: Brookings Institution, 105–39.

—— (1993). *Industrial Relations and European State Traditions*. Oxford: Clarendon Press.

—— (1999). *Social Change in Western Europe*. Oxford: Oxford University Press.

—— (2001). 'Breaking Open Black Boxes: The Implications for Sociological Theory of European Integration'. In A. Menon and V. Wright (eds.), *From the Nation State to Europe? Essays in Honour of Jack Hayward*. Oxford: Oxford University Press.

—— (2005*a*). *Capitalist Diversity and Change: Recombinant Governance and Institutional Pioneers*. Oxford, Oxford University Press.

—— (2005*b*). 'The Governance of *emersione*: Preparing the Approach'. Working Document for Project 23, NewGov Research Programme, European Union Framework Programme. Florence: European University Institute.

—— and Farrell, H. (2004). 'Breaking the Path of Institutional Development? Alternatives to the New Determinism', *Rationality and Society* 16/1: 5–43.

—— and Keune, M. (2005). 'Changing Dominant Practice: Making use of Institutional Diversity in Hungary and the United Kingdom'. In Streeck and Thelen (eds).

—— —— (2005). 'Rapid Change by Endogenous Actors: The Utility of Institutional Incongruence'. In Streeck and Thelen (eds.).

—— and O'Mahoney, J. (2004). 'Machine Tooling in the United Kingdom'. In Crouch et al. (eds.).

—— and Streeck, W. (1997). 'Introduction: The Future of Capitalist Diversity'. In Crouch and Streeck.

—— —— (eds.) (1997). *Political Economy of Modern Capitalism: Mapping Convergence and Diversity*. London: Sage.

—— and Trigilia, C. (2001). 'Conclusions: Still Local Economies in Global Capitalism?'. In Crouch et al..

—— Finegold, D., and Sako, M. (1999). *Do Skills Matter? A Political Economy of Skill Formation in Advanced Societies*. Oxford: Clarendon Press.

—— Le Galès, P., Trigilia, C., and Voelzkow, H. (eds.) (2001). *Local Production Systems in Europe: Rise or Demise?* Oxford: Oxford University Press.

—— —— —— —— (eds.) (2004). *Changing Governance of Local Economies: Response of European Local Production Systems*. Oxford: Oxford University Press.

—— Streeck, W., Boyer, R., Amable, B., Hall, P. A., and Jackson, G. (2005). 'Dialogue on "Institutional Complementarities and Political Economy"'. *Socio-Economic Review* 3: 359–82.

Culpepper, P. D. (2001). 'Employers, Public Policy, and the Politics of Decentralized Cooperation in Germany and France'. In Hall and Soskice (eds.)

—— (2003) *Creating Cooperation: How States Develop Human Capital in Europe*. Ithaca NY: Cornell University Press.

—— (2005). 'Institutional Change in Contemporary Capitalism: Coordinated Financial Systems since 1990'. *World Politics* 57: 173–99.

—— Hall, P. A. and Palier, B. (eds) (2006). *Changing France: The Politics that Markets Make*, London: Palgrave-Macmillan.

Daly, M. (2000). 'A Fine Balance: Women's Labour Market Participation in International Comparison'. In Scharpf and Schmidt (eds.).

Dasgupta, P. and Stoneman, P. (eds) (1987). *Economic policy and technological performance*. Cambridge : Cambridge University Press.

David, P. A. (1992*a*). 'Path Dependence and Economics'. Center for Economics Research Working Paper. Stanford: Stanford University.

—— (1992*b*). 'Path Dependence in Economic Processes: Implications for Policy Analysis in Dynamic System Contexts'. Center for Economics Research Working Paper. Stanford: Stanford University.

—— (2000). 'Path Dependence, its Critics and the Quest for "Historical Economics"'. In Garrouste and Ioannides (eds.).

Deeg, R. (2001*a*). *Institutional Change and the Uses and Limits of Path Dependency: The Case of German Finance*. MPIfG Discussion Paper 01/6. Cologne: Max Planck Institut für Gesellschaftsforschung.

—— (2001*b*). 'Path Dependence and National Models of Capitalism: Are Germany and Italy on New Paths?' Paper presented at the Annual Meeting of the American Political Science Association, San Francisco. Aug. 30–Sep. 2.

—— (2004). 'Change from Within: German and Italian Finance in the 1990s' In Streeck and Thelen (eds.).

—— (2005*a*). *Complementarity and Institutional Change: How Useful a Concept?* Discussion Paper SP 11 2005–21. Berlin: WZB.

—— (2005*b*). 'Path Dependency, Institutional Complementarity, and Change in National Business Systems'. In Morgan, Whitley, and Moen (eds.).

Deutsche Bundesbank (1997): *Quarterly Report*. November.

Die Zeit (1997): 'Unser Modell will keiner mehr'. 5 September.

DiMaggio, P. (1998). 'The New Institutionalisms: Avenues of Collaboration'. *Journal of Institutional and Theoretical Economics* 154/4: 697–705.

—— (ed.) (2001). *The Twenty-First Century Firm: Changing Economic Organization in Comparative Perspective*. Princeton, NJ: Princeton University Press.

—— and W. W. Powell (1991). 'Introduction'. In Powell and DiMaggio (eds.).

Djelic, M.-L. (1999). 'From a Typology of Neo–Institutional Arguments to Their Cross–Fertilization'. Unpublished paper, ICC Workshop. Evanston: Kellogg Institute.

—— and Quack, S. (2003). 'Conclusion: Globalization as a Double Process of Institutional Change and Institution Building'. In Djelic and Quack (eds.).

—— —— (eds.) (2003) *Globalization and Institutions: Redefining the Rules of the Economic Game*. Cheltenham: Edward Elgar.

Dobbin, F. (1994a). 'Cultural Models of Organization: The Social Construction of Rational Organizing Principles'. In D. Crane (ed.), *The Sociology of Culture*. Oxford, Blackwell, 117–191.

—— (1994b). *Forging Industrial Policy: The United States, Britain and France in the Railway Age*. New York: Cambridge University Press.

Dodd, L. C., and C. Jillson (eds.) (1994). *The Dynamics of American Politics*. Boulder, CO: Westview.

Dore, R. (1997). 'The Distinctiveness of Japan'. In Crouch and Streeck (eds).

—— (2000). *Stock Market Capitalism: Welfare Capitalism.* Oxford: Oxford University Press.

—— Bertoldi, M., and Regini, M. (2003). 'Varièta e dinamiche del capitalismo'. *Stato e Mercato* 69: 365–83.

—— Boyer, R., and Mars, Z. (eds.) (1994). *The Return of Incomes Policy.* London: Pinter.

Douglas, M. (1987). *How Institutions Think.* London: Routledge.

Drago, M. E. (1998). 'The Institutional Bases of Chile's Economic "Miracle": Institutions, Government *Discretionary Authority* (DA). Economic Performance under Two Policy Regimes'. Ph.D. thesis: European University Institute, Florence.

Durkheim, E. (1984 [1893]). *The Division of Labor in Society.* New York: The Free Press.

Easterbrook, F., and Fischel, D. (1991). *The Economic Structure of Corporate Law.* Cambridge, MA: Harvard University Press.

Eaton, J., and Kortum, S. (1999). 'International Technology Diffusion: Theory and Measurement'. *International Economic Review* 40/3: 537–70.

Ebbinghaus, B. (2001). 'When Labour and Capital Collude: The Political Economy of Early Retirement in Europe, Japan and the USA'. In Ebbinghaus and Manow (eds.).

—— and Manow, P. (2001). 'Introduction: Studying Varieties of Welfare Capitalism'. In Ebbinghaus and Manow (eds.).

—— —— (eds.) (2001). *Comparing Welfare Capitalism. Social Policy and Political Economy in Europe, Japan and the USA.* London: Routledge.

Edquist, C. (ed.) (1997). *Systems of Innovation: Technologies, Institutions, and Organizations.* New York: Pinter.

Edwards, P. N. (1996). *The Closed World: Computers and the Politics of Discourse in Cold War America.* Cambridge, MA: MIT Press.

Eichengreen, B. (2007): *The European Economy Since 1945: Coordinated Capitalism and Beyond.* Princeton. NJ: Princeton University Press.

Eliasson, G. (2003). Global Economic Integration and Regional Attractors of Competence'. *Industry and Innovation* 10/1: 75–102.

Elster, J. (1989). *Nuts and Bolts for the Social Sciences.* Cambridge: Cambridge University Press.

—— (1989). *The Cement of Society: A Study of Social Order.* Cambridge: Cambridge University Press.

—— (2003). 'Authors and Actors'. Paper presented at the Conference on Crafting and Operating Institutions, Yale University. 11–13 April.

Ernst and Young (1998*a*). *European Life Sciences 1998.* London: Ernst and Young.

—— (1998*b*). *Aufbruchstimmung 1998: First German Biotechnology Survey.* Munich: Ernst and Young.

Ernst, E. C. (2002). 'Financial Systems, Industrial Relations, and Industry Specialization: An Econometric Analysis of Institutional Complementarities'. Unpublished manuscript.

Esping-Andersen, G. (1990) *The Three Worlds of Welfare Capitalism.* Princeton, NJ: Princeton University Press.

Estevez-Abe, M., Iversen, T., and Soskice, D. (2001). 'Social Protection and the Formation of Skills: A Reinterpretation of the Welfare State'. In Hall and Soskice (eds.).

Evans, A. (2005). 'Preemptive Modernisation and the Politics of Sectoral Defense: Adjustment to Globalisation in the Portuguese Pharmacy Sector'. *Comparative Politics* 40: 253–72.

Ferrera, M. (1997). *Le trappole del welfare*. Bologna: Il Mulino.

—— and Hemerijck, A. (2003). 'Recalibrating Europe's Welfare Regimes'. In Zeitlin and Trubeck (eds.).

—— —— and Rhodes, M. (2000). *The Future of Social Europe: Recasting Work and Welfare in the New Economy*. Lisbon: Report for the Portuguese Presidency of the European Union.

Fioretos, O. (2001). 'The Domestic Sources of Multilateral Preferences: Varieties of Capitalism in the European Community'. In Hall and Soskice (eds.).

Fligstein, N. (1990). *The Transformation of Corporate Control*. Cambridge, MA: Harvard University Press.

—— (1997). 'A Political Cultural Approach to Market Institutions'. *American Sociological Review* 4: 656–73.

—— (2001). *The Architecture of Markets: An Economic Sociology of Twenty-First-Century Capitalist Societies*. Princeton, NJ: Princeton University Press.

Freeman, C. (1995). 'The National System of Innovation in Historical Perspective'. *Cambridge Journal of Economics* 19/1: 5–24.

Frieden, J., and Rogowski, R. (1996) 'The Impact of the International Economy on National Policies: An Analytical Overview'. In Keohane, R. O. and Milner, H. V. (eds.).

Friedman, M. (1962). *Capitalism and Freedom*. Chicago: University of Chicago Press.

Friedman, T. (2000). *The Lexus and the Olive Tree*. New York. Anchor Books.

Gamble, A. (1988). *The Free Economy and the Strong State: The Politics of Thatcherism*. Basingstoke: Macmillan.

Garfield, E. (1979). *Citation Indexing: Its Theory and Application in Science, Technology, and Humanities*. New York: John Wiley & Sons.

Garfinkel, I., Rainwater, L., and Smeeding, T. (2007). *The American Welfare State: Laggard or Leader?* New York: Russell Sage Foundation.

Garrett, G. (1998). *Partisan Politics in the Global Economy*. Cambridge: Cambridge University Press.

—— (2000). 'Shrinking States? Globalization and National Autonomy'. In N. Woods (ed.).

Garrouste, P. and S. Ioannides (eds.) (2000). *Evolution and Path Dependence in Economic Ideas: Past and Present*. Cheltenham: Edward Elgar.

Garud, R., and Karnøe, P. (2001*a*). 'Preface'. In Garud and Karnøe (eds.).

—— —— (2001*b*). 'Path Creation as a Process of Mindful Deviation'. In Garud and Karnøe (eds.).

—— —— (eds.) (2001). *Path Dependence and Creation*. Mahwah, NJ: Lawrence Elbaum Associates.

Giddens, A. (1976). *New Rules of Sociological Method: A Positive Critique of Interpretative Sociologies.* London: Heinemann.

Gilson, R. (1999). 'The Legal Infrastructure of High Technology Industrial Districts: Silicon Valley, Route 128, and Covenants not to Compete'. *New York University Law Review* 74: 572–629.

—— (2003). 'Engineering a Venture Capital Market: Lessons from the American Experience'. *Stanford Law Review* 1067–1103.

Glanzel, W., and Moed, H. F. (2002). 'Journal Impact Measures in Bibiliometric Research'. *Scientometrics* 53/2: 171–93.

Glassmann, U. (2004). 'Refining National Policy: The Machine-Tool Industry in the Local Economy of Stuttgart'. In Crouch et al. (eds.) 2004.

—— and Voelzkow, H. (2001). 'The Governance of Local Economies in Germany'. In Crouch et al. (eds.).

Glyn, A. (2006). *Capitalism Unleashed.* Oxford: Oxford University Press.

Goldthorpe, J. H. (1978). 'The Current Inflation: Towards a Sociological Account'. In Hirsch, F. and Goldthorpe, J. H. (eds).

—— (2001). 'Causation, Statistics, and Sociology'. *European Sociological Review* 17: 1–20.

—— (ed.) (1984). *Order and Conflict in Contemporary Capitalism.* New York and Oxford: Oxford University Press.

Goodin, R. (2003). 'Choose Your Capitalism?'. *Comparative European Politics* 1/2: 203–14.

—— Headey, B., Muffels, R., and Dirven, H.-J. (1999). *The Real Worlds of Welfare Capitalism.* Cambridge: Cambridge University Press.

Gould, S. J. (2002). *The Structure of Evolutionary Theory.* Cambridge, MA: Harvard University Press.

Gourevitch, P. A., and Shinn, J. (2005). *Political Power and Corporate Control: The New Global Politics of Corporate Governance.* Princeton, NJ: Princeton University Press.

Goyer, M. (2005). 'Institutional Complementarity and Change: Assessing the Impact of the Transformation of Corporate Governance in France and Germany'. Paper presented to a Workshop on Institutional Change in Contemporary Capitalism, London School of Economics. June.

—— (2006). 'The Transformation of Corporate Governance in France'. In Culpepper, Hall, and Palier (eds.).

—— (2007). 'Capital Mobility, Varieties of Institutional Investors and the Transforming Stability of Corporate Governance in France and Germany'. In Hancké, Rhodes, and Thatcher (eds.).

Grabher, G. (1993*a*). 'Rediscovering the Social in the Economics of Interfirm Relations'. In Grabher (ed.) 1993: 1–32.

—— (1993*b*). 'The Weakness of Strong Ties: The Lock-in of Regional Development in the Ruhr Area'. In Grabher (ed.).

—— (ed.) (1993). *The Embedded Firm: On the Socioeconomics of Industrial Networks.* London: Routledge.

—— (2002). 'Cool Projects, Boring Institutions'. *Regional Studies* 36: 205–14.

Granovetter, M. (1973). 'The Strength of Weak Ties'. *American Journal of Sociology* 78/6: 1360–80.

—— (1985). 'Economic Action and Social Structure: The Problem of Embeddedness'. *American Journal of Sociology* 91/3: 481–510.

—— (1990). 'The Old and the New Economic Sociology'. In R. Freedland and A. F. Robertson (eds.).

Grant, W. (1997). 'Perspectives on Globalization and Economic Coordination'. In Hollingsworth and Boyer (eds.).

Grebel, T., Pyka, A., and Hanusch, H. (2003). 'An Evolutionary Approach to the Theory of Entrepreneurship'. *Industry and Innovation* 10/4: 493–514.

Greenwood, J., Pyper, R., and Wilson, D. (2002). *New Public Administration in Britain.* London: Routledge.

Greif, A. and David, L. (2004). 'A Theory of Endogenous Institutional Change'. *American Political Science Review* 98: 633–52.

—— (2003). 'How do Self-Enforcing Institutions Endogenously Change?' Unpublished manuscript: Stanford University.

Griliches, Z. (1990). 'Patents Statistics as Economic Indicators: A Survey'. *Journal of Economic Literature* 28/4: 1661–707.

—— (ed.) (1984). *R&D, Patents, and Productivity.* Chicago: University of Chicago Press.

—— Hall, B. H., and Pakes, A. (1987). 'The Value of Patents as Indicators of Inventive Activity'. Dasgupta, P. and P. Stoneman (eds.) (1987), 68–103.

Gruber, L. (2000). *Ruling the World: Power Politics and the Rise of Supranational Institutions.* Princeton, NJ: Princeton University Press.

Guillen, M. (2000). 'Corporate Governance and Globalization: Is There Convergence Across Countries?'. *Advances in International Comparative Management* 13: 175–204.

Hacker, J. (2005). 'Policy Drift: The Hidden Politics of US Welfare State Retrenchment'. In Streeck and Thelen (eds.).

Hage, J., and Alter, C. (1997). 'A Typology of Interorganizational Relationships and Networks'. In Hollingsworth and Boyer (eds.).

—— —— and Hollingsworth, J. R. (2000). 'A Strategy for the Analysis of Idea Innovation Networks and Institutions'. *Organization Studies* 21/5: 971–1004.

Hall, B. H. (2001). 'The NBER Patent Citations Data File: Lessons, Insights, and Methodological Tools'. Working Paper 8498. Cambridge, MA: National Bureau of Economic Research.

—— Jaffe, A., and Trajtenberg, M. (2000). 'Market Value and Patent Citations: A First Look'. Working Paper 7741. Cambridge, MA: National Bureau of Economic Research.

Hall, P. A. (1986). *Governing the Economy: The Politics of State Intervention in Britain and France.* New York: Oxford University Press.

—— (1987). 'The Evolution of Economic Policy under Mitterrand'. In Ross, G., Hoffmann, S. and Malzacher, S. (eds).

—— (1992). 'The Movement from Keynesianism to Monetarism: Institutional Analysis and British Economic Policy in the 1970s'. In Steinmo, Thelen, and Longstreth (eds.)

Hall, P. A. (1993). 'Policy Paradigms, Social Learning and the State: The Case of Economic Policy Making in Britain'. *Comparative Politics* 25/3: 275–96.

—— (1994). 'Central Bank Independence and Coordinated Wage Bargaining: Their Interaction in Germany and Europe'. *German Politics and Society* 31: 1–23.

—— (1998). 'Institutions and Economic Performance: The Evolution of the Field from the Perspective of Political Science'. Lecture to the GAAC Workshop on Institutions and Economic Performance in Advanced Economies since 1945, Berlin: WZB. July.

—— (1999). 'The Political Economy of Europe in an Era of Interdependence'. In Kitschelt et al. (eds.).

—— (2000). 'Organized Market Economies and Unemployment in Europe: Is it Finally Time to Accept Liberal Orthodoxy?'. In Bermeo (ed.).

—— (2005). 'Preference Formation as a Political Process: The Case of Monetary Union in Europe'. In Katznelson and Weingast (eds.).

—— (2007). 'The Evolution of Varieties of Capitalism in Europe'. In Hancké, Rhodes, and Thatcher (eds.).

—— and Franzese, R. Jr. (1998). 'Mixed Signals: Central Bank Independence, Coordinated Wage Bargaining, and European Monetary Union'. *International Organisation* 52: 502–36.

—— and Gingerich, D. (2004). *Varieties of Capitalism and Institutional Complementarities in the Macro-Economy*. Discussion Paper 04/5. Cologne: Max Planck Institut für Gesellschaftsforschung.

—— and Soskice, D. (2001). 'Introduction'. In Hall and Soskice (eds.).

—— —— (eds.) (2001). *Varieties of Capitalism: The Institutional Foundations of Comparative Advantage*. Oxford, Oxford University Press.

—— —— (2003). 'Varieties of Capitalism and Institutional Change: A Response to Three Critics'. *Comparative European Politics* 1/2: 241–50.

—— and Thelen, K. (2009). 'Institutional Change in Varieties of Capitalism'. *Socio-Economic Review*, 7(1):7–34.

Hancké, B. (2001). 'Revisiting the French Model: Coordination and Restructuring in French Industry'. In Hall and Soskice (eds.).

—— (2002). *Large Firms and Institutional Change: Industrial Renewal and Economic Restructuring in France*. Oxford: Oxford University Press.

—— and Herrmann, A. (2007). 'Wage Bargaining and Comparative Advantage in EMU'. In Hancké, Rhodes and Thatcher (eds.).

—— Rhodes, M., and Thatcher, M. (eds.) (2007). *Beyond Varieties of Capitalism: Conflict, Contradictions and Complementarities in the European Economy*. Oxford, Oxford University Press.

Handelsblatt (1998). 'Co-Investments machen Deutschland zum Mekka der Start-up Finanziers'. 21 October.

Harhoff, D., Narin, F., Scherer, F. M., and Vopel, K. (1999). 'Citation Frequency and the Value of Patented Inventories'. *Review of Economics and Statistics* 81/3: 511–15.

Hassel, A., and Williamson, H. (2004). 'The Evolution of the German Model: How to Judge the Reforms in Europe's Largest Economy'. Paper prepared for the Anglo-German Foundation for the Study of Industrial Society.

Hay, C. (2002). 'Common Trajectories, Variable Paces, Divergent Outcomes? Models of European Capitalism under Conditions of Complex Economic Interdependence'. Paper presented to the Conference of Europeanists, Chicago. March.

Hayek, F. A. (1960). *The Constitution of Liberty.* Chicago: University of Chicago Press.

—— (1973). *Rules and Order.* London: Routledge and Kegan Paul.

Hechter, M. (1990). 'The Emergence of Cooperative Social Institutions'. In M. Hechter, K.-D. Opp, and R. Wippler (eds.).

Hechter, M., Opp, K.-D. and Wippler, R. (eds) (1990). *Social institutions. Their Emergence, Maintenance and Effects.* Berlin: Walter de Gruyter.

Hedström, P., and Swedberg, R. (1996). 'Social Mechanisms'. *Acta Sociologica* 39: 281–308.

Helleiner, E. (1994). *States and the Reemergence of Global Finance.* Ithaca, NY: Cornell University Press.

Helper, S., MacDuffie, J. P., and Sabel, C. (2000). 'Pragmatic Collaborations: Advancing Knowledge while Controlling Opportunism'. *Industrial and Corporate Change* 9/3: 443–88.

Helpman, E. (1984). 'Increasing Returns, Imperfect Markets, and Trade Theory'. *Handbook of International Economics.* Amsterdam: North Holland, 325–65.

Hemerijck, A. (1992). 'The Historical Contingencies of Dutch Corporatism'. D.Phil. thesis: University of Oxford.

—— and Schludi, M. (2000). 'Sequences of Policy Failures and Effective Policy Responses'. In Scharpf and Schmidt (eds.), (2000).

—— Unger, B., and Visser, J. (2000). 'How Small Countries Negotiate Change: Twenty-Five Years of Policy Adjustment in Austria, the Netherlands, and Belgium'. In Scharpf and Schmidt (eds.).

Herrigel, G. (1993). 'Power and the Redefinition of Industrial Districts: The Case of Baden-Württemberg'. In G. Grabher (ed.).

—— (2000). 'American Occupation, Market Order, and Democracy: Reconfiguring the Steel Industry in Japan and Germany after the Second World War'. In Zeitlin and Herrigel (eds.).

—— (2008). *Manufacturing Possibilities: Creative Action and the Recomposition of Industrial Practice in the U.S., Germany and Japan.* Oxford: Oxford University Press.

—— and Wittke, Volker (2005). 'Varieties of Vertical Disintegration: The Global Trend Toward Heterogeneous Supply Relations and the Reproduction of Difference in US and German Manufacturing'. In Morgan, Whitley, and Moen (eds.).

Hicks, A., and Kenworthy, L. (1998). 'Cooperation and Political Economic Performance in Affluent Democratic Capitalism'. *American Journal of Sociology* 103: 1631–72.

Hicks, D. (1999). 'The Difficulty of Achieving Full Coverage of International Social Science Literature and the Bibliometric Consequences'. *Scientometrics* 44/2: 193–215.

Hirsch, F. and Goldthorpe, J. H. (eds.) (1978). *The Political Economy of Inflation.* London : Martin Robertson, 1978.

Hirst, P., and Thompson, G. (1997). 'Globalization in Question: International Economic Relations and Forms of Public Governance'. In Hollingsworth and Boyer (eds.).

Hobbes, T. (1651). *Leviathan: or, the Matter, Forme and Power of a Commonwealth, Ecclesiasticall and Civil.* London.

Hodgson, G. (2002). 'Institutional Blindness in Modern Economics'. In Hollingsworth, Müller, and Hollingsworth (eds.).

Hollingsworth, J. R. (1997) 'The Institutional Embeddedness of American Capitalism'. In Crouch and Streeck (eds.).

—— (1997). 'Continuities and Changes in Social Systems of Production: The Cases of Japan, Germany, and the United States'. In Hollingsworth and Boyer (eds.).

—— (2000). 'Doing Institutional Analysis: Implications for the Study of Innovations'. *Review of International Political Economy* 7/4: 595–644.

—— (2002). 'On Institutional Embeddedness'. In Hollingsworth, Müller, and Hollingsworth (eds.).

—— (2004). Oral Presentation at the Conference on Health Care Industries, European University Institute, Florence.

—— and Boyer, R. (eds.) (1997). *Contemporary Capitalism: The Embeddedness of Institutions.* Cambridge: Cambridge University Press.

—— and Hollingsworth, E. J. (2000). 'Major Discoveries and Biomedical Research Organizations: Perspectives on Interdisciplinarity, Nurturing Leadership, and Integrated Structure and Cultures'. In Weingart and Stehr (eds.) 2000: 215–44.

—— Müller, K. H., and Hollingsworth, E. J. (eds.) (2002). *Advancing Socio-Economics: An Institutionalist Perspective.* Lanham: Rowman and Littlefield.

—— Schmitter, P. C., and Streeck, W. (eds.) (1994). *Governing Capitalist Economies: Performance and Control of Economic Sectors.* New York: Oxford University Press.

Hopkins, T. K., and Wallerstein, I. (1982). *World-Systems Analysis: Theory and Methodology.* Beverly Hills, CA: Sage.

Höpner, M. (2001). *Corporate Governance in Transition: Ten Empirical Findings on Shareholder Value and Industrial Relations in Germany.* MPIfG Discussion Paper 01/5. Cologne: Max Planck Institut für Gesellschaftsforschung.

—— (2003*a*). *European Corporate Governance Reform and the German Party Paradox.* MPIfG Discussion Paper 03/4. Cologne: Max Planck Institut für Gesellschaftsforschung.

—— (2003*b*). 'What Connects Industrial Relations with Corporate Governance? A Review on Complementarity'. Complementarity group unpublished paper. Cologne: Max Planck Institut für Gesellschaftsforschung.

—— (2004). *Unternehmensmitbestimmung unter Beschuss.* MPIfG Discussion Paper 04/8. Cologne: Max Planck Institut für Gesellschaftsforschung.

—— (2005) 'What Connects Industrial Relations and Corporate Governance? Explaining Institutional Complementarity'. *Socio-Economic Review* 3/2: 331–58.

—— (2007) *Coordination and Organization: The Two Dimensions of Nonliberal Capitalism.* MPIfG Discussion Paper 07/12. Cologne: Max Planck Institut für Gesellschaftsforschung.

—— and Jackson, G. (2001). *An Emerging Market of Corporate Control? The Case of Mannesmann and German Corporate Governance.* MPIfG Discussion Paper 01/4. Cologne: Max Planck Institut für Gesellschaftsforschung.

Howell, C. (2003). 'Varieties of Capitalism: and then there was one?'. *Comparative Politics*. 36/1: 103–24.

Huber, E., and Stephens, J. D. (2001). *Development and Crisis of the Welfare States: Parties and Policies in Global Markets*. Chicago, IL: University of Chicago Press.

Hyde, A. (1998). 'The Wealth of Shared Information: Silicon Valley's High-Velocity Labor Market, Endogenous Economic Growth, and the Law of Trade Secrets'. Manuscript. Available at <http://newark.rutgers.edu/~hyde/>.

Immergut, E. (2005). 'Historical-Institutionalism and the problem of Change'. In Wimmer and Köessler (eds.).

Iversen, T. (1999). *Contested Institutions*. New York: Cambridge University Press.

—— and Cusack, T. (2000). 'The Causes of Welfare State Expansion: Deindustrialization or Globalization'. *World Politics* 52: 313–49.

—— , Pontusson, J. and Soskice, D. (eds.) (2000). *Unions, Employers, and Central Banks: Macroeconomic Coordination and Institutional Change in Social Market Economies*. Cambridge: Cambridge University Press.

—— and Soskice, D. (2007). 'Distribution and Redistribution: The Shadow from the Nineteenth Century'. Working Paper, Department of Government, Harvard University.

—— and Wren, A. (1998). 'Equality, Employment and Budgetary Restraint'. *World Politics* 50: 507–46.

—— and Soskice, D. (2006). 'Electoral Institutions and the Politics of Coalitions: Why Some Democracies Redistribute More than Others'. *American Political Science Review* 100/2: 165–81.

Jaccoby, S. (1990). 'The New Institutionalism: What Can It Learn from the Old?'. *Industrial Relations* 29: 316–59.

Jackson, G. (2001). 'The Origins of Nonliberal Corporate Governance in Germany and Japan'. In Streeck and Yamamura (eds.).

—— (2004). 'Contested Boundaries: Ambiguity and Creativity in the Evolution of German Co-Determination'. In Streeck and Thelen (eds.).

—— (forthcoming). 'Varieties of Capitalism: A Review'.

Jaffe, A. B., Trajtenberg, M., and Fogarty, M. (2000). 'The Meaning of Patent Citations: Report of the NBER/Case Western Reserve Survey of Patentees'. Working Paper 7631. Cambridge, MA: National Bureau of Economic Research.

Jong Kon Chin, S. (2002). 'Covenants not to Compete, Trade Secrets and the Emergence of High Tech Clusters'. M.Phil. thesis: Management Studies, University of Cambridge.

—— (forthcoming). 'The Birth, Dispersion and Adaptation of New Institutions Across Institutional Systems: A Study of the Emergence and Performance of Biotech Firms and Technology Transfer Officers in and Around Publicly Funded Research Centres in Three Regions'. Ph.D. thesis: European University Institute, Florence.

Jürgens, U., and Naschold, F. (1994). 'Arbeits- und industriepolitische Entwicklungsengpässe der deutschen Industrie in den neunziger Jahren'. In Zapf and Dierkes (eds.).

Karl, T. (1997). *The Paradox of Plenty: Oil Booms and Petro-states*. Berkeley, CA: University of California Press.

Katzenstein, P. (ed.) (1978). *Between Power and Plenty*. Madison, WI: University of Wisconsin Press.

Katzenstein, P. (1987). *Policy and Politics in West Germany: Towards the Growth of a Semisovereign State.* Philadelphia: Temple University Press.
—— (1989) 'Stability and Change in the Emerging Third Republic'. In Katzenstein (ed.).
—— (ed.) (1989). *Industry and Politics in West Germany.* Ithaca, NY: Cornell University Press.
—— (1985) *Small States in World Markets.* Ithaca, NY, Cornell University Press.
Katznelson, I. (2003). 'Periodization and Preferences: Reflections on Purposive Action in Comparative Historical Social Science'. In Mahoney and Rueschemeyer (eds.).
—— and Milner, H. (eds.) (2002). *Political Science: The State of the Discipline.* New York: W. W. Norton.
—— and Weingast, B. (eds.) (2005). *Preferences and Situations.* New York, Russell Sage Foundation.
Keller, B. 1991: *Einführung in die Arbeitspolitik.* Munich: Oldenbourg.
Kenney, M. (2000). 'Introduction'. In Kenney (ed.).
—— (ed.) (2000). *Understanding Silicon Valley: The Anatomy of an Entrepreneurial Region.* Stanford: Stanford University Press.
—— and Florida, R. (2000). 'Venture Capital in Silicon Valley: Fuelling New Firm Foundation'. In Kenney (ed.).
—— and von Burg, U. (2000). 'Institutions and Economics: Creating Silicon Valley'. In Kenney (ed.) 2000.
Kenworthy, L. (1995). *In Search of National Economic Success: Balancing Competition and Cooperation.* Thousand Oaks, CA: Sage.
—— (2003). 'Do Affluent Countries Face an Incomes–Jobs Tradeoff?'. *Comparative Political Studies* 36: 1180–209.
—— (2006). 'Institutional Coherence and Macroeconomic Performance'. *Socio-Economic Review* 4: 69–91.
Keohane, R.O. and Milner, H. V. (1996). *Internationalization and Domestic Politics.* Cambridge: Cambridge University Press, 1996.
Keune, M., with Kiss, J. P., and Tóth, A. (2004). 'Innovation, Actors and Institutions: Change and Continuity in Local Development Policy in Two Hungarian Regions'. *International Journal of Urban and Regional Research* 28: 586–600.
King, D., and Wood, S. (1999). 'The Political Economy of Neoliberalism: Britain and the United States in the 1980s'. In Kitschelt et al. (eds.).
Kitschelt, H., Lange, P., Marks, G., and Stephens, J. (1999a). 'Convergence and Divergence in Advanced Capitalist Democracies'. In Kitschelt et al. (eds.).
—— —— —— —— (eds.) (1999). *Continuity and Change in Contemporary Capitalism.* Cambridge: Cambridge University Press.
Kjær, P., and Pedersen, O. K. (2001). 'Translating Liberalization: Neoliberalism in the Danish Negotiated Economy'. In Campbell and Pedersen (eds.).
Knight, J. (1992). *Institutions and Social Conflict.* New York: Cambridge University Press.
—— (1995). 'Models, Interpretations and Theories: Constructing Explanations of Institutional Emergence and Change'. In Knight and Sened (eds.).
—— (2001). 'Explaining the Rise of Neoliberalism: The Mechanisms of Institutional Change'. In Campbell and Pedersen (eds.) 2001: 27–50.

Knight, J., and Sened, I (eds.) (1995). *Explaining Social Institutions.* Ann Arbor, MI: University of Michigan Press.

Koch, R., and J. Reuling (eds.) (1995). *The European Dimension in Vocational Training.* Bielefeld: Bertelsmann.

Kooiman, T. (1993). *Modern Governance.* London: Sage.

Korpi, W. (1983). *The Democratic Class Struggle.* London: Routledge Kegan Paul.

—— (2006). 'Power Resources and Employee-Centred Approaches in Explanations of Welfare States and Varieties of Capitalism'. *World Politics* 58/2: 167–206.

Krasner, S. D. (1988). Sovereignty: An Institutional Perspective. *Comparative Political Studies* 21/1: 66–94.

Kreile, M. (1978). 'West Germany: Dynamics of Change'. In Katzenstein (ed.) 1978: 191–224.

Krippner, G. (2001). 'The Elusive Market: Embeddedness and the Paradigm of Economic Sociology'. *Theory and Society* 30: 775–810.

Kristensen, P. H. (1997). 'National Systems of Governance and Managerial Prerogatives in the Evolution of Work Systems: England, Germany, and Denmark Compared'. In Whitley and Kristensen (eds.).

Krugman, P. (1991). *Geography and Trade.* Cambridge, MA: MIT Press.

—— (ed.) (1986). *Strategic Trade Policy and the New International Economics.* Cambridge, MA: MIT Press.

Kume, I., and Thelen, K., (2006). 'Coordination as a Political Problem in Coordinated Market Economies'. *Governance* 19: 11–42.

Kuran, T. (1991). 'Now out of Never: The Element of Surprise in the East European Revolution of 1989'. *World Politics* 44/1: 7–48.

Kurzer, P. (1993) *Business and Banking: Political Change and Economic Integration in Western Europe.* Ithaca, NY: Cornell University Press.

Lane, C. (1995). *Industry and Society in Europe: Stability and Change in Britain, Germany and France.* London: Edward Elgar.

Lange, P., and Garrett, G. (1985). 'The Politics of Growth'. *Journal of Politics* 47: 794–809.

Lanjouw, J. O. (1999). 'The Quality of Ideas: Measuring Innovation with Multiple Indicators'. Working Paper 7345. Cambridge, MA: National Bureau of Economic Research.

—— and Schankerman, M. (1997). 'Stylized Facts of Patent Litigation: Value, Scope, and Ownership'. Working Paper 6297. Cambridge, MA: National Bureau of Economic Research.

Lash, S., and Urry, J. (1987). *The End of Organized Capitalism.* Cambridge: Polity Press.

Layard, R., Nickell, S., and Jackman, R. (1991). *Unemployment.* Oxford, Oxford University Press.

Lazonick, W. (1991). *Business Organization and the Myth of the Market Economy.* Cambridge: Cambridge University Press.

—— and O'Sullivan, M. (1996). 'Organization, Finance and International Competition'. *Industrial Corporate Change* 5: 1–49.

Lazonick, W. (1997). 'Big Business and Skill Formation in the Wealthiest Nations: The Organizational Revolution in the Twentieth Century'. In Chandler, Amatori, and Hikino (eds.).

Le Grand, J. (2003). *Motivation, Agency and Public Policy.* Oxford: Oxford University Press.

Leach, R., and Percy-Smith, J. (2001). *Local Governance in Britain.* London, Palgrave.

Lepsius, M. R. (1990). *Interessen, Ideen und Institutionen.* Opladen: Westdeutscher Verlag.

Leslie, S. W. (2000). 'The Biggest "Angel" of Them All: The Military and the Making of Silicon Valley'. In Kenney (ed.) 2000: 48–67.

Levi, M. (1996). 'Social and Unsocial Capital: A Review Essay of Robert Putnam's *Making Democracy Work*'. *Politics and Society* 24/1: 45–55.

Lévi-Strauss, C. (1962). *La Pensée Sauvage.* Paris: Agora.

Levy, J. D. (2004). 'Redeploying the State: Liberalization and Social Change in France'. In Streeck and Thelen (eds.).

Luhmann, N. (1980). *Gesellschaftsstruktur und Semantik.* Frankfurt am Main: Suhrkamp.

Lundvall, B.-A. (ed.) (1992). *National Systems of Innovation: Towards a Theory of Innovation and Interactive Learning.* London: Pinter.

Lütz, S. (2000). 'From Managed to Market Capitalism? German Finance in Transition'. *German Politics* 9: 149–70.

—— (2003). *Governance in der politischen Ökonomie.* MPIfG Discussion Paper 03/5. Cologne: Max Planck Institut für Gesellschaftsforschung.

Macneil, I. (2001). *The Relational Theory of Contract: Selected Works of Ian Macneil* (ed. David Campbell). London: Sweet and Maxwell.

Magnusson, L. (2001). 'The Role of Path Dependence in the History of Regulation'. In Magnusson and Ottoson (eds.).

—— —— (eds.) (2001). *The State, Regulation and the Economy.* Cheltenham: Edward Elgar.

Mahoney, J. (2000). 'Path Dependence in Historical Sociology'. *Theory and Society* 29: 507–48.

—— and D. Rueschemeyer (eds.) (2003). *Comparative Historical Analysis in the Social Sciences.* New York: Cambridge University Press.

Manow, P., and Seils, E. (2000). 'Adjusting Badly: The German Welfare State, Structural Change and the Open Economy'. In Scharpf and Schmidt (eds.).

March, J. G., and Olsen, J. P. (1989). *Rediscovering Institutions: The Organizational Basis of Politics.* New York: Free Press.

—— and Simon, H. A. (1958). *Organizations.* New York: Wiley.

Mares, I. (2001). 'Firms and the Welfare State: When and How Does Social Policy Matter to Employers'. In Hall and Soskice (eds.).

—— (2003) *The Politics of Social Risk.* New York: Cambridge University Press.

Mason, G., and Wagner, K. (1999). 'Knowledge Transfer and Innovation in Germany and Britain: "Intermediate Institution" Models of Knowledge Transfer under Strain?'. *Industry and Innovation* 6/1: 85–109.

Matzner, E., and Streeck, W. (eds.) (1992). *Beyond Keynesianism.* London and Aldershot: Edward Elgar.

Mayntz, R. (2004). *Organizational Forms of Terrorism: Hierarchy, Network, or a Type sui generis?* MPIfG Discussion Paper 04/4. Cologne: Max Planck Institut für Gesellschaftsforschung.

—— and Scharpf, F. (1995). 'Der Ansatz der akteurzentrierten Institutionalismus'. In R. Mayntz and F. Scharpf (eds.), *Steuerung und Selbstorganisation in staatsnahen Sektoren.* Frankfurt am Main: Campus, 39–72.

McDonald, T. J. (ed.) (1996). *The Historic Turn in the Human Sciences.* Ann Arbor, MI: University of Michigan Press.

McMillan, G. S., and Hamilton, R. D. (2000). 'Using Bibliometrics to Measure Firm Knowledge: An Analysis of the U.S. Pharmaceutical Industry'. *Technology Analysis & Strategic Management* 12/4: 465–75.

Meyer, J., and Rowan, B. (1991). 'Institutionalized Organizations: Formal Strategy as Myth and Ceremony'. In Powell and DiMaggio (eds.).

Middlemas, K. (1979). *Politics in Industrial Society: The Experience of the British System since 1911.* London: Deutsch.

—— (1986–91). *Power, Competition and the State.* 3 vols. Basingstoke: Macmillan.

Milgrom, P., and Roberts, J. (1992). *Economics, Organization and Management.* Englewood Cliffs, NJ: Prentice Hall.

Moe, T. (2003). 'Power and Political Institutions'. Paper presented at the Conference on Crafting and Operating Institutions, Yale University. April 11–13.

—— (2005). 'Power and Political Institutions'. *Perspectives on Politics* 3: 215–34.

Mokyr, J. (1990). *The Lever of Riches: Technological Creativity and Economic Progress.* New York: Oxford University Press.

Molina, O., and Rhodes, M. (2007). 'The Political Economy of Adjustment in Mixed Market Economies: A Study of Spain and Italy' in Hancké, Rhodes and Thatcher (eds.).

Moore, B. (1979). *Injustice: The Social Bases of Obedience and Revolt.* New York: Random House.

Morgan, G. (2005). 'Introduction'. In Morgan, Whitley, and Moen (eds.).

—— Whitley, R., and Moen, E. (eds.) (2005). *Changing Capitalisms? Complementarities, Contradictions and Capability Development in an International Context.* Oxford: Oxford University Press.

Morin, F. (2000). 'A Transformation in the French Model of Shareholding and Management'. *Economy and Society* 29/1: 36–53.

Morris, J., and Imrie, R. (1992). *Transforming Buyer–Supplier Relations.* London: Macmillan.

Mowery, D. C. (ed.) (1996). *The International Computer Software Industry: a Comparative Study of Industry Evolution and Structure.* Oxford: Oxford University Press.

—— and Rosenberg, N. (1979). 'The Influence of Market Demand Upon Innovation: A Critical Review of Some Recent Empirical Studies'. *Research Policy* 8/2: 102–53.

Myles, J., and Pierson, P., (2001). 'The Comparative Political Economy of Pension Reform'. In Pierson (ed.).

Naldini, M. (1999). 'Evolution of Social Policy and the Institutional Definition of Family Models: The Italian and Spanish Cases in Historical and Comparative Perspective'. Ph.D. thesis: European University Institute, Florence.

National Bureau of Economic Research (2001). *The NBER U.S. Patent Citation Data File: Lessons, Insights, and Methodological Tools.* Available at www.nber.org/patents; accessed 24 March 2004.

National Science Board (2002). *Science and Engineering Indicators – 2002.* Washington, DC: National Science Board.

Nelson, R. R. (1993). *National Innovation Systems: A Comparative Analysis.* Oxford: Oxford University Press.

—— (2000). *Knowledge Management in the Learning Society.* Paris: OECD.

—— and Winter, S. G. (1982). *An Evolutionary Theory of Economic Change.* Cambridge, MA: Harvard University Press.

Nielson, K., Jessop, B., and Hausner, J. (1995). 'Institutional Change in Post-Socialism'. In J. Hausner, B. Jessop, and K. Nielsen (eds.).

North, D. C. (1990a). *Institutions, Institutional Change, and Economic Performance.* Cambridge: Cambridge University Press.

—— (1990b). 'A Transaction Cost Theory of Politics'. *Journal of Theoretical Politics* 2/4: 355–68.

—— and Thomas, R. P. (1973). *The Rise of the Western World: A New Economic History.* Cambridge: Cambridge University Press.

Nugent, J. B. (2005). 'The New Institutional Economics: Can It deliver for Change and Development?'. In Wimmer and Kössler (eds.).

OECD (1994). *The Jobs Study.* Paris: OECD.

—— (1997). 'Economic Performance and the Structure of Collective Bargaining'. In *OECD Employment Outlook.* Paris: OECD, 63–93.

—— (2004a). *OECD Labour Force Statistics Database.* Available at <www1.oecd.org/scripts/cde/members/lfsdataauthenticate.asp>.

—— (2004b). *OECD Statistical Compendium.* Edition 01#2004, Paris, OECD.

—— (2004c). *Revenue Statistics, 1965–2003.* Paris, OECD.

Offe, C., and Wiesenthal, H. (1985) 'Two Logics of Collective Action: Theoretical Notes on Social Class and Political Form'. In Offe and Keane (eds.) 1985: 170–220.

—— and Keane, J. (eds.) (1985). *Disorganized Capitalism: Contemporary Transformations of Work and Politics.* Cambridge, MA: The MIT Press.

Ohmae, K. (1985). *Triad Power: The Coming Shape of Global Competition.* New York: Free Press.

Olson, M. (1982) *The Rise and Decline of Nations.* New Haven, CT: Yale University Press.

Orren, K., and Stephen S. (1994). 'Beyond the Iconography of Order: Notes for a "New" Institutionalism'. In Dodd and Jillson (eds.).

—— —— (2004). *The Search for American Political Development.* New York: Cambridge University Press.

O'Sullivan, M. (2001). 'Equity Markets and the Corporate Economy in France'. Unpublished manuscript.

—— (2007). 'Acting Out Institutional Change: Understanding the Recent Transformation of the French Financial System'. *Socio-Economic Review* 5: 389–436.

Pagano, M. and Volpin, P. (2002). 'The Political Economy of Corporate Governance'. Centro Stude in Economia e Finanza, Departimento di Scienze Economiche, Universitya degli Studi di Salerno, Working Paper No. 29.

Pakes, A. (1986). 'Patents as Options: Some Estimates of the Value of Holding European Patent Stocks'. *Econometrica* 54/4:755–84.

Palier, B. (2005). 'Ambiguous Agreement, Cumulative Change: French Social Policy in the 1990s'. In Streeck and Thelen (eds.).

—— and Thelen, K. (2008). 'Dualizing CMEs: Flexibility and Change in Coordinated Market Economies'. Paper presented at the 16th Conference of the Council for European Studies, Chicago. 6–8 March.

Parsons, T., and Bales, R. F. (1955). *Family, Socialization and Interaction Process.* New York: Free Press.

Pekkarinen, J., Pohjola, M., and Rowthorn, B. (eds.) (1992). *Social Corporatism: A Superior Economic System?* Oxford: Clarendon Press.

Pempel, T. J. (1998). *Regime Shift: Comparative Dynamics of the Japanese Political Economy.* Ithaca, NY: Cornell University Press.

Penan, H. (1996). 'R&D Strategy in a Techno-Economic Network: Alzheimer's Disease Therapeutic Strategies'. *Research Policy* 25: 337–58.

Penrose, E. (1959). *The Theory of the Growth of the Firm.* Oxford: Blackwell.

Phelps, E. S. (2006). 'Understanding the Great Changes in the World: Gaining Ground and Losing Ground since World War II'. *Capitalism and Society.* 1/2.

Pierre Audoin Conseil (1998). *1998 Survey: Software and I.T. Services in Europe.* Paris: Pierre Audoin Conseil.

Pierson, P. (1993). 'When Effect Becomes Cause: Policy Feedback and Political Change'. *World Politics* 45: 595–628.

—— (1994). *Dismantling the Welfare State? Reagan, Thatcher, and the Politics of Retrenchment.* New York, Cambridge University Press.

—— (1996). 'The Path to European Integration: A Historical Institutionalist Approach'. *Comparative Political Studies* 29/2: 123–63.

—— (2000a). 'The Limits of Design: Explaining Institutional Origins and Change'. *Governance* 13/4: 475–99.

—— (2000b). 'Increasing Returns, Path Dependence, and the Study of Politics'. *American Political Science Review* 94/2: 251–67.

—— (ed.) (2001). *The New Politics of the Welfare State.* New York, Oxford University Press.

—— (2004). *Politics in Time: History, Institutions, and Political Analysis.* Princeton, NJ: Princeton University Press.

Piore, M. J., and Sabel, C. F. (1984). *The Second Industrial Divide.* New York: Basic Books.

Pizzorno, A. (1983). 'Sulla razionalità della scelta democratica'. *Stato e Mercato* 7, 3–46.

Polanyi, K. (1944). *The Great Transformation.* New York: Rinehart.

Pontusson, J. (2005) 'Varieties and Commonalities of Capitalism'. In Coates (ed.).

Pontusson, J. and Swenson, P. (1996). 'Labor Markets, Production Strategies and Wage Bargaining Institutions'. *Comparative Political Studies* 29: 223–50.

Porter, M. E. (1990). *The Competitive Advantage of Nations*. New York: Free Press.

Powell, W. (1996). 'Inter-Organisational Collaboration in the Biotechnology Industry'. *Journal of Institutional and Theoretical Economics* 152/1: 197–225.

—— and DiMaggio, P. (eds.) (1991). *The New Institutionalism in Organizational Analysis*. Chicago: University of Chicago Press.

—— and Jones, D. L. (eds.) (forthcoming). *Bending the Bars of the Iron Cage*. Chicago: University of Chicago Press.

Prevezer, M. (1998). 'Clustering in Biotechnology in the USA'. In Swann, Prevezer, and Stout (eds.).

Proudfoot, N. (forthcoming). 'The Governance of Innovation: Comparisons from the European Biopharmaceuticals Industry'. Ph.D. thesis: European University Institute, Florence.

Przeworski, A. (1985). *Capitalism and Social Democracy*. Cambridge: Cambridge University Press.

Putnam, R. D. (1993a). 'The Prosperous Community: Social Capital and Public Life'. *The American Prospect*. Spring: 35–42.

—— (1993b). *Making Democracy Work: Civic Traditions in Modern Italy*. Princeton, NJ: Princeton University Press.

Quack, S., and Djelic, M.-L. (2005). 'Adaptation, Recombination and Reinforcement: The Story of Antitrust and Competition Law in Germany and Europe'. In Streeck and Thelen (eds.).

Quack, S., and Djelic, M.-L. (2005). 'Adaptation and Recombination: The Story of Antitrust and Competition Law in Germany and Europe'. In Streeck and Thelen (eds.).

—— and Morgan, G. (2000). 'National Capitalisms, Global Competition and Economic Performance: An Introduction'. In Quack, Morgan, and Whitley (eds.).

Quack, S., Morgan, G. and Whitley, R. (eds.) (2000). *National Capitalisms, Global Competition and Economic Performance*. Amsterdam: John Benjamins.

Quéré, M. (2003). 'Knowledge Dynamics: Biotechnology's Incursion into the Pharmaceutical Industry'. *Industry and Innovation* 10/3: 255–74.

Radice, H. (1998). ' "Globalization" and National Differences'. *Competition and Change* 3: 263–91.

—— (2000). 'Globalization and National Capitalisms: Theorizing Convergence and Differentiation'. *Review of International Political Economy* 7/4: 719–42.

Ragin, C. (2000). *Fuzzy-Set Social Science*. Chicago: University of Chicago Press.

Regini, M. (1996). 'Le imprese e le istituzioni: domanda e produzione sociale di risorse umane nelle regioni europee'; and 'Conclusioni'. In Regini (ed.).

—— (ed.) (1996). *La produzione sociale delle risorse humane*. Bologna: Il Mulino.

—— (2003). 'Dal neo-corporativismo alle varietà del capitalismo'. *Stato e Mercato* 69: 388–93.

Rhodes, M. (1997). 'Globalisation, Labour Markets and Welfare States: A Future of "Competitive Corporatism"?'. In Rhodes and Meny (eds.).

—— and Meny, Y. (eds.) (1997). *The Future of European Welfare.* London, Macmillan.

Rhodes, R. (1997). *Understanding Governance.* Buckingham: Open University Press.

Rieger, E., and Leibfried, S. (2003). *Limits to Globalization.* Oxford: Polity.

Rodríguez-Pose, A. (1998). *Dynamics of Regional Growth in Europe: Social and Political Factors.* Oxford: Oxford University Press.

—— (1999). 'Convergence or Divergence? Types of Regional Responses to Socio-Economic Change in Western Europe'. *Tijdschrift voor Economische en Sociale Geografie* 90/4: 363–78.

Roe, M. (2003). *Political Determinants of Corporate Governance.* Oxford: Oxford University Press.

—— (1994). *Strong Managers, Weak Owners.* Princeton, NJ: Princeton University Press.

Romer, P. M. (1990). 'Endogenous Technological Change'. *Journal of Political Economy* 98/5: 71–102.

Rosenau, J. N. (1992). 'Governance, Order and Change in World Politics'. In Rosenau and Czempiel (eds.).

Rosenau, N. D., and E. O. Czempiel (eds.) (1992). *Governance without Government.* Cambridge: Cambridge University Press.

Rosenberg, N., and Birdzell, L. E. Jr. (1986). How the West Grew Rich: The Economic Transformation of the Industrial World. New York: Basic Books.

Ross, G., Hoffmann, S. and Malzacher, S. (eds) (1987). *The Mitterrand Experiment: Continuity and Change in Modern France.* Oxford: Polity.

Rothstein, B. (2005). *Social Traps and the Problem of Trust.* Cambridge: Cambridge University Press.

—— (1998). *Just Institutions Matter: The Moral and Political Logic of the Universal Welfare State.* New York: Cambridge University Press.

Rueda, D., and Pontusson, J. (2000). 'Wage Inequality and Varieties of Capitalism'. *World Politics* 52: 350–83.

Sabel, C., and Zeitlin, J. (eds.) (1997). *World of Possibilities: Flexibility and Mass Production in Western Industrialization.* Cambridge: Cambridge University Press.

Samuels, R. J. (1994). *'Rich Nation, Strong Army': National Security and the Technological Transformation of Japan.* Ithaca, NY: Cornell University Press.

Saxenian, A.-L. (1994). *Regional Advantage: Culture and Competition in Silicon Valley and Route 128.* Cambridge, MA: Harvard University Press.

Scharpf, F. (1997). *Games Real Actors Play: Actor-Centered Institutionalism in Policy Research.* Boulder, CO: Westview.

Scharpf, F., and Schmidt, V. (eds.) (2000*a*). *Welfare and Work in the Open Economy.* Vol. 1: *From Vulnerability to Competitiveness.* Oxford: Oxford University Press.

—— —— (eds.) (2000*b*). *Welfare and Work in the Open Economy.* Vol. 2: *Diverse Responses to Common Challenges.* Oxford: Oxford University Press.

Scherer, F. M. (1965). 'Firm Size, Market Structure, Opportunity, and the Output of Patented Innovations'. *American Economic Review* 55/5:1097–125.

Schickler, E. (1999). 'Disjointed Pluralism and Congressional Development: An Overview'. Paper presented at the 95th Annual Meeting of the American Political Science Association, Atlanta. 2–5 September.

Schickler, E. (2001). *Disjointed Pluralism: Institutional Innovation and the Development of the U.S. Congress.* Princeton, NJ: Princeton University Press.

Schmidt, V. (2002). *The Futures of European Capitalism.* Oxford, Oxford University Press.

Schmitter, P., and Streeck, W. (1985). *Private Interest Government.* London, Sage.

Schmookler, J. (1966). *Invention and Economic Growth.* Cambridge, MA: Harvard University Press.

Schneiberg, M. (n.d.). 'Combining New Institutionalisms: Market Failures, Models of Order, and Endogenous Institutional Change in American Property Insurance'. Reed College Manuscript. Portland, OR.

—— and Clemens, E. S. (forthcoming). 'The Typical Tools for the Job: Research Strategies in Institutional Analysis'. In Powell and Jones (eds.).

Schumpeter, J. A. (1934). *The Theory of Economic Development: An Inquiry into Profits, Capital, Credit, Interest, and the Business Cycle.* Cambridge, MA: Harvard University Press.

Schwartz, A. (1992). 'Relational Contracts and the Courts'. *Journal of Legal Studies* 21: 780–822.

—— and Zysman, J. (eds.) (1998). *Enlarging Europe: The Industrial Foundations of a New Political Reality.* International and Area Studies, Research Series. Berkeley, CA: University of California Press.

Scott, W. R. (2001). *Institutions and Organizations,* 2nd edn. Thousand Oaks, CA: Sage.

Selznick, P. (1957). *Leadership in Administration.* New York: Harper & Row.

Sewell, W. H. (1992). 'A Theory of Structure: Duality, Agency, and Transformation'. *American Journal of Sociology* 98/1: 1–29.

—— (1996). 'Three Temporalities: Toward an Eventful Sociology'. In McDonald (ed.).

—— (2008) 'The Temporalities of Capitalism'. *Socio-Economic Review* 6: 517–37.

Shepsle, K. (1986) 'Institutional Equilibrium and Equilibrium Institutions'. In Weisberg, H. (ed.).

Shonfield, A. (1964). *Modern Capitalism.* Oxford: Oxford University Press.

Sinclair, T. J. (2001). 'The Infrastructure of Global Governance: Quasi-Regulatory Mechanisms and the New Global Finance'. *Global Governance* 7: 441–51.

Skocpol, T. (1992). *Protecting Soldiers and Mothers: The Political Origins of Social Policy in the United States.* Cambridge, MA: Belknap.

Skowronek, S. (1995). 'Order and Change'. *Polity* 28/1: 91–6.

Smith, M. R., and Marx, L. (eds.) (2004). *Does Technology Drive History: The Dilemma of Technological Determinism.* Cambridge, MA: MIT Press.

Solokoff, K. L., and Engerman, S. (2000). 'Institutions, Factor Endowments, and Paths of Development in the New World'. *Journal of Economic Perspectives* 14/3: 217–32.

Solow, R. M. (1957). 'Technical Change and the Aggregate Production Function'. *Review of Economics and Statistics* 39/3: 312–20.

Soskice, D. (1990). 'Wage Determination: The Changing Role of Institutions in Advanced Industrialized Countries'. *Oxford Review of Economic Policy* 6/4: 36–61.

—— (1994). 'Innovation Strategies of Companies: A Comparative Institutional Analysis of Some Cross-Country Differences'. In Zapf (ed.).

—— (1995). 'A Comparative Review of National Training Models: Germany, the UK, the USA, Japan'. In Koch and Reuling (eds.).

—— (1997). 'German Technology Policy, Innovation, and National Institutional Frameworks'. *Industry and Innovation* 4: 75–96.

—— (1999). 'Divergent Production Regimes: Coordinated and Uncoordinated Market Economies in the 1980s and 1990s'. In Kitschelt et al. (eds.).

Stark, D. (1995). 'Not by Design: The Myth of Designer Capitalism in Eastern Europe'. In Hausner, Jessop, and Nielsen (eds.).

—— (2001). 'Ambiguous Assets for Uncertain Environments: Heterarchy in Postsocialist Firms'. In DiMaggio (ed.).

Steinmo, S., Thelen, K., and Longstreth, F. (eds.) (1992). *Structuring Politics: Historical Institutionalism in Comparative Analysis*. Cambridge: Cambridge University Press.

Stewart, M. (1972). *Keynes and After*. Harmondsworth: Penguin.

—— (1977). *The Jekyll and Hyde Years: Politics and Economic Policy since 1964*. London: J. M. Dent.

Stinchcombe, A. L. (1968). *Constructing Social Theories*. New York: Harcourt, Brace and World.

Streeck, W. (1984). *Industrial Relations in West Germany: A Case Study of the Car Industry*. New York: St. Martin's Press.

—— (1989). 'Successful Adjustment in Turbulent Markets: The Automobile Industry'. In Katzenstein (ed.).

—— (1991) 'On the Institutional Conditions for Diversified Quality Production'. In Matzner and Streeck (eds.).

—— (1992). *Social Institutions and Economic Performance*. London: Sage.

—— (1994). 'Pay Restraint without Incomes Policy: Institutionalized Monetarism and Industrial Unionism in Germany'. In Dore, Boyer and Mars (eds.).

—— (1996). 'Lean Production in the German Automobile Industry? A Test Case for Convergence Theory'. In Berger and Dore (eds.).

—— (1997*a*). 'The German Economic Model: Does It Exist? Can it Survive?'. In Crouch and Streeck (eds.).

—— (1997*b*). 'Beneficial Constraints: On the Economic Limits of Rational Voluntarism'. In Hollingsworth and Boyer (eds.).

—— (2001). 'Introduction: Explorations into the Origins of Nonliberal Capitalism in Germany and Japan'. In Streeck and Yamamura (eds.).

—— (2004). 'Taking Uncertainty Seriously: Complementarity as a Moving Target'. Workshop Proceedings of the Oesterreichische Nationalbank, 1, 101–115.

—— (2005*a*). 'Requirements for a Useful Concept of Complementarity'. *Socio-Economic Review* 3/2: 363–6.

—— (2005*b*) 'Rejoinder: On Terminology, Functionalism, (Historical) Institutionalism and Liberalism'. *Socio-Economic Review* 3: 577–87.

—— (2009). *Re-Forming Capitalism: The Liberalization of the German Political Economy*. Oxford: Oxford University Press.

Streeck, W. and Thelen, K. (2005). 'Institutional Change in Advanced Political Economies'. In Streeck and Thelen (eds.) 2005: 1–39.

—— —— (eds.) (2005). *Beyond Continuity: Institutional Change in Advanced Political Economies*. Oxford: Oxford University Press.

—— and Yamamura, K. (eds.) (2001). *The Origins of Nonliberal Capitalism: Germany and Japan in Comparison*. Ithaca, NY: Cornell University Press.

Sturgeon, T. J. (2000). 'How Silicon Valley Came to Be'. In Kenney (ed.).

Suchman, M. C. (2000). 'Dealmakers and Counselors: Law Firms as Intermediaries in the Development of Silicon Valley'. In M. Kenney (ed.).

Swank, D. (2002). '21-Nation Pooled Time-Series Data Set: Political Strength of Political Parties by Ideological Group in Capitalist Democracies'. Manuscript. Department of Political Science, Marquette University.

—— Martin, C. J. and Thelen, K. (2008). 'Institutional Change and the Politics of Social Solidarity in Advanced Industrial Democracies'. Paper presented at the Conference of Europeanists, Chicago. March.

Swann, G. M. P. (1998). 'Clusters in the US Computing Industry'. In Swann, Prevezer, and Stout (eds.).

—— and Prevezer, M. (1998). 'Introduction'. In Swann, Prevezer, and Stout (eds.).

—— —— and Stout, D. (eds.) (1998). *The Dynamics of Industrial Clustering: International Comparisons in Computing and Biotechnology*. Oxford: Oxford University Press.

Swedberg, R. (1987). 'Economic Sociology: Past and Present'. *Current Sociology* 35/1: 1–221.

Swenson, P. (1991). 'Bringing Capital Back In, or Social Democracy Reconsidered: Employer Power, Cross-Class Alliances and Centralization of Industrial Relations in Denmark and Sweden'. *World Politics* 43: 513–44.

—— (2001). *Capitalists Against Markets*. New York, Oxford University Press.

Swidler, A. (1986). 'Culture in Action: Symbols and Strategies'. *American Sociological Review* 51: 273–86.

Tate, J. (2001). 'National Varieties of Standardization'. In Hall and Soskice (eds.).

Taylor, M. Z. (2004). 'Empirical Evidence against Varieties of Capitalism's Theory of Technological Innovation'. *International Organization* 58/3: 601–31.

Temple, P. (1998). 'Clusters and Competitiveness: A Policy Response'. In Swann, Prevezer, and Stout (eds.).

Teubner, G. (2001). 'Legal Irritants: How Unifying Law Ends up in New Divergences'. In Hall and Soskice (eds.).

Thatcher, M. (2007). 'Reforming National Regulatory Institutions: the EU and Cross-National Variety in European Networked Industries'. In Hancké, Rhodes, and Thatcher (eds.).

The Economist (1996). Special insert on the software industry. 25 May.

Thelen, K. (1991). *Union of Parts: Labor Politics in Postwar Germany*. Ithaca, NY: Cornell University Press.

—— (1999). 'Historical Institutionalism in Comparative Politics'. *Annual Review of Political Science* 2: 369–404.

—— (2000). 'Why German Employers Cannot Bring Themselves to Dismantle the German Model'. In Iversen, et al. (eds.).

—— (2001). 'Varieties of Labor Politics in the Developed Democracies'. In Hall and Soskice (eds.).

—— (2002). 'The Political Economy of Business and Labor in the Developed Democracies: Agency and Structure in Historical-Institutional Perspective'. In Katznelson and Milner (eds.).

—— (2003). 'How Institutions Evolve: Insights from Comparative Historical Analysis'. In Mahoney and Rueschemeyer (eds.).

—— (2004). *How Institutions Evolve: The Political Economy of Skills in Germany, Britain, the United States, and Japan.* Cambridge: Cambridge University Press.

—— and Kume, I. (1999). 'The Effects of Globalization on Labor Revisited: Lessons from Germany and Japan'. *Politics and Society* 27: 477–505.

—— and van Wijnbergen, C. (2003). 'The Paradox of Globalization: Labor Relations in Germany and Beyond'. *Comparative Political Studies* 36/8: 859–80.

Tiberghien, Y. (2002). *Political Mediation of Global Market Forces.* Ph.D. thesis: Stanford University.

Trajtenberg, M. (1990). 'A Penny for Your Quotes: Patent Citations and the Value of Innovations'. *RAND Journal of Economics* 21/1: 172–87.

Trampusch, C. (2005). 'Institutional Resettlement: The Case of Early Retirement in Germany'. In Streeck and Thelen (eds.).

Trigilia, C. (1998). *Sociologia Economica.* Bologna: Il Mulino.

—— (2004). 'The Governance of High-Tech Districts'. In Crouch et al. (eds.).

Tylecote, A., and Conesa, E. (1999). 'Corporate Governance, Innovation Systems and Industrial Performance'. *Industry and Innovation* 6/1: 25–50.

Tyson, L. D'A. (1993). *Who's Bashing Whom? Trade Conflicts in High-Technology Industries.* Washington, DC: Institute for International Economics.

Utterback, J. M. (1994). *Mastering The Dynamics of Innovation: How Companies Can Seize Opportunities in the Face of Technological Change.* Boston: Harvard Business School Press.

Uzzi, B. (1997). 'Social Structure and Competition in Inter-Firm Networks: The Paradox of Embeddedness'. *Administrative Science Quarterly* 42: 35–67.

—— (1999). 'Embeddedness in the Making of Financial Capital: How Social Relations and Networks Benefit from Firms Seeking Financing'. *American Sociological Review* 64: 481–505.

Van Iterson, A., and Olie, R. (1992). 'European Business Systems: The Dutch Case'. In R. Whitley (ed.).

Van Waarden, F. (2002). 'Market Institutions as Communicating Vessels: Changes between Economic Coordination Principles as a Consequence of Deregulation Policies'. In Hollingsworth, Müller, and Hollingsworth (eds.).

Viebrock, E. (2004). 'The Role of Trade Unions as Intermediary Institutions in Unemployment Insurance: A European Comparison'. Ph.D. thesis: European University Institute, Florence.

Visser, J., and Hemerijck, A. (1997). *A Dutch 'Miracle'.* Amsterdam: Amsterdam University Press.

Vitols, S. (1995). 'Are German Banks Different?'. WZB Discussion Paper FS95–1, 308.

—— Casper, S., Soskice, D., and Woolcock, S. (1997). *Corporate Governance in Large British and German Companies.* London: Anglo-German Foundation.

Vogel, S. (2004). 'Routine Adjustment and Bounded Innovation: The Changing Political Economy of Japan'. In Streeck and Thelen (eds.).

Voss, T. R. (2001). 'Institutions'. In Neil J. Smelser and Paul B. Baltes (eds.), *International Encyclopedia of the Social and Behavioral Sciences.* Vol. 7. Amsterdam: Elsevier, 7561–6.

Waterman, R. H. Jr. (1994). *What America Does Right.* New York, Penguin Books.

Watson, M. (2003). 'Ricardian Political Economy and the Varieties of Capitalism Approach: Specialisation, Trade and Comparative Institutional Advantage'. *Comparative European Politics* 1: 227–40.

Weber, M. (1922). *Wirtschaft und Gesellschaft.* Tübingen: Mohr.

—— (1978 [1956]). *Economy and Society.* Berkeley, CA: University of California Press.

Weingart, P., and N. Stehr (eds.) (2000). *Practising Interdisciplinarity.* Toronto: Toronto University Press

Weingast, B. (2002). 'Rational-Choice Institutionalism'. In Katznelson and Milner (eds.).

—— and Marshall, W. J. (1988). 'The Industrial Organization of Congress; or, Why Legislatures, like Firms, are not Organized as Markets'. *Journal of Political Economy* 96/1: 132–63.

Weisberg, H. (ed.) (1996). *Political Science: The Science of Politics.* New York: Agathon.

Western, B. (2000). 'Bayesian Thinking about Macrosociology'. Working Paper 2000/152. Istituto Juan, Madrid. March.

Whitley, R. (1997). 'The Social Regulation of Work Systems: Institutions, Interest Groups, and Varieties of Work Organization in Capitalist Societies'. In Whitley and Kristensen (eds.).

—— (1999). *Divergent Capitalisms: The Social Structuring and Change of Business Systems.* Oxford, Oxford University Press.

—— (2005). 'How National Are National Business Systems? The Role of States and Complementary Institutions in Standardising Systems of Economic Coordination and Control at the National Level'. In Morgan, Whitley, and Moen (eds.).

Whitley, R., and Kristensen, P. H. (eds.) (1997). *Governance at Work: The Social Regulation of Economic Relations.* Oxford: Oxford University Press.

Wilensky, H. L. (2002). *Rich Democracies.* Berkeley, CA: University of California Press.

Williamson, O. E. (1975). *Markets and Hierarchies: Analysis and Antitrust Implications.* New York: Free Press.

—— (1985). *The Economic Institutions of Capitalism: Firms, Markets, Relational Contracting.* New York: Free Press.

—— and Masten, S. E. (1995). *Transaction Cost Economics.* Aldershot: Edward Elgar.

Wimmer, A., and Kössler, A. (eds.) (2005). *Understanding Change: Models, Methodologies and Metaphors.* London: Palgrave.

Windolf, P. (2002). *Corporate Networks in Europe and the United States.* Oxford: Oxford University Press.

Wirtschaftswoche (1998). 'Schneller Aufstieg'. 24 September: 134–9.

Wood, S. (1997). 'Capitalist Constitutions: Supply Side Reform in Britain and West Germany 1960–1990'. Ph.D. thesis: Harvard University.

—— (2001a). 'Employer Preferences, State Power and Labor Market Policy and Germany and Britain'. In Hall and Soskice (eds.).

—— (2001b). 'Business, Government and Patterns of Labor Market Policy in Britain and the Federal Republic of Germany'. In Hall and Soskice (eds.).

Woods, N. (ed.) (2000). *The Political Economy of Globalization*. New York: Macmillan.

Wrong, Dennis (1961). 'The Oversocialized Conception of Man in Modern Sociology'. *American Sociological Review* 26/2: 183–93.

Yamamura, K., and Streeck, W. (eds.) (2003). *The End of Diversity? Prospects for German and Japanese Capitalism*. Ithaca, NY: Cornell University Press.

Zapf, W. and Dierkes, M. (ed.) (1994). *Institutionvergleich und Institutionsdynamik*. Berlin: Sigma.

Zeitlin, J. (2003). 'Introduction: Governing Work and Welfare in a New Economy: European and American Experiments'. In Zeitlin and Trubek (eds.).

—— and Herrigel, G. (eds.) (2000). *Americanization and its Limits: Reworking US Technology and Management in Post-War Europe and Japan*. New York: Oxford University Press.

—— and Trubek, D. (eds.) (2003). *Governing Work and Welfare in a New Economy: European and American Experiments*. Oxford: Oxford University Press.

Zukin, S., and DiMaggio, P. (1990). *Structures of Capital: The Social Organization of the Economy*. Cambridge: Cambridge University Press.

Zysman, J. (1983). *Governments, Markets, and Growth: Financial Systems and the Politics of Industrial Change*. Ithaca, NY: Cornell University Press.

Index